TREASURES
in the
PSALMS

TREASURES
in the
PSALMS

Henry M. Morris
with Henry M. Morris III

Foreword by Tim LaHaye

Master
Books

First printing: June 2000
Second printing: March 2001

ISBN: 0-89051-298-1
Library of Congress Number: 00-102652

Library of Congress Cataloging in Publication Data
    Morris, Henry Madison, 1918-
    Treasures in the Psalms

    1   Bible. O. T. Psalms English — Commentaries. I. Title.

Cover design by Farewell Communications
Cover illustration by Brian Miller
Interior design by Judy Lewis

Printed in the United States of America

Please visit our website for other great titles:
www.masterbooks.net

For information regarding publicity for author interviews
please contact Dianna Fletcher at (870) 438-5288.

Acknowledgments

My good friend and colleague over many years, Dr. Tim LaHaye has written a very kind Foreword for this book. Although I am afraid he was too generous in his comments, I do appreciate this very much, and hope the book will measure up to his evaluation.

I also want to thank Mrs. Mary Smith and Mrs. Mary Thomas, both of whom worked extensively on typing and editing the manuscript. Thanks also to the editorial and publishing staff at Master Books for their work in getting the book ready for publication.

Finally, my oldest son, Dr. Henry M. Morris III, reviewed the entire manuscript, and then he himself made a special contribution to the book, consisting of chapters 54 through 59. He is a gifted Bible teacher in his own right, and I appreciate his sharing this way in the book.

Contents

Part I — Message and Method in the Psalms

Part II — Prophecies of Christ in the Psalms

Part III — Events of the Second Coming

Part IV — Scientific Foregleams in the Psalms

V. The Songs of Degrees and the Christian Life

VI. Psalms of Comfort and Guidance
(The Maschil Psalms)

VII. The Book-End Psalms

VIII. Psalms of Encouragement and Blessing
(Henry Morris III)

IX. The Praise Psalms of the Redeemed

Foreword

Anything written by Dr. Henry M. Morris is well worth reading. He was a Phi Beta Kappa student at Rice University and earned a Ph.D. from the University of Minnesota in the scientific field of engineering hydrology. In an age when the academic community is obsessed with the unscientific theory of evolution, he has been the foremost advocate for biblical creationism. He sees the handiwork of God in Scripture, in nature, and in everything about him. He not only has a well-developed belief in creation, but a personal faith in and knowledge of the Creator and Savior, born out of years of intimate study of the Holy Scriptures.

I first met Dr. Morris in January of 1970, while we were guest speakers at the Torrey Memorial Bible Conference sponsored by Biola College. I had read several of his books and was deeply impressed with the clear and easy way he had of writing about complicated subjects so that even we non-scientists could understand complex ideas. At the urging of the Holy Spirit I asked him if he would be interested in helping my associate pastor, Dr. Arthur Peters, and me to start a Christian college in San Diego, the second largest city in the state. Little did I realize that he had been the head of what was then the third largest civil engineering department in American universities for 13 years and would have to leave tenure and security behind to do so. He prayed about it, accepted the invitation, then in June moved his family by faith to San Diego, and in September we started the college with ten students. Today the college is fully accredited and there are more than a thousand graduates all across the country serving in ministry, missions, teaching, counseling, medicine, and many fields of science. Without the initial services of Dr. Henry Morris as academic vice president, there would not have been a Christian Heritage College. He developed the curriculum and standards of academic and biblical excellence that have continued to this day.

One of the great honors of my life as the senior minister of the sponsoring church was to serve as pastor for Dr. Morris and his wife and several of his very dedicated children. All six of his children have been a testimony to him and his wife, Mary Louise, and their lives "rise up to call them blessed." My wife Beverly and I also had the honor of assisting Dr. Morris in the original founding of what has become the most effective creation science organization in the world, the Institute for Creation Research. ICR today has ten full-time scientists on its staff and dozens of others from across the country who participate with them in the advancement of the truth of creation by the direct act of God in opposition to the evolutionary propaganda that emanates from Christ-rejecting scientists and the educational institutions they represent. The scientifically accurate and biblically based books, magazines, and other literature that have come from ICR have rescued thousands from the false teachings of evolution, and as a result many of these are carrying on this same God-honoring crusade in their own communities.

As great a scientist and as brilliant a writer as he is, there is something about Henry Morris that stands out in my mind even more. He is a man deeply devoted to the God of the Bible, His Son, Jesus Christ, and of course, to the ministry of the Holy Spirit in his life. And while his scientific books have had an incredible influence on the entire body of Christ today, he has also been very influential in making the Book of Psalms practical and meaningful in the minds of readers. If you were to ask him which of the Bible's books were his favorites, he would probably say Genesis, Revelation, and everything in between, particularly the psalms. He saw things in the psalms I had never seen before, particularly the Messianic and end-time prophecies featuring the second coming of Jesus. Studying his commentary on the psalms will help you appreciate even more the words inspired by the same divine author as Genesis, Job, and Revelation, three other books of the Bible on which Dr. Morris has written commentaries.

Many times I asked him to preach in the church when I was there, and, of course, I heard him speak in the college chapel many times. He would often speak from the psalms, and it was obviously a book that he had studied often and deeply, letting God speak to him through its pages.

Psalms is one of the most-loved books of the Old Testament by Christians and is worthy of every believer's study. They exalt Jesus the Messiah, honor God the Father, and bring His mercy and grace to an art form that inspires readers to praise and worship the Lord. You cannot help being blessed by studying the Book of Psalms, particularly through the eyes, mind, and heart of a man who truly knew the God who inspired them. *Treasures in the Psalms* will give readers a unique devotional and illuminating reading experience that will be a worthy addition to the able library of books by Henry M. Morris.

Tim LaHaye, Litt. D.
Author, Minister

Introduction

The Book of Psalms has been a delight and blessing to the people of God for a hundred generations. In more ways than one, it is at the very heart of the Bible. The central chapter of the Bible is Psalm 117, which is also the shortest chapter in the Bible. The next chapter contains the central verse of the Bible, Psalm 118:8, which affirms very appropriately that: "It is better to trust in the Lord than to put confidence in man." Then the next chapter, Psalm 119, is the longest and most amazing chapter in the Bible.

But more importantly, the Book of Psalms is the heart of the Bible in that it speaks to our own hearts more eloquently and fervently than does any other book. It is the book of praise, the book of singing — but also the book of comfort and even sometimes the book of anger. It is a book of testimony and a book of prayer. It speaks of joy in the midst of sorrow and hope in the midst of despair.

In our own family devotionals, extending now every day through the past 60 years, the Scripture readings have been from the Book of Psalms more than from any other book of the Bible. Speaking personally (and, no doubt many other Christians would agree), although I love and try to study the entire Bible, the Book of Psalms is my *favorite* book!

I believe that the Book of Genesis is the most *important* book of the Bible, since it is the foundation of all the rest. Similarly, the Book of Revelation is the most *thrilling* book of the Bible, because it is the climax of all the rest, ushering us into the very vestibule of eternity. Nevertheless, the Book of Psalms is my favorite, because here I experience more direct communion between my own heart and the heart of God than anywhere else in Scripture.

A verse-by-verse study of any of the psalms inevitably yields a great harvest of spiritual blessing. They are far more than mere devotional poems for pious reading. Each contains depths of revelation that seem inexhaustible. Furthermore, there are probably more direct and concrete marks of divine inspiration in the psalms than in any other book. There are numerous scientific insights far in advance of their discovery by scientists, many amazingly fulfilled prophecies of the coming Savior, and even many evidences of remarkable geometric structure in the very combinations of words and concepts that are inexplicable except in terms of inspiration by the Holy Spirit.

This book is written with the purpose of sharing with others some of the blessings I have experienced in studying the marvelous Book of Psalms. There are, of course, 150 chapters in the entire Book of Psalms, and I have covered only half of them in this particular volume. The ones discussed, however, are among the most remarkable psalms, both in their evidences of divine inspiration and in their impact on our hearts and souls as we study them.

The beauty of the psalms is brought out most effectively in the King James translation, and this is the translation followed herein. In most cases, the study proceeds verse by verse (or at least section by section), so the text of each psalm is fully incorporated in the exposition.

I only hope that these studies — admittedly taking a somewhat different approach to the exposition of this tremendous book — will yield as much blessing to the reader as they have to the writer. As we proceed to the study, there are no words more appropriate than those of the Psalmist himself:

> I will worship toward thy holy temple, and praise thy name for thy lovingkindness and for thy truth: for thou hast magnified thy word above all thy name (Ps. 138:2).

Part I

Message and Method in the Psalms

Chapter 1

Songs in the Night

T he Book of Psalms is unique in the Bible. It was the hymnbook of Israel and, to a great extent, has been the pattern for all the other hymnbooks used by God's people through the ages. The Jews called it "The Hallal Book" — "The Book of Praises." It is replete with songs of praise, of course, but it contains also a strong component of songs of suffering, songs of battle, and even songs of imprecation.

The word for "psalms" (Hebrew *mizmer*) means "songs," probably implying songs which were to be sung with musical accompaniment. Most of them were written originally by David, but some had other authors (even Moses), and many are anonymous. They were collected by some unknown process of selection into five books, with a total of 150 psalms comprising 2,461 verses in all.

The Theme of Conflict

Although the note of praise does sound often in the psalms, the theme of spiritual warfare is even more frequent. In almost every psalm, the element of conflict is either implicit or explicit. The great conflict of the ages is the struggle between truth and deception, between sin and righteousness, between the godly and ungodly, between the chosen nation and the heathen, and finally between God and Satan.

The 1st Psalm contains the definitive statement on this conflict and is the foundation for all the other psalms. The final psalm (150) speaks of the final and eternal victory of God and His purposes. This victory is foreshadowed in the 1st Psalm, but the conflict is very real throughout all the intervening psalms.

It is singularly appropriate, of course, for a book whose theme is songs of praise to be also a book of warfare and struggle and suffering. This present world is groaning and travailing together in pain (Rom. 8:22), and "man is born unto trouble, as the sparks fly upward" (Job 5:7).

But it is trust in God that enables the believer to be joyful in spite of trouble. "As unknown, and yet well known; as dying, and, behold, we live; as chastened, and not killed; As sorrowful, yet always rejoicing; as poor, yet making many rich; as having nothing, and yet possessing all things" (2 Cor. 6:9–10).

Such is the note sounded throughout the psalms. The world is in darkness, but the light of God's promises continually illumines the way. "Deep calleth unto deep at the noise of thy waterspouts: all thy waves and thy billows are gone over me. Yet the Lord will command His lovingkindness in the daytime, and in the night His song shall be with me, and my prayer unto the God of my life" (Ps. 42:7–8).

It is significant that the first actual reference to singing in the psalms is in the verse immediately following the first of the so-called "imprecations" in the psalms. Note the contrast: "Destroy thou them, O God; let them fall by their own counsels; cast them out in the multitude of their transgressions; for they have rebelled against thee. But let all those that put their trust in thee rejoice; let them ever shout for joy [same as "sing for joy"], because thou defendest them: let them also that love thy name be joyful in thee" (Ps. 5:10–11).

Structure of the Book of Psalms

The Book of Psalms actually consists of five "books," composed as follows:

Book I	Psalms 1 through 41	=	41 psalms
Book II	Psalms 42 through 72	=	31 psalms
Book III	Psalms 73 through 89	=	17 psalms
Book IV	Psalms 90 through 106	=	17 psalms
Book V	Psalms 107 through 145	=	39 psalms
Epilogue	Psalms 146 through 150	=	5 psalms

No one knows the original reason for the compilations as listed. Probably they represent ancient chronological compilations, but the details are obscure. Most Bibles indicate the last five psalms to have been a part of Book V, but, for reasons to be discussed in the last section of this volume, it appears more likely that they are intended as a grand epilogue to the entire five books.

The ancient Jewish commentators believed the five groupings corresponded to the five books of Moses, the "Pentateuch." Any supposed correlation in subject matter based on this idea seems quite tenuous, however.

Authors named in the traditional inscriptions on the psalms may account in part for the collections. For example, Book I consists almost entirely of Davidic psalms, and so may represent the first collection of his psalms as published either by David or possibly by Solomon. Altogether, seven different authors are found listed in these inscriptions, but fully a third of the psalms carry no name. Authorship is divided among the various books in accordance with the following tabulation.

Author	Book I	Book II	Book III	Book IV	Book V	Epilogue	Total
David	37	18	1	2	15		73
Asaph		1	11				12
Sons of Korah		7	3				10
Moses				1			1
Solomon		1			1		2
Heman			1				1
Ethan			1				1
Anonymous	4	4		14	23	5	50
Total	41	31	17	17	39	5	150

Actually, one of the anonymous psalms in Book I (Psalm 2) is attributed to David in Acts 4:25, and Psalm 72, called "A Psalm of Solomon," closes with the words, "The prayers of David the son of Jesse are ended," so that it may well have been written by David instead of Solomon. Also, Psalm 127, is called "A Song of Degrees *for* Solomon," and the ten psalms attributed to the Sons of Korah were actually inscribed as "*for* the Sons of Korah." Thus the total may, with these revisions, become somewhat more symmetrical.

Author	Book I	Book II	Book III	Book IV	Book V	Epilogue	Total
David	38	19	1	2	15		75
Asaph		1	11				12
Moses				1			1
Heman			1				1
Ethan			1				1
Anonymous	3	11	3	14	24	5	60
Total	41	31	17	17	39	5	150

Many of the "anonymous" psalms, of course, may well have been written by David or one of the other Psalmists listed above.

One significant feature of the five books is that each ends with a great doxology. These are:

I. Psalm 41:13. "Blessed be the Lord God of Israel from everlasting, and to everlasting. Amen, and Amen."

II. Psalm 72:19. "And blessed be his glorious name forever: and let the whole earth be filled with His glory: Amen, and Amen."

III. Psalm 89:52. "Blessed be the Lord for evermore. Amen, and Amen."

IV. Psalm 106:48. "Blessed be the Lord God of Israel from everlasting to everlasting: and let all the people say, Amen. Praise ye the Lord."

V. Psalm 145:21. "My mouth shall speak the praise of the Lord; and let all flesh bless His holy name for ever and ever."

The Epilogue ends not with a similar "blessing," but with an even greater exhortation and doxology:

Let everything that hath breath praise the Lord. Praise ye the Lord (Ps. 150:6).

Just prior to each of these grand book-ending doxologies, however, had been a testimony of great conflict between the enemies of God and God's people. Psalm 145:20 is representative: "The Lord preserveth all them that love Him: but all the wicked will He destroy."

Such is the Book of Psalms — God's gracious assurances to all who love Him in the midst of a sinful world, to the accompaniment of their praises and their songs in the night.

Chapter 2

Two Ways and Two Destinies

Psalm 1
The Foundation Psalm

The 1st Psalm is an introductory psalm, laying the foundation for all the others. Appropriately, its author is anonymous, but he outlines in graphic language the great theme of the age-long conflict between the ungodly and the righteous, with their two ends. The first three verses describe the way of the righteous man and the last three verses the way of the ungodly. The righteous will be sustained in the midst of an ungodly world, but the ungodly will ultimately be destroyed in the judgment. Though men commonly claim there are many ways and all lead to God, the Scriptures make it clear from beginning to end that there are only two ways, one leading to heaven and one to hell. The Lord Jesus made this fact forever clear: "Enter ye in at the strait gate: for wide is the gate, and broad is the way, that leadeth to destruction, and many there be which go in thereat: Because strait is the gate, and narrow is the way, which leadeth unto life, and few there be that find it" (Matt. 7:13–14).

The two ways and the two destinies constitute the theme of innumerable other Scriptures. For example:

And I will put enmity between thee and the woman, and between thy seed and her seed; it shall bruise thy head, and thou shalt bruise his heel (Gen. 3:15).

And many of them that sleep in the dust of the earth shall awake, some to everlasting life, and some to shame and everlasting contempt (Dan. 12:2).

Then shall ye return, and discern between the righteous and the wicked, between him that serveth God and him that serveth him not (Mal. 3:18).

Marvel not at this: for the hour is coming, in the which all that are in the graves shall hear his voice, And shall come forth; they that have done good, unto the resurrection of life; and they that have done evil, unto the resurrection of damnation (John 5:28–29).

[God] will render to every man according to his deeds: To them who by patient continuance in well doing seek for glory and honour and immortality, eternal life: But unto them that are contentious, and do not obey the truth, but obey unrighteousness, indignation and wrath, Tribulation and anguish, upon every soul of man that doeth evil (Rom. 2:6–9).

The conflict has many faces and forms. Behind it all is the primeval and continuing satanic rebellion against God. Satan has gained dominion over the world once given to Adam, and this will continue until God's final victory over him at the end of the age. In the interim, God, through Christ, has paid the price of redemption and is recovering many souls from the snare of the devil, their salvation being accomplished through their faith in His word. The spiritual battle rages primarily now in the minds of men, who must decide between "the counsel of the ungodly" and "the law of the Lord" (verses 1–2), but this decision of the mind and will has all manner of consequences in life and character. The counsel of the ungodly is nothing less than the philosophy of the natural man who seeks to understand his existence and control his destiny without regard to God. It is man-centered rather than God-centered, humanistic rather than theistic, based on the myth of evolution instead of the fact of creation. Standing in stark contrast is the infallible Word of God, revealing the Lord as sovereign Creator and judge, and man as hopelessly lost without God's salvation.

The Way of the Righteous
Verses 1–3

Blessed is the man that walketh not in the counsel of the ungodly, nor standeth in the way of sinners, nor sitteth in the seat of the scornful.

But his delight is in the law of the LORD; and in his law doth he meditate day and night.

And he shall be like a tree planted by the rivers of water, that bringeth forth his fruit in his season; his leaf also shall not wither; and whatsoever he doeth shall prosper.

The psalm begins with the wonderful word "Blessed." This word (Hebrew *ashere*) means "happy," and is often so translated. It occurs in the Book of Psalms more than in all the rest of the Bible put together. Thus, even though the theme of conflict is prominent throughout the psalms, they begin on a note of happiness and end (Ps. 150:6) on a note of praise.

We do not know who wrote this psalm, although most of the psalms in Book I (Ps. 1–41) were written by David. Its terminology (particularly the word "scornful" is unique to this particular psalm, perhaps seeming more appropriate for the Book of Proverbs than the Book of Psalms. Possibly it was originally written by Solomon as an introduction to the first compilation of his father's writings. In any case, these first verses constitute a marvelous testimony of assurance. If one desires happiness, here is the key.

Verse one indicates the separation of the happy man from the broad way leading to destruction, while verse two describes his commitment to the narrow way leading to life. Note the progression in verse one — "walketh not," — "nor standeth" — "nor sitteth." This corresponds to the progression of commitment to the humanistic world view. First, the unwary soul would hearken to the "counsel of the ungodly;" then he would begin to associate with "the way of sinners;" finally, he would settle down permanently in "the seat of the scornful." This is always the order. First, one is impressed by the high-sounding philosophy of ungodly intellectuals; then, having rejected God's truth, he falls away from God's standard of righteousness in practice, and, in the end, he assumes an attitude of scoffing superiority to all who believe God, becoming one who himself offers the "counsel of the ungodly" to those who have neglected God's Word.

Such a pathway, however attractive it may seem to the natural man, can never produce true happiness. "There is a way which seemeth right unto a man; but the end thereof are the ways of death" (Prov. 14:12). The way of the ungodly shall perish.

Happy is the man who, despite the inducements of temporal acclaim of wealth or pleasure, refuses to be intimidated by the humanistic, naturalistic, evolutionistic wisdom of this world — "the counsel of the ungodly" — and who, instead, takes his knowledge and counsel from God in His Word. "Happy is that people, that is in such a case: yea, happy is that people, whose God is the LORD" (Ps. 144:15).

Such a man is characterized by love for the Scriptures. "His delight is in the law [Hebrew *torah*] of the LORD." The "law" was essentially the only part of the Scriptures then available to the Psalmist, whereas we today have the complete revelation of God, and therefore far greater reason to delight in it even than he had. Furthermore, this godly man meditates in the law day and night — not that he never thinks of anything else, but rather that all his thoughts and actions are governed by his deliberate desire to be obedient to God's Word in every way. No doubt his terminology was inspired by the testimony of Joshua, with which the Psalmist was familiar: "This book of the law shall not depart out of thy mouth; but thou shalt meditate therein day and night, that thou mayest observe to do all that is written therein: for then thou shalt make thy way prosperous, and then thou shalt have good success." (Josh. 1:8).

It is noteworthy that the Scriptures are set in direct confutation of the counsel of the ungodly. This is a very necessary truth for us to learn today. Ungodly counsel, sinful ways, and a scornful heart may be answered and corrected not by human wisdom and good resolutions, but only by the Word of God!

The godly man is also likened to a deep-rooted tree growing along a natural watercourse, whose leaves never wither because of drought and whose fruit is produced regularly and abundantly. The "rivers of water" may speak of the Holy Spirit (John 7:38–39) and the "bringing forth of fruit in season" of the godly life and productive witness produced in that man by the Spirit (John 15:16; Eph. 5:9) through the Word. As God had promised to Joshua, such a man would prosper in all he set out to do — because, of course, all of his undertakings would be directed by the Lord. "In all thy ways, acknowledge him, and he shall direct thy paths" (Prov. 3:6). In contrast to the tree of the righteous, the tree of the wicked is described in Psalm 37:35–36: "I have seen the wicked in great power, and spreading himself like a green bay tree. Yet he passed away, and, lo, he was not: yea, I sought him, but he could not be found." The second half of Psalm 1 focuses on the ungodly man.

The Way of the Ungodly
Verses 4–5

The ungodly are not so: but are like the chaff which the wind driveth away.

Therefore the ungodly shall not stand in the judgment, nor sinners in the congregation of the righteous.

The grain was commonly flayed on the summit of a high and windy hill, so that the lighter chaff could be easily separated. The Psalmist used such wind-driven chaff to illustrate how the ungodly would one day vanish from the earth. Though ungodly philosophies, all centered in evolutionary humanism, now spread themselves abroad in great power, like a green bay tree, they will soon pass away and never be found again. The day is coming when all ungodliness will be revealed for what it is. "And then shall that Wicked be revealed, whom the Lord shall consume with the spirit of his mouth, and shall destroy with the brightness of his coming" (2 Thess. 2:8). Even now, in the minds and hearts of right-thinking people, such systems quickly dissipate in the light of God's Word.

Of course, it should not be forgotten that all of us are among the "ungodly" until redeemed by Christ. None are truly in "the way of the righteous." "There is none righteous; no, not one" (Rom. 3:10). All were originally "in the way of sinners," because "all have sinned and come short of the glory of God" (Rom. 3:23).

We were all ungodly people, but "when we were yet without strength, in due time Christ died for the ungodly" (Rom. 5:6). Though we could in no way ever earn salvation, "to him that worketh not, but believeth on him that justified the ungodly, his faith is counted for righteousness" (Rom. 4:5). Even though we could never find and follow the way of the righteous ourselves, Jesus said: "I am the way" (John 14:6), so when we are "in Christ," we are indeed in the way of the righteous. In fact, Christ is not only the Way, but He also is the very personification of righteousness. He is "Jesus Christ the righteous" (1 John 2:1), and He is made righteousness unto us (1 Cor. 1:30; 2 Cor. 5:21). In the final analysis, the battle is the Lord's. Jesus Christ is the ultimate righteous one: the Antichrist is the ultimate ungodly one. In fact, the word "ungodly" in Psalm 1 is the same word as "wicked," and the final great Antichrist is "that Wicked [one]" in 2 Thessalonians 2:8.

Since Christ is not only "the Way of the Righteous," but also will be the judge (John 5:22), it is clear that "the ungodly shall not stand in the judgment." The "great congregation" of the redeemed cannot include any that are unrepentant and therefore still among the ungodly. There will finally have to be an eternal separation of the wheat from the chaff. "The wicked shall be turned into hell, and all the nations that forget God" (Ps. 9:17).

Verse 6

For the LORD knoweth the way of the righteous: but the way of
the ungodly shall perish.

This climactic verse of the first psalm thus becomes the key verse of the entire Book of Psalms. Though the heathen rage and earth's leaders seek to break the rule of God and His Christ (see the second psalm!), the way of the ungodly shall perish. Therefore, for all eternity, "Blessed is the man who walketh not in the counsel of the ungodly," and, furthermore, "Blessed are all they that put their trust in Him" (Ps. 2:12).

Part II

Prophecies of Christ
in the Psalms

Chapter 3

The Son of God

Psalm 2

I n one sense, practically all the psalms could be understood as prophetic of the coming Savior. In type, if nothing else, each one seems to foreshadow in one way or another either "the sufferings of Christ" or "the glory that should follow" (1 Pet. 1:11).

There are a number of psalms, however, which are so explicitly clear in their description of the person or work of Christ that practically all Bible-believing Christian writers after Christ, as well as even some Jewish rabbis before Christ, have recognized them as peculiarly "messianic" psalms. Their prophetic descriptions are so accurate as to be outside the range of speculative probabilities, and thus they provide uniquely powerful evidence of divine inspiration.

The first, and one of the greatest, of these messianic psalms is Psalm 2, the psalm immediately following the great introductory psalm. The two groups of mankind categorized in Psalm 1 quickly become personalized in Psalm 2, which describes a great council of Christ-hating leaders arrayed against Christ and His followers.

The second psalm is unique among the psalms in three interesting respects. It is actually referred to by number in the New Testament (Acts 13:33), a fact which indicates that the chapter divisions were present in the Book of Psalms right from the start. Secondly, its Davidic authorship is confirmed in the New Testament (Acts 4:25), even though the heading of the psalm itself, contrary to the usual situation, does not say who the author is.

This psalm is also one of the greatest of the messianic psalms. It is one of the very few Old Testament passages — and the only one in the psalms — which refers to the Son of God by that name (verses 7 and 12).

The psalm is written in the form of a great dramatic poem, in four stanzas of three verses each. The first stanza is written directly in terms of David's perspective and the second stanza stresses the viewpoint of God the Father. The third is in the form of a direct statement by God the Son. The final stanza is a testimony which most appropriately would come from God, the Holy Spirit.

The Kings of the Earth
Verses 1–3

Why do the heathen rage, and the people imagine a vain thing?

The kings of the earth set themselves, and the rulers take counsel together, against the Lord, and against his anointed, saying,

Let us break their bands asunder, and cast away their cords from us.

In the first stanza, it is as though David were carried forward in the Spirit to a future time. In his vision, he sees great assemblages of people coming together, perhaps from many different times and places, and, as he listens to their speeches and deliberations, he is greatly disturbed and perplexed at what he hears. Finally, he cries out: "Why?"

"Why do the heathen rage and the people imagine a vain thing?" The word "heathen" refers especially to the Gentile nations, and "people" (by parallelism) to the people of those nations and probably of the Jewish nation as well. The word "rage" is literally, "tumultuously assemble." Evidently the people of various nations are coming together, through their representatives, in a great convocation, and they are boisterous and riotous. Their purpose is to "imagine" (literally, "study" or "plan") a "vain thing." The latter phrase is one word in the Hebrew, but the translation is accurate.

And what is the vain thing which the nations are planning? "The kings of the earth set themselves, and the rulers take counsel together against the Lord, and against His anointed." The word "anointed," of course, is *Messiah*, the Hebrew equivalent of the Greek *Christ*. Thus, the assembly has been called together to plan a concerted rebellion and opposition against Jehovah and against Jesus Christ!

The prophecy was fulfilled in a precursive way at the trial of Christ. After quoting this very verse, the Early Church then applied it thus: "For of a truth against thy holy child Jesus, whom thou hast anointed, both Herod and Pontius Pilate with the Gentiles, and the people of Israel, were gathered together" (Acts 4:27).

The ultimate fulfillment, however, will no doubt be at the very end of the age, in the last great rebellion against God, of both men and devils. "For they are the spirits of devils, working miracles, which go forth unto the kings of the earth and of the whole world, to gather them to the battle of that great day of God Almighty" (Rev. 16:14). This "gathering together" is to Armageddon (Rev. 16:16), but there is even another such assemblage after the millennium. "[Satan] shall go out to deceive the nations which are in the four quarters of the earth, Gog and Magog, to gather them together to battle" (Rev. 20:8).

Between the initial fulfillment of this prophecy, at the trial of Christ, and the final fulfillment at the end of the age, there have been innumerable other partial fulfillments. The word "rulers" in verse 2 can be applied to leaders of any sort. Whenever there is an educational convocation, a scientific convention, a political conference, an industrial gathering, the almost universal practice is to ignore the leadership of God and His Christ, and in some cases, actively to oppose them. Men operate under the awful delusion that they can plan and decide things on their own, without consulting the will of God.

Perhaps the most conspicuous example is the Assembly of the United Nations. Another was the great Darwinian Centennial Convocation in 1959 at the University of Chicago, where the convocation keynote speaker, Sir Julian Huxley, boasted that "Darwinism had removed the very concept of God from the sphere of rational discussion." More recently, the American Humanist Association, in its 1973 Manifesto, blatantly declared: "No deity will save us, we will save ourselves."

The essential man-centered theme of all such assemblies is, as David foresaw, "Let us break their bands asunder, and cast away their cords from us." What little restraint is still practiced among men because of the fear of God must be fully removed. God and His Word, Christ and His salvation, must be banished from the schools, the airwaves, and the press, and the atheistic or pantheistic bondage (such as now exists in many of the world's nations) replace the bonds of love and cords of compassion which constrain all who serve God.

Truly, this is a *vain thing* which the people *imagine*! "Because that, when they knew God, they glorified Him not as God, neither were thankful; but became *vain in their imaginations*, and their foolish heart was darkened. Professing themselves to be wise, they became fools" (Rom. 1:21–22).

Heavenly Derision
Verses 4–6

He that sitteth in the heavens shall laugh: the Lord shall have them in derision.

Then shall he speak unto them in his wrath, and vex them in his sore displeasure.

Yet have I set my king upon my holy hill of Zion.

One of the most tragic verses in the entire Bible opens the second stanza of this psalm. "He that sitteth in the heavens shall laugh: the Lord shall have them in derision." When men take counsel to dethrone God, it hardly provokes Him to fear or flight! It provokes Him to derisive laughter. The fact that men foolishly reject God as their Creator does not mean He did not really create them. "Because I have called, and ye refused; I have stretched out my hand, and no man regarded; but ye have set at naught all my counsel, and would none of my reproof; I also will laugh at your calamity; I will mock when your fear cometh" (Prov. 1:24–26).

The scene thus shifts in this stanza to the heavens, where God the Father sits on the throne. After laughing at the fools who say there is no God (Ps. 14:1), then He speaks. "Then shall he speak unto them in his wrath, and vex them in his sore displeasure." First, He laughs at them, then speaks to them, and finally "troubles" them. There is coming a day of "vengeance on them that know not God, and that obey not the gospel of our Lord Jesus Christ" (2 Thess. 1:8).

When God finally does break His long and patient silence, these will be His words: "Yet have I set my king upon my holy hill of Zion." Though men would take counsel together and plot against the Lord, finally even condemning His anointed one to be crucified, it was all merely in the accomplishment of God's plan. "For to do whatever thy hand and thy counsel determined before to be done" (Acts 4:28).

There are two senses, of course, in which God will set His king upon the hill of Zion. The word used for "set" actually means either "offer" or "pour out." It is translated "offer," for example, in Psalm 16:4. "Their drink offerings of blood will I not offer." Thus, the reference here is first of all to God's offering of His anointed one on Mount Zion, pouring out His blood in atonement for sin. What divine irony! When men and devils took counsel together to put the Savior to death, it was only that "through death he might destroy him that had the power of death, that is the devil" (Heb. 2:14).

But then also He will be anointed on Mount Zion not only for death, but as King. "Rejoice greatly, O daughter of Zion . . . behold, thy King cometh unto thee" (Zech. 9:9). "And it shall be in that day, that living waters shall go out from Jerusalem . . . And the LORD shall be king over all the earth" (Zech. 14:8–9). "For out of Zion shall go forth the law, and the word of the LORD from Jerusalem" (Isa. 2:3).

The Son of God Speaks
Verses 7–9

I will declare the decree: the Lord hath said unto me, Thou art my Son; this day have I begotten thee.

Ask of me, and I shall give thee the heathen for thine inheritance, and the uttermost parts of the earth for thy possession.

Thou shalt break them with a rod of iron; thou shalt dash them in pieces like a potter's vessel.

In the third stanza is heard the voice of the Son of God, the one who had been offered up as a sacrifice on the holy hill of Zion, the one against whom the world's leaders would take counsel together, whose cords they would, age after age, seek to unloose. If there was a mystery concerning how He could be anointed both as sacrifice and king, it is resolved in this stanza. He could not only suffer death, but would, in the process, *conquer* death!

"I will declare the decree." "No man hath seen God at any time; the only begotten Son, which is in the bosom of the Father, He hath declared Him" (John 1:18). The Father made the decree, the Son declared it. He is the *Word* of God, and when we hear Him, we hear the Father. And what is that decree?

He quotes from the Father: "The Lord has said unto me, Thou art my son; this day have I begotten thee." There are several senses in which Jesus Christ is the only-begotten Son of God, but here the emphasis is on His resurrection from the dead. He had been condemned and crucified, and, if that had been all, no one would have believed on Him. But He was "declared to be the Son of God with power . . . by the resurrection from the dead" (Rom. 1:4). He was the "firstborn from the dead" (Col. 1:18). He is "the faithful witness, and the first begotten of the dead, and the prince of the kings of the earth" (Rev. 1:5).

Any question that this verse refers to His resurrection is dispelled by its quotation in the New Testament: "And we declare unto you glad tidings, how that the promise which was made unto the fathers, God hath fulfilled the same unto us their children, in that he hath raised up Jesus again, as it is also written in the second psalm, Thou art my Son, this day have I begotten thee" (Acts 13:32–33). This same verse is also restated in Hebrews 5:5.

Because of His victory over death, He will triumph over all lesser enemies. Continuing His declaration of God's decree, He quotes the Father: "Ask of me, and I shall give thee the heathen [or, 'nations'] for thine inheritance, and the uttermost parts of the earth for thy possession." The Son is also the heir and He is to be "heir of all things" (Heb. 1:2). Since He "created all things" (Col. 1:16), is "upholding all things" (Heb. 1:3), and died to "reconcile all things" (Col. 1:20), therefore, eventually He will "gather together in one all things in Christ" (Eph. 1:10).

"Thou shalt beat them with a rod of iron, thou shalt dash them in pieces like a potter's vessel." The kings and rulers and leaders of the earth, with few exceptions, will not submit willingly unto Him, and so He must "put down all rule and all authority and power" (1 Cor. 15:24). "And out of his mouth goeth a sharp sword, that with it he should smite the nations: and he shall rule them with a rod of iron: and he treadeth the winepress of the fierceness and wrath of Almighty God" (Rev. 19:15). "And he that overcometh, and keepeth my works unto the end, to him will I give power over the nations: And he shall rule them with a rod of iron; as the vessels of a potter shall they be broken to shivers: even as I received of my Father" (Rev. 2:26–27). These great promises will, so far as we can tell from Scripture, all be fulfilled literally in the coming Tribulation and Millennium periods. The Good Shepherd shall constrain all rebels in the flock with a rod of iron.

The Exhortation
Verses 10–12

Be wise now therefore, O ye kings: be instructed, ye judges of the earth.

Serve the LORD with fear, and rejoice with trembling.

Kiss the Son, lest he be angry, and ye perish from the way, when his wrath is kindled but a little. Blessed are all they that put their trust in him.

The last trilogy of verses contains an exhortation, a warning, and an invitation. Though the Psalmist does not say so specifically, it is appropriate to think of these as the direct urgings of God the Holy Spirit. It is His ministry to "reprove the world of sin, and of righteousness, and of judgment" (John 16:8), and that is exactly what these verses do.

"Be wise now therefore, O ye kings: be instructed, ye judges of the earth." The emphasis is on *now*. Don't persist in your rebellion until that day when every knee shall be forced to bow, and every tongue compelled to confess Christ as Lord. "Behold, now is the accepted time; behold, now is the day of salvation" (2 Cor. 6:2). The kings and rulers who vainly imagine they can do away with God and His Christ, though professing themselves to be wise, have become fools, for "fools despise wisdom and instruction" (Prov. 1:7).

"Serve the Lord with fear, and rejoice with trembling." These are parallels and are strongly emotional terms. Serving the Lord is joyful, but is to be with great reverence and holy awe. "Wherefore we [receive] a kingdom which cannot be moved, let us have grace, whereby we may serve God acceptably with reverence and godly fear" (Heb. 12:28).

"Kiss the Son, lest he be angry and ye perish from the way, when his wrath is kindled but a little." This is the other Hebrew word for "son." In verse 7 it is *ben*; here it is *bar*. There is no doubt, however, that both verses identify Him as the Son of God. Some versions (e.g., Revised Standard, Living Bible, etc.) either replace or modify this command by "kiss his feet," but such a translation reveals more about the bias than the skill of the translators. The "kiss" is one of true and selfless love. Not only are men to serve the Lord, but also to love the Lord. "If any man love not the Lord Jesus Christ, let him be Anathema Maranatha [literally 'accursed, for our Lord is coming']" (1 Cor. 16:22).

The word for "but a little" is also in other passages rendered "soon," and it may be that such is the emphasis here. The day of the "wrath of the Lamb" (Rev. 6:16) is soon coming and then it will be too late. Men should be wise *now*, therefore!

This great psalm concludes with a beautiful gospel invitation: "Blessed [or 'happy'] are all they that put their trust in him." This invitation down through the ages has been accepted and proved by many kings and leaders, even by evolutionists and atheists, as well as by multitudes of ordinary "people" in all "nations." It is still a promise in God's Word and will still prove true today, for all who believe.

Chapter 4

The Garden Prayer and the Empty Tomb

Psalm 16

The greatest event in history since the very creation of the world itself, as well as the crowning proof of the truth of Christianity, is the bodily resurrection of the Lord Jesus Christ. Psalm 16 contains a thrilling prophecy of this resurrection, written by David a thousand years before its fulfillment.

As the Apostles went forth to preach after Christ's ascension, in accordance with His Great Commission, the record tells that "with great power gave the apostles witness of the resurrection of the Lord Jesus: and great grace was upon them all" (Acts 4:33). Furthermore, they referred to the Scriptures (Acts 13:35–37), and used this psalm as the keystone of their preaching that the Scriptures foretold Christ's resurrection. We are, therefore, well justified in applying the psalm to Christ. Indeed, it is one of the greatest of all the Messianic psalms.

One of the first things to note is that although Psalm 16 is written by David in the first person, no doubt against a background of his own experiences, it goes far beyond anything that could be applied merely to him. It clearly is a prayer from the very heart of Christ, and we should read it as though Christ himself is speaking the words.

The Garden of Gethsemane
Verses 1–4

Preserve me, O God: for in thee do I put my trust.

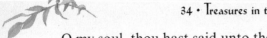

O my soul, thou hast said unto the LORD, Thou art my Lord: my goodness extendeth not to thee;

But to the saints that are in the earth, and to the excellent, in whom is all my delight.

Their sorrows shall be multiplied that hasten after another god: their drink-offerings of blood will I not offer, nor take up their names into my lips.

Although He speaks of the Resurrection (verse 10), it is evident that the resurrection is placed in the future tense. Thus, the prayer predates the Resurrection, and, for that matter, evidently predates the Cross as well. Yet both the Cross and the empty tomb are clearly in the very immediate future. All things considered, the context fits perfectly the conclusion that this psalm can be nothing less than the prayer uttered by Christ in the Garden of Gethsemane, the night before His crucifixion. The exposition below will proceed on that assumption.

He had just prayed: "O my Father, if this cup may not pass away from me, except I drink it, thy will be done" (Matt. 26:42). Having accepted the bitter cup, He then turned himself over to the care of His loving Father:

"Preserve me, O God: for in thee do I put my trust. O my soul . . . Thou art my Lord: my goodness extendeth not to thee" (verses 1 and 2). That is, though He was holy and sinless, He was not offering His goodness to God as justification for escaping the wrath of God deserved by sinners. For He, himself, was about to be "made sin for us, who knew no sin, that we might be made the righteousness of God in him" (2 Cor. 5:21).

Instead of offering His righteousness to God, it was to be offered "to the saints that are in the earth, and to the excellent, in whom is all my delight" (verse 3). It was His delight to offer the free gift of His own righteousness to those whose hearts desired forgiveness, the "saints" (that is, the "ones set apart") and the "excellent" (those who would gladly respond to His grace and love, and to whom thus could be imputed His own excellence).

On the other hand, there would be many others who would not have Him. They would, instead, "hasten after another god" (literally, "exchange for others"). There would be many excuses offered, and many other ways tried, to avoid responding to Him. But, since His righteousness is the only righteousness acceptable before a holy God, the end of all such dissimulating can only be that "their sorrows will be multiplied." Ever since the great Curse on the ground (Gen. 3:17), the lot of fallen man has been one of sorrow. Christ has offered deliverance from sorrow and death, but for those who reject Him there can only be left an endless multiplication of sorrows.

Not that such people were irreligious. Sacrifices and offerings without end have always been found among those who reject Christ — even "drink offerings of blood," as though the gods were thirsty for the blood of men and beasts! These were utterly repugnant, however, to the Savior.

Yet He, himself, was about to drink the bitterest cup of all, and to offer up His own precious blood, in order that God's holiness might be vindicated and sinners be saved. There were, indeed, drink offerings prescribed in the Mosaic Laws (Num. 15:7), and even before the time of Moses (Gen. 35:14), but these were of wine, not blood, the wine symbolizing the blood which He would one day shed on the cross. Furthermore, these drink offerings were to be "poured out" at the altar, not drunk, as the heathen did. The people of Israel were specifically forbidden to eat or drink blood — the blood was given on the altar as an atonement for their souls (Lev. 17:11–14), not as some mystical source of life and power, as the heathen believed. For such as these, He could not "take up their names into my lips." For each one who would truly confess His name, however, He would turn gladly to "confess his name before my Father" (Rev. 3:5).

The Cup and the Heritage
Verses 5–7

The LORD is the portion of mine inheritance and of my cup: thou maintainest my lot.

The lines are fallen unto me in pleasant places; yea, I have a goodly heritage.

I will bless the LORD, who hath given me counsel; my reins also instruct me in the night seasons.

The next three verses (5–7) seem particularly appropriate in the context of Christ's prayer to His Father concerning the "cup" which He was to drink, and the comfort and assurance granted to Him even in light of that dread prospect. Verse 5 even mentions the cup: "The LORD is the portion of my inheritance and of my cup: thou maintainest my lot."

When the tribes of Israel entered the Promised Land, each family received a certain "lot," determined by the "casting of lots," to serve as its inheritance. Jesus Christ, however, in His humanity never had a home or even any place to "lay His head" (Matt. 8:20). The Lord was *His* inheritance, and that was sufficient. Furthermore, that lot was kept up and assured also by the Lord. "The Father hath not left me alone; for I do always those things that please him" (John 8:29).

But that inheritance involved a "cup" as well — a word which comprehended one's entire life experience, especially that portion of his experience which might involve testing or suffering. The specific cup which was to be taken by the Lord Jesus was the most bitter cup ever offered, that containing the wine of God's wrath against the sin of the world (Rev. 14:19; Matt. 26:27–28).

And yet He, "for the joy that was set before him, endured the cross, despising the shame" (Heb. 12:2). In spite of all the infinite suffering He must endure in order to redeem lost men, He could look forward to the great inheritance awaiting Him beyond the cross.

"The lines [that is, the surveying lines outlining the 'lot' of His inheritance] are fallen unto me in pleasant places; yea, I have a goodly heritage" (verse 6).

His inheritance is nothing less than the entire world of the redeemed. "I shall give thee the [nations] for thine inheritance, and the uttermost parts of the earth for thy possession" (Ps. 2:8). Indeed, He is to be "appointed heir of all things" (Heb. 1:2). And because He drank the cup on our behalf, we have the inestimable privilege of being "heirs of God, and joint heirs with Christ" (Rom. 8:17).

In the Gospel accounts, it is recorded that, after His ordeal of prayer and travail that night in the Garden of Gethsemane, when even "His sweat was as it were great drops of blood falling down to the ground" (Luke 22:44), "there appeared an angel unto Him from heaven, strengthening him" (Luke 22:43). It is apparently this event that is prophesied in verse 7 of the psalm. "I will bless the Lord, who hath given me counsel; my reins also instruct me in the night seasons."

The Bodily Resurrection
Verses 8–11

I have set the LORD always before me: because he is at my right hand, I shall not be moved.

Therefore my heart is glad, and my glory rejoiceth: my flesh also shall rest in hope.

For thou wilt not leave my soul in hell; neither wilt thou suffer thine Holy One to see corruption.

Thou wilt shew me the path of life: in thy presence is fulness of joy; at thy right hand there are pleasures for evermore.

The last four verses of the psalm (all restated in Acts 2:25–28) do contain a remarkable summary of the events following the prayer in the Garden, especially His death and resurrection. Immediately after the prayer Judas came, and He was arrested and taken to prison and judgment. The several pseudo-trials that followed, accompanied by insults and mockery and, finally, beatings and condemnation to death, were unjust in the extreme, yet He bore it patiently and without resistance. This is all implied in verse 8: "I have set the Lord always before me: because he is at my right hand, I shall not be moved." He had no public defender or counsel — only accusers and judges. Nevertheless, the Lord was both before Him for protection and at His right hand for guidance, so that He was not alone.

As a result of His Father's assurance and presence, He could look forward with joy even to the experience of death itself. "Therefore my heart is glad, and my glory rejoiceth." The word "glory," following the Septuagint, is rendered by the word "tongue" in Peter's quotation of this verse in Acts 2:26 — "my tongue is glad."

This might seem like an unusual interchange of meanings, especially if ordinary men were in view. For such men, their tongues are hardly instruments of glory! In fact, James says, "But the tongue can no man tame; it is an unruly evil, full of deadly poison" (James 3:8). Of the Lord Jesus, however, even His enemies testified: "Never man spake like this man" (John 7:46). Another Psalmist, speaking prophetically of this same man, said, "Thou art fairer than the children of men: grace is poured into thy lips" (Ps. 45:2). Of the one who was the very Word of God incarnate, speaking words which would last forever (Matt. 24:35), it is beautifully fitting to equate His tongue with His glory!

"My flesh also shall rest in hope." After His trial and His death would come His burial, with the battered flesh of His body resting in Joseph's tomb. However, that body would not return to dust, even though every other dead body since the beginning of time had so disintegrated. *His* body would merely rest until His spirit returned to it after accomplishing a vital mission in the heart of the earth. His ministry of substitution and propitiation would have already been fully accomplished on the cross, as testified by the victory cry, "It is finished!" (John 19:30) immediately before He withdrew His spirit from its body. His body could be committed to the sepulchre in full confidence of resurrection. And because of Him, all who believe in Him likewise "sorrow not, even as others which have no hope. For if we believe that Jesus died and rose again, even so them also which sleep in Jesus will God bring with him" (1 Thess. 4:13–14).

"Neither wilt thou suffer thine Holy One to see corruption." Not only would His body not return to the dust; it would not even begin the normal process of post-mortem decay. It would simply "rest" in death until He returned. In the meantime, for the three days His body was in the grave, Christ was still alive in His spirit, "By which he went and preached unto the spirits in prison; Which sometime were disobedient, when the longsuffering of God waited in the days of Noah" (1 Pet. 3:19–20). This was not a preaching of the Gospel, but a proclaiming of victory and judgment to those evil spiritual powers (the same ones of whom Peter also spoke in his second epistle). These were the "angels that sinned" and who were "cast down to hell" and were "to be reserved unto judgment" (2 Pet. 2:4), who had tried to thwart God's plan of redemption through corrupting all flesh in the original world before the flood. Following this visit to their great prison in the depths of the earth, He would return to His body waiting in the tomb, fashion it into an eternal body of glory, rise from the dead, and ascend to heaven. "Who is gone into heaven, and is on the right hand of God; angels and authorities and powers being made subject unto him" (1 Pet. 3:22).

Furthermore, He would return with "the keys of [Hades] and of death" (Rev. 1:18), together with the spirits of all who had previously died in faith. "When He ascended up on high, He led captivity captive" after He had "also descended first into the lower parts of the earth" (Eph. 4:8–9).

If anyone should be inclined to reject the idea of a prison (or "hell" or "pit" — various terms are used in Scripture with essentially the same place under consideration) in the deep interior of the earth on the ground that geologists reject such a notion, he should remember that no geological instruments are capable of determining whether or not such a region exists. Therefore, no geologist or other scientist is capable of refuting the clear testimony of the Bible that it does exist.

Furthermore, if anyone is disposed to reject the bodily resurrection predicted there on the basis that this is scientifically impossible, let him realize that this is the very point. God, not the scientists, ordained those principles in nature which we now call laws of science. Miracles, therefore, are possible — in fact, a miracle could well be defined as an event that is impossible by the laws of science, but which happens nonetheless. The historic *fact* of the bodily resurrection of Christ meets all the objective criteria of historicity as well as, or better than, any other fact of history.

The final verse of Psalm 16 looks forward to His resurrection, ascension, and "session" at the right hand of His Father in heaven. "Thou wilt show me the path of life." Actually, the word "life" is in the plural, perhaps referring to the multitudes that have also received endless life through His mighty act. "In thy presence is fulness of joy." Back in the presence of His Father, He would enter forever into the "joy that was set before him" (Heb. 12:2) as He prepared to drink the "cup" and "endure the cross." This was the joy of seeing God's purpose in creation finally accomplished, with multitudes of redeemed souls brought into God's presence and fellowship forever.

The psalm concludes with the magnificent testimony, "At thy right hand there are pleasures for evermore." This is the very first reference in the Bible to Christ's presence in heaven at the right hand of God, but far from the last. In all, there are 21 such references, and they can be arranged nicely into three groups of seven each.

The first such group consists of two references in the Book of Psalms (the other being Ps. 110:1), and the five places in the New Testament that quote Psalm 110:1 (Matt. 22:44; Mark 12:36; Luke 20:42; Acts 2:34; and Heb. 1:13). Psalm 16:11 emphasizes the right hand of God as a place of fellowship; Psalm 110:1 as a source of power!

The second group consists of seven general references to Christ at God's right hand in Paul's epistles (Rom. 8:34; Eph. 1:20; Col. 3:1; Heb. 1:3, 8:1, 10:12, and 12:2). The third group consists of seven references in other books of the New Testament (Matt. 26:64; Mark 14:62; 16:19; Luke 22:69; Acts 7:55; 7:56; and 1 Pet. 3:22).

At the right hand of the Father there is, therefore, both full joy and eternal joy. No more sorrow, no more pain, no more tears, no more death! (Rev. 21:4). "If ye then be risen with Christ, seek those things which are above, where Christ sitteth on the right hand of God" (Col. 3:1).

Chapter 5

Christ on the Cross

Psalm 22

A thousand years before Christ, David wrote this remarkable poem of suffering and praise, taken in part from his own experience, but then going far beyond anything which he could ever have known in his own limited understanding.

The psalm constitutes a remarkable evidence of divine inspiration, as it outlines in minute prophetic detail the sufferings of Christ on the cross, as well as His victory over sin and the subsequent preaching of His gospel in all the world. As we shall see, there are aspects of the very structure of the psalm, which still further confirm its divine inspiration.

The 22nd Psalm is quoted at least seven times in the New Testament, all in reference to Jesus Christ, so there is no doubt that it was understood by the Apostles as a messianic psalm. It describes accurately the agony of death by crucifixion, in spite of the fact that this method of execution was virtually unknown at the time of David, especially among the Jews. The reader is given an insight, not only into the physical sufferings of Christ, but also into the very thoughts of His heart. It is almost as though we were there ourselves with the soldiers and Pharisees around the cross, when "sitting down they watched him there" (Matt. 27:36).

Forsaken by the Father
Verses 1–5

My God, my God, why hast thou forsaken me? Why art thou so far from helping me, and from the words of my roaring?

O my God, I cry in the daytime, but thou hearest not; and in the night season, and am nor silent.

But thou art holy, O thou that inhabitest the praises of Israel.

Our fathers trusted in thee: they trusted, and thou didst deliver them.

They cried unto thee, and were delivered: they trusted in thee, and were not confounded.

The psalm begins with the awful cry from the cross: "My God, my God, why hast thou forsaken me?" (See Matt. 27:46 and Mark 15:34.) Of the famous "seven words from the cross," this cry is the central "word," and the central word in this central word is the most important question ever to be answered: "*Why?*"

Why, indeed, should the pure and spotless Lamb be impaled on a cross to die? The queries continue in His soul: "Why art thou so far from helping me [!] and from the words of my roaring?"

The Lord Jesus was not, of course, roaring on the cross. He was utterly silent, and in some translations the scholars have thought it more appropriate to say He was "groaning." Nevertheless the Hebrew word really is "roaring," the same word as used for the roaring of a lion.

The clue to the answer to these questions is found later in the 32nd Psalm, written after David's sin in the matter of Bathsheba and Uriah. There David wrote: "When I kept silence, my bones waxed old through my roaring all the day long" (Ps. 32:3). David was silent on the outside, but "roaring" inwardly because of the pressing guilt of his sin. The soul of the Lord Jesus likewise was roaring inwardly, because of the guilt of the sins of the whole world, which He was bearing in His own body on the tree (1 Pet. 2:24). His Father had turned His back on Him, as it were, because He was "of purer eyes than to behold evil" or to "look on iniquity" (Hab. 1:13).

He, who had always been in perfect communion with His Father, now was separated from Him because of sin. This, of course, is the essence of what hell will be (that is, complete separation from God). In those three terrible hours of darkness on the cross, Jesus Christ endured hell itself, in order to save sinners from the eternal separation from God (2 Thess. 1:9) which they deserved.

Verse 2 of the psalm notes His suffering in the morning hours and then in "the night season," when the sun was darkened supernaturally in mid-day. The answer to His own question is given in verse 3. "Thou art holy." That is, the only possible reason that the Father could ever forsake His own beloved Son is because He was made sin for us, and God's holiness requires that sin be judged.

The three hours of darkness were not caused by a solar eclipse, for no such eclipse occurred at that time in astronomic history. The event was entirely miraculous. It was as though darkness had vanquished light, for He who was "the light of the world" was dying. But it would be only for a short season, for God's purpose in creation can never be defeated. His light must inevitably conquer satanic darkness.

And what a beautiful figure is Christ's testimony here (verse 3) of God's dwelling place, "thou that *inhabitest the praises of Israel!*" He who would one day become the heir of all God's promises to Israel, even now could recall all God's promises and deliverances for His people, and how He had never failed when they called on Him. Yet God would not hear *Him!*

The Scarlet Worm
Verse 6

But I am a worm, and no man; a reproach of men, and despised of the people.

In verse 6, He is recorded to have said in His heart, "But I am a worm, and no man; a reproach of men, and despised of the people." In Isaiah 52:14 it would be said prophetically that "his visage was so marred more than any man, and His form more than the sons of men." That is, from the awful beatings He endured in connection with His trial and crucifixion, He no longer even looked like a man. Isaiah 53:3 said, "He is despised and rejected of men."

These statements, however, hardly explain fully the identification of himself as a worm. The key seems to lie in the recognition that this was a specific type of worm — the *scarlet worm*. As a matter of fact, the Hebrew word translated "worm" in this passage (*tolath*) is also frequently translated "scarlet" (e.g., Exod. 25:4) or "crimson" (Isa. 1:18). The reason for this odd equivalence is because the scarlet worm was the source of a fluid from which the people of ancient times made their scarlet dyes.

Christ's portrayal of himself as stained crimson on the cross thus immediately speaks to us in the words of Colossians 1:20. "Having made peace through the blood of his cross, by him to reconcile all things unto himself."

But no doubt the deeper significance of His identification of himself as the Scarlet Worm lies in the remarkable life-death cycle of this unique animal. For when the mother worm of this species is ready to give birth to her baby worms, she will implant her body in a tree somewhere, or a post or a stick of wood, so firmly that she can never leave again.

Then, when the young are brought forth, the mother's body provides protection and sustenance for her young until they reach the stage where they can leave home and fend for themselves. Then the mother dies.

And as she dies, the scarlet fluid in her body emerges to stain her body and the bodies of her progeny and the wood of the tree where they were given life by their dying mother.

What a picture of the blood-stained cross, and how "it became him, for whom are all things, and by whom are all things, in bringing many sons unto glory, to make the captain of their salvation perfect through sufferings" (Heb. 2:10). "A woman when she is in travail hath sorrow because her hour is come: but as soon as she is delivered of the child, she remembereth no more the anguish, for joy that a man is born into the world" (John 16:21).

Throughout the realm of the animal kingdom, new life is always preceded by a time of travail and possibly death, and this is always a divine portrait of bringing forth sons to spiritual life through spiritual death. Thus, it is said prophetically of Christ, "He shall see of the travail of his soul and shall be satisfied" (Isa. 53:11). Because of His death, not only are individual souls delivered unto everlasting life through a "new birth," but so, ultimately, "the [creation] itself also shall be delivered from the bondage of corruption" at the "manifestation of the sons of God" (Rom. 8:19–21). The redemption price was great, but the result is endless joy and glory.

Principalities and Powers
Verses 7–13

All they that see me laugh me to scorn: they shoot out the lip, they shake the head, saying,

He trusted on the LORD that he would deliver him: let him deliver him, seeing he delighted in him.

But thou art he that took me out of the womb: thou didst make me hope when I was upon my mother's breasts.

I was cast upon thee from the womb: thou art my God from my mother's belly.

Be not far from me; for trouble is near; for there is none to help.

Many bulls have compassed me: strong bulls of Bashan have beset me round.

They gaped upon me with their mouths, as a ravening and a roaring lion.

Verses 7 through 21 of this 22nd Psalm comprise one of the most remarkable passages ever written, describing in intimate detail the events that would take place a thousand years later on Calvary. The events are told through the eyes and heart of the one hanging on the "tree" planted there.

> All they that see me laugh me to scorn: they shoot out the lip, they shake the head, saying, he trusted on the LORD that he would deliver him: let him deliver him, seeing he delighted in him.

Instead of compassion for the innocent victim and sorrow over His suffering, there is nothing but gloating and mocking. Listen to the record of its fulfillment: "And they that passed by reviled him, wagging their heads. . . . Likewise also the chief priests mocking him, with the scribes and elders, said, He saved others; himself he cannot save. . . . He trusted in God; let him deliver him now, if he will have him: for he said, I am the Son of God" (Matt. 27:39–43).

In the next two verses of the psalm, He recalls His unique conception and birth, when He entered the world in human flesh. "Thou art he that took me out of the womb: Thou didst make me hope when I was upon my mother's breasts." He had left His throne in heaven to take up residence in a body "prepared" for Him (Heb. 10:5) in a virgin's womb, and He had been conscious of His Father's presence and fellowship even when in the embryonic and infant stages of the growth of that body. Throughout His human pilgrimage, He knew that "He that sent me is with me: the Father hath not left me alone; for I do always those things that please him" (John 8:29). Yet, finally, here on the cross, He prays in anguish: "Be not far from me; for trouble is near; for there is none to help." Even His Father had apparently forsaken Him.

Trouble, indeed, was very near! A malevolent horde of the demonic hosts of darkness surrounded him, invisible to human eyes but viciously real, anticipating imminent victory over their age-long enemy. "This was [their] hour, and the power of darkness" (Luke 22:53). "That old serpent" (Rev. 12:9) was inflicting his violent sting of death on the seed of the woman (Gen. 3:15), and like a rabid menagerie of wild animals, his demonic spirits were closing in for the kill. There were "many bulls . . . strong bulls of Bashan" compassing Him. These wicked bull-spirits had long ago corrupted the Canaanites in the kingdom of Bashan, producing and possessing an evil race of giants (note Gen. 6:4 and Deut. 3:1–12), which had been destroyed by the Israelites through the strength of their God.

There, also, He could see that "dogs have compassed me" — perhaps referring to the vicious demons controlling the Gentile soldiers who had so cruelly scourged and mocked Him (verse 16). "Unicorns" were there also (a term referring to the mighty *aurochs*, long extinct, but of unexcelled ferocity when living), aptly symbolizing the other fierce spirits hovering over Him (verse 21). Furthermore, there were "ravening and roaring lions" — including Satan himself (1 Pet. 5:8) — "gaping upon Him with their mouths" (verse 13) and seeking to devour Him.

"The assembly of the wicked have enclosed me!" (verse 16). That evil congregation dancing around their victim (apostate priests and brutal soldiers, jeering rabble and hordes of invisible demonic powers) little realized that they were only securing their own eternal doom. A great transaction was there being effected, planned long before the foundation of the world.

"Blotting out the handwriting of ordinances that was against us, which was contrary to us, [He] took it out of the way, nailing it to his cross; having spoiled principalities and powers, he made a shew of them openly, triumphing over them in it" (Col. 2:14–15). "Forasmuch then as the children are partakers of flesh and blood, he also himself likewise took part of the same; that through death he might destroy him that had the power of death, that is, the devil; And deliver them who through fear of death were all their lifetime subject to bondage" (Heb. 2:14–15).

Though the serpent had bruised His heel, He would crush the head of that wicked one, destroying him and all who followed him, whether man or angel, in everlasting fire (Matt. 25:41). The accomplishment of this great work, however, required that He must first satisfy the righteous justice of a Holy God, in offering His own suffering and death in substitution for the deserved penalty of eternal death pronounced for the sins of the world. He must first "by the grace of God . . . taste death for every man" (Heb. 2:9).

The Agony of Crucifixion
Verses 14–18

I am poured out like water, and all my bones are out of joint: my heart is like wax; it is melted in the midst of my bowels.

My strength is dried up like a potsherd; and my tongue cleaveth to my jaws; and thou hast brought me into the dust of death.

For dogs have compassed me: the assembly of the wicked have inclosed me: they pierced my hands and my feet.

I may tell all my bones; they look and stare upon me.

They part my garments among them, and cast lots upon my vesture.

In verses 14 through 18 of Psalm 22 are described prophetically, a thousand years in advance, the details of the physical sufferings and indignities that Christ must endure in His crucifixion. "I am poured out like water . . . all my bones are out of joint . . . my heart is like wax . . . melted in the midst of my bowels." Suspended by spikes which "pierced my hands and my feet," the unnatural strains forced His bones to tear out of their joints, the body to dehydrate, the heart eventually to collapse and rupture. Probably the most agonizingly painful form of execution ever invented by human cruelty, the hideous Cross will remain forever as the ultimate measure of man's wickedness and of God's love. Almost unnoticed as we view His awful sufferings is the remarkable evidence of divine inspiration which this psalm provides. The mathematical probability of David's being able to predict these events in such detail without the guidance of the Holy Spirit is, for all practical purposes, absolutely zero!

"My strength is dried up like a potsherd; and my tongue cleaveth to my jaws." Jesus had become like a desiccated piece of splintered clay, and the thirst was beyond imagination. Even the normal fluids of the mouth had dried away in the burning sun that had preceded the noonday darkness. "Thou hast brought me into the dust of death." Because of Adam's sin, all men must return to the dust, of course, but God had promised that the body of the second Adam would never see corruption (Ps. 16:10). He would enter and experience death, therefore, but its "dust" does not here refer to the destiny of His body. The term must refer rather to the enduring of every tiny element of suffering that anyone would ever have to endure.

To the physical agonies, of course, were added the mental humiliations. The first Adam had been provided a coat of skins to cover his nakedness (Gen. 3:21). The last Adam had every garment stripped from Him, as He hung suspended before the leers of the carnal and bestial mob around Him. "I may tell all my bones; they look and stare upon me."

The Scriptures mercifully spare both Him and us of any further chronicling of the obscene curses and physical torments inflicted on Him during the horrible hours on the cross. However, there is one remarkable incident which is mentioned. "They part my garments among them, and cast lots upon my vesture" (verse 18). This is almost the only specific event at the cross which is mentioned in all four of the Gospels (Matt. 27:35; Mark 15:24; Luke 23:34; and John 19:23–24). There must be a special reason why this one event is emphasized in this way.

So far as the record goes, these few items of clothing were the only personal possessions ever owned by the Lord Jesus Christ (Maker of heaven and earth!) during His life on earth. "Though he was rich, yet for your sakes he became poor" (2 Cor. 8:9). Though He has been "appointed heir of all things" (Heb. 1:2), the only inheritance He left at His death was the "New Testament" and its "promise of eternal inheritance" (Heb. 9:15). And even His pitiful scraps of clothing were stolen and appropriated by His executioners, not allowing even those to be given to His grieving mother. What He had taught by precept, He also taught by example: "Lay not up for yourselves treasures upon earth" (Matt. 6:19). No doubt, there will be great embarrassment when we enter one day into His presence, as He asks us concerning the possessions that we have left upon earth!

The Climax of Suffering
Verses 19–21

> But be not thou far from me, O LORD: O my strength, haste thee to help me.
>
> Deliver my soul from the sword; my darling from the power of the dog.
>
> Save me from the lion's mouth: for thou hast heard me from the horns of the unicorns.

In verses 19, 20, and 21 we have the climax of His prayer, at the very peak of His suffering during the three hours of hell's darkness. In agony and urgency, He calls upon God to help Him before Satan's triumph is complete. He has endured all the sufferings of earth and hell, and it is unthinkable that the Son of God can die forever, with Satan usurping the throne of the universe.

"Deliver my soul from the sword; my darling from the power of the dog." The word for "darling" is, in the Septuagint, translated *monogenes* — the same word as in John 3:16 — "only begotten." The Father surely will not forever turn His back on His beloved Son, once the price for sin is paid. "The power of the dog," in addition to its demonic implications, may also refer to leering Sodomites savoring the scene at the cross, for such were called "dogs" by God in the Mosaic laws (Deut. 23:17–18).

"Save me from the lion's mouth . . . from the horns of the unicorns." Satan, the roaring lion, is about to devour Him, and the mighty bulls to impale Him. But, then, the Father's silence finally is broken! "Thou hast heard me!" (verse 21).

No more, from this verse on, is heard the roaring of the lions and the bellowing of the bulls, the barking dogs, or the hissing serpents, or the jeering and cursing of the bloodthirsty mob. The hour of darkness is past; the light has dawned. Satan is a defeated foe, and Christ "hath abolished death, and hath brought life and immortality to light through the gospel" (2 Tim. 1:10).

The Son of Praise
Verse 22

I will declare thy name unto my brethren: in the midst of the congregation will I praise thee.

There are several themes in these latter verses — resurrection, witnessing, and victory — but probably the most important concept is that of praise. In fact, there is a very remarkable structural pattern that comes to the surface when we consider this theme of praise.

In a real sense, the very reason for the unique phenomenon of *language* is in order that God might be able to communicate His will and His plans to men, and that men might in turn respond to God in *praise*! The ability of communicating in intelligible, abstract, symbolic vocabularies and phonologies is an ability shared equally by all tribes among mankind, but an ability which is completely absent among animals. The phenomenon of language has no evolutionary explanation — it is uniquely an attribute of the image of God in man. And the highest function of human language is to praise the Lord.

This Book of Psalms is the longest book in the Bible and is uniquely a book of praise. In fact, it is commonly called the *Hallal* Book — the book of the "praises" of Israel. Furthermore, it has a unique structure. The other books of the Bible originally had no chapter and verse divisions — these were developed much later by medieval scholars as a matter of convenience. The chapter and verse divisions of the Book of Psalms, however, were there right from the start. Each psalm comprises a chapter, and the verses correspond to the obvious poetic divisions.

It is also significant that the medium in which God first chose to communicate His eternal Word in written form to man was the Hebrew language. The Hebrew language, in turn, is built around an alphabet of 22 letters, so that this number (22) seems often associated in the Bible with both the written Word and the living Word, Jesus Christ. Christ, in fact, called himself the "Alpha and Omega" (that is, the first and last letters of the Greek language in which the New Testament was written — see Rev. 22:13), thus emphasizing that He is, himself, the very Word of God (John 1:1, 14).

Now, although the great theme of the Book of Psalms is that of praise, it is remarkable that the verb "to praise" (Hebrew *hallal*) is never used in the first 21 of the psalms. The Holy Spirit seemingly refrained from using this word until it could first be recorded as coming from the lips of the suffering Savior, here in this 22nd Psalm.

It must be much more than coincidence, considering the fact that this number "22" represents both the Word and the very purpose of language, that it is found for the first time (at least in the Book of Psalms) here in this 22nd verse of the 22nd Psalm! "I will declare thy name unto my brethren: in the midst of the congregation will I *praise* thee!" Right at the very pinnacle of His suffering, He sings out a great note of praise, for His Father had heard and delivered Him. He had not, after all, really "hid His face from Him," nor had He "abhorred the affliction of the afflicted" (verse 24); He had, indeed, heard His cry, and when the cup of suffering had been emptied, He hastened once again to His presence.

This 22nd verse is quoted in the Book of Hebrews, in the very chapter to which we have already frequently referred in this exposition. But there it is rendered: "For both he that sanctifieth and they who are sanctified are all of one [i.e., of one Father]: for which cause he is not ashamed to call them brethren, Saying, I will declare thy name unto my brethren, in the midst of the church will I sing praise unto thee" (Heb. 2:11–12). The congregation in which He is the great "Song-Leader," the "Praise-Leader," is thus the church. The "assembly of the wicked" around Him had been routed, but there was left around the cross a very little flock — the remnants of that first church that He had established upon the rock of His deity and the salvation He would provide through His blood (note Matt. 16:18, 18:17; Acts 20:28). It was in the midst of *that* congregation (John the beloved, his mother, and the other women) that He first offered up the sacrifice of praise, but since that day, "where two or three are gathered together in my name, there am I in the midst of them" (Matt. 18:20). In His prayer the previous night in the Upper Room, He said, "I have manifested thy name unto the men which thou gavest me out of the world" (John 17:6). That name was "Father," and He was not ashamed to call them His "brethren."

The Victory and the Commission
Verses 23–31

Ye that fear the LORD, praise him; all ye the seed of Jacob, glorify him; and fear him, all ye the seed of Israel.

For he hath not despised nor abhorred the affliction of the afflicted; neither hath he hid his face from him; but when he cried unto him, he heard.

My praise shall be of thee in the great congregation: I will pay my vows before them that fear him.

The meek shall eat and be satisfied: they shall praise the LORD that seek him: your heart shall live for ever.

All the ends of the world shall remember and turn unto the LORD: and all the kindreds of the nations shall worship before thee.

For the kingdom is the LORD's: and he is the governor among the nations.

All they that be fat upon earth shall eat and worship: all they that go down to the dust shall bow before him: and none can keep alive his own soul.

A seed shall serve him; it shall be accounted to the LORD for a generation.

They shall come, and shall declare his righteousness unto a people that shall be born, that he hath done this.

At verse 23, there is a change of person. In the first 22 verses the entire psalm is a prayer, with the one on the cross praying to His God and Father, the pronouns "I" and "thee" appearing almost continuously. At this point, however, the psalm becomes an exhortation to its readers. The Holy Spirit himself, through David, speaks of Christ in the third person and directly to His readers in the second person.

The theme thus now turns sharply from one of suffering to one of praise. Christ first offered praise because of victory over death and Satan. Now we may continually (Heb. 13:15) offer the sacrifice of praise, giving thanks to Him for His great love for us. "Ye that fear the LORD, praise him! — glorify him! — fear him!"

Then comes the natural response to this great exhortation, in verse 25: "My praise shall be of thee in the great congregation: I will pay my vows before them that fear him." This is the testimony of the redeemed. As the Lord even now leads our praises in each little congregation, so we shall all one day share our testimonies in that great congregation, as we enter "the city of the living God, the heavenly Jerusalem, and to an innumerable company of angels, To the general assembly and church of the firstborn, which are written in heaven, and to God the Judge of all, and to the spirits of just men made perfect, And to Jesus the mediator of the new covenant" (Heb. 12:22–24).

And in that great day, "The meek shall eat and be satisfied: they shall praise the LORD that seek him: your heart shall live forever. All the ends of the world shall remember and turn unto the LORD: and all the kindreds of the nations shall worship before thee. For the kingdom is the LORD's: and he is the governor among the nations" (verses 26–28). In these verses are summed up all the great prophecies and promises of all the ages, when God's great purposes in creation will have finally been accomplished. Every knee shall bow and every tongue shall confess that the Lamb who was on the altar is the King on the eternal throne. Both those that prosper ("the fat upon the earth") and those who die ("all they that go down to the dust") shall bow down to Him. Though "none can keep alive his own soul," we shall forever thank Him for the travail through which He passed in order to keep our souls alive through the endless ages.

In the meantime, we that have been thus "born again" through receiving His life by faith comprise "a seed that shall serve him" (verse 30). Remember again the scarlet worm and the many sons brought forth through suffering. This innumerable spiritual progeny will continue serving Him until the coming day when He will be recognized as governor among the nations. The latter part of verse 30 says literally: "This shall be accounted of the Lord for a generation." That is, each succeeding generation would continue recounting the same old, but always new, story of the great love of the one who had died to bring life. "One generation shall praise thy works to another, and shall declare thy mighty acts" (Ps. 145:4).

This is the final refrain of Psalm 22. "They shall come, and shall declare his righteousness unto a people that shall be born, that he hath done this."

This very last phrase is, literally, "He hath finished!" The mighty act which the scarlet one had been about ever since He left the presence of His Father in glory, to be "cast upon [Him] from the womb" (verse 10), culminating in the cross, has been accomplished. The victory cry, "It is finished!" still echoes through the centuries, and provides continuing comfort and counsel for the seed that serves Him.

Chapter 6

The Shepherd and His Sheep

Psalm 23

Although the 23rd Psalm is one of the Bible's shortest chapters, its six verses contain many evidences of divine inspiration, in terms of both its interesting structure and also its wonderful message. It is quite likely the best-loved chapter in the Bible, one of the first learned by Sunday school children and the last requested for deathbed reading by dying Christians. It was written by David, and its shepherd theme no doubt grew out of his own experiences as a shepherd boy. But its message far transcends anything that could be devised by David or any other man, speaking with great power and blessing to all people of every time and place.

The psalm's shepherd, of course, is none other than the Lord Jesus Christ. He frequently spoke of himself as the shepherd (John 10:14; Matt. 25:32, 26:31, etc.). He called himself the good shepherd, dying for His sheep (John 10:11); Paul spoke of Him as the great shepherd, guiding His sheep (Heb. 13:20–21; and Peter saw Him as the chief shepherd, rewarding His sheep (1 Pet. 5:4).

The psalm also refers to Him as the Lord (i.e., *Jehovah*). This Old Testament name of God has been appropriated and applied to Christ in the New Testament — for example, Acts 2:21, 36, quoting Joel 2:32. Thus, "Jehovah my Shepherd" in Psalm 23:1 is to be understood as none other than Jesus Christ.

The Intriguing Structure of the Twenty-third Psalm

Psalm 23 is probably the greatest testimony to the believer's security to be found in the Bible, at least in the Old Testament. This theme of security is woven into the very structure of the psalm.

All six verses are intensely subjective, with the writer opening his deepest heart in his expressions about, and to, the Lord. There is beautiful symmetry in the respective verse themes, which can be summarized as follows:

Verse one	Statement of faith in the present
Verse two	Testimony of God's faithfulness
Verse three	Testimony of God's faithfulness
Verse four	Prayer of thanksgiving
Verse five	Prayer of thanksgiving
Verse six	Statement of faith for the future

These themes are accompanied by 12 references to the Lord, organized symmetrically as follows:

Verse one	"The LORD" (once)
Verse two	"He" (twice)
Verse three	"He" (thrice)
Verse four	"Thou" (thrice)
Verse five	"Thou" (twice)
Verse six	"The LORD" (once)

It seems obvious that this remarkable arrangement could not be attributed to chance, and almost as unlikely that David contrived it. It can best be explained by inspiration of the Holy Spirit. Six is a number usually associated with human weakness and incompleteness, but the number 12 seems always associated with God's special provision for mankind in calling and organizing chosen servants for dealing with the spiritual needs of His people.

Note also that there are no less than 17 references in the psalm to the believer himself, through use of the first person pronouns (I, me, my, etc.), and this number commonly is peculiarly connected with the doctrine of assurance and security in Christ. For example, there are 17 categories of opposition to the Christian listed in Romans 8:35–39 which can *never* "separate us from the love of God which is in Christ Jesus, our Lord." The ark of safety which carried believers through the awful judgment of the cataclysmic deluge rested "on the seventeenth day of the month," after the flood had come on" the seventeenth day of the month" five months earlier (Gen. 8:4, 7:11 — the first mention of 17 in the Bible).

In John 21:11 there were "153 great fishes" brought to shore by the disciples in a net which did not break. This symbolically represents those believers in all nations who would be won to Christ through the witnessing of those "fishers of men" whom Christ would send forth into all the world, and who would be brought safely to shore in the gospel net. The number 153 seems to have been particularly mentioned because it is the sum of all the numbers 1 through 17 and the product of 9 by 17. The sum of its digits (1 + 5 + 3) equals the other factor, 9, while the sum of the cubes of its digits again equals 153.

But while such mathematical features are interesting, and while they provide incidental evidences of divine origin of the psalm's structure, it is the message of the words themselves which brings blessing and the assurance of salvation and security to the heart of the believer.

All Needs Supplied by Christ
Verse 1

The LORD is my shepherd; I shall not want.

In each of the last five verses of Psalm 23 two vital needs are mentioned, needs shared by all men but probably felt most openly by the believing Christian who, like a lost sheep in a dangerous country, is living in a world which is at enmity with God. He desperately needs care and direction which he himself cannot provide, just as the sheep needs the shepherd. Verse one simply contains the comforting assurance that all these needs will be supplied. "The LORD is my shepherd." Jehovah is the great covenant and redemptive name of God, and the expression here is actually a compound name — "Jehovah my Shepherd." The immediate conclusion that necessarily follows is: "I cannot lack!" A human shepherd may occasionally be careless or ineffective, but not Jehovah. "My God shall supply all your need according to his riches in glory by Christ Jesus" (Phil. 4:19).

Rest and Peace
Verse 2

He maketh me to lie down in green pastures: He leadeth me beside the still waters.

The first need is rest. God rested from His great work of creation, and the lost sinner needs to find rest for his own soul. He has attempted unsuccessfully to find rest in his own way and to provide his own needs. A great burden is lifted when he finally places complete trust in the Shepherd. "There remaineth therefore a rest to the people of God. For he that is entered into his rest, he also hath ceased from his own works, as God did from his" (Heb. 4:9–10).

That rest is symbolized here in Psalm 23:2 by the resting in "grassy pastures." The phrase "maketh me to lie down" is one word in the Hebrew and does not intend to indicate a forced rest, but rather can be expressed as "causeth me to rest."

The Christian may not often be able to rest physically, but even in the midst of great physical or mental toil as he serves the Lord, he does again and again lie down in great ease spiritually in God's green, grassy meadows, in living fellowship with the Lord.

And the Lord also gives great peace: He "leadeth me" means "gently guideth me." The "still waters" are not stagnant waters, but "stilled waters," waters that have been brought to rest by the Lord's power. Even though the great storm may almost overwhelm us, He says, "Peace, be still" (Mark 4:39), and we find peace in the midst of turmoil. "Your strength is to sit still," God told the fearful Israelites; "In returning and rest shall ye be saved; in quietness and confidence shall be your strength" (Isa. 30:15). The Lord is well in control of every situation, and our peace is simply to be where He is!

Health and Guidance
Verse 3

> He restoreth my soul: he leadeth me in the paths of righteousness for his name's sake.

"He restoreth my soul," means literally "bringeth back life." Genuine health is one of God's choice provisions for His people. Rest and peace are, in themselves, the best medicines. "Trust in the Lord with all thine heart; and lean not unto thine own understanding. In all thy ways acknowledge him, and he shall direct thy paths. Be not wise in thine own eyes: fear the Lord, and depart from evil. It shall be health to thy navel, and marrow to thy bones" (Prov. 3:5–8).

The Christian normally does not need to worry excessively about what he eats (Matt. 6:25; 1 Tim. 4:4; Rom. 14:17) or what exercise he gets (1 Tim. 4:8), as long as he is placing God's will and His kingdom first (Matt. 6:33). God, of course, is able to heal our diseases in answer to prayer if it is His will, but even if we have a "thorn in the flesh" which He elects not to remove, we always have His gracious assurance: "My grace is sufficient for thee; for my strength is made perfect in weakness" (2 Cor. 12:7–10).

One of our greatest needs, of course, is to know His will. And so, He also provides guidance. When the psalm says in this verse, "He leadeth me," it is a different word from that in verse 2. There, "He gently guides me"; here, "He forcibly guides me." If we stray out of His will, that is, He will constrain us back into the "paths [literally 'tracks'] of righteousness." "The steps of a good man are ordered by the Lord; and he delighteth in his way. Though he fall, he shall not be utterly cast down: for the Lord upholdeth him with his hand" (Ps. 37:23–24). All of this is for our good (Rom. 8:28; Heb. 12:11), but even more, it is "for His name's sake." That He will show us His will (through His word, through circumstances, through inner conviction) without the necessity of falling and being chastised, if we are really willing to follow it, is obvious from such Scriptures as John 7:17; Romans 12:1–2; and others.

Courage and Comfort
Verse 4

Yea, though I walk through the valley of the shadow of death, I will fear no evil: for thou art with me; thy rod and thy staff they comfort me.

If we are in His will, we need not fear either man or devil. The word "evil" in this verse can refer to evil men, evil phenomena, or to dangers of any kind. Even "the shadow of death" (one word in the original connoting "the nearness of death") need generate no fears in the believer. God can deliver us either from death, or through death, depending on His will, and since "to live is Christ, and to die is gain" (Phil. 1:21), we are victors in either case! The dark "valley of [weeping]" can be transformed into a flowing well (Ps. 84:6) of living water.

"Thy rod" (literally, "thy club" or "thy sceptre") and "thy staff" (literally "thy cane" or "thy crook") suffice either to force us back or pull us back, as need may dictate, into the right tracks. This might seem at first a strange way of bringing "comfort," until one notes that the same word also means "repent." God's chastenings and corrections are calculated to bring us to repentance, and we have here His gracious assurance that we, as His sheep, will never be allowed to be comfortable when out of His will.

Protection and Provision
Verse 5

Thou preparest a table before me in the presence of mine enemies: thou anointest my head with oil; my cup runneth over.

There are enemies all around the believer in this world, both human and demonic, but He provides all our needs right in the very "presence of our enemies," and they are powerless to prevent it. "The angel of the Lord encampeth round about them that fear him, and delivereth them" (Ps. 34:7). "And the Lord shall deliver me from every evil work, and will preserve me unto His heavenly kingdom" (2 Tim. 4:18).

"Thou anointest my head with oil; my cup runneth over." The word "anoint" here is actually "fatten." Not only will the Shepherd protect the sheep from the enemies surrounding him, but also He will fatten (greatly bless and prosper) him, beyond measure, to God's glory and his enemies' discomfiture.

Love and Life
Verse 6

> Surely goodness and mercy shall follow me all the days of my
> life: and I will dwell in the house of the LORD for ever.

All this and heaven, too! Not only does the believer have rest and peace, health and guidance, courage and comfort, protection and provision, in Christ, he also has the promise of His unfailing love throughout this life and the endless life to come.

God's "goodness and mercy [literally, 'loving-kindness'] will follow him all the days of his [earthly] life." The word "follow" is a strong word, meaning "chase after." In addition to "leading me" (verses 2 and 3), He will pursue after me, like the great hound of heaven, never allowing retreat or escape. "Whither shall I go from thy spirit? Or whither shall I flee from thy presence? If I ascend up into heaven, thou art there: if I make my bed in hell, behold, thou art there. If I take the wings of the morning, and dwell in the uttermost parts of the sea; even there shall thy hand lead me, and thy right hand shall hold me" (Ps. 139:7–10).

Then, when this life is over, the believer "will dwell" with the Lord and His people "forever." The "house of the LORD" means "the family of the LORD" (like "the house of David," etc.; note Eph. 2:19–22; Rev. 21:2–3). "In the ages to come" (Eph. 2:7), we will enjoy the fellowship of all the redeemed, as well as the Lord himself.

Listen again to the Lord Jesus: "My sheep hear my voice, and I know them, and they follow me: And I give unto them eternal life; and they shall never perish, neither shall any man pluck them out of my hand" (John 10:27–28).

Chapter 7

Incarnation and Virgin Birth

Psalm 40
The Christmas Psalm

The true testimony of Christmas, at least to the Christian, is the incarnation. When Christ came into the world — that is, when God became man — the age-long barrier between earth and heaven was finally crossed. This grand theme, along with the great work of salvation He came to accomplish, is the message of the 40th Psalm.

Although the psalm was written by David and is in the first person, it is clear from the New Testament references to it that the person speaking is actually the Lord Jesus Christ, himself. The context, furthermore, indicates that, most likely, it represents the inward meditation of His heart as He hung on the cross dying for the sin of the world. In this respect, it is a corollary of Psalm 22, which likewise reveals His thoughts during the hours of His darkest sufferings, when even His Heavenly Father had forsaken Him (Ps. 22:1; Matt. 27:46).

The 40th psalm seems probably to contain His testimony during the interval following the three hours of darkness on the cross, but before His actual physical demise. No longer was He separated from His Father (Luke 23:46); the actual experience of hell (separation from God) was "finished" (John 19:30). All that remained was for Him, in the Spirit, to proclaim His victory to the wicked spirits in the heart of the earth (1 Pet. 3:18–19; Matt. 12:40); to set the captives free (Isa. 61:1; Eph. 4:8–10); and to return to His own body resting in death in the tomb, with the very keys to death and hell, alive forevermore (Rev. 1:18).

Testimony of Deliverance
Verses 1–5

I waited patiently for the LORD; and he inclined unto me, and heard my cry.

He brought me up also out of an horrible pit, out of the miry clay, and set my feet upon a rock, and established my goings.

And he hath put a new song in my mouth, even praise unto our God: many shall see it, and fear, and shall trust in the LORD.

Blessed is that man that maketh the Lord his trust, and respecteth not the proud, nor such as turn aside to lies.

Many, O Lord my God, are thy wonderful works which thou hast done, and thy thoughts which are to us-ward: they cannot be reckoned up in order unto thee: if I would declare and speak of them, they are more than can be numbered.

In His testimony, as recorded in Psalm 40, He expresses thankfulness for the great deliverance already experienced, and continues to pray for the full accomplishment of God's purpose in His suffering. With this context in mind, let us now take a verse-by-verse journey through this marvelous psalm.

"I waited patiently for the LORD; and He inclined unto me, and heard my cry." The Scripture admonishes, "For ye have need of patience, that, after ye have done the will of God, ye might receive the promise" (Heb. 10:36). He had come to do God's will (verse 8), and had finally accomplished it. For three long hours, especially, He had endured hell itself, suffering patiently what others deserved to suffer, but from which they could now be freed. Finally, He uttered the sad cry of desolation, and God heard and answered.

"He brought me up also out of an horrible pit, out of the miry clay, and set my feet upon a rock, and established my goings." When God heard, then He lifted His soul out of the darkness. All others who had died had been forced to confinement in Hades, the horrible pit in the depths of the earth. (The fact that men ridicule the idea of such a prison enclosure far down in the earth's core does not prove it is not there; there is ample room, and no seismic instruments yet developed can determine otherwise.) Even those who had died in faith were there, because no efficacious offering, which would purge their sins, had yet been made. But *He* could not be bound there! "For thou wilt not leave my soul in hell" (Ps. 16:10). Otherwise, "what profit is there in my blood, when I go down to the pit?" (Ps. 30:9).

"And He hath put a new song in my mouth, even praise unto our God: many shall see it, and fear, and shall trust in the LORD." The glorious "song of the Lamb" (Rev. 15:3–4), which we shall hear in His presence one day, is such a testimony of praise: "Great and marvelous are thy works, Lord God Almighty; just and true are thy ways, thou King of saints." The message of salvation which His great work released has led multitudes to trust in the Lord, everyone testifying in his own turn that he also has been delivered from the miry clay and his path established on the solid rock. "Upon this Rock I will build my church," He said, "and the gates of hell shall not prevail against it" (Matt. 16:18).

"Blessed is that man that maketh the Lord his trust, and respecteth not the proud, nor such as turn aside to lies." This is both a personal testimony on the part of Jesus and a promise to all others. He, as the perfect man, the second Adam, had resisted Satan, the proud one (Isa. 14:12–14; Ezek. 28:17) and the father of lies (John 8:44). "He that committeth sin is of the devil," but "in him is no sin" (1 John 3:7, 8). Though he could not deceive Jesus, even in the physical weakness of His humanity (Matt. 4:10), Satan continues to this very hour as the deceiver of the whole world (Rev. 12:9), seeking to turn men away from "the true God, and eternal life" (1 John 5:19–20). Yet, "blessed are all they that put their trust in Him" (Ps. 2:12).

"Many, O Lord my God, are thy wonderful works which thou hast done, and thy thoughts which are to us-ward: they cannot be reckoned up in order unto thee: if I would declare and speak of them, they are more than can be numbered." Even in the midst of His sufferings on the cross, the Lord Jesus could continually meditate on both the works and the words of the infinite God. This testimony, no doubt, includes God's works in creation as well as those in salvation. Every system in nature — even the most insignificant microorganisms, and even the very structure of matter itself — provide further insight to the thoughts of their Creator. All are marvels of design, so that even the study of science is nothing but "thinking God's thoughts after Him," as some of the greatest scientists have testified. Even greater are His redemptive works. "O the depth of the riches both of the wisdom and knowledge of God! . . . For of him, and through him, and to him are all things: to whom be glory for ever" (Rom. 11:33–36).

The Prepared Body
Verses 6–8

Sacrifice and offering thou didst not desire; mine ears hast thou opened: burnt-offering and sin-offering hast thou not required.

Then said I, Lo, I come: in the volume of the book it is written of me.

I delight to do thy will, O my God: yea, thy law is within my heart.

"Sacrifice and offering thou didst not desire; mine ears hast thou opened: burnt-offering and sin-offering hast thou not required." We now enter the very heart of the psalm, as well as that of the Savior, as He rehearses the reason for His incarnation. Not any of the four great offerings and sacrifices of the Levitical system — the "sacrifice" (that is, the "peace offering" of Lev. 3) or the "offering" (that is, the "meat offering" of Lev. 2) or the "burnt offering" (Lev. 1) or the "sin offering" (Lev. 4) — were either desired or required by God as true sacrifices for sin. They could only, as evidence of the offerer's faith, serve as a temporary atonement (literally "covering") for sin, but they could never really "take away sins" (Heb. 10:4).

For this a greater sacrifice was required — "The Lamb of God, which taketh away the sin of the world" (John 1:29). But before He could take away the sin of the world, He would have to come into the world. Though He had created man, He must Himself *become* man, then die for man, in order to save man from his sins. And for this, the Son of God must declare to His Father His willingness to become the Son of Man.

This He did, in token whereof "mine ears hast thou opened." The symbolism of this remarkable action speaks of complete submission of one's body to do the will of his master. When an indentured servant in ancient Israel was due to be set free following his term of service, he could instead make the decision to remain in servitude forever, if he so chose. In token of this decision, "his master shall bore his ear through with an aul; and he shall serve him for ever" (Exod. 21:6). The meaning of this ritual was apparently the complete submission of the servant's ear to the voice of his master. Whatever his master commanded, his servant would do forthwith. The Son thus completely yielded himself to do the will of His Father, and this will required Him to become man.

This is the passage quoted in the New Testament that definitely identifies the 40th Psalm as Messianic. Remarkably, however, the Holy Spirit used the Septuagint translation, which renders the clause by "a body hast thou prepared me" (Heb. 10:5). The opening of the ear, by divine inspiration, is thus, in this case, interpreted as synonymous with taking on a specially prepared human body. Thus, the verse speaks of the unique work of incarnation, when God became man. ". . . the Word was made flesh, and dwelt among us" (John 1:14).

"Then said I, Lo, I come: in the volume of the book it is written of me." After submitting himself to the will of the Father in this way, the Son proceeded to come to earth. The testimony recorded here must have been given prior to His coming to earth, but it had been written down in the volume of the book even before that. Both the book of God's Word (note Ps. 119:89, 160 — "thy word forever settled in heaven" and "thy word true from the beginning") and the "book of life" (see Rev. 13:8) containing the names of the redeemed were written before the foundation of the world. God the Creator does not have "second thoughts" or "afterthoughts"!

But exactly how could such a remarkable transition be accomplished? How could God become man — and, especially, how could God become man without ceasing to be God? Man, ever since the Fall, has been in sin from his very birth. "Behold, I was shapen in iniquity; and in sin did my mother conceive me" (Ps. 51:5). If He were *only* man, then how could He save man?

These mysteries are resolved in the miracle of the virgin birth. "A body hast thou prepared me" (Heb. 10:5, referring to His coming into the world). He did not enter the world at the time of the virgin birth, of course, but nine months earlier, at the time of His miraculous conception in the womb of the virgin Mary. The remarkable nature of this "preparation" of His body by God is pointed up by the fact that the same Greek word is used in the next chapter of Hebrews to tell how God created the universe — "the worlds were *framed* by the word of God" (Heb. 11:3).

Such a body must be fully human and so must be formed from the elements of the earth as Adam's body had been (Gen. 2:7), but it must also be free of inherent sin or genetic defects, as Adam's body had been originally. He must "in all things . . . be made like unto his brethren" (Heb. 2:17) and be tested "like as we are, yet without sin" (Heb. 4:15). Though He could receive no genetic inheritance from His earthly parents or ancestors (otherwise, there would be no non-miraculous way in which He would not likewise have inherited both the sin nature and its accompanying genetic defects from both his human parents), yet He must also be of the "seed of the woman" (Gen. 3:15), the "seed of Abraham" (Heb. 2:16), and the "seed of David" (Rom. 1:3). These biblical requirements could only be met by a perfect human body supernaturally "framed" by God and placed as a single living cell (equivalent to the cell normally formed by the penetration of the "egg" of a woman by a male "seed") in the womb of a virgin descended from Abraham and David. In His growth from this one-celled stage, He would then share in all the experiences of mankind, from conception to death, yet be (as was the first Adam) without inherent sin.

"I delight to do thy will, O my God: yea, thy law is within my heart." As the Son left the Father's home in heaven and took up a new residence ("dwelt [tabernacled] among us" — John 1:14) in the body God had prepared for Him, He set forth to do the Father's will, even though that will included the Cross. God's law was in His heart, a condition yet future for other men (Heb. 8:10).

Results of the Incarnation
Verses 9–17

I have preached righteousness in the great congregation: lo, I have not refrained my lips, O Lord, thou knowest.

I have not hid thy righteousness within my heart; I have declared thy faithfulness and thy salvation: I have not concealed thy lovingkindness and thy truth from the great congregation.

Withhold not thou thy tender mercies from me, O Lord: let thy lovingkindness and thy truth continually preserve me.

For innumerable evils have compassed me about: mine iniquities have taken hold upon me, so that I am not able to look up; they are more than the hairs of mine head: therefore my heart faileth me.

Be pleased, O Lord, to deliver me: O Lord, make haste to help me.

Let them be ashamed and confounded together that seek after my soul to destroy it; let them be driven backward and put to shame that wish me evil.

Let them be desolate for a reward of their shame that say unto me, Aha, aha.

Let all those that seek thee rejoice and be glad in thee: let such as love thy salvation say continually, The Lord be magnified.

But I am poor and needy; yet the Lord thinketh upon me: thou art my help and deliverer; make no tarrying, O my God.

"I have preached righteousness in the great congregation: lo, I have not refrained my lips, O Lord, thou knowest." Continuing His meditation there on the cross, the Savior recalled His ministry, preaching God's Word to God's people — not only in the land of Israel, but also anticipating in the Spirit His future preaching throughout the world throughout the ages. As He had prayed the night before, "I have given them thy word" (John 17:14). There is also mention of this "great congregation" in Psalm 22:25, in the same connection, but looking to the future. Quite possibly it includes not only the believers of all ages, but even the holy angels (Heb. 12:23).

"I have not hid thy righteousness within my heart; I have declared thy faithfulness and thy salvation: I have not concealed thy lovingkindness and thy truth from the great congregation." No man has seen God at any time, but the Son has declared him. Note all the magnificent attributes of God which Christ revealed: "thy righteousness, thy faithfulness, thy salvation, thy lovingkindness, thy truth," also "thy will, thy law"(verse 8), and "thy tender mercies" (verse 11). What an array of testimonies! Not only had Christ told of God in word, He had himself displayed the attributes of God in person. "In him dwelleth all the fullness of the Godhead bodily" (Col. 2:9).

"Withhold not thou thy tender mercies from me, O Lord: let thy lovingkindness and thy truth continually preserve me." In His prefect humanity, the Lord Jesus fully exhibited the life of prayer and trust in God that pleases Him and serves as an example for us. Even in the midst of excruciating pain and suffering, and facing imminent physical death, He trusted the overshadowing mercy and love of His Father.

"For innumerable evils have compassed me about: mine iniquities have taken hold upon me, so that I am not able to look up; they are more than the hairs of mine head: therefore my heart faileth me." Surrounding Him there at the Cross was a great host of wicked spirits — the "assembly of the wicked" (Ps. 22:16), the "principalities and powers" of darkness over whom He would soon triumph in His death (Col. 2:15). Not only so, but the sins of all the world were laid upon Him, and His "iniquities" (literally, "punishments") were so heavy and so many that His head began to sink and His heart to break. That perfect, sinless body which had been prepared for Him by God when He came into the world was now unspeakably bruised and disfigured as He was about to leave the world. "His visage was so marred more than any man" (Isa. 52:14). "But he was wounded for our transgressions, he was bruised for our iniquities: the chastisement of our peace was upon him; and with his stripes we are healed" (Isa. 53:5). "Who his own self bare our sins in his own body on the tree" (1 Pet. 2:24). Our key passage in the tenth chapter of Hebrews says that He had come into the world to do God's will through that prepared body, "By the which will we are sanctified through the offering of the body of Jesus Christ once for all" (Heb. 10:10).

"Be pleased, O Lord, to deliver me: O Lord, make haste to help me." In His closing moments of life, the dying Savior prayed to the Father for His presence through death and the work yet to be accomplished. His body must be delivered from the wicked ones surrounding Him (and indeed, God shortly sent the loving hands of Joseph and Nicodemus to care for that body and place it in Joseph's new tomb).

"Let them be ashamed and confounded together that seek after my soul to destroy it; let them be driven backward and put to shame that wish me evil." This prayer also was soon answered. Satan and his hosts of evil were there and no doubt believed they were gaining a great victory as they contrived to destroy His soul. But it was this very death that sealed their shame and doom forever! "Blotting out the handwriting of ordinances that was against us, which was contrary to us, and took it out of the way, nailing to his cross; And having spoiled principalities and powers, He made a shew of them openly, triumphing over them in it" (Col. 2:14–15). ". . . that through death he might destroy him that had the power of death, that is, the devil; And deliver them who through fear of death were all their lifetime subject to bondage" (Heb. 2:14–15).

"Let them be desolate for a reward of their shame that say unto me, Aha, aha." This exclamation of His enemies is a Hebrew expression of malicious joy, with no real English equivalent. Those who take such delight in iniquity and, especially, in the suffering of the righteous, are at last to receive their equitable reward. They will be consigned finally to "shame and everlasting contempt" (Dan. 12:2).

"Let all those that seek thee rejoice and be glad in thee: let such as love thy salvation say continually, The Lord be magnified." In contrast to the unbelieving, whether men or demons, those whose hearts are right toward God may now be satisfied and full of joy, world without end. The word "salvation" is the Hebrew *yeshuah*, essentially the same as the human name given Him when God became man. This verse could even be read: "Let such as love thy Jesus say continually, the Lord be magnified." The promise of Christmas is fulfilled in the cross! No wonder the holy angels announcing His birth spoke of tidings of great joy. "But this man, after He had offered one sacrifice for sins for ever, sat down on the right hand of God" (Heb. 10:12).

"But I am poor and needy; yet the Lord thinketh upon me: thou art my help and my deliverer; make no tarrying, O my God." No matter how weak and helpless one may be, the Lord knows and cares. We may freely "cast all our cares upon him" (1 Pet. 5:7), for He never will leave us nor forsake us. If that were true, He would surely not be deaf to the prayers of His Holy One. The suffering for sin was over; He would now enter into the joy set before Him. In verse 13 was recorded His prayer for deliverance and help. In this final verse, He testified: "Thou *art* my help and deliverer." His prayer was answered. He who had waited in infinite patience as He had done the will of God (verse 1; compare Heb. 10:36) was now ready to receive the promise fulfilled.

And so shall we! "For yet a little while, and he that shall come will come, and will not tarry" (Heb. 10:37).

Chapter 8

Setting the Captives Free

Psalm 68

We have discussed a few of the great messianic psalms with their marvelous prophetic insights into the future coming of the Messiah — both His first and second comings, along with the many events that were to accompany His two comings. But there are still others! A great many of the psalms of David and the other Psalmists, while rooted in their own experiences and meditations, also prophesy or foreshadow in some way "the sufferings of Christ, and the glory that should follow" (1 Pet. 1:11).

When the risen Christ was comforting His grieving disciples, He reminded them "that all things must be fulfilled, which are written in the law of Moses, and in the prophets, and in the psalms concerning me" (Luke 24:44). There are indeed a great many glorious truths "in the psalms" concerning Jesus.

All of the messianic psalms discussed in this section have been cited in the New Testament as applying to the Lord Jesus Christ. This is evidence enough that the psalm as a whole must be messianic. Psalm 23 is not quoted directly, but the references to Christ as our shepherd are so clear and numerous that most writers consider it to be messianic.

Another of these is Psalm 68, a great psalm of victory, focussing especially on Christ's descent into Hades and his triumphant return with the spirits of faithful believers in God's Word. Their tentative imprisonment there had been ended when Christ finally had paid for their sins on the cross. We know that it is basically a messianic psalm because of its being quoted by Paul in Ephesians 4:7–16, quoting especially Psalm 68:18, which is the middle verse of this psalm, with 17 verses before and after.

Verses 1–4

Let God arise, let his enemies be scattered: let them also that hate him flee before him.

As smoke is driven away, so drive them away: as wax melteth before the fire, so let the wicked perish at the presence of God.

But let the righteous be glad; let them rejoice before God: yea, let them exceedingly rejoice.

Sing unto God, sing praises to his name: extol him that rideth upon the heavens by his name JAH, and rejoice before him.

Psalm 68, written by David, is believed by some to have been written in connection with the return of the ark to Jerusalem after its earlier capture by the Philistines (2 Sam. 6:12). This may be suggested by its opening words, in relation to the times with Moses in the wilderness, whenever God would lead the Israelites to move forward. "And it came to pass, when the ark set forward, that Moses said, Rise up, Lord, and let thine enemies be scattered; and let them that hate thee flee before thee" (Num. 10:35).

But this prayer, uttered both by Moses and David, was fulfilled only partially and locally in those long-ago times. Its final accomplishment, worldwide in scope, was yet future. Its initial phase began with the resurrection of the rejected and crucified Messiah. The ancient prayer, "Let God arise" was answered marvelously when Christ arose from the dead. The enemies that slew Him soon were scattered over the earth, like smoke driven away. The total fulfillment, however, awaits His second coming. Then, once again the Lord will arise, this time from His heavenly throne at the right hand of the Father, to return to earth, there to judge the nations. Then the wicked shall "perish at the presence of God," while the righteous shall "rejoice before God."

He whose name is JAH "rideth upon the heavens" — indeed "upon the heavens of heavens" (verse 33), and He shall return seated on a great white horse as He "treadeth the winepress of the fierceness and wrath of Almighty God." (Rev. 19:11–15). This is the only place in the Bible where the name JAH is used, except when the word "hallelujah" ("praise the Lord") is used as an exhortation (note the discussion of the Hallelujah psalms, 146–150, in chapters 60 through 65). As a contraction of "Jehovah" (or "*Yahweh*"), it clearly refers to the Lord Jesus in this context. Surely the wonderful promise that He will arise some day to drive all His enemies far away "from the presence of the Lord, and from the glory of his power" (2 Thess. 1:9), is abundant reason for those who love Him to "sing praises to his name" and to "rejoice before him."

Verses 5–10

A father of the fatherless, and a judge of the widows, is God in his holy habitation.

God setteth the solitary in families: He bringeth out those which are bound with chains: but the rebellious dwell in a dry land.

O God, when thou wentest forth before the people, when thou didst march through the wilderness; Selah:

The earth shook, the heavens also dropped at the presence of God: even Sinai itself was moved at the presence of God, the God of Israel.

Thou, O God, didst send a plentiful rain, whereby thou didst confirm thine inheritance, when it was weary.

Thy congregation hath dwelt therein; thou, O God, hast prepared of thy goodness for the poor.

Verse 6 is very fascinating when one studies the individual words, though none of the regular translations seem to recognize this. The word for "solitary" is the same word translated "darling" in Psalm 22:20 and Psalm 35:17. In the Greek Septuagint, "darling" is rendered by *monogenes,* meaning literally "only begotten." The Hebrew for "families" is translated many different ways, most often "home," and frequently "temple" or "palace." The word for "setteth" is really "sets down" or "sits down."

Putting all this together, the first part of verse 6 might read: "God sets down His only begotten in His own home (or heavenly temple)." Following our previous inference that verse 1 refers ultimately to Christ's resurrection, this ties in beautifully with such Scriptures as Ephesians 1:20: "[God] raised him from the dead, and set him at his own right hand in the heavenly places."

Then the last part of verse 6 anticipates verse 18 (see below). When Christ rose from the dead, His Spirit returning from Sheol (or Hades), "He bringeth out those which are bound (that is, those who had died in faith, but had to remain in Hades until Christ became the sacrifice for their sins) into freedom." The word for "chains" is actually "freedom" or "prosperity," as many translations render it. In contrast, the ones who died still in rebellion against God must be left in the prison — "a dry land" (literally, "parched land"; compare Luke 16:24).

In verses 7–10, the Psalmist reminds his readers of God's great deliverance of the past, when He saved His people out of cruel bondage in Egypt. The mighty miracles He performed then constituted a type, as well as assurance, that He would someday do an even greater work when He would deliver all who believed on Him from the bondage of sin and death. He had marched with them for 40 years through the wilderness, and they had seen the earth shake and the mountain breathe fire and smoke at Sinai. They knew the judgments of the Lord, but also His tender mercies. Even when they were faithless, He remained faithful (2 Tim. 2:13).

Verses 11–19

The Lord gave the word: great was the company of those that published it.

Kings of armies did flee apace: and she that tarried at home divided the spoil.

Though ye have lien among the pots, yet shall ye be as the wings of a dove covered with silver, and her feathers with yellow gold.

When the Almighty scattered kings in it, it was white as snow in Salmon.

The hill of God is as the hill of Bashan; an high hill as the hill of Bashan.

Why leap ye, ye high hills? this is the hill which God desireth to dwell in; yea, the LORD will dwell in it for ever.

The chariots of God are twenty thousand, even thousands of angels: the Lord is among them, as in Sinai, in the holy place.

Thou hast ascended on high, thou hast led captivity captive: thou hast received gifts for men; yea, for the rebellious also, that the Lord God might dwell among them.

Blessed be the Lord, who daily loadeth us with benefits, even the God of our salvation. Selah.

Note how frequently the names of God are invoked in this psalm. The majestic name Elohim ("God") occurs in the first and last verses, and 30 times altogether. As noted above, the name JAH is used only once in the Bible, and that was in verse 4. He is called "Lord" (Hebrew *Adonai*) here in verse 11, and then seven more times. He is "the Almighty" (Hebrew *Shaddai*) in verse 14, "the LORD" (*Jehovah*) in verse 16, "the Lord God" (*Adonai Elohim*) in verse 18, "God the Lord" (*Jehovah Adonai*) in verse 20, and "my King" in verse 24. Forty-two times altogether (7x6) in the thirty-five (7x5) verses of the psalm is God mentioned by name. Thus, the presence of God is evident throughout, especially the presence of God the Son, in this remarkable messianic psalm.

In this section of the psalm, David seems gradually to return in his vision to the prophetic future, and the great victories that would result from Messiah's death and resurrection. Expressed initially in terms of their experiences towards the end of their wilderness journeys as they won great victories over the nations adjacent to Canaan, the testimony of the past seems to merge with the promise of the future.

"The Lord gave the word" (literally, the "commandment"). This may well apply first to God's command to proceed with the conquest of the Promised Land, but then also later to the Great Commission of Christ to His followers after His resurrection, "great was the company of those that published it." The original language indicates that the "publishers" or proclaimers, of His word would include both men and women, all His disciples. The word translated "published" implies not shouts of battle but rather a proclamation of glad tidings. Again, this relates mainly to the post-Resurrection preaching of the joyous gospel of salvation.

The succeeding verses can then also be interpreted in this context. The fleeing armies are the hosts of darkness routed by the advance of the gospel. The gospel messengers, though of humble circumstances, many even working among the pots (or flesh-hooks; some versions translate this word as "stalls"), will become beautiful as they publish the message. As Isaiah prophesied, "How beautiful upon the mountains are the feet of him . . . that publisheth salvation: that saith unto Zion, Thy God reigneth!" (Isa. 52:7).

Even kings shall be defeated and scattered by the Almighty as God's truth prevails. This prophecy will finally be fulfilled literally in the ultimate triumph of Christ when He returns (Rev. 17:14). The reference to Salmon becoming white as snow is difficult as long as Salmon is considered to be a mountain, as most commentators assume. However, there is no other mention of this mountain in the Bible, and no one knows where it was. The word itself means "shady" or "dark," and "white as snow" is only one word in the Hebrew. Perhaps the reference is to the transformation of darkness into snowy-whiteness as the kings of darkness are scattered. As Isaiah said, "Though your sins be as scarlet, they shall be as white as snow" (Isa. 1:18).

The kingdom of Bashan had been conquered by the Israelites while still under Moses (Num. 21:33–35). It was a fertile land with many beautiful hills, east of the Jordan. Still, God had chosen the hill of Zion (Ps. 132:13). "This is the hill which God desireth to dwell in . . . forever" (verse 16; see also Heb. 12:22).

The people of Israel knew there had been many angels at Sinai (Deut. 33:2). They were also present when Christ was born and when He died (Luke 2:9–14; Matt. 26:53). They were present when He arose (Luke 24:23) and will be with Him when He comes again (2 Thess. 1:7).

Then verse 18 returns to the great theme of His resurrection and ascension. This is the central verse and the key verse of Psalm 68, for it is quoted in Ephesians 4:8 and identified with the risen Christ. This is the verse which justifies us in recognizing Psalm 68 as a messianic psalm and thus understanding the whole psalm as referring primarily to the person and work of the Lord Jesus Christ. Allusions in the psalm to the wilderness wanderings and the return of the ark to Jerusalem are there primarily as types of the future ministry of Christ.

Thus Paul applies it as follows: "Wherefore he saith, When he ascended up on high, he led captivity captive, and gave gifts unto men. (Now that he ascended, what is it but that he also descended first into the lower parts of the earth? He that descended is the same also that ascended up far above all heavens, that he might fill all things)" (Eph. 4:8–10).

During the time between His crucifixion and resurrection, Christ in His Spirit descended into Sheol, the great prison in the heart of the earth, where the spirits of those who had died in faith were awaiting His promised coming to atone for their sins and set them free. There He finally did come "to proclaim liberty to the captives, and the opening of the prison to them that are bound" (Isa. 61:1).

Then He "carried captivity captive," taking them with Him from Sheol, and then even into bodily resurrection when He himself arose bodily from His tomb. "And the graves were opened, and many bodies of the saints which slept arose, and came out of the graves after His resurrection, and went into the holy city, and appeared unto many" (Matt. 27:52–53).

Following their brief appearance back on earth, these resurrected saints of the old covenant, were evidently taken to heaven with Christ (note Luke 23:43 and John 20:17), and they are still there today.

Like the leader of a conquering army carrying His captives back to his homeland, the Lord Jesus then distributed gifts to those rejoicing with Him in the great victory. These gifts, according to Paul, were "apostles; and some, prophets; and some, evangelists, and some, pastors and teachers" (Eph. 4:11), as gifts to the saints of the new covenant as they were about to begin their own ministry of publishing the good news of salvation.

At this point, David, enthralled by the great vision he was receiving, paused to interject a special doxology (verse 19), and then urged his readers to meditate on what had just been revealed. "*Selah*," he said, concluding the first half of his psalm.

Verses 20–23

He that is our God is the God of salvation; and unto God the Lord belong the issues from death.

But God shall wound the head of his enemies, and the hairy scalp of such an one as goeth on still in his trespasses.

The Lord said, I will bring again from Bashan, I will bring my people again from the depths of the sea:

That thy foot may be dipped in the blood of thine enemies, and the tongue of thy dogs in the same.

Following his prophecy of resurrection and ascension, the Psalmist jumps ahead to the ultimate consummation of Christ's victory at the cross and the tomb. The great promise in Eden that He would crush the head of the old serpent (Gen. 3:15) is in view when David says that God will "wound the head of his enemies" (or enemy), the one who never ceases in "his trespasses" — that is, Satan, the ancient leader of the angelic rebellion against the Creator. All of God's true people will be rescued and resurrected, whether their bodies died in the hills of Bashan or were drowned in the sea. Then, at Armageddon, the blood of the still-living enemies of God will flow so deeply when Christ wields the sword out of His mouth that it will reach "unto the horse bridles" and His vesture shall be "dipped in blood" (Rev. 14:20, 19:13 and 15).

Verses 24–32

They have seen thy goings, O God; even the goings of my God, my King, in the sanctuary.

The singers went before, the players on instruments followed after; among them were the damsels playing with timbrels.

Bless ye God in the congregations, even the Lord, from the fountain of Israel.

There is little Benjamin with their ruler, the princes of Judah and their council, the princes of Zebulun, and the princes of Naphtali.

Thy God hath commanded thy strength: strengthen, O God, that which thou hast wrought for us.

Because of thy temple at Jerusalem shall kings bring presents unto thee.

Rebuke the company of spearmen, the multitude of the bulls, with the calves of the people, till every one submit himself with pieces of silver: scatter thou the people that delight in war.

Princes shall come out of Egypt; Ethiopia shall soon stretch out her hands unto God.

Sing unto God, ye kingdoms of the earth; O sing praises unto the Lord; Selah.

This closing section of the psalm looks beyond the destruction at Armageddon to the Millennium, the great kingdom age. At the newly built temple in Jerusalem, many musicians will sing and play as they observe the "goings" of God — that is Christ the King, who will reign over the earth during these great days to come.

The tribes of Israel, re-gathered to their promised land, will all be there, and all the leaders of the other nations will bring presents (note Zech. 14:16). Swords will be turned into plowshares, and spears into pruning hooks: "nation shall not lift up sword against nation, neither shall they learn war any more." (Isa. 2:4).

Verses 33–35

To him that rideth upon the heavens of heavens, which were of old; lo, he doth send out his voice, and that a mighty voice.

Ascribe ye strength unto God: his excellency is over Israel, and his strength is in the clouds.

O God, thou art terrible out of thy holy places: the God of Israel is he that giveth strength and power unto his people. Blessed be God.

Psalm 68 then closes with an exhortation to praise and bless the God who has done and will do all these wonderful acts. He is not only the King whose "goings" are in the earthly sanctuary (verse 24): He is the mighty One who rides on the heavens of heavens. He resides "above all heavens" (Eph. 4:10), where He ascended after His resurrection, "that he might fill all things."

He is greater than the infinite cosmos, for He created and upholds and fills it. And yet He cares about His people! "He giveth strength and power unto his people. Blessed be God."

Chapter 9

Man of Sorrows

Psalm 69

The contrast between Psalm 68 and Psalm 69 is striking, yet both are messianic psalms. Psalm 69 emphasizes "the sufferings of Christ," whereas Psalm 68 focuses on "the glory that should follow" (1 Pet. 1:11). As with Psalm 16, the first verses of the psalm seem to reflect His tearful prayers in Gethsemane. Then come tragic verses indicative of His prayers on the cross, as in Psalm 22. Next come prayers of imprecation against His implacable enemies, and finally thanksgiving for God's ultimate blessing through it all.

Verses 1–7

Save me, O God; for the waters are come in unto my soul.

I sink in deep mire, where there is no standing: I am come into deep waters, where the floods overflow me.

I am weary of my crying: my throat is dried: mine eyes fail while I wait for my God.

They that hate me without a cause are more than the hairs of mine head: they that would destroy me, being mine enemies wrongfully, are mighty: then I restored that which I took not away.

O God, thou knowest my foolishness; and my sins are not hid from thee.

Let not them that wait on thee, O Lord God of hosts, be ashamed for my sake: let not those that seek thee be confounded for my sake, O God of Israel.

Because for thy sake I have borne reproach; shame hath covered my face.

As with several other psalms, David's personal experiences provide
the background for Psalm 69. However, by inspiration, he seems here to
be anticipating the prayers of His greater son, the Lord Jesus, as He faced
the cross. Whether or not these words are really a part of Christ's prayer
in the Garden of Gethsemane on the tragic night of His betrayal, they
could have been, and it helps us to understand and relate to them better if
we think of them in that light. Jesus knew Judas would soon be coming
with the soldiers and He then would be vilified and tortured and put to a
horrible death. It was as though He had begun to sink down into deep
quicksand, more water than sand, in fact, with no escape.

Yet, "for the joy that was set before Him" (Heb. 12:2), He would
endure it all. Soon He would be able to praise God, saying: "He brought
me up also out of an horrible pit, out of the miry clay" (Ps. 40:2). For the
present, however, He "offered up prayers and supplications with strong
crying and tears unto him that was able to save him from death" (Heb.
5:7), until He was "weary of my crying" and "mine eyes fail" (verse 3).

He knew that His enemies were many and powerful, yet He had come
to save them from sin and death. He had strongly rebuked them for their
sinful practices, but instead of causing them to repent and believe on Him
as Messiah and Savior, they became still more embittered against Him. They
"hate me without a cause," He prayed, and "would destroy me" (verse 4).

Jesus spoke of "my sins," but He himself had done no sin. Nevertheless, He had come to effect a great transaction, and the weight of the price
He must pay was already crushing Him. For God was about to make
"Him to be sin for us, who knew no sin; that we might be made the righteousness of God in him" (2 Cor. 5:21). He was also praying, not just for
himself, but for "them that wait on thee" that they not "be confounded
for my sake" (verse 6).

Verses 8–15

I am become a stranger unto my brethren, and an alien unto
my mother's children.

For the zeal of thine house hath eaten me up; and the reproaches
of them that reproached thee are fallen upon me.

When I wept, and chastened my soul with fasting, that was to
my reproach.

I made sackcloth also my garment; and I became a proverb to
them.

They that sit in the gate speak against me; and I was the song of the drunkards.

But as for me, my prayer is unto thee, O LORD, in an acceptable time: O God, in the multitude of thy mercy hear me, in the truth of thy salvation.

Deliver me out of the mire, and let me not sink: let me be delivered from them that hate me, and out of the deep waters.

Let not the waterflood overflow me, neither let the deep swallow me up, and let not the pit shut her mouth upon me.

Verses 8 and 9 clearly let us identify this psalm as preeminently a psalm of Messiah, the man of sorrows, for they are quoted in the New Testament and applied to Jesus. One would think that His brothers, who had known and observed Him all their lives, would have sided with Him, even if their mother, Mary, had not told them about the angel Gabriel and the other events surrounding His birth. Yet "neither did His brethren believe in Him" (John 7:5). Note also that the psalm speaks of "my mother's children;" Jesus had no human father, so could not call them "my father's children."

When Jesus drove the moneychangers out of the temple, "His disciples remembered that it was written, The zeal of thine house hath eaten me up" (John 2:17), and they knew that Psalm 69:9 was speaking prophetically of Him. The apostle Paul also realized that the second part of this verse applied mainly to Christ. He wrote, "For even Christ pleased not himself; but, as it is written, The reproaches of them that reproached thee fell on me" (Rom. 15:3).

There is no record of Jesus wearing sackcloth, though David did (1 Chron. 21:16) and it is certainly possible that the Lord did, especially during His 40 days of fasting as the devil was testing Him in the wilderness (Matt. 4:2). In any case, He was repeatedly being reproached and ridiculed, with attempts even made on His life (e.g., Luke 4:29 and John 10:39).

"They that sit in the gate" (verse 12) — that is, the judges and religious leaders of the Jews — certainly had spoken against Him, and would very soon condemn Him to death. Nevertheless, He would continue to pray and trust His Father. His Father would, after the great work was done, deliver His beloved Son out of the deep miry waters. It could never swallow Him up and have the gates of Hades shut forever upon Him. Though He had become the Son of man, and would very soon be dying for all the sins of man, He was still the eternal Son of God, and God can never die eternally, for He is the very Creator of life, and of salvation. The dark pit could never shut her mouth upon the Lord Jesus Christ, for He was the one who had created the earth itself. Instead, He would storm its very gates, and set its captives free.

Verses 16–21

Hear me, O LORD; for thy loving kindness is good: turn unto me according to the multitude of thy tender mercies.

And hide not thy face from thy servant; for I am in trouble: hear me speedily.

Draw nigh unto my soul, and redeem it: deliver me because of mine enemies.

Thou hast known my reproach, and my shame, and my dishonour: mine adversaries are all before thee.

Reproach hath broken my heart; and I am full of heaviness: and I looked for some to take pity, but there was none; and for comforters, but I found none.

They gave me also gall for my meat; and in my thirst they gave me vinegar to drink.

It is probably at this point that the scene in the psalm shifts from the Garden to the Cross. There, while suffering bitter agonies of soul (bearing the shame of all the world's sin) and of body (the indescribable tortures of crucifixion), the Lord nevertheless continues to pray to the Father. Certain prayers were actually heard by those at the Cross (that is, the famous "seven last words"), but most were silent, known only to himself and the Father.

For a while, even the Father seems not to hear. "Hide not thy face from thy [suffering] servant," He prays, "hear me speedily" (verse 17). But for three awful hours, even the Father seems to have forsaken Him, for He has been made sin for us, and the Father is "of purer eyes than to behold evil, and canst not look on iniquity" (Hab. 1:13).

"Mine adversaries are all before thee," He prays. And indeed they were! Not only the cruel soldiers and mocking priests, but also Satan and the demons of hell were there at the Cross.

"Many bulls have compassed me . . . as a ravening and roaring lion . . . the assembly of the wicked have inclosed me" (Ps. 22:12–16).

"Reproach hath broken my heart," He cries. "My heart is like wax; it is melted in the midst of my bowels" (Ps. 22:14). The Lord Jesus Christ, maker of heaven and earth, died — literally and spiritually — of a broken heart!

Then, in verse 21, is inserted another amazingly fulfilled prophecy — the vinegar and gall. In fact, Jesus himself took special pains to assure its fulfillment. "After this, Jesus knowing that all things were now accomplished, that the scripture might be fulfilled, saith, I thirst. Now there was set a vessel full of vinegar: and they filled a sponge with vinegar, and put it upon hyssop, and put it to his mouth" (John 19:28–29).

Earlier, even before they nailed Him to the cross, "they gave him vinegar to drink mingled with gall" (Matt. 27:34), but He would not drink it, since it would have deadened some of the pain, and He knew He must drink the bitter cup of God's wrath to the full. After it was all finished, however, in order to fulfill this very Scripture, He drank a bit of the vinegar, and then died, crying out a great victory cry, "It is finished!" (John 19:30).

Verses 22–29

Let their table become a snare before them: and that which should have been for their welfare, let it become a trap.

Let their eyes be darkened, that they see not; and make their loins continually to shake.

Pour out thine indignation upon them, and let thy wrathful anger take hold of them.

Let their habitation be desolate; and let none dwell in their tents.

For they persecute him whom thou hast smitten; and they talk to the grief of those whom thou hast wounded.

Add iniquity unto their iniquity: and let them not come into thy righteousness.

Let them be blotted out of the book of the living, and not be written with the righteous.

But I am poor and sorrowful: let thy salvation, O God, set me up on high.

"Let their table become a snare." This sudden change of subject from the one suffering to those who have caused it is cited by Paul in reference to those Jews who were opposing the advance of the gospel. He quoted Psalm 69:22–23 in noting that their actions had been responsible in part at least for God going to the Gentiles (Rom. 11:9–10).

Once the suffering for sin has been complete, the tenor of Christ's prayer (presumably after His death) takes on the aspect of strong imprecation. With respect to the Roman soldiers, merely carrying out their commanded duties, He had prayed earlier: "Father, forgive them, for they know not what they do" (Luke 23:34).

The political and religious leaders who had condemned Him to death, however, knew very well what they were doing. They were familiar with His teachings, His miracles, His righteousness, the Scriptures He had fulfilled — all the evidences that He was the long-promised Messiah. But He was a serious threat to their own power and ill-gotten wealth, and that was more important to them than the word of God. They had willfully and knowingly rejected the Savior who had come to save them, and that is the unforgivable sin. Thus, it became appropriate for Christ to pray for their irrevocable destruction, before they could lead others down the path to hell.

Judas, the traitor, was certainly one of these. After three years of daily contact with the Lord Jesus and the 11, he still betrayed the Lord, knowing that would inevitably lead to Christ's crucifixion. The apostle Peter quoted verse 25 as being particularly fulfilled in Judas. Speaking of this heinous act by Judas, Peter said, "For it is written in the book of Psalms, Let his habitation be desolate, and let no man dwell therein: and his bishoprick let another take" (Acts 1:20). The Greek word for "bishoprick" simply means "overseer," or "officer." In this case, the result of Judas' betrayal of the Lord was the election of Matthias to the honorable office he had forfeited.

One of the imprecations in Christ's prayer was especially fearful: "Add iniquity unto their iniquity: and let them not come into thy righteousness" (verse 27). Not only are such apostates forever cut off from access to Christ's imputed righteousness, but their unforgiven sinfulness will continually increase, even in hell. Of these, the angel says in the Bible's very last chapter: "He that is unjust, let him be unjust still; and he which is filthy, let him be filthy still" (Rev. 22:11). The word "still" here actually means "more." Thus, their eternal habitation is a "world of iniquity" (James 3:6). All who willfully reject (or simply ignore) the gift of righteousness through Christ indicate that they prefer to live in a world where there is complete freedom to continue in sin, and so — in perfect equity — that is what God will give them. In the lake of fire, Jesus said, "their worm dieth not, and the fire is not quenched" (Mark 9:44).

Another of his imprecations was to "let them be blotted out of the book of the living" (verse 28). This is not a reference to physical death but to the second death (Rev. 20:6) — that is, being "cast into the lake of fire" (Rev. 20:14).

The "book of the living" is the same as "the book of life." The many references to this book in the Bible indicate that all who are born (or even conceived) have their names initially inscribed in this book of life, or book of the living. But those who finally and willfully reject Christ and His

Word will have their names blotted out of the book of life (Rev. 3:5, 22:19, etc.). "And whosoever was not found written in the book of life was cast into the lake of fire" (Rev. 20:15).

Verses 30–36

> I will praise the name of God with a song, and will magnify him with thanksgiving.
>
> This also shall please the LORD better than an ox or bullock that hath horns and hoofs.
>
> The humble shall see this, and be glad: and your heart shall live that seek God.
>
> For the LORD heareth the poor, and despiseth not his prisoners.
>
> Let the heaven and earth praise him, the seas, and every thing that moveth therein.
>
> For God will save Zion, and will build the cities of Judah: that they may dwell there, and have it in possession.
>
> The seed also of his servants shall inherit it: and they that love his name shall dwell therein.

After the suffering of the man of sorrows was finished, and the judgment set for the ungodly, then follows the joyful testimony of the ones who were redeemed through His sacrifice and whose sins therefore have been forgiven. The final seven verses of this great psalm are testimonies of praise and thanksgiving. Such "sacrifices of praise" (Heb. 13:15) are far more pleasing to God than sacrifices of animals.

Eventually, after Christ's triumph over the hosts of darkness at Armageddon, the whole creation — "heaven and earth . . . the seas, and every thing that moveth therein" (verse 34) — will join in grateful praise to their Creator and Redeemer (Ps. 148:1–14). In particular the believing remnant of God's chosen people will be able to dwell in peace and fruitfulness in Zion and the other cities of Judah and throughout the whole land promised to Abraham long ago (Gen. 15:18).

The believing remnant in every nation will likewise praise God for His great gift of love and His wonderful work of salvation. The promise is not only to nations as a whole but to every individual who has acknowledged his own utter unworthiness and trusted in Christ's loving sacrifice for His own salvation. "The humble shall see this and be glad" (verse 32).

Chapter 10

Human "Gods" and the Son of God

Psalm 82

This short psalm, written by David's musician, Asaph, is included among the messianic psalms primarily because of the unique use of it made by Christ in dealing with the religious leaders who were accusing Him of blasphemy. See the account of this confrontation in John 10:22–39.

Verses 1–2

God standeth in the congregation of the mighty; he judgeth among the gods.

How long will ye judge unjustly, and accept the persons of the wicked? Selah.

The term "gods" in verse 1 is actually *elohim,* the basic Hebrew name for God, especially in His identification as omnipotent Creator of all things. However, its *im* ending marks it as a uni-plural noun ("God" or "gods"), depending on context and the associated verb. It is frequently used in reference to the false gods of the heathen — for example, "all the gods of the nations are idols" (Ps. 96:5). It is translated "angels" in Psalm 8:5, "made him a little lower than the angels."

But it is also used occasionally for human leaders — especially judges — whom God has allowed to represent Him in applying and enforcing His divine laws among people here on earth. It is actually translated judges" in Exodus 21:6: "His master shall bring (his servant) unto the judges," as well as in a few other places.

Psalm 82 opens with what seems like a vision of God himself standing in the midst of an assemblage of "gods." The initial impression might be one of God judging a congregation of fallen angels, especially since the Hebrew for "mighty" here is *el*, a word also occasionally translated as "God" or "gods."

However, such a meaning is immediately negated in the context, as these particular *elohim* are acting unjustly as human rulers judging other human beings. The "congregation" therefore, is an earthly gathering of human judges being called to account by the divine "Judge of all the earth" (Gen. 18:25).

So far as we know, there has never been such a congregation assembled in a literal sense (although it is conceivable that this might happen in the great judgment period yet to come when Christ returns). Thus, the Psalmist, in effect, has been given a grand vision of God speaking in the Spirit and through His word to all the human judges in Israel, and implicitly to all human rulers who exercise authority over fellow men in every nation in every age. As we shall see, Christ applied it to the Jewish religious leaders of His day. Remember, however, that such leaders — whether elected, appointed, or inherited — are ultimately chosen by God, who has allowed them to hold office and to whom, therefore, they are accountable. "For there is no power but of God: the powers that be are ordained of God" (Rom. 13:1).

God's charge against these powers-that-be is twofold. First, they are rendering unjust judgments; not acting impartially in accordance with the laws and principles of God's revealed word, but in accordance with their own interests instead. Second, they are consorting with wicked men, no doubt to their own profit. Their counselors and agents also promote and enforce these ungodly policies.

It is sad but true that political and religious leaders in every nation, whether in theocracies like ancient Israel, monarchies like imperial Rome, or democracies or republics like modern America, all too often have become guilty of these two crimes against the divine Judge and His will here on earth. Therefore, they must all give account to God someday in a great court of heaven. "For unto whomsoever much is given, of him shall be much required" (Luke 12:48).

Verses 3–5

Defend the poor and fatherless: do justice to the afflicted and needy.

Deliver the poor and needy: rid them out of the hand of the wicked.

They know not, neither will they understand; they walk on in darkness: all the foundations of the earth are out of course.

These heavenly orders to the judges and other leaders in the nations are gracious opportunities given them by God to use their offices properly, in accordance with God's revealed will, before they are really called to final account by God. It is especially important that they provide protection and support for those who, through no fault of their own, are not able to provide for themselves.

Verse 5 even associates the social evil of unjust political and religious "powers" with disturbances in the very foundations of the earth. The context could hardly refer to the earth's physical foundations, of course, so the implication is that stable and just human government is the very foundation of world order as God has planned it.

This has been the case ever since the great flood. The antediluvian world had no government structure except that of the family. The end result was that "the wickedness of man was great in the earth, and that every imagination of the thoughts of his heart was only evil continually" (Gen. 6:5). Finally, God had to cleanse the whole earth with the flood.

In the world after the flood, God established a new social order to be implemented by the descendants of Noah and his family. This was developed around the basic principle of human government — that of human authority to punish murderers with their own death. "Whoso sheddeth man's blood, by man shall his blood be shed" (Gen. 9:6). In order to carry out this command, it was necessary to establish organizations to enact and enforce regulations for all those human activities (stealing, adultery, etc), which, if unrestrained, would lead to murder and, then, to capital punishment. This fundamental command did not specify the form, but only the fact, of human government.

This arrangement was better than the anarchism of the pre-flood world, but human rebellion soon surfaced again, and this eventually led to the divine confusion of tongues and scattering of the families at Babel (Gen. 11). As these developed into various tribes and nations, many forms of government were developed, but human sinfulness eventually became dominant in all of them.

Therefore, God then chose a special nation and provided detailed written laws for its governance. The theocratic government which God established in Israel was, according to the Lord's own testimony, the best form that could ever be devised for implementation by sinful human beings. "What nation is so great, that hath statutes and judgments so righteous as all this law, which I set before you this day?" (Deut. 4:8).

But even the judges of Israel, and later the kings of Israel, and their religious leaders, also failed. Still later, the American colonists formed a constitutional republic, with laws and elected leaders largely based on biblical principles, and many authorities have argued that *this* was the best system every developed.

But the American government also has become, in these latter days, permeated with scandal and corruption and anti-biblicism and the people seem pleased with it, so there seems little hope for significant return to its original principles. The same is evidently true with every government in the world. There are individual exceptions here and there — honest, God-fearing judges, governors, legislators, etc. — maybe even some kings and presidents.

But by and large, the condemnation of these human "gods" in Psalm 82 is well warranted everywhere, not just in ancient Israel. As verse 5 says: "They know not, neither will they understand; they walk on in darkness: all the foundations of the earth are out of course." The time for the Judge of all the earth to intervene must be drawing near, for "if the foundations be destroyed, what can the righteous do?" (Ps. 11:3).

Verses 6–8

I have said, Ye are gods; and all of you are children of the most High.

But ye shall die like men, and fall like one of the princes.

Arise, O God, judge the earth: for thou shalt inherit all nations.

God has ordained these "powers that be" and entrusted them with great position and power, even calling them after His own name — "gods." He has considered them as his specially privileged "children." The Hebrew word here is *ben*, most commonly translated as "son" or "sons." Thus, in God's arrangement, they are both "gods" and "sons of God." The name for God here is "Most High" (Hebrew *Elyon*, a name used often in emphasizing God's position as supreme ruler of the universe).

What a high privilege is theirs, called to represent God in maintaining order and equity in His creation! But only rarely do any of them ever view these exalted positions in that light.

They are not really gods, of course, but men, and God has reminded them here that they will die just like other men. Then, "as it is appointed unto men once to die, but after this the judgment" (Heb. 9:27), they will be judged just like other men, only more severely because of their greater responsibility. They shall "fall" from their high position as "one of the princes" called by God (the word for "princes" applies also to "governors" or any other positions of power). Verse 7 can also be translated: "Ye shall fall as one, O ye rulers."

It is this passage — especially verse 6 — that Jesus used in defending His claim to be the Son of God. The account is found in John 10:23–39. When Jesus called himself God, as one with the Father, the Jewish rulers (mostly Pharisees) accused Him of blasphemy.

> Jesus answered them, Is it not written in your law, I said, Ye are gods? If he called them gods, unto whom the word of God came, and the scripture cannot be broken; Say ye of him, whom the Father hath sanctified, and sent into the world, Thou blasphemeth; because I said, I am the Son of God? (John 10:34–36).

Note, in passing, that Jesus, stressing the truth that "the Scripture cannot be broken," showed that He himself believed not only in general inspiration but in the verbal inspiration of the Scriptures. He based His vital argument on just one single word — "gods" — in this very short and relatively obscure psalm.

He also noted that even the Book of Psalms should be considered as a part of God's "law," as well as all the other books of the Old Testament canon.

There was irony in His answer to the Pharisees. He reminded them that they, as well as the other "judges" in Israel had been called "gods," as well as "sons of God" by God himself, so it seemed out of order for them to question His own claim to be the Son of God. Furthermore, calling their attention in this way to Psalm 82 would point up the fact that they had — as the psalm stresses — failed in their responsibilities and were headed for judgment themselves.

He noted, too, that, although they, like He, had been given the privilege of teaching and judging as God's representatives on earth, His own mission was far more significant. They were merely men "unto whom the word of God came," whereas He himself was the living Word whom the Father had sent into the world.

Nowhere do we read that "the word of God came to Jesus," as had been frequently said in relation to human "gods." He could speak on His own authority since He was not a human "god" representing God, but God himself, incarnate in human flesh.

The Pharisees surely understood this claim, as they "sought again to take him, but he escaped out of their hand" (John 10:39).

They also knew that when He talked about God judging these "gods," He had stated that He himself would be their judge, so that Psalm 82 was really speaking about Him. On a previous occasion, when "the Jews sought the more to kill him" (John 5:18), He had responded by saying that "the Father . . . hath committed all judgment unto the Son" (John 5:18–22). So, instead of accepting His rebuke and repenting, their anger and hatred became more intense than ever.

The final verse of the psalm makes it abundantly clear that He is actually the one who is speaking to "the congregation of the mighty" and who "judgeth among the gods" (verse 1). This is so because the one who "judgeth the earth" is the same one who shall "inherit all nations" (verse 8).

It is the Son of God who is to be "the heir of all things" (Heb. 1:2). "Ask of me," the Father has said to the Son, "and I shall give thee the (nations) for thine inheritance, and the uttermost parts of the earth for thy possession" (Ps. 2:8).

Therefore, "Be wise now . . . O ye kings: be instructed, ye judges of the earth. Serve the Lord with fear, and rejoice with trembling" (Ps. 2:10–11). "For yet a little while, and he that shall come will come, and will not tarry" (Heb. 10:37).

The psalm closes with the exhortation: "Arise, O God, judge the earth," and there will never be truly just judgment on earth until He does. Then, however, "with righteousness shall he judge the poor, and reprove with equity for the meek of the earth: and he shall smite the earth with the rod of his mouth, and with the breath of his lips shall he slay the wicked" (Isa. 11:4).

Chapter 11

Victorious and Eternal Savior

Psalm 102

Psalm 102 is accepted as a messianic psalm because its climactic verses (25–27) are quoted in Hebrews 1:10–12, and applied to Christ as the eternal Creator. Yet much of the psalm centers on the afflictions experienced by Him in His human incarnation. In fact, the inspired title of the psalm is, "A prayer of the afflicted, when he is overwhelmed, and poureth out His complaint before the Lord" The author of the psalm is unknown, but evidently he had endured much opposition and suffering because of his faithfulness to God. His "complaint" to the Lord was, nevertheless, offered in genuine faith that the Lord would intervene in His own time and way to accomplish His perfect will for His people.

He and his experiences thus became a fitting type of the future sufferings of Christ and the glory to follow. We can be confident that this is the primary application of the psalm because of its use in Hebrews 1:10–12. As we shall see, this passage makes it clear that the Lord Jesus Christ is the Creator and is, therefore, the one addressed in the psalm. Yet, in the first part of the psalm, Christ in His suffering human incarnation is also seen as praying to the Father.

Verses 1–11

Hear my prayer, O Lord, and let my cry come unto thee.

Hide not thy face from me in the day when I am in trouble; incline thine ear unto me: in the day when I call answer me speedily.

For my days are consumed like smoke, and my bones are burned as an hearth.

My heart is smitten, and withered like grass; so that I forget to eat my bread.

By reason of the voice of my groaning my bones cleave to my skin.

I am like a pelican of the wilderness: I am like an owl of the desert.

I watch, and am as a sparrow alone upon the house top.

Mine enemies reproach me all the day; and they that are mad against me are sworn against me.

For I have eaten ashes like bread, and mingled my drink with weeping,

Because of thine indignation and thy wrath: for thou hast lifted me up, and cast me down.

My days are like a shadow that declineth; and I am withered like grass.

The first 11 verses of the psalm are a prayer of lamentation and a cry to God for comfort and help. The Psalmist seems to be going through trials much like those of Job, not because of personal sins but because God has allowed it for other reasons. If we read it in a messianic context, if becomes much like Psalms 22, 40, and 69, reflecting the thoughts of Christ on the cross. We shall assume that this is the primary intent of the Holy Spirit who was speaking through the unknown Psalmist.

The plea of the suffering one for God to hear His prayer and not to hide His face (verses 1 and 2), seems to echo Christ's cry on the cross to His Father not to forsake Him (Ps. 22:1–2; Matt. 27:46). When Christ says, "my bones are burned," He is using the same Hebrew word as in the parallel messianic Psalm 69:3 when He says that "my throat is dried." The ordeal of crucifixion led Him finally to cry, "I thirst" (John 19:28).

"My heart is smitten, and withered like grass" (verse 4). This lament parallels Psalm 22:14: "My heart is like wax." "The voice of my groaning" is more accurately "the voice of my sighing," the latter being a more common translation of the Hebrew word. The Lord Jesus was not "groaning" on the cross, but suffering in silence and, no doubt, sighing over the sins of the men and women for whom He was suffering and dying.

Three lonely birds are taken by Him as picturing His own loneliness on the cross, forsaken by His disciples and even by His Father — a pelican (or cormorant) out in the wilderness, a desert owl and a lone sparrow on the roof (verses 6–7). He is continually reproached — "despised and rejected of men, a man of sorrows, and acquainted with grief" (Isa. 53:3) — and has "mingled my drink with weeping" (verse 8–9).

And all of this is "because of thine indignation and thy wrath" (verse 10). God "hath laid on him the iniquity of us all" (Isa. 53:6), and He had to drink deeply of the cup of the wrath of God which we deserved — not He. "Thou hast lifted me up" (verse 10) on the brutal cross (John 12:32–33), He says, and then "cast me down" into the "dust of death" (Ps. 22:15).

"My days are like a [lengthening] shadow," He said (verse 11), and "I am withered like grass." It was the darkening sunset of His life, and He was dying. Nevertheless, although "the grass withereth, and the flower thereof falleth away," His Father had not really forsaken Him, for "the word of the Lord endureth forever" (1 Pet. 1:24–25).

Verses 12–15

But thou, O Lord, shalt endure for ever; and thy remembrance unto all generations.

Thou shalt arise, and have mercy upon Zion: for the time to favour her, yea, the set time, is come.

For thy servants take pleasure in her stones, and favour the dust thereof.

So the heathen shall fear the name of the Lord, and all the kings of the earth thy glory.

If the word of the Lord endures forever, the Lord himself must surely endure forever (verse 12), and it is the Lord of whom the psalm is speaking. He must die for our sins, but death cannot hold Him, for He is the Creator of life. "Thou shalt arise" is the promise (verse 13) first from the grave to ascend back *to* His throne in heaven, then — at the set time — *from* His throne in heaven to complete "the redemption of His purchased possession" (Eph. 1:14), back on earth.

Then, when that set time finally arrives, all the ancient promises will be fulfilled. "The Lord shall yet comfort Zion, and shall yet choose Jerusalem. . . . Sing and rejoice, O daughter of Zion: for, lo, I come, and I will dwell in the midst of thee, saith the Lord. . . . And the Lord shall inherit Judah His portion in the holy land, and shall choose Jerusalem again" (Zechariah 1:17–2:12).

But when is that set time? "It is not for you to know the times or the seasons," said Jesus, "which the Father hath put in His own power" (Acts 1:7). "Of that day and that hour knoweth no man, no, not the angels which are in heaven, neither the Son, but the Father" (Mark 13:32).

We do know, however, that it will be after "the time of Jacob's trouble"

(Jer. 30:7). It will also be after "the fulness of the Gentiles (has) come in. And so all Israel shall be saved" (Rom. 11:25–26). The prophet Amos said: "In that day will I raise up the tabernacle of David that is fallen. . . . And I will plant them upon their land, and they shall no more be pulled up out of their land which I have given them, saith the LORD thy God" (Amos 9:11–15, note also Acts 15:13–18).

There are many other biblical prophecies to the same effect. The Promised Land will be fully restored to Israel after the great Tribulation and their national repentance and acceptance of the Lord Jesus as their Messiah and Redeemer (see Zech. 12:9–13:1; Matt. 24:29–31; etc). Exactly when that "set time" will be, only God knows. In the meantime, the biblical signs of the nearness of His coming before the beginning of this tribulation period seem to be increasing daily.

But that's another study. The emphasis here in this psalm is that the time is coming when Zion (that is, Jerusalem) will be fully rebuilt (including its temple and all "her stones"). At that time, all the other nations "shall fear the name of the LORD, and all the kings of the earth thy glory" (verse 15). In that day, "many nations shall come, and say, Come, and let us go up to the mountain of the LORD, and to the house of the God of Jacob, and he will teach us of his ways, and we will walk in his paths: for the law shall go forth of Zion, and the word of the LORD from Jerusalem" (Mic. 4:2).

In that day, the great thousand-year reign of peace on earth will begin. The Lord Jesus "shall speak peace unto the heathen, and His dominion shall be from sea even to sea, and from the river even to the ends of the earth" (Zech. 9:10).

Verses 16–22

When the LORD shall build up Zion, he shall appear in his glory.

He will regard the prayer of the destitute, and not despise their prayer.

This shall be written for the generation to come: and the people which shall be created shall praise the LORD.

For he hath looked down from the height of his sanctuary; from heaven did the LORD behold the earth;

To hear the groaning of the prisoner; to loose those that are appointed to death;

To declare the name of the LORD in Zion, and his praise in Jerusalem;

When the people are gathered together, and the kingdoms, to serve the LORD.

When the "set time" has come, and the Lord builds up Zion once again, the great millennial age will begin. Those who have had "part in the first resurrection . . . shall be priests of God and of Christ, and shall reign with him a thousand years" (Rev. 20:6). At the beginning of that time, "when the Son of man shall come in his glory, and all the holy angels with him, then shall he sit upon the throne of his glory" (Matt. 25:31). He had previously promised His disciples that "when the Son of man shall sit in the throne of his glory, ye also shall sit upon twelve thrones, judging the twelve tribes of Israel" (Matt. 19:28).

As He judges the nations (Matt. 25:32), He will indeed "regard the prayer of the destitute" (verse 17). This great prophecy, the Psalmist says, is "written for the generation to come," evidently for that generation that survives the tribulation and the judgment of the nations, and is then allowed to form the beginning population for the thousand-year kingdom age.

"The people which shall be created" (verse 18) is almost certainly a reference to the new nation of Israel which the Lord will "create" at that time. These will not be newly created men and women (as were Adam and Eve) but rather a miraculously regenerated nation, born in a day. "For I will take you from among the heathen, and gather you out of all countries, and will bring you into your own land. . . . A new heart also will I give you, and a new spirit will I put within you. . . . And ye shall dwell in the land that I gave to your fathers; and ye shall be my people, and I will be your God" (Ezek. 36: 24–28).

The Psalmist then takes a retrospective look at the conditions in the world — especially among the Israelites during that fierce "time of Jacob's trouble" (Jer. 30:7) — which had just preceded these events and had led to the Lord's coming down from His heavenly temple (verse 19). He will come "in the clouds of heaven, with power and great glory," and His angels will "gather together" His suffering people from all over the world (Matt. 24:30–31).

Then, all the "elect" will declare the Lord's "praise in Jerusalem" (verse 21). As they are all "gathered together," the great kingdom will be established on earth, and they will all (at least in its early generations) "serve the LORD" (verse 22).

Verses 23–28

He weakened my strength in the way; he shortened my days.

I said, O my God, take me not away in the midst of my days: thy years are throughout all generations.

Of old hast thou laid the foundation of the earth: and the heavens are the work of thy hands.

They shall perish, but thou shalt endure: yea, all of them shall wax old like a garment; as a vesture shalt thou change them, and they shall be changed:

But thou art the same, and thy years shall have no end.

The children of thy servants shall continue, and their seed shall be established before thee.

In this last portion of the psalm, the unknown author, having seen the wonderful vision of the ultimate coming of the Lord, the restoration of Zion, and the glories of the future kingdom, realizes that he himself will die before his prophecies are to be fulfilled. He longs to be there himself (actually, he will be there, because the Resurrection will have taken place, but his revelation did not deal explicitly with that aspect of the future).

Thus, he seems almost to be complaining that the Lord has "shortened my days" and will take him away "in the midst of my days" (verses 23–24. But then, he quickly realizes that the same God who has spoken through him will be there "throughout all generations," and that is what counts.

The next three verses contain a remarkable scientific insight, as well as a beautiful testimony of the creation in relation to its Creator. Furthermore, this is the section that is quoted in Hebrews in reference to the Son of God and His deity. Note, "But unto the Son, he [that is, the Father] saith, Thy throne, Oh God, is for ever and ever. . . . And, Thou, Lord, in the beginning hast laid the foundation of the earth; and the heavens are the works of thine hands: They shall perish; but thou remainest; and they all shall wax old as doth a garment: And as a vesture shalt thou fold them up, and they shall be changed: but thou are the same, and thy years shall not fail" (Heb. 1:8–12).

This beautiful testimony of praise acknowledges that the Son of God (the same person whose "afflictions" as the Son of man are described so graphically in the first 11 verses of the psalm) is actually the one who created the heavens and the earth. Note also the chronological order of these acts of creation, the same as in Genesis 1, with the earth mentioned first, then the handiwork of the heavens. This is sharply contrary to modern speculation about stellar and planetary evolution, which have the heavens evolving from the big bang billions of years before the evolution of the earth.

This testimony also notes the scientific fact of stellar decay, thousands of years before the formulation of the scientific law that governs it. There are, indeed, changes taking place in the heavens: stars (including the sun) are burning up their supplies of fuel; occasionally stars disintegrate in great explosions; asteroids, comets, and meteorites are breaking up. All of this is in accord with the principle of increasing entropy (disorder), better known as the second law of thermodynamics, which was recognized and formulated as a universal scientific law only a little over a century ago.

This law, which has no known exception, not only contradicts the whole notion of evolution but also points up the sharp contrast between the Creator and His creation. All the elements of God's creation are now under His curse because of man's sin, so that "the whole creation groaneth and travaileth in pain together until now" (Rom. 8:22). "Heaven and earth (are passing) away" Jesus said, "but my words shall not pass away" (Matt. 24:35). "They shall perish," declares the Psalmist, "but thou shalt endure" (verse 26). "All of them shall wax old . . . and they shall be changed. But thou art the same, and thy years shall have no end" (verse 26–27).

The prophet Isaiah noted the same great principle. "The heavens shall vanish away like smoke, and the earth shall wax old like a garment, and they that dwell therein shall die in like manner" (Isa. 51:6). That is, living creatures, including man, are under the same bondage to aging and death as the earth — all are under God's curse because of man's sin.

The same is true of plant life. "As for man, his days are as grass: as a flower of the field, so he flourisheth. For the wind passeth over it, and it is gone" (Ps. 103:15–16). In fact, "all flesh is grass: The grass withereth, the flower fadeth" (Isa. 40:6–7).

But all such assertions of universal decay are then contrasted with the permanence of God and His word and His promises: "But my salvation shall be for ever, and my righteousness shall not be abolished" (Isa. 51:6). "But the mercy of the Lord is from everlasting to everlasting upon them that fear him" (Ps. 103:17). "But the word of our God shall stand for ever" (Isa. 40:8).

The last verse of the psalm provides the same firm assurance of eternity to those created and redeemed by the mighty Creator and gracious dying-and-living Redeemer, none other than the Lord Jesus Christ. The "children of the servants shall continue, and their seed shall be established before thee" (verse 28). Because He suffered and died for us, we are saved and shall live forever with Him.

Chapter 12

A Priest Forever

Psalm 110

Although it only contains seven verses, the 110th Psalm is surely one of the most remarkable of all the messianic psalms. It is quoted at least a dozen times in the New Testament, always in reference to the Lord Jesus Christ. While a number of the messianic psalms stress His exalted position as eternal King, reigning over His creation (Ps. 45, Ps. 72, etc.), Psalm 110 also presents Him as the eternal priest, forever mediating God's blessings to His redeemed creation.

Verse 1

The LORD said unto my Lord, Sit thou at my right hand, until I make thine enemies thy footstool.

As we have noted in other chapters, many of the messianic psalms are identified as such by being quoted in the New Testament in reference to Christ. But Psalm 110 is almost unique in being so quoted and applied by Christ himself. Because the Pharisees and Sadducees were rejecting His messianic claims and mission, He asked them: "What think ye of Christ? Whose son is he? They say unto him, The Son of David. He saith unto them, How then doth David in spirit call him Lord, saying, The Lord said unto my Lord, Sit thou on my right hand, till I make thine enemies thy footstool? If David then call him Lord, how is he his son?" (Matt. 22:42–45).

The Jews all acknowledged Psalm 110 to be prophetic of the coming Messiah. Yet it was written by David "in (the) Spirit," and David obviously recognized this Messiah as his Lord. The Jews also recognized that Messiah would be of "the seed of David." Jesus pointed out to them that this could only mean that Messiah must be God incarnate in human flesh.

This amazing verse is quoted four other times in the New Testament. The same incident is recorded in Mark 12:35–37 and Luke 20:41–44. After Christ's resurrection, Peter also quoted the verse in reference to Christ's deity (Acts 2:34–35). Finally, Hebrews 1:13 does likewise, showing Christ's superiority to the angels: "But to which of the angels said he at any time, Sit on my right hand, until I make thine enemies thy footstool?"

Not only does the verse indicate the deity of Christ, it also implies the uni-plurality of the godhead, with one of the divine persons addressing another. The verse actually reads "Jehovah said unto Adonai, Sit thou at my right hand." These are two of the most frequently used names for God.

As noted in connection with Psalm 16, in chapter 4, there are no less than 21 references in the Bible to Christ being at the Father's right hand after His resurrection and ascension. Only two are in the Old Testament (Ps. 16:11 and Ps. 110:1), the rest are in the New. The 21 follow an interesting pattern of three sevens. In addition to the seven already cited, there are seven in the epistles of Paul (Rom. 8:34; Eph. 1:20; Col. 3:1; Heb. 1:3, 8:1, 10:12, 12:2) and seven in the other books of the New Testament (Matt. 26:64; Mark 14:62; 16:19; Luke 22:69; Acts 7:55–56; 1 Pet. 3:22). The Lord Jesus Christ, in His glorified human body (yet still also God the Son) has been at the right hand of the Father ever since He returned to heaven, and will be there until He finally fulfills His promise to return again to earth. That, also, is one of the great themes of this 110th Psalm.

The psalm begins with the Father (identified here as Jehovah (or Yahweh) speaking to the Son (here addressed as Adonai), inviting Him to leave His enemies on earth and to return to His throne in Heaven. These enemies, who think they have triumphed over Him, will eventually become His "footstool;" but, until that time comes, He will remain at the right hand of the Father on high.

This prophecy, written 1,000 years before it was fulfilled, clearly refers to the rejection of the Messiah by the leaders of His chosen people, and then His ascension back to Heaven. In the meantime, His work on earth would be carried on by His disciples. "And he said unto them, Go ye into all the world, and preach the gospel to every creature. . . . So then after the Lord had spoken unto them, he was received up into heaven, and sat on the right hand of God" (Mark 16:15–19).

The enemies of Messiah, responsible for His rejection and crucifixion, had said, "Let him be crucified. . . . His blood be on us, and on our children" (Matt. 27:23–25).

And so it has been. Jesus had said, weeping: "That upon you may come all the righteous blood shed upon the earth. . . . O Jerusalem, Jerusalem. . . . Behold, your house is left unto you desolate. For I say unto you, Ye shall not see me henceforth, till ye shall say, blessed is he that cometh in the name of the Lord." (Matt. 23:35–39).

That day will come, however. "God at the first did visit the Gentiles, to take out of them a people for his name. . . . After this I will return, and build again the tabernacle of David, which is fallen down; and I will build again the ruins thereof, and I will set it up" (Acts 15:14–16). "And so all Israel shall be saved: . . . There shall come out of Sion, the Deliverer, and shall turn away ungodliness from Jacob" (Rom. 11: 26).

Verses 2–3

The LORD shall send the rod of thy strength out of Zion: rule thou in the midst of thine enemies.

Thy people shall be willing in the day of thy power, in the beauties of holiness from the womb of the morning: thou hast the dew of thy youth.

When the Deliverer (that is, Redeemer — see Isa. 59:20, from which Rom. 11:26 is quoted) does finally come back to Zion (that is, Jerusalem), though "the enemy shall come in like a flood, the Spirit of the LORD shall lift up a standard against him" (Isa. 59:19). "Then shall the LORD go forth, and fight against those nations. . . . And his feet shall stand in that day upon the mount of Olives, which is before Jerusalem on the east . . . and the LORD my God shall come, and all the saints with thee" (Zech. 14:3–5).

Then He shall indeed rule in the midst of His enemies, and His own chosen people will finally be willing to believe Him and serve Him. "I will pour upon the house of David, and upon the inhabitants of Jerusalem the spirit of grace and of supplications: and they shall look upon me whom they have pierced, and they shall mourn for him, as one mourneth for his only son" (Zech. 12:10). "In that day there shall be a fountain opened to the house of David and to the inhabitants of Jerusalem for sin and for uncleanness" (Zech. 13:1).

Not only in Zion itself will He rule. "The LORD" — that is Jehovah, His Father—"shall send the rod of thy strength out of Zion" to all the nations of the world "I shall give thee the (nations) for thine inheritance, and the uttermost parts of the earth for thy possession. Thou shalt break them with a rod of iron, thou shalt dash them in pieces like a potter's vessel" (Ps. 2:8–9). "And he shall rule them with a rod of iron" (Rev. 19:15).

The phrase "beauties of holiness" may well refer to the "beautiful sanctuary" of the millennial temple which will be built in Jerusalem when

Christ returns as King ("holiness" and "sanctuary" are the same word in the Hebrew). Some have suggested that it may also refer to the beautiful garments of the high priest.

Like the early dew of the morning, the Messiah (that is, Christ) will still have the "dew of youth" when He returns. Even though He will have been in Heaven — still in His human body — for almost two thousand years, He still has His same youthful strength as when He was on earth before. However, His body had been transformed into a "glorious body" when He defeated death and rose from the dead, although it was still the same identifiable body in which He had lived on earth for 33 years (note John 20:20; Rev. 1:13–16). There is no "aging process" in Heaven!

And it is wonderful to note, just in passing, that, when He comes back for us from Heaven, He "shall change our vile body, that it may be fashioned like unto His glorious body" (Phil. 3:21). "We know that, when he shall appear, we shall be like him; for we shall see him as he is" (1 John 3:2). Perhaps we shall be young again if we are now old, or at the "optimum age" (as when He died and rose again) if we were still young at death or at the rapture. In any case, He will still have "the dew of thy youth" when He comes again, and He is "the same yesterday, today, and for ever" (Heb. 13:8).

It is worth noting also that the word "willing" in this passage is more commonly used to designate a "freewill offering." Thus, His people are not just "willing" to accept Him this second time, but will even offer themselves completely to Him, as He had long ago offered His own body as a sacrifice for them and their sins. This is the sense of the apostle Paul's challenge to all believers: "I beseech you therefore, brethren, by the mercies of God, that ye present your bodies a living sacrifice, holy, acceptable unto God, which is your reasonable service" (Rom. 12:1).

Verse 4

The LORD hath sworn, and will not repent, Thou art a priest for ever after the order of Melchizedek.

This is an amazing verse, one expounded at some length in the seventh chapter of Hebrews. The King Messiah, of whom the Psalmist is speaking, is not only to rule forever but also to serve as a priest forever.

Normally the roles of king and priest were kept completely separate, and God judged severely anyone who would intrude into the other's office (e.g., 1 Sam. 13:9–14, where Saul's heirs were denied any kingly succession because Saul had usurped Samuel's authority as priest). However, after the return from the Babylonian captivity, a remarkable prophecy was given through Zechariah, confirming that the Messiah would indeed be both king and priest. "Thus speaketh the LORD of hosts, saying, Behold the man whose name is the BRANCH. . . . Even he shall build the temple of the LORD; and he shall bear the glory, and shall sit and rule upon his throne; and he shall be a priest upon his throne; and the counsel of peace shall be between them both" (Zech. 6:12–13).

But the priesthood of Israel had been promised to the seed of Aaron and the kingdom to the seed of Judah, so how could one man serve as both priest and king? The answer is that He must be of a different priestly order than that of Aaron, for He would serve as High Priest to both Jewish and Gentile believers "one Mediator between God and men, the man Christ Jesus" (1 Tim. 2:5). Thus, He was made "a priest for ever after the order of Melchizedek." This key verse was quoted in Hebrews 5:6, 5:10, 6:20, 7:11, 7:17, and 7:21, and Melchizedek is mentioned by name nine times altogether in these three chapters of Hebrews. One gathers that this verse provides an important component of God's revelation!

But who is Melchizedek, and what is his priestly order? The only other mention of him is in connection with the experience of Abraham, after his victory over the invading armies from the north: "And Melchizedek, king of Salem brought forth bread and wine: and he was the priest of the most high God. And he blessed him, and said, Blessed be Abram of the most high God, possessor of heaven and earth: And blessed be the most high God, which hath delivered thine enemies into thy hand. And he gave him tithes of all" (Gen. 14:18–20).

The almost universal interpretation of Melchizedek, both ancient and modern, is that he was a tribal king of the small city-state of Salem, or Jerusalem, and that he not only worshiped the true God of creation, but also was serving as God's priest to the inhabitants of the town.

But this naturalistic interpretation raises a number of hard questions and involves the biblical record in a significant internal contradiction.

If Melchizedek's priesthood was so important as to include Christ himself, in the same order, why is there no record of its establishment, as in the case of Aaron? What about Noah or Shem or even Job? And who was in the priestly succession between Melchizedek and Christ? If there were no others, why not? Aaron's priestly successors continued up to and beyond the incarnation of Christ.

Also, if there was already a godly community in Canaan, with such a wonderful king and priest, why did God call Abram out of paganism to go there to establish just such a community? Abram settled not far from Jerusalem, so why didn't he join up with this godly man and community already there? Why did he later have to send back to Syria to find a God-fearing wife for Isaac? Surely there would have been some good women there in Jerusalem.

As a matter of fact, when we next hear of Jerusalem, it is ruled by a pagan king named Adonizedek (Josh. 10:1), and its inhabitants are the ungodly Jebusites, who were living in Canaan even before Abraham arrived there (Gen. 10:16, 15:21). The city was apparently founded by a Canaanite named Jebus (Judg. 19:10).

In fact, the Bible indicates that until David conquered it, Jerusalem (or Jebus) had *always* been a pagan city. God, through the prophet Ezekiel, reminded the inhabitants of Jerusalem of this fact, as follows: "Son of man, cause Jerusalem to know her abominations, And say, Thus saith the Lord God unto Jerusalem: Thy birth and thy nativity is of the land of Canaan: thy father was an Amorite, and thy mother a Hittite" (Ezek. 16:2–3). Thus, from its very beginnings, Jerusalem had been part of the Canaanite culture that God called abomination.

There is thus no real evidence whatever, in either the Bible or archaeology, that Jerusalem was ever a godly community governed by a priest/king such as Melchizedek. Until David, it had always been an ungodly pagan city.

But, then who *was* Melchizedek? The inspired Psalmist says that the divine Son, of whom he was writing, was to be a priest forever after Melchizedek's order. The Son, as just indicated, is one of the persons of the godhead, and therefore eternal by His very nature. If Melchizedek were the first priest of that same order, it would follow that he also must have been eternal for that seems to be an implied characteristic of the "order of Melchizedek."

The inspired commentary in Hebrews confirms this. "For this Melchizedek, king of Salem, priest of the most high God . . . first being by interpretation King of righteousness [that is, the meaning of the name Melchizedek], and after that also King of Salem, which is, King of peace; Without father, without mother, without descent, having neither beginning of days, nor end of life; but made like unto the Son of God; abideth a priest continually" (Heb. 7:1–3).

Thus, Melchizedek is not only an eternal person, but also the very personification of righteousness and peace. But such a description could apply only to God himself! In other words, Melchizedek could have been none other than the Lord Jesus Christ in a pre-incarnate theophany. Jesus Christ is "the same yesterday, and today, and forever" (Heb. 13:8). He has always been the one true King of righteousness and King of peace, as well as eternal priest — the one mediator between God and man.

It is unfortunately true that most modern commentators demean this great person by saying that the exalted language describing him in

Hebrews means only that his parents were not listed and the dates of his birth and death not given. They make him to be merely a tribal chieftain of a minor town of Amorites and Hittites in Canaan.

The parents of most of Christ's disciples (even including Paul) have not been listed in Scripture, nor their times of birth and death, yet none of them has ever been described as without parents or beginning and end of life.

Such language seems utterly inappropriate unless it is meant to be taken literally. It would have been easier and more understandable for the writer (inspired by God the Holy Spirit) to note that neither Melchizedek's parents nor how long he lived, were known and that these facts somehow made him "like unto the Son of God," if that was what he meant. Still, if Melchizedek was just a man, that very fact would make any such comparison inappropriate, for the parents and birth and death of the *human* Jesus *were* known.

The only interpretation of this remarkable verse which fits all the facts and the language itself is that Melchizedek was none other than the Son of God himself in a pre-incarnate theophany. The King of peace and righteousness, before His human incarnation, was thus for a brief time, "made like" He would eventually be like on earth, in order to give special assurance and comfort to Abraham at a very critical time in the life of that patriarch. He brought "bread and wine" to him, just as Christ would do one day to his disciples, at their last supper.

Verses 5–7

The Lord at thy right hand shall strike through kings in the day of his wrath.

He shall judge among the heathen, he shall fill the places with the dead bodies; he shall wound the heads over many countries.

He shall drink of the brook in the way: therefore shall he lift up the head.

The central verse of Psalm 110 (verse 4) sets forth the great truth of Christ's everlasting priesthood, but the first three verses, and now the last three, all speak of His victorious and eternal reign as King. The psalmist David is here carried forward in his vision to Christ's ultimate triumph at Armageddon.

All "the kings of the earth and of the whole world" will be gathered together in the last days, "into a place called in the Hebrew tongue

Armageddon" (Rev. 16:14–16), where they will be cast "into the great winepress of the wrath of God" (Rev. 14:19). In that "great day of his wrath" (Rev. 6:17). He "shall fill the places with the dead bodies" until "all the fowls (are) filled with their flesh" (Rev. 19:21).

And in the process of judging these "nations" (same word as "heathen"), He will "wound the heads over many countries."

The Hebrew word for "wound" in verse 6 is the same as "strike through" in verse 5, implying that He will inflict a deadly wound on the beast (the word "heads" is actually in the singular); in the last days there will be just one head over the nations of the world. "Power was given him over all kindreds, and tongues, and nations" (Rev. 13:7).

But when "the Lord at thy right hand strikes through kings in the day of his wrath," then "the beast (will be) taken, and with him the false prophet. . . . These both (will be) cast alive into a lake of fire burning with brimstone" (Rev. 19:20).

All the Lord's enemies will have been made His footstool in that day. As the mighty conqueror, His foot will (symbolically) have been placed on their prostrate bodies, in the ancient token of conquest, and He will thenceforth serve forever as the King and priest for His redeemed people.

He can rest then in His kingdom of perfect peace and righteousness. He and His weary people will "drink of the brook" (or better, "river") and He will "lift up (his) head" Then they shall all "drink of the river of thy pleasures" (Ps. 36:8). In order to be their eternal priest and King, He had long ago "thirsted" on the cross, and then "bowed his head" in death (John 19:28–30). Now, on the throne, He shall "drink of the river" of holy pleasures and "lift up His head" forever.

Chapter 13

The Chief Cornerstone

Psalm 118

The 118th Psalm is certainly one of the most clearly messianic of all the messianic psalms. It is quoted or referred to over a dozen times in the New Testament, and (like Ps. 110) Christ himself quoted it as referring to His own ministry.

Neither the author nor the occasion for writing it is known. Some attribute it to Moses and the wilderness experience, others to David, others to some unknown writer after the Babylonian exile. It has been suggested rather frequently that it was sung by Israelites on their way to Jerusalem or by worshipers approaching the temple. No one knows for certain.

Since, however, it is clearly a messianic psalm, quoted as such by the Lord Jesus himself, that is the emphasis placed on it in this exposition.

Verses 1–4

O give thanks unto the LORD; for he is good: because his mercy endureth for ever.

Let Israel now say, that his mercy endureth for ever.

Let the house of Aaron now say, that his mercy endureth for ever.

Let them now that fear the LORD say, that his mercy endureth for ever.

The first four verses of the psalm seem to be a direction to various groups by their worship leader to sing their thanks to the Lord in turn — first the saved Israelites as a whole, then the priests in particular, then all the redeemed of the Lord. Perhaps we can think of the worship leader as the Lord Jesus Christ himself, leading the praises of "the great congregation" (see Ps. 22:25 and its exposition in chapter 5) when all are gathered together at "the general assembly" in heaven (Heb. 12:23). Or perhaps we can think of Him as our worship leader (in spiritual presence) in each local assembly as well, as He then reviews the great events that culminated in our redemption and His exaltation.

Four times we are reminded (then once again, in the last verse of the psalm), that God's mercy, through Christ, will endure throughout eternity. We shall never deserve it, but, nevertheless, "in the ages to come he (will show) the exceeding riches of his grace in his kindness toward us through Christ Jesus" (Eph. 2:7).

Verses 5–9

I called upon the LORD in distress: the LORD answered me, and set me in a large place.

The LORD is on my side; I will not fear: what can man do unto me?

The LORD taketh my part with them that help me: therefore shall I see my desire upon them that hate me.

It is better to trust in the LORD than to put confidence in man.
It is better to trust in the LORD than to put confidence in princes.

Verse 5 reminds us of another messianic psalm, in which the Lord Jesus was speaking prophetically through David. "He brought me up also out of an horrible pit, out of the miry clay, and set my feet upon a rock" (Ps. 40:2). The word "distress" in the Hebrew actually means a very tight place. The Lord is contrasting the "strait" through which He was passing with the "large place" into which His Father finally brought Him. "For the joy that was set before him (he) endured the cross" (Heb. 12:2).

Verses 6 and 7 also correlate with the experience of Christ in His ministry on earth, followed by His crucifixion, resurrection, and then the resulting judgment on Israel and her worldwide dispersion. But they can also be applied to His followers. For example, verse 6 is actually quoted in Hebrews 13:6 as encouragement to those who are being persecuted for Christ's sake. "We may boldly say, The Lord is my helper, and I will not fear what man shall do unto me."

Verse 8 is a unique verse in a special sense. In the providence of God, when the biblical text was organized into chapters and verses, this verse turned out to be the middle verse of the Bible. We should not think of these verse divisions as divinely inspired in the same way as the text itself, of course (with the exception of the psalms, where the verse divisions follow naturally from the structure of the poetry, and the chapter divisions are dictated by the individual psalms). Nevertheless, it is natural and appropriate to think of these divisions as having been guided providentially by the Holy Spirit. They were developed in prayer and with the worthy motive of encouraging more study of the Scriptures. There are so many remarkable "coincidences" that can be noted in the divisions and which do lead often to special insight and blessing, that we can well believe that God was pleased with this contribution.

One such "coincidence" is that Psalm 118:8 would turn out to be the central verse. What could be more appropriate as a succinct central thought of God's revelation than just this? "It is better to trust in the Lord than to put confidence in man." It is simple trust in Christ and His completed work that brings us our eternal salvation. No man-made religion or philosophy can do this. "There is a way that seemeth right unto a man, but the end thereof are the ways of death" (Prov. 14:12, 16:5).

Putting one's trust in "princes" (or scientists, presidents, professors, or any other human leaders) instead of the Lord and His inspired Word will lead to eternal death, but "whosoever shall call upon the name of the Lord shall be saved" (Rom. 10:13).

Verses 10–18

All nations compassed me about: but in the name of the LORD will I destroy them.

They compassed me about; yea, they compassed me about: but in the name of the LORD I will destroy them.

They compassed me about like bees; they are quenched as the fire of thorns: for in the name of the LORD I will destroy them.

Thou hast thrust sore at me that I might fall: but the LORD helped me.

The LORD is my strength and song, and is become my salvation.

The voice of rejoicing and salvation is in the tabernacles of the righteous: the right hand of the LORD doeth valiantly.

The right hand of the LORD is exalted: the right hand of the LORD doeth valiantly.

I shall not die, but live, and declare the works of the LORD.

The LORD hath chastened me sore: but He hath not given me over unto death.

Verses 10 and 11 note no less than four times that Christ was "compassed about" with enemies seeking to destroy Him. The first of these says that "all nations" were surrounding Him, and this could only be true if the speaker were Christ himself.

In Psalm 22, the great prophetic psalm of His crucifixion, describing His inner thoughts while hanging on the cross, He said that "dogs have compassed me: the assembly of the wicked have enclosed me" (Ps. 22:16). The Roman soldiers, the Jewish priests, and a mixed multitude, plus the demons of hell, were all there around His cross "Many bulls have compassed me: strong bulls of Bashan have beset me round" (Ps. 22:12).

But, "in the name of the LORD will I destroy them," He had said, three times in three verses. His suffering and death on the cross not only provided salvation for believers, but also ultimate judgment and destruction for His enemies. "Through death he (shall) destroy him that had the power of death, that is, the devil" (Heb. 2:14).

There is yet to be one more time when He will be compassed about by Satan and His enemies, right at the end of His future thousand-year reign on the earth. "And when the thousand years are expired, Satan shall be loosed out of his prison. And shall go out to deceive the nations which are in the four quarters of the earth . . . to gather them together to battle: . . . And they compassed the camp of the saints about, and the beloved city" (Rev. 20:7–9).

The beloved city, of course, is the beautiful millennial Jerusalem, where the Lord Jesus will have been reigning over the earth for a thousand years of peace and prosperity. In spite of this, Satan will be able to recruit a great multitude whom, while outwardly submissive, are inwardly rebellious and resentful against the Lord. This time, however, God's longsuffering patience is exhausted, "and fire came down out of heaven, and devoured them. And the devil that deceived them was cast into the lake of fire . . . and shall be tormented day and night for ever and ever" (Rev. 20:9–10).

In verse 13, the phrase "thrust sore" is one word in the original, and can be translated various ways. The Lord Jesus seems here to address Satan, saying, in effect: "Thou hast thrust me down, but the Lord saved me, giving me strength and a song."

Three times in verses 15 and 16, "the right hand of the LORD" is seen in action, doing valiantly and being exalted. Thus, this "hand" can be none other than Jesus Christ who, after His death and resurrection, "was received up into heaven, and sat on the right hand of God" (Mark 16:19).

Then, when He says, "I shall not die, but live" (verse 17), He points to His resurrection. "I am he that liveth, and was dead: and behold, I am alive for evermore" (Rev. 1:18). He was "chastened sore" by the Lord, even to death, dying for our sins, but death could not hold the Creator of life. He could never be simply "given over to death." Although He suffered spiritual death on the cross, being utterly separated from His Father during those hours of darkness, He was still physically alive. Then, while He was physically dead in the tomb, His spirit was very much alive, proclaiming victory in Hades (1 Pet. 3:18–19).

Although there is much of mystery here as we seek to relate all these passages to Christ, it is surely clear that the statements of this psalm could never really fit David, or any other man. That the psalm is fully and essentially messianic becomes even more certain as we look at the next section.

Verses 19–24

Open to me the gates of righteousness: I will go into them, and I will praise the LORD:

This gate of the LORD, into which the righteous shall enter.

I will praise thee: for thou hast heard me, and art become my salvation.

The stone which the builders refused is become the head stone of the corner.

This is the LORD's doing; it is marvelous in our eyes.

This is the day which the LORD hath made; we will rejoice and be glad in it.

Following the death and resurrection of the Lord, He would return to the gates of the heavenly city. This is the grand theme of Psalm 24 (see chapter 16). "Lift up your hands, O ye gates; and be ye lift up, ye everlasting doors; and the King of glory shall come in" (Ps. 24:7). Only the righteous can enter these gates of righteousness, and He is "Jesus Christ the righteous" (1 John 2:1).

However, He is also our "advocate with the Father," and through His grace, we who have been redeemed by His precious blood have been "made the righteousness of God in him" (2 Cor. 5:21). Therefore, we also one day shall see those 12 gates, each of one great pearl (Rev. 21:21), and "enter in through the gates into the city" (Rev. 22:14). Only those can enter "which are written in the Lamb's book of life" (Rev. 21:27).

Verse 21 could be understood either as praise from the Son to His Father for delivering Him through the ordeal of the cross or as praise from the souls for whom He died to provide salvation, or perhaps as both. The verses before verse 21 presumably were the testimonies of Christ, both recalling His time on the cross and also looking forward to the ultimate consummation that He would carry out as a result of His victory there. Then the succeeding verses express the inspired testimony of the Psalmist about Him, in effect speaking for all those who have been redeemed.

But that very testimony was later appropriated by Jesus Christ as having been fulfilled in himself. "Jesus saith unto them, Did ye never read in the scriptures, The stone which the builders rejected, the same is become the head of the corner: this is the LORD's doing, and it is marvelous in our eyes?" (Matt. 21:42).

There is a Jewish tradition that, during the construction of Solomon's temple, such a situation had actually occurred. The stones for the temple had all been cut and dimensioned away from the temple site, so that no construction noises could be "heard in the house, while it was in building" (1 Kings 6:7). The tradition says that one stone did not seem to fit anywhere, so the construction crew laid it aside for later disposal. But when they came to lay the "head stone of the corner," that was the only stone that would fit.

The Psalmist clearly was prophesying that, when the Messiah about whom he was writing would finally come, the religious leaders of Israel would reject Him. Jesus interpreted it thus, and indicated that it would be fulfilled in Him.

After it *had* been fulfilled, the apostle Peter, forced to appear before the priests, with the elders and scribes, rebuked these rulers by referring to the same Scripture. Speaking of the man they had recently crucified, but who had risen from the dead, he said: "This is the stone which was set at nought of you builders, which is become the head of the corner. Neither is there salvation in any other, for there is none other name under heaven, given among men, whereby we must be saved" (Acts 4:11–12).

The prophet Isaiah had used a similar metaphor in prophesying of the coming Messiah. "Therefore thus saith the Lord God, Behold, I lay in Zion for a foundation a stone, a tried stone, a precious corner stone, a sure foundation." (Isa. 28:16).

Peter, in his epistle, referred to both these prophecies as being fulfilled in Christ. "Wherefore also it is contained in the scripture, Behold, I lay in Sion a chief corner stone, elect, precious. . . . Unto you therefore which believe he is precious: but unto them which be disobedient, the stone which the builders disallowed, the same is made the head of the corner" (1 Pet. 2:6–7).

The apostle Paul also called the Lord Jesus Christ "the chief corner stone" (Eph. 2:20) of the great spiritual temple now being erected by the Lord composed of all believers, "for an habitation of God through the Spirit" (Eph. 2:22). Obviously, all "this is the LORD's doing" and it is "marvelous [the Hebrew word actually means 'miraculous'] in our eyes" (verse 23).

The next verse notes that "this is the day which the LORD hath made" (verse 24). The day of which he was prophesying was almost certainly the day on which Christ entered the city of Jerusalem on the little donkey, in effect claiming to be the Messiah (as predicted specifically in Zech. 9:9) and Israel's promised King. When they rejected Him, He wept over Jerusalem, saying: "If thou hadst known, even thou, at least in this thy day, the things which belong unto thy peace! but now they are hid from thine eyes" (Luke 19:42).

Verses 25–29

Save now, I beseech thee, O LORD: O LORD, I beseech thee, send now prosperity.

Blessed be he that cometh in the name of the LORD: we have blessed you out of the house of the LORD.

God is the LORD, which hath showed us light: bind the sacrifice with cords, even unto the horns of the altar.

Thou art my God, and I will praise thee: thou art my God, I will exalt thee.

O give thanks unto the LORD; for he is good: for his mercy endureth for ever.

At first, when Jesus rode into the city on that "day which the LORD hath made," the common people welcomed Him gladly, crying out "Hosanna to the Son of David: Blessed is he that cometh in the name of the Lord; Hosanna in the highest" (Matt. 21:9).

They were, in effect, quoting verses 25 and 26 of our psalm, but only in part. "Save now" (verse 25) is the meaning of "Hosanna," and then they repeated part of verse 26. "Blessed be the King that cometh in the name of the Lord" (Luke 19:38). But the same multitude, just a few days later, was following the priests in calling for His crucifixion. Thus, Jesus had to say to the city and the house of Israel as a whole: "Behold, your house is left unto you desolate. For I say unto you, Ye shall not see me henceforth, till ye shall say, Blessed is he that cometh in the name of the Lord" (Matt. 23:38–39).

That day will come, of course, when "all Israel shall be saved" (Rom. 11:26) and will finally recognize that Jesus was their Messiah, who "cometh in the name of the Lord," the great "Deliverer," who "shall turn away ungodliness from Jacob."

At the time when He was rejected, however, those who had seemingly welcomed Him were soon calling for His blood. He had, indeed, come to be the sacrificial "Lamb of God, which taketh away the sin of the world" (John 1:29). "Bind the sacrifice with cords, even unto the horns of the altar," they cried out in effect. "We have a law, and by our law He ought to die, because He made himself the Son of God" (John 19:7). And so they crucified Him.

But all this was done "by the determinate counsel and foreknowledge of God," and God soon raised Him up again, "having loosed the pains of death: because it was not possible that he should be holden of it" (Acts 2:23–24). "Christ died for our sins according to the Scriptures; and . . . rose again the third day according to the scriptures" (1 Cor. 15:3–4). And it is this wonderful gospel by which we are saved!

"God is the LORD, which hath shewed us light" (verse 27). This could also — perhaps better — be translated, "Mighty is Jehovah, who has shown us the light." Now we, who have seen the light and believed on Him, are ourselves willing to be "living sacrifices" (Rom. 12:1), bound to His altar, seeking to live for Him, who died for us. "Thou art my God, and I will praise thee." We "give thanks unto the LORD; for he is good; for his mercy endureth forever."

Chapter 14

The Living Word of God

Psalm 119
Introduction

In many ways, the 119th Psalm is one of the most remarkable chapters in the Bible. With 176 verses, it is by far the longest chapter in the Bible. It is almost the middle chapter, but the central chapter is actually the shortest chapter, the two-verse-long 117th Psalm. The middle verse of the Bible is Psalm 118:8 — "It is better to trust in the Lord than to put confidence in man."

But the most striking feature of the psalm is its constant emphasis on God's written word, the Holy Scriptures. Practically every verse is a testimony to the value of the Scriptures, a fact which is all the more remarkable since the writer of the psalm had only a small portion of the complete Bible available in his day. If the Scriptures were such a blessing to him, how much more should they be so to us! Even though this psalm is never quoted in the New Testament as specifically messianic, its structure and theme clearly point to Christ as God's Living Word.

The 119th psalm is of unknown authorship, 1 of the 50 anonymous psalms in the Book of Psalms. The real author, of course, is the Holy Spirit, and there is probably no chapter in the Bible containing more clear internal evidences of divine inspiration than this one.

Numerical Structure

All of God's physical creation is filled with evidences of design and order, capable of being described and analyzed mathematically. It is not too surprising, then, that His written revelation (which is far superior to His revelation in nature) should likewise exhibit evidences of order and structure. Occasionally these are actually in the form of numerical patterns, and this is especially true of Psalm 119.

The most obvious numerical pattern is the psalm's division into 22 stanzas of 8 verses each. Each of the 22 stanzas is headed by one of the 22 letters of the Hebrew alphabet. In the original Hebrew, the psalm is a remarkable acrostic, with the first letter of each verse consisting of the letter corresponding to its stanza. Thus, each of the first eight verses begins with the Hebrew letter *aleph*, each of the second eight with *beth*, the third eight with *gimel*, and so on.

It was the Hebrew language, of course, in which God chose to convey His Word to mankind originally, and it is appropriate that this unique psalm of the Word should be structured so strikingly around the Hebrew alphabet. The New Testament revelation was given in the Greek language, and it is significant that He who is the living Word said in His last revelation, "I am Alpha and Omega" (Rev. 1:8, 22:13). Alpha and omega, of course, are the first and last letters of the Greek alphabet, and this claim of the Lord Jesus identifies Him as the very author of all language. In fact, the gift of language is a unique gift of God to man, not shared in any degree by animals and completely inexplicable on any kind of evolutionary basis. Evidently the very purpose of language is to enable God to reveal himself and His will to men, and for men to respond in praise to God.

It is not so immediately obvious why each stanza of the psalm has eight verses, but this also is singularly appropriate. The number eight in the Bible is symbolic of resurrection and eternal life, and it is the living Word who gives eternal life through the written Word. "Being born again, not of corruptible seed, but of incorruptible, by the word of God, which liveth and abideth forever" (1 Pet. 1:23).

It is universally acknowledged that the number seven in the Bible represents completeness and rest. The week of seven days regularly commemorates God's primeval week of creation. By the same token, the number six represents incompleteness, and the number eight represents a new beginning. Man was created on the sixth day, and always "comes short of the glory of God" in his sin and rebellion, so that six seems in the Bible commonly associated with man as separated from God. Conversely, eight represents the perfect man, Jesus Christ, especially in His resurrected state, and thus also all who have received new life through faith in Him.

Christ was raised from the dead on the "eighth" day, the first day of a new week, after He had rested in the tomb on the Sabbath day. It is significant that there are eight other specific "resuscitations" (not true resurrections, since these all died again later) mentioned in the Bible. There were three in the ministry of Elijah and Elisha — 1 Kings 17:22; 2 Kings 4:34–35, and 13:21; three in the ministry of Jesus — Matthew 9:24–25; Luke 7:15; and John 11:44; and two in the ministry of the apostles — Acts 9:40–41 and 20:9–12).

In the 119th Psalm it is striking that there are exactly eight different words which are used to refer to the Scriptures. The number of occurrences of each forms the following pattern:

Torah (= "law")	25	Imrah (= "word")	19
Edah (= "testimony")	23	Mishpat (= "judgment")	21
Dabar (= "word")	23	Piqqu (= "precept")	21
Chuggah (= "statute")	22	Mitzvah (= "commandment")	22

Sum of each pair of most and least frequent occurrences = 44
Total occurrences = 4 x 44 = number of verses in the psalm = 176

The above arrangement could hardly have been deliberately contrived by the writer, and yet it is far too regular and symmetrical to have occurred by chance. The verbal inspiration of the Scriptures by the Holy Spirit is the most satisfying explanation. It is interesting that six verses in the psalm (3, 37, 90, 91, 122, and 132) contain *no* reference to the Scriptures, but six verses contain *two* references to the Scriptures (16, 43, 48, 160, 168, and 172).

But that is not all. It is well known that numbers in both the Hebrew and Greek languages were expressed by letters in the alphabet, each letter representing also a certain number. The Jews and Greeks did not use unique symbols such as the Arabic numerals which we today use with the English language. Therefore, each Hebrew and Greek word also had a distinct "numerical value," which was simply the total of the numbers represented by the letters of the alphabet used in the word.

This is the plain literal meaning of the admonition in Revelation 13:17–18 to "count the number of his name" — that is, "add up the numerical values of the letters used in his name." The name of this coming beast, the man of sin, will have a numerical value (presumably when transliterated into the New Testament Greek language) of 666, which is "the number of a man," and which will enable those believers in that day who "have wisdom" to identify him before he is openly revealed.

About one in every 10,000 names will have the numerical value of 666, but presumably there will be only one important political leader in that day with this identification. The significant point about this in connection with Psalm 119, however, is that the name "Jesus" in the Koine Greek has the number 888! The three-fold 8 probably connotes the triune godhead, "all the fulness" of which dwells bodily in Jesus (Col. 2:9). The three-fold 6 in 666 may similarly suggest the counterfeit trinity of the dragon, the beast, and the false prophet (Rev. 16:13).

The full resurrection name of Christ is "Lord Jesus Christ." In the

Greek the name "Lord" has a numerical value of 8 x 100, "Jesus" a value of 8 x 111, and "Christ" a value of 8 x 185. So "Lord Jesus Christ" has a numerical value of 8 x 396, which is also the number 176 x 18, where 176 is the number of verses in this 119th Psalm.

Another point of interest is that there are exactly 8 combinations of this name ("Lord," "Jesus," "Christ," "Jesus Christ," "Christ Jesus," "Lord Jesus," "Lord Christ," and "Lord Jesus Christ") which are used in the New Testament. In addition to His name, the New Testament uses many titles for Christ. It is perhaps significant that Christ referred to himself most frequently as the Son of Man, a title which He used 80 times.

There are, no doubt, many other significant structural and numerical patterns to be found in this tremendous psalm, but these should suffice to make the point that it manifests by its very form that it is divinely inspired. Such designs in the Bible can be explained neither by chance nor by human ingenuity, and thus can only be attributed to God.

Furthermore, there are numerous claims in the psalm itself to the absolute authority and integrity of the Scriptures. For example, note the following:

I know, O LORD, that thy judgments are right (verse 75).

For ever, O LORD, thy word is settled in heaven (verse 89).

I have more understanding than all my teachers: for thy testimonies are my meditation (verse 99).

I esteem all thy precepts concerning all things to be right (verse 128).

Thy word is very pure (verse 140).

The righteousness of thy testimonies is everlasting (verse 144).

Concerning thy testimonies, I have known of old that thou hast founded them for ever (verse 152).

Thy word is true from the beginning: and every one of thy righteous judgments endureth for ever (verse 160).

Purpose and Nature of the Psalm

As noted before, all 176 verses of Psalm 119 stress the written Word of God. The numerical structure, as well as its own claims, indicate that it (as well as the entire Bible) came ultimately from the Spirit of God. However, the message of the psalm is much more than merely a testimony to the divine inspiration of the Scriptures.

The Scriptures were inspired for a purpose, "All Scripture is given by inspiration of God . . . that the man of God may be perfect, throughly furnished unto all good works" (2 Tim. 3:16–17). This is the primary message of Psalm 119: the Holy Scriptures are profitable in every way and able to meet every need in time and eternity.

When one first reads this psalm, it seems there is little or no continuity from one verse to the next. It all seems like a miscellaneous collection of sayings, arranged in no particular sequence or order except to fit the acrostic structure. But it is unlikely that a writer giving such attention to numeric and alphabetic order would not give at least as much attention to order of content.

As a matter of fact, the psalm takes on beautiful significance if one will read it as sort of a spiritual diary, written at various times during the long life of a believer, one who has experienced many and varied circumstances of life, but has found the Word of God able to give guidance and victory in all situations.

The psalm does not itself say that this was the background of its composition, so one cannot be dogmatic. But since it does not preclude such an interpretation, and since this does seem to fit naturally, we can at least think of it in this frame of reference. In a way, therefore, the psalm may record the spiritual growth of its writer, from his youthful decision to believe and obey God's Word down to the time when he is expecting shortly to meet the Lord. Each stanza centers on a dominant theme, representing the primary experiences of that stage of his life. At the same time, each stanza contains "overtones" of other themes, both past and future, since many experiences in a believer's life are repeated in greater or lesser degree throughout his life. With this concept in mind, let us journey through his diary, comparing his circumstances with our own today, and noting with him that God can meet every need through His Word.

Aleph: Conviction of Sin through the Word
Verses 1–8

Blessed are the undefiled in the way, who walk in the law of the LORD.

Blessed are they that keep his testimonies, and that seek him with the whole heart.

They also do no iniquity: they walk in his ways.

Thou hast commanded us to keep thy precepts diligently.

O that my ways were directed to keep thy statutes!

Then shall I not be ashamed, when I have respect unto all thy commandments.

I will praise thee with uprightness of heart, when I shall have learned thy righteous judgments.

I will keep thy statutes: O forsake me not utterly.

The first eight verses constitute the writer's recognition that God's blessings are reserved for those who obey God's laws, followed by an affirmation that He will, indeed, do just that. But it is significant that only six of the eight words used in Psalm 119 for the Scriptures occur in this stanza, and all six emphasize the Scriptures as God's many *commandments*. Thus:

Verse 1 — "walk in the law [*torah*] of the LORD"
Verse 2 — "keep his testimonies [*eduth*]"
Verse 4 — "keep thy precepts [*piqqudim*] diligently"
Verse 5 — "keep thy statutes! [*chuqqah*]"
Verse 6 — "have respect unto all thy commandments [*mitzvah*]"
Verse 7 — "learned thy righteous judgments [*mishpat*]"

Resolutions to keep God's commandments are all well and good, but "by the law is the knowledge of sin" (Rom. 3:10). The better one knows the holiness of God's statutes, the more he realizes he is unable to measure up to God's standard. "For as many as are of the works of the law are under the curse: for it is written, Cursed is every one that continueth not in all things which are written in the book of the law to do them" (Gal. 3:10).

This was the experience of the Psalmist. Immediately after making the sweeping boast "I will keep thy statutes!" he seems to have suddenly been overwhelmed with the utter impossibility of such a claim and closes the stanza by throwing himself completely on God's mercy. "O forsake me not utterly."

Beth: Regeneration and Victory by the Word
Verses 9–16

Wherewithal shall a young man cleanse his way? by taking heed thereto according to thy word.

With my whole heart have I sought thee: O let me not wander from thy commandments.

Thy word have I hid in mine heart, that I might not sin against thee.

Blessed art thou, O Lord: teach me thy statutes.

With my lips have I declared all the judgments of thy mouth.

I have rejoiced in the way of thy testimonies, as much as in all riches.

I will meditate in thy precepts, and have respect unto thy ways.

I will delight myself in thy statutes: I will not forget thy word.

In response to his cry and the sincere searching in his heart (verse 10), God brings cleansing and salvation through His Word. In this stanza, the last two words for the Scriptures are used, both of which are translated "word."

The first verse (9) is powerful. "Wherewithal shall a young man cleanse his way? By taking heed thereto according to thy word [*dabar*]." And then, equally powerful is verse 11. "Thy word [*imrah*] have I hid in mine heart, that I might not sin against thee." The first "word" speaks of cleansing and the second "word" speaks of victory over sin. Thus, the Scriptures not only convict of sin, but also bring regeneration and power to live a godly life in obedience to God's commandments. Verse 9 tells of "the washing of water by the word" (Eph. 5:26), and verse 11 of being "sanctified" through the word of truth (John 17:17). It is only in the Scriptures, of course, that a person can learn of God's salvation through faith in Christ and His work.

The rest of this stanza stresses the joy of a young believer, forgiven of sin and desiring to grow in grace through diligent study of the Scriptures. At the end of the first stanza he had cried futilely, "I will keep thy statutes," but at the end of the second stanza he testifies joyfully, "I will delight myself in thy statutes." The law is no longer a burden, but a delight!

Gimel: Nurture and Growth Through the Word
Verses 17–24

Deal bountifully with thy servant, that I may live, and keep thy word.

Open thou mine eyes, that I may behold wondrous things out of thy law.

I am a stranger in the earth: hide not thy commandments from me.

My soul breaketh for the longing that it hath unto thy judgments at all times.

Thou hast rebuked the proud that are cursed, which do err from thy commandments.

Remove from me reproach and contempt; for I have kept thy testimonies.

Princes also did sit and speak against me: but thy servant did meditate in thy statutes.

Thy testimonies also are my delight and my counsellors.

Time and space do not facilitate a verse-by-verse analysis of all the remaining stanzas of Psalm 119, but only an annotation concerning the dominant theme of each stanza, remembering that each stanza also contains overtones from earlier and later themes. Immediately after regeneration, the need is for spiritual growth. "As newborn babes, desire the sincere milk of the word, that ye may grow thereby" (1 Pet. 2:2). This is the prayer of the young believer in this stanza: "Open thou mine eyes that I may behold wondrous things out of thy law" (verse 18). "Thy testimonies also are my delight and my counsellors" (verse 24).

Daleth: Confession of Sin and Renewed Victory through the Word
Verses 25–32

My soul cleaveth unto the dust: quicken thou me according to thy word.

I have declared my ways, and thou heardest me: teach me thy statutes.

Make me to understand the way of thy precepts: so shall I talk of thy wondrous works.

My soul melteth for heaviness: strengthen thou me according unto thy word.

Remove from me the way of lying: and grant me thy law graciously.

I have chosen the way of truth: thy judgments have I laid before me.

I have stuck unto thy testimonies: O LORD, put me not to shame.

I will run the way of thy commandments, when thou shalt enlarge my heart.

The first flush of joy and victory in a young convert is often followed by a sudden lapse into sin and defeat, from which he must be restored by confessing and forsaking the sin. "My soul cleaveth unto the dust: quicken thou me according to thy word. . . . My soul melteth for heaviness: strengthen thou me according unto thy word. Remove from me the way of lying. . . . I have chosen the way of truth" (verses 25–30).

He: Continued Instruction in the Word, For True Character Growth
Verses 33–40

Teach me, O LORD, the way of thy statutes; and I shall keep it unto the end.

Give me understanding, and I shall keep thy law: yea, I shall observe it with my whole heart.

Make me to go in the path of thy commandments; for therein do I delight.

Incline my heart unto thy testimonies, and not to covetousness.

Turn away mine eyes from beholding vanity: and quicken thou me in thy way.

Stablish thy word unto thy servant, who is devoted to thy fear.

Turn away my reproach which I fear: for thy judgments are good.

Behold, I have longed after thy precepts: quicken me in thy righteousness.

The godly man does not arrive at spiritual maturity instantaneously. It is a lifelong process, but every stage of that growth must come from the Word. "Teach me, O LORD, the way of thy statutes; and I shall keep it unto the end. . . . Incline my heart unto thy testimonies, and not to covetousness" (verses 33–36).

Vau: Witnessing of the Word to Others
Verses 41–48

Let thy mercies come also unto me, O LORD, even thy salvation, according to thy word.

So shall I have wherewith to answer him that reproacheth me: for I trust in thy word.

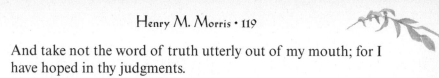

And take not the word of truth utterly out of my mouth; for I have hoped in thy judgments.

So shall I keep thy law continually for ever and ever.

And I will walk at liberty: for I seek thy precepts.

I will speak of thy testimonies also before kings, and will not be ashamed.

And I will delight myself in thy commandments, which I have loved;

My hands also will I lift up unto thy commandments, which I have loved; and I will meditate in thy statutes.

The true believer desires to tell of his faith to others and to lead them to salvation, answering their problems and objections through his growing knowledge of God's Word. As Peter commands, we are to "be ready always to give an answer to every man that asketh you a reason of the hope that is in you" (1 Pet. 3:15). This was the Psalmist's chief concern at this stage of his growth. "So shall I have wherewith to answer him that reproacheth me: for I trust in thy word. . . . I will speak of thy testimonies also before kings, and will not be ashamed" (verses 42–46).

Zain: Comfort in Suffering from the Word
Verses 49–56

Remember the word unto thy servant, upon which thou hast caused me to hope.

This is my comfort in my affliction: for thy word hath quickened me.

The proud have had me greatly in derision: yet have I not declined from thy law.

I remembered thy judgments of old, O Lord; and have comforted myself.

Horror hath taken hold upon me because of the wicked that forsake thy law.

Thy statutes have been my songs in the house of my pilgrimage.

I have remembered thy name, O Lord, in the night, and have kept thy law.

This I had, because I kept thy precepts.

As to everyone, a time of suffering comes to the writer at this period, probably resulting from his bold testimony. But God's Word was his own answer. "This is my comfort in my affliction: for thy word hath quickened me. . . . Thy statutes have been my song in the house of my pilgrimage" (verses 50–54).

Cheth: The Fellowship of Believers in the World
Verses 57–64

Thou art my portion, O Lord: I have said that I would keep thy words.

I intreated thy favour with my whole heart: be merciful unto me according to thy word.

I thought on my ways, and turned my feet unto thy testimonies.

I made haste, and delayed not to keep thy commandments.

The bands of the wicked have robbed me: but I have not forgotten thy law.

At midnight I will rise to give thanks unto thee because of thy righteous judgments.

I am a companion of all them that fear thee, and of them that keep thy precepts.

The earth, O Lord, is full of thy mercy: teach me thy statutes.

A pilgrim needs not only the comfort of God and His Word, but also the fellowship of others on the same pilgrimage. "I am a companion of all them that fear thee, and of them that keep thy precepts" (verse 63).

Teth: Chastisement Following Disobedience to the Word
Verses 65–72

Thou hast dealt well with thy servant, O Lord, according unto thy word.

Teach me good judgment and knowledge: for I have believed thy commandments.

Before I was afflicted I went astray: but now have I kept thy word.

Thou art good, and doest good; teach me thy statutes.

The proud have forged a lie against me: but I will keep thy precepts with my whole heart.

Their heart is as fat as grease: but I delight in thy law.

It is good for me that I have been afflicted; that I might learn thy statutes.

The law of thy mouth is better unto me than thousands of gold and silver.

Suffering is sometimes from God's chastening hand, and this possibility must always be considered, at least, even by those who have been faithful in times past. When one continues in disobedience to the teachings of Scripture, God may have to force repentance through chastisement, but this is far better than allowing an erring child to continue uncorrected. "Before I was afflicted I went astray: but now have I kept thy word. . . . It is good for me that I have been afflicted; that I might learn thy statutes" (verses 67–71).

Jod: Submission to God's Word under Affliction
Verses 73–80

Thy hands have made me and fashioned me: give me understanding, that I may learn thy commandments.

They that fear thee will be glad when they see me; because I have hoped in thy word.

I know, O LORD, that thy judgments are right, and that thou in faithfulness hast afflicted me.

Let, I pray thee, thy merciful kindness be for my comfort, according to thy word unto thy servant.

Let thy tender mercies come unto me, that I may live: for thy law is my delight.

Let the proud be ashamed; for they dealt perversely with me without a cause: but I will meditate in thy precepts.

Let those that fear thee turn unto me, and those that have known thy testimonies.

Let my heart be sound in thy statutes; that I be not ashamed.

The believer must learn to submit willingly to the instruction and light of Scripture when under God's chastening. "I know, O LORD, that thy judgments are right and that thou in faithfulness hast afflicted me. . . . Let my heart be sound in thy statutes; that I be not ashamed" (verses 75–80).

Ceph: Persecution and Deliverance, Through the Word
Verses 81–88

My soul fainteth for thy salvation: but I hope in thy word.

Mine eyes fail for thy word, saying, When wilt thou comfort me?

For I am become like a bottle in the smoke; yet do I not forget thy statutes.

How many are the days of thy servant? When wilt thou execute judgment on them that persecute me?

The proud have digged pits for me, which are not after thy law.

All thy commandments are faithful: they persecute me wrongfully; help thou me.

They had almost consumed me upon earth; but I forsook not thy precepts.

Quicken me after thy lovingkindness; so shall I keep the testimony of thy mouth.

Not all suffering is chastisement, of course, and often the faithful witness will suffer real persecution because of the Word. But the Word is itself the needed comfort and deliverer. "They had almost consumed me upon earth; but I forsook not thy precepts. Quicken me after thy lovingkindness; so shall I keep the testimony of thy mouth" (verses 87–88).

Lamed: Security in the Word
Verses 89–96

For ever, O LORD, thy word is settled in heaven.

Thy faithfulness is unto all generations: thou hast established the earth, and it abideth.

They continue this day according to thine ordinances: for all are thy servants.

Unless thy law had been my delights, I should then have perished in mine affliction.

I will never forget thy precepts: for with them thou hast quickened me.

I am thine, save me; for I have sought thy precepts.

The wicked have waited for me to destroy me: but I will consider thy testimonies.

I have seen an end of all perfection: but thy commandment is exceeding broad.

The second half of Psalm 119 opens with the tremendous testimony, "For ever, O LORD, thy word is settled in heaven. Thy faithfulness is unto all generations: thou hast established the earth, and it abideth. They continue this day according to thine ordinances: for all are thy servants" (verses 89–91). When one puts his trust in the God of the Bible, he is following no will-o-the-wisp, but the eternal Word of the God of creation. That the Word is everlasting and immutable is the testimony of many other Scriptures as well (Isa. 40:8; Matt. 24:35; Ps. 19:9; 1 Pet. 1:24–25, etc.).

Mem: Understanding the Word
Verses 97–104

O, how I love thy law! It is my meditation all the day.

Thou through thy commandments hast made me wiser than mine enemies: for they are ever with me.

I have more understanding than all my teachers: for thy testimonies are my meditation.

I understand more than the ancients, because I keep thy precepts.

I have refrained my feet from every evil way, that I might keep thy word.

I have not departed from thy judgments: for thou hast taught me.

How sweet are thy words unto my taste! Yea, sweeter than honey to my mouth.

Through thy precepts I get understanding: therefore I hate every false way.

The Psalmist here returns to the theme of studying the Word, for this is, indeed, a lifelong occupation. "O how love I thy law! It is my meditation all the day. . . . I have more understanding than my teachers: for thy testimonies are my meditation. . . . How sweet are thy words unto my taste! Yea, sweeter than honey to my mouth!" (verses 97–103). As a matter of fact, the older one grows in the Lord and the more varied his experiences and deliverances, the more blessed the Word becomes.

Nun: Guidance By the Word
Verses 105–112

Thy word is a lamp unto my feet, and a light unto my path.

I have sworn, and I will perform it, that I will keep thy righteous judgments.

I am afflicted very much: quicken me, O LORD, according unto thy word.

Accept, I beseech thee, the freewill-offerings of my mouth, O LORD, and teach me thy judgments.

My soul is continually in my hand: yet do I not forget thy law.

The wicked have laid a snare for me: yet I erred not from thy precepts.

The testimonies have I taken as a heritage for ever: for they are the rejoicing of my heart.

I have inclined mine heart to perform thy statutes alway, even unto the end.

Nor does a believer ever grow so mature in spiritual experience as to be able to proceed independently of the Word. "Thy word is a lamp unto my feet, and a light unto my path. . . . Thy testimonies have I taken as a heritage for ever: for they are the rejoicing of my heart" (verses 105–111).

Samech: Protection By God's Promises in the Word
Verses 113–120

I hate vain thoughts: but thy law do I love.

Thou art my hiding place and my shield: I hope in thy word.

Depart from me, ye evildoers: for I will keep the commandments of God.

Uphold me according unto thy word, that I may live: and let me not be ashamed of my hope.

Hold thou me up, and I shall be safe: and I will have respect unto thy statutes continually.

Thou hast trodden down all them that err from thy statutes: for their deceit is falsehood.

Thou puttest away all the wicked of the earth like dross: therefore I love thy testimonies.

My flesh trembleth for fear of thee; and I am afraid of thy judgments.

The more powerful the testimony of the believer, the more powerful and bitter become his enemies. But God's Word is adequate for this need, too. "Thou art my hiding place and my shield: I hope in thy word. . . . Thou puttest away all the wicked of the earth like dross: therefore, I love thy testimonies" (verses 114–119).

Ain: Settled Obedience to the Word
Verses 121–128

I have done judgment and justice: leave me not to mine oppressors.

Be surety for thy servant for good: let not the proud oppress me.

Mine eyes fail for thy salvation, and for the word of thy righteousness.

Deal with thy servant according unto thy mercy, and teach me thy statutes.

I am thy servant; give me understanding, that I may know thy testimonies.

It is time for thee, LORD, to work: for they have made void thy law.

Therefore I love thy commandments above gold; yea, above fine gold.

Therefore I esteem all thy precepts concerning all things to be right; and I hate every false way.

As the writer continues to grow in grace and knowledge, doubts and rebellions are increasingly vanquished in his mind. "Therefore I love thy commandments above gold; yea, above fine gold. Therefore, I esteem all thy precepts concerning all things to be right; and I hate every false way" (verses 127–128).

Pe: Light and Victory through the Word
Verses 129–136

Thy testimonies are wonderful: therefore doth my soul keep them.

The entrance of thy words giveth light; it giveth understanding unto the simple.

I opened my mouth, and panted: for I longed for thy commandments.

Look thou upon me, and be merciful unto me, as thou usest to do unto those that love thy name.

Order my steps in thy word: and let not any iniquity have dominion over me.

Deliver me from the oppression of man: so will I keep thy precepts.

Make thy face to shine upon thy servant; and teach me thy statutes.

Rivers of waters run down mine eyes, because they keep not thy law.

All true instruction must come from the Word of God. "The entrance of thy words giveth light; it giveth understanding to the simple" (verse 130). Through the entering and illuminating Word comes victory in every trial, against both internal and external dangers. "Order my steps in thy word: and let not any iniquity have dominion over me. Deliver me from the oppression of man: so will I keep thy precepts" (verses 133–134).

Tzaddi: Zeal for the Truth of God's Word
Verses 137–144

Righteous art thou, O Lord, and upright are thy judgments.

Thy testimonies that thou hast commanded are righteous and very faithful.

My zeal hath consumed me, because mine enemies have forgotten thy words.

Thy word is very pure: therefore thy servant loveth it.

I am small and despised: yet do not I forget thy precepts.

Thy righteousness is an everlasting righteousness, and thy law is the truth.

Trouble and anguish have taken hold on me: yet thy commandments are my delights.

The righteousness of thy testimonies is everlasting: give me understanding, and I shall live.

With increasing experience in God's Word comes increasing zeal in its defense because of increasing confidence in its integrity. "My zeal hath consumed me, because mine enemies have forgotten thy words. Thy word is very pure: therefore thy servant loveth it. . . . The righteousness of thy testimonies is everlasting: give me understanding, and I shall live" (verses 139–144).

Koph: Increasing Faith in the Word
Verses 145–152

I cried with my whole heart; hear me, O LORD: I will keep thy statutes.

I cried unto thee; save me, and I shall keep thy testimonies.

I prevented the dawning of the morning, and cried: I hoped in thy word.

Mine eyes prevent the night watches, that I might meditate in thy word.

Hear my voice according unto thy lovingkindness: O LORD, quicken me according to thy judgment.

They draw nigh that follow after mischief: they are far from thy law.

Thou art near, O LORD; and all thy commandments are truth.

Concerning thy testimonies, I have known of old that thou hast founded them for ever.

The believer's love and longing for the Word should continue to increase all his life long. Furthermore, increasing obedience to the Word generates increasing sensitivity to disobedience and a longing to be utterly free from the sin nature which perpetually resists one's growth in the Lord. "I prevented the dawning of the morning, and cried; I hoped in thy word. Mine eyes prevent the night watches, that I might meditate in thy word. . . . Concerning thy testimonies, I have known of old that thou hast founded them for ever" (verses 147–152).

Resh: Deliverance From all Evils by the Word
Verses 153–160

Consider mine affliction, and deliver me: for I do not forget thy law.

Plead my cause, and deliver me: quicken me according to thy word.

Salvation is far from the wicked: for they seek not thy statutes.

Great are thy tender mercies, O LORD: quicken me according to thy judgments.

Many are my persecutors and mine enemies; yet do I not decline from thy testimonies.

I beheld the transgressors, and was grieved; because they kept not thy word.

Consider how I love thy precepts: quicken me, O LORD, according to thy lovingkindness.

Thy word is true from the beginning: and every one of thy righteous judgments endureth for ever.

The final verse of this stanza is a tremendous affirmation of the eternal and plenary inspiration and authority of the written Word of God.

"Consider mine affliction and deliver me: for I do not forget thy law. Plead my cause and deliver [same word here as 'redeem'] me: quicken me according to thy word. . . . Thy word is true from the beginning: and every one of thy righteous judgments endureth for ever" (verses 153–160).

Schin: Settled Peace through the Word
Verses 161–168

Princes have persecuted me without a cause: but my heart standeth in awe of thy word.

I rejoice at thy word, as one that findeth great spoil.

I hate and abhor lying: but thy law do I love.

Seven times a day do I praise thee, because of thy righteous judgments.

Great peace have they which love thy law: and nothing shall offend them.

LORD, I have hoped for thy salvation, and done thy commandments.

My soul hath kept thy testimonies; and I love them exceedingly.

I have kept thy precepts and thy testimonies: for all my ways are before thee.

Though oppositions and conflicts with the ungodly continue throughout the believer's life, the Word gives increasing rest and peace. Here the Psalmist, who began as a young man, now is old, but enjoying confident peace through his lifelong companionship with the Word of God. "Princes have persecuted me without a cause: but my heart standeth in awe of thy word. . . . Great peace have they which love thy law: and nothing shall offend them. . . . I have kept thy precepts and thy testimonies; for all my ways are before thee" (verses 161–168).

Tau: Final Salvation by the Word
Verses 169–176

Let my cry come near before thee, O LORD: give me understanding according to thy word.

Let my supplication come before thee: deliver me according to thy word.

My lips shall utter praise, when thou hast taught me thy statutes.

My tongue shall speak of thy word: for all thy commandments are righteousness.

Let thine hand help me; for I have chosen thy precepts.

I have longed for thy salvation, O LORD; and thy law is my delight.

Let my soul live, and it shall praise thee; and let thy judgments help me.

I have gone astray like a lost sheep: seek thy servant; for I do not forget thy commandments.

Salvation, of course, is first from the penalty of sin, daily from the power of sin, and ultimately from the presence of sin. As the Psalmist neared the end of his long pilgrimage, he increasingly desired to see his Lord. "I have longed for thy salvation, O LORD; and thy law is my delight" (verse 174). Actually the word "salvation" in Hebrew is *yeshua*, the same as "Jesus." The closer one comes to the end of his life and the more conscious he becomes of soon entering into God's presence, the more keenly he becomes aware of his unworthiness, and the more he returns to his first simple faith in the saving grace of God's Word. It is most appropriate, therefore, that Psalm 119 ends as it began, with a simple confession of faith and prayer for salvation; "I have gone astray like a lost sheep; seek thy servant; for I do not forget thy commandments."

Part III

Events of the Second Coming

Chapter 15

Judgment of the Nations

Psalm 9

In chapters 3–14, 12 of the great messianic psalms were discussed, and some of these (e.g., Ps. 2) involved both His first and second comings. However, there are other psalms that also deal with the great events surrounding the second coming of Christ, and we want to consider some of these in this section of the book. We shall begin by looking at the great scenes of judgment as revealed in Psalm 9.

Psalms 9 and 10 actually seem to go together, by virtue of a rather unique feature. The first ten verses of Psalm 9 are in the form of an acrostic, with the first letter of each verse consisting successively of the first ten letters of the Hebrew alphabet. Then the first seven verses of Psalm 10 are also an acrostic, utilizing the *next* seven letters of the Hebrew alphabet.

It is thus likely that David wrote Psalm 10 as well as Psalm 9, even though Psalm 10 is one of only four psalms in Book I of the Psalms (Psalms 1–41) that do not have an author indicated. All the other 37 psalms in Book I are ascribed to David.

Nevertheless, the two psalms are quite properly listed as separate psalms. Both deal with the opposition of the ungodly to God's people, but Psalm 9 stresses also their ultimate fate in the coming judgment. It is this latter aspect that we want to focus on particularly in this discussion.

This psalm has an enigmatic heading: "To the chief musician upon Muth-labben." The meaning of this latter phrase is clearly "The Death of the Son," but expositors seem mystified as to what this title could have to do with the content of the psalm. The usual guess is that this was the name of the tune to which the psalm was sung by "the chief musician."

That is not an explanation consistent with biblical inspiration, however. There has to be some connection of the title with the content of the psalm. As noted above, the recurring note throughout the psalm is that of God's eventual judgment of all the nations. We know from our vantage point on this side of Calvary that this judgment has been committed by God the Father to God the Son. "For the Father judgeth no man, but hath committed all judgment unto the Son. That all men should honour the Son, even as they honour the Father" (John 5:22–23).

And why has the Father given this responsibility to the Son? Jesus said, "Therefore doth my Father love me, because I lay down my life, that I might take it again" (John 10:17). The Son was willing to suffer and die for the sins of the whole world (1 John 2:2), thereby making faith in Him the one criterion by which men are to be judged for heaven or hell. "For God sent not His Son into the world to condemn the world: but that the world through Him might be saved. He that believeth on Him is not condemned; but he that believeth not is condemned already because he hath not believed in the name of the only begotten Son of God" (John 3:17–18).

"The Death of the Son" is thus an appropriate name for a psalm that tells us of God's (that is, the Son's) ultimate righteous judgment of the world (note also verses 8 and 11).

Verses 1–3

I will praise thee, O LORD, with my whole heart: I will shew forth all thy marvelous works.

I will be glad and rejoice in thee: I will sing praise to thy name, O thou most High.

When mine enemies are turned back, they shall fall and perish at thy presence.

Although David was sincerely giving here his own praise to God, the context justifies our transposing it to the lips of that greater Son of David, the Messiah, in prophetic anticipation of that great day to come when all rebellion will be put down. After all, it is only He who could say in truth: "I will shew forth all thy marvelous works," and who will finally be able to say that "mine enemies . . . shall fall and perish at thy presence."

Verses 4–6

For thou hast maintained my right and my cause; thou satest in the throne judging right.

Thou hast rebuked the heathen, thou hast destroyed the wicked, thou hast put out their name for ever and ever.

O thou enemy, destructions are come to a perpetual end: and
thou hast destroyed cities; their memorial is perished with them.

Again, it is appropriate to hear these exultant affirmations as coming
from the lips of King Messiah, for only he could know that the name of
the wicked [that is Satan and his cohorts] will have been "put out . . . for
ever and ever" and that their destructiveness has "come to a perpetual
end." In that great day, "He shall smite the earth with the rod of His mouth,
and with the breath of His lips shall he slay the wicked" (Isa. 11:4).

Thus, will God have "rebuked the heathen," and the whole creation
will acknowledge that God on His throne has judged rightly. With our
very limited understanding in this present age, we find it difficult to understand why God often allows the wicked to prosper and faithful believers often to suffer loss and even persecution, but someday everyone will
acknowledge that the "Judge of all the earth" has done right (Gen. 18:25).

Verses 7–10

But the LORD shall endure for ever: he hath prepared his throne
for judgment.

And he shall judge the world in righteousness, he shall minister
judgement to the people in uprightness.

The LORD also will be a refuge for the oppressed, a refuge in
times of trouble.

And they that know thy name will put their trust in thee; for
thou, LORD, hast not forsaken them that seek thee.

Though the name of the wicked shall be silenced (verse 5) forever,
the Lord's name shall endure forever. Those who are wise, therefore, "will
put their trust" in Him (verse 10). And again the Psalmist envisions God's
judgment throne (see also verse 4) when He will shortly be judging the
whole world in perfect righteousness.

The apostle Paul, speaking to representatives of the "heathen" (same
word as nations) in Athens, again affirmed what Christ had said to the
Jews. "[God] hath appointed a day, in which he will judge the world in
righteousness by that man whom he hath ordained; whereof he hath given
assurance unto all men, in that he hath raised him from the dead" (Acts
17:31). The fact that Jesus Christ alone of all the religious leaders of past
and present is qualified to judge the world has been demonstrated not
only by His uniquely and totally righteous human life but also, conclu-
sively, by His bodily resurrection three days after dying for our sins. Only

the Creator of life could defeat death; therefore only He can save and judge for salvation in perfect righteousness.

Verses 11–12

Sing praises to the LORD, which dwelleth in Zion: declare among the people his doings.

When he maketh inquisition for blood, he remembereth them: He forgetteth not the cry of the humble.

The second half of the psalm begins at verse 10 and with it there appears to be a change of speaker. Messiah is speaking in the first half, testifying of God's righteousness in the last days on His throne of judgment. In the last half it seems that a representative of those that have been redeemed is voicing their testimony of thanksgiving, exhorting all the others to join him in his song of praise.

The Hebrew word for "maketh inquisition for" is flexible, being translated several different ways, depending on context. Most frequently it is translated "seek" or "require." In its first occurrence it is rendered "require" (Gen. 9:5), in reference to "requiring the blood" of those who have shed blood. If that usage is followed here in verse 11, in deference to the defining principle of first mention, then the speaker in verse 11 is in effect saying, "When He (that is, God) requires blood, He is remembering those who have put their trust in Him (see verse 10), those who in humility have confessed their need of forgiveness and salvation."

The New Testament tells us that "without shedding of blood is no remission" (Heb. 9:22). God requires the shedding of blood for forgiveness of sins and, on this side of the cross of Christ, we know that "the blood of Jesus Christ his Son cleanseth us from all sin" (1 John 1:7).

It may well be that it is in this great truth that the mystery of the psalm's title, "The Death of the Son," is resolved. God has required the precious blood of His own Son in substitution for the sins of the people He would redeem, and therefore it will be His Son by whom the world — both believers and unbelievers — will be judged in righteousness.

Verses 13–16

Have mercy upon me, O LORD; consider my trouble which I suffer of them that hate me, thou that liftest me up from the gates of death:

That I may shew forth all thy praise in the gates of the daughter of Zion: I will rejoice in thy salvation.

The heathen are sunk down in the pit that they made: in the net which they hid is their own foot taken.

The LORD is known by the judgment which He executeth: the wicked is ensnared in the work of his own hands. Higgaion. Selah.

In answer to his cry for mercy (compare Luke 18:13) on the basis of the blood shed on his behalf, the redeemed sinner will indeed be lifted up from the gates of death, and thus desires to show forth the praises of his Savior and the joy of his salvation. The wicked, on the other hand, relying on their works, are snared in their own net. The works in which they trust will be their condemnation, for they (like Cain) arrogantly presume to offer their own self-righteousness instead of standing under the sacrificial blood of the death of God's Son.

In verse 15, these unbelievers are called "the heathen," as also in verses 5 and 19. The Hebrew word here is *goy* (plural *goyim*), which is also translated "nations" in verses 17 and 20. In other places it is "Gentiles." The same word is rendered these three ways, thus indicating that "heathen," "nations," and "Gentiles" are essentially synonymous terms in the Old Testament. Thus, to the Old Testament Hebrew, every non-Israelite was a "Gentile," every non-believer in the Scriptures was a "heathen," every ethnic group other than the chosen people was merely a "nation." In the New Testament, the same phenomenon occurs. "Gentiles," "heathen," and "nations" are all translations of the same Greek word *ethnos*, depending on context.

The terms "*Higgaion*" and "*Selah*" are interjections probably indicating that the reader should pause at this point for grateful meditation on the great truths just revealed.

Verses 17–20

The wicked shall be turned into hell, and all the nations that forget God.

For the needy shall not always be forgotten: the expectation of the poor shall not perish forever.

Arise, O LORD; let not man prevail; let the heathen be judged in thy sight.

Put them in fear, O LORD: that the nations may know themselves to be but men. Selah.

Those who have trusted in their own righteousness are actually considered "the wicked" in God's sight, having rejected, ignored, or forgotten the saving grace of God through the sacrificial death of His Son. As the prophet said later, "all our rightousnesses are as filthy rags" (Isa. 64:6), and as the apostle Paul would say still later, "By the deeds of the law shall no flesh be justified in his sight" (Rom. 3:20).

At the last great judgment, of which this psalm is speaking, we read: "They were judged every man according to their works. . . . And whosoever was not found written in the book of life was cast into the lake of fire" (Rev. 20:13–15).

Thus, "the wicked shall be turned into hell." And we need again to remember that all are "wicked" because "there is none righteous, no, not one" (Rom. 3:10), until they have been redeemed through faith in the substitutionary death of the Son of God. They are the "nations" — that is, the "heathen" — who "forget God." They are "but men" (verse 20), and lost men at that, until they "put their trust in thee" (verse 10). "Selah."

Chapter 16

Ascension and Rapture

Psalm 24

Psalms 22, 23, and 24 are sometimes viewed as a trilogy, with Psalm 22 speaking of Christ as our suffering Savior, Psalm 23 representing Him as our daily Lord, and Psalm 24 as our coming King. Psalm 22 and 23 have been discussed previously, as messianic psalms. Psalm 24 also features Christ, but now as victorious over death and sin, preparing to complete His purpose in creation and to establish His eternal kingdom.

Verses 1–2

The earth is the LORD's and the fulness thereof; the world, and they that dwell therein.

For he hath founded it upon the seas, and established it upon the floods.

This great assertion follows directly upon the beautiful closing promise of the 23rd psalm just preceding it. Those who follow the Lord Jesus as their great Shepherd "shall dwell in the house of the Lord forever." That wonderful house is both a spiritual house ("the household of faith" — Gal. 6:10) and also eventually an actual physical mansion, the "place" that Christ is now preparing for all His disciples (John 14:3).

Thus, it is appropriate for the 24th Psalm to deal with that future home and our ultimate arrival there. That God can indeed assure us of that home follows from the fact that He shall have regained control over the earth from Satan, who had usurped dominion over it from Adam.

At this present time, however, Satan is "the god of this world" (2 Cor. 4:4), and thus "we know that . . . the whole world lieth in wickedness"

(1 John 5:19). The word "wickedness" in this verse actually means "the wicked one" — that is, Satan — the same word as used in 1 John 2:13–14.

When Christ returns, Satan will be defeated and eventually consigned forever to "the lake of fire" (Rev. 20:10). Then it will again be completely true, as it was in the beginning prior to Adam's fall, that "the earth is the Lord's and the fulness thereof."

And who are "they that dwell therein"? The place that the Lord has prepared for us is "the holy city" (Rev. 21:2) where "there shall in no wise enter into it any thing that defileth, . . . but they which are written in the Lamb's book of life" (Rev. 21:27).

The pristine earth as God had created it in the beginning had been "founded . . . upon [or, better 'above'] the seas, and established [above] . . . the floods" (or 'rivers'). That was evidently accomplished on the third day of creation week, when God "laid the foundations of the earth" (Job 38:4), separating out the solid earth material from the primeval waters which had covered the world initially (Gen. 1:2). The completed world, with its human and animal inhabitants had all been "very good" at first (Gen. 1:31), but God's curse had fallen on it when Adam sinned.

Finally, however, after thousands of years of satanic dominion, the curse will have been removed (Rev. 22:3) and the earth made new again, prepared as the eternal home for the redeemed. Even the seas of that first world will have been taken away, and the rivers will be rivers of living water from the throne of the Lamb (Rev. 21:1, 22:1). That new earth, with all its fullness, will belong to the Lord Jesus Christ, who created the first earth, then later redeemed it with His precious blood, and one day will have made it all new once again.

Verses 3–6

Who shall ascend into the hill of the LORD? Or who shall stand in his holy place?

He that hath clean hands, and a pure heart: who hath not lifted up his soul unto vanity, nor sworn deceitfully.

He shall receive the blessing from the LORD, and righteousness from the God of his salvation.

This is the generation of them that seek him, that seek thy face, O Jacob. Selah.

But who will inhabit Christ's renewed earth? The earthly hill of the Lord was Mount Zion and the holy place was the tabernacle, then, later the temple. But these are mere types of the mountainous celestial city and heavenly temple that are in view here.

The context surely suggests a greater mountain and greater sanctuary than in ancient Jerusalem. Most likely it is the one described in the New Testament as follows: "But ye are come unto Mount Sion and unto the city of the living God, the heavenly Jerusalem, and to an innumerable company of angels. To the general assembly and church of the firstborn" (Heb. 12:22–23).

And who can stand there? Only "the spirits of just men made perfect." Or, as the Psalmist says: "He that hath clean hands, and a pure heart." No man, in his imperfect state, has clean hands and a pure heart, of course, so his spirit must be "*made* perfect." The only ones with clean hands and pure hearts are those whose hands have been cleansed and whose hearts have been made pure by the blood of Christ. "The blood of Jesus Christ His Son cleanseth us from all sin" (1 John 1:7). Thus, verse 4 could be read: "He that hath *cleansed* hands and a *purified* heart." We can ascend, as Christ did after His resurrection, into God's holy hill and His holy sanctuary, because we have been cleansed and purified by His shed blood.

There is a further description. One whose hands and hearts have been *truly* cleansed and purified by the blood of Christ can be further identified, humanly speaking, as one "who hath not lifted up his soul unto vanity, nor sworn deceitfully."

The phrase "lifted up his soul unto vanity" is describing an attitude of worship. Such a person is not worshiping his Creator and Savior, however, but something else that has in effect become his god — his idol. Such worship is pure vanity, an icon of his own invention or dedication. Whatever has been his outward profession of faith, his true worship is toward someone or something else, and is completely in vain.

Neither will he have "sworn deceitfully" if his hands and heart have truly been redeemed and cleansed. That is, he is not a perjurer, one who deliberately lies while under oath. How can one who is indwelt by the Spirit of truth (John 16:13) so blatantly yield to the father of lies (John 8:44)? In fact, the biblical warning is explicit: "All liars, shall have their part in the lake which burneth with fire and brimstone: which is the second death" (Rev. 21:8).

All who have indeed had their sins washed away by the cleansing blood will have been beautifully arrayed with the righteousness of Christ, the garments of salvation (2 Cor. 5:21; Isa. 61:10). Finally, there is one other identifying characteristic of these who have so richly "received the blessing from the Lord" (verse 5). That is, these are men and women who *wanted* salvation, who have sought the face of the Lord. "For he that cometh to God must believe that he is, and that he

is a rewarder of them that diligently seek him" (Heb. 11:6).

There is an intriguing question that is raised just before the "Selah" pause for reflection at the end of verse 6. Why is the section addressed to "Jacob," when one would have thought it should be to the "God of Jacob"? Although the scope of Psalm 24 ultimately includes all the redeemed, it was originally inspired in the context of pre-Calvary Israel. It was originally read and believed by godly Israelites, men and women of the seed of Jacob, people of the nation chosen as God's elect nation, to whom God had always identified himself as the God of Abraham, Isaac, and Jacob (e.g., Matt. 22:32).

Perhaps David, in writing "O Jacob" here, was thinking of Israel as so identified with God that he would be understood as really writing "O God of Jacob." Perhaps more likely he was thinking of "Jacob" as a prophetic name for the promised Messiah, and was earnestly seeking His face and desiring His coming. Jacob had, indeed, been at least a type of Christ, in that he had gained victory over his carnal brother Esau, showing the triumph of "spirit" in conflict with "flesh," and then spending many years in a far country before returning to His kingdom (compare Luke 19:11–12).

Verses 7–10

> Lift up your heads, O ye gates; and be ye lift up, ye everlasting doors; and the King of glory shall come in.
>
> Who is this King of glory? The LORD strong and mighty, the LORD mighty in battle.
>
> Lift up your heads, O ye gates; even lift them up, ye everlasting doors; and the King of glory shall come in.
>
> Who is this King of glory? The LORD of hosts, He is the King of glory. Selah.

The last four verses of the psalm are especially intriguing. This "hill of the LORD" and its "holy place" are evidently to be entered through "gates" and "everlasting doors." But why are they *twice* exhorted to be lifted up?

When this magnificent "hill" — most likely referring to "that great city, the holy Jerusalem" (Rev. 21:10) — which "lieth foursquare," with its length and breath and height each extending twelve thousand furlongs (equivalent to about 1380 miles — note Rev. 21:16), eventually descends from heaven to the renewed earth, its pearly gates "shall not be shut at all" (Rev. 21:25) after that.

Until the victorious King of glory ascended to the great city after His victory over death and hell, however, the gates must have been shut, for there were as yet none who were qualified to enter. But Christ has now overcome, and the gates must be opened for Him and for all those to whom He has given clean hands and a pure heart by His great sacrifice. So the heads of the mighty gates and the everlasting doors are lifted wide open, so the King of glory can enter, followed by all His redeemed ones.

When David wrote this psalm (by divine, inspiration, of course), this great event was yet future. The spirits of all those who had died in faith were still in the heart of the earth, awaiting their future resurrection. Then in the fullness of God's time, God sent forth His Son to "put away sin by the sacrifice of Himself" (Heb. 9:26), and to make it possible for them to be set free.

Isaiah also prophesied of Him: "He hath sent me . . . to proclaim liberty to the captives, and the opening of the prison to them that are bound" (Isa. 61:1). While His body was in Joseph's tomb, His spirit "descended into the lower parts of the earth." Then, He did indeed proclaim liberty and the opening of the prison to all those believers who had died in faith. "When he ascended up on high, he led captivity captive" (see Eph. 4:8–10). Thus, at some stage of His glorious ascension, He must have called together all those who had been raised following His own resurrection. He did not ascend alone to the heavenly city!

This seems to be the conclusion we must draw from a mysterious passage in Matthew's record of the resurrection: "And the graves were opened; and many bodies of the saints which slept arose, and came out of the graves after his resurrection, and went into the holy city, and appeared unto many" (Matt. 27:52–53).

The spirits of the Old Testament saints had been set free by Christ when He descended into their temporary prison in the lower parts of the earth and evidently were then reunited with their long-dead bodies following His own resurrection. There were "many" of them and they were seen by numerous people in the city, probably during the same 40 days during which the resurrected Christ was still on earth (Acts 1:3).

While the references to this great event are few and enigmatic, and hardly justify dogmatic interpretation, it does seem that this is the best way in which they can be understood. If so, this tells us that a great host of Old Testament believers, now in their glorified immortal bodies, accompanied the Lord Jesus Christ when He ascended on high to enter the gates of pearl through the everlasting doors.

As they approached the great celestial city, it was probably the angelic host that cried out for the King of glory to come in. He had defeated the great enemy and his horde of fallen angels when He paid the awful price of redemption on the cross; "having spoiled principalities and powers, He made a shew of them openly, triumphing over them in it" (Col. 2:15). He is "strong and mighty, the LORD mighty in battle" — not mere physical battles, but spiritual battles, battles in the heavens with the great enemy of souls. He had taken all our sins in His own body to die in our place, "that through death he might destroy him that had the power of death, that is, the devil; And deliver them who through fear of death were all their lifetime subject to bondage" (Heb. 2:14–15). He is now "alive for evermore," having gained forever "the keys of hell and of death" (Rev. 1:18).

Yet the devil still is alive and well today, and sin and death still prevail in the earth. The heavenly gates had been opened to admit the King of glory and His Old Testament saints, but presumably then had to be closed again.

But the Psalmist in his vision then heard again the great cry: "Lift up your heads, O ye gates: even lift them up, ye everlasting doors: and the King of glory shall come in" (verse 9). The great King will again leave the holy city to go to earth, but this time He will not be alone.

During the long period following that first great ascension to the heavenly city with His saints from pre-Calvary times, His church is being formed on earth. When New Testament believers die, their spirits no longer descend into Hades but rather go "to be with Christ" (Phil. 1:23), while their bodies await His coming back to earth for their own resurrection.

And when He finally comes, He will bring them with Him to be finally reunited with their own resurrected and glorified bodies. This will be the promised "coming of our Lord Jesus Christ with all his saints" (1 Thess. 3:13).

What a wonderful gathering that will be! "For the Lord himself shall descend from heaven with a shout, with the voice of the archangel, and with the trump of God: and the dead in Christ shall rise first: Then we which are alive and remain shall be caught up together with them in the clouds, to meet the Lord in the air: and so shall we ever be with the Lord" (1 Thess. 4:16–17).

That will, indeed, be a great resurrection day! The Lord Jesus Christ, descending from heaven, will instantaneously "change our vile body, that it may be fashioned like unto his glorious body" (Phil. 3:21). "We shall all be changed, In a moment, in the twinkling of an eye, at the last trump: for the trumpet shall sound, and the dead shall be raised incorruptible, and we shall be changed" (1 Cor. 15:51–52).

And then, with our great Creator and loving Savior, we shall all ascend to the heavenly Jerusalem. Once again, the great cry will sound from the city: "Lift up your heads, O ye gates: even lift them up, ye everlasting doors; and the King of glory shall come in." And He that went forth

144 · Treasures in the Psalms

weeping, bearing that precious seed, sowing himself, that good seed, the living Word of God (compare Luke 8:4–11) into the prepared ground to die and rise again (note John 12:23–24), "shall doubtless come again with rejoicing, bringing his sheaves with him" (Ps. 126:6).

"The LORD of hosts, he is the King of glory." And what a great host that will be! "But ye are come unto mount Sion, and unto the city of the living God, the heavenly Jerusalem, and to an innumerable company of angels . . . and to God the Judge of all, and to the spirits of just men made perfect, and to Jesus the mediator of the new covenant, and to the blood of sprinkling, that speaketh better things than that of Abel." (Heb. 12:22–24).

Selah!

Chapter 17

When Wars Finally Cease

Psalm 46

One of the great themes of the Old Testament is the promise of the future messianic kingdom, when Messiah will come to put down all rebellion against God and finally bring universal peace to the earth. In that great day, "He shall judge among the nations, and shall rebuke many people; and they shall beat their swords into plowshares, and their spears into pruninghooks: nation shall not lift up sword against nation, neither shall they learn war any more" (Isa. 2:4).

But before this wonderful millennial age can begin (note Rev. 20:2–7, where its thousand-year duration is mentioned six times), the earth and its population must go through a terrible period of divine judgment and purgation, known as the period of tribulation (Matt. 24:21), or the day of God's wrath.

All of this is in the perspective of Psalm 46. It is written from the viewpoint of the believing Jewish remnant suffering during that terrible period as it nears its end. The prophet Jeremiah spoke of it as follows: "Alas! for that day is great, so that none is like it; it is even the time of Jacob's trouble; but he shall be saved out of it" (Jer. 30:7).

"Jacob" — that is, the believing Jews who will finally receive the Lord Jesus as their Messiah and Savior — will ultimately be delivered out of the tribulation period to enter the millennial kingdom, and this also is in view in this stirring psalm. The most wonderful aspect of this kingdom age, of course, will be the glorious return and ongoing presence of Christ himself, finally to be "exalted in the earth" (Ps. 46:10).

Verses 1–3

God is our refuge and strength, a very present help in trouble.

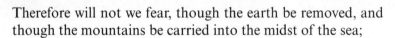

Therefore will not we fear, though the earth be removed, and though the mountains be carried into the midst of the sea;

Though the waters thereof roar and be troubled, though the mountains shake with the swelling thereof. Selah.

The Jewish remnant will indeed need a "very present help in trouble," for they will be going through that "time of Jacob's trouble." The great "man of sin" will have become the world ruler and will seek to slay all who refuse to worship his image, the Jews in particular, as well as all who have turned to Christ during the earlier days of the tribulation period. All of these will have to trust God as both their refuge and strength — that is, as both their shield and sword, their protection and enabler.

This same promise has been dear to God's people all through the centuries, but it will be especially meaningful to believers in these final fearful days.

The earth itself will be going through terrifying physical trauma at that time, the most severe since the great flood in the days of Noah. It was literally true, in that earlier time of worldwide judgment, that the flood waters removed great masses of earth from the lands into the seas; in fact, the mountains themselves were eroded away and their soils and vegetation carried down into the midst of the sea. One can observe many of the cataclysmic effects of this great deluge and its associated upheavals in the vast sedimentary rock systems and their many fossil graveyards all around the earth. During the flood, there were also great earthquakes and volcanic eruptions, the mountains "shaking with the swelling thereof."

These terrible convulsions of the earth in Noah's day have been long forgotten, but they will again become terrifyingly real during the coming tribulation period. Great earthquakes will move the very mountains out of place and, finally the greatest quake in all history will literally level the earth. As John described it in his vision, "Every island fled away, and the mountains were not found" (Rev. 6:14, 16:18–20). Throughout the earth there will be "distress of nations, with perplexity . . . Men's hearts failing them for fear, and for looking after those things that are coming on the earth" (Luke 21:25–26).

But God's people will know that God is in control, and so they can say: "Therefore will not we fear." For "God is our refuge and strength." "The Lord is my rock, and my fortress, and my deliverer; my God, my strength, in whom I will trust; my buckler, and the horn of my salvation, and my high tower" (Ps. 18:2).

Just as they will be able to trust their Maker and Redeemer in those awful days to come, so we can trust Him today, in whatever trials or persecutions He may call on us to bear in the present age.

Actually the word "removed" in verse 2 really means "changed," and is so translated every time it appears except in this one verse. The earth will indeed be drastically *changed* during the tribulation, as it is being prepared for the kingdom age. The end result of the great shakings and rushing waters will be that "every valley shall be exalted, and every mountain and hill shall be made low; and the crooked shall be made straight, and the rough places plain." (Isa. 40:4). "Selah!"

Verses 4–7

There is a river, the streams whereof shall make glad the city of God, the holy place of the tabernacles of the most High.

God is in the midst of her; she shall not be moved: God shall help her, and that right early.

The heathen raged, the kingdoms were moved: He uttered His voice, the earth melted.

The LORD of hosts is with us; the God of Jacob is our refuge. Selah.

But once the shaking is done and all the rebels purged out of it, then will come the wonderful peace of the kingdom age. At this point in the psalm, the writer suddenly sees in his vision the beauties of that age to come, first the millennial temple and then the surpassing beauty of the holy city and the eternal ages even beyond the millennium.

In the original garden where God had dwelt with His first people, there was a river flowing out of it and parting into four streams (Gen. 2:10) which went out to water the primeval lands. This was a type of the great river that will flow out of the millennial temple. Christ will dwell there, and Ezekiel saw in *his* vision of *that* temple that "the glory of the LORD filled the house" (Ezek. 43:5). Then he saw the river. "Behold, waters issued out from under the threshold of the house eastward . . . and it was a river that I could not pass over" (Ezek. 47:1–5).

But even *this* future river is itself only a type of the magnificent river of life in the new earth following the millennium and the fiery renovation of the present world. John in *his* vision saw "a pure river of water of life, clear as crystal, proceeding out of the throne of God and of the Lamb" (Rev. 22:1). "And let him that is athirst come. And whosoever will, let him take the water of life freely" (Rev. 22:17).

In this final city, however, the temple will have been removed, for the Lord God Almighty and the Lamb are the temple of it. Indeed the city itself is "the tabernacle of God" (Rev. 21:3), where He will dwell eternally with His people. It is from the great throne of the Lamb, probably in the center and highest summit of the holy city, that the great river will flow, serving perpetually as a reminder of the water and the blood that flowed from that same Lamb of God as He died on the cross (John 19:34). It then divides (like the river in Eden) into a number of streams of living water that will course probably through the whole earth. In fact, the word translated "streams" (plural) is elsewhere usually translated "rivers." Thus, as in Eden, the future river of life will divide into many rivers, so that "whosoever will" can freely drink of its waters.

God is in the midst of the city, so it can never be moved. The millennial city, with its temple will itself have lasted for a thousand years, but must eventually be displaced by the New Jerusalem, which will then last forever.

After this the Psalmist returns to his vision of the awful tribulation that must precede the kingdom age. Although "the heathen raged" (note also Ps. 2:1), and all "the kings of the earth" follow the reigning Antichrist in the very last days, setting themselves "against the LORD, and against His anointed [Hebrew *Messiah*], saying, Let us . . . cast away their cords from us" (Ps. 2:2–3), they will soon be utterly broken with God's "rod of iron" (Ps. 2:9). "These shall make war with the Lamb, and the Lamb shall overcome them: for He is Lord of lords, and King of kings" (Rev. 17:14).

And *how* shall He overcome them? Merely by the sound of His voice! "He shall smite the earth with the rod of his mouth, and with the breath of his lips shall he slay the wicked" (Isa. 11:4). "Out of his mouth goeth a sharp sword, that with it he should smite the nations: and he shall rule them with a rod of iron" (Rev. 19:15). Thus, verse 6 of our psalm says that when "He uttered his voice, the earth melted." None can stand before our God "when he ariseth to shake terribly the earth" (Isa. 2:21).

Therefore, during the great Tribulation, the remnant of God's people still living at that time can repeat, over and over, no matter what dangers and sufferings they encounter: "The LORD of hosts is with us, the God of Jacob is our refuge."

And this same testimony should be on the lips of God's people in every age and nation and circumstance. "God is with us." He has said, "I will never leave thee, nor forsake thee" (Heb. 13:5).

Verses 8–11

Come, behold the works of the LORD, what desolations He hath made in the earth.

He maketh wars to cease unto the end of the earth; He breaketh the bow, and cutteth the spear in sunder; He burneth the chariot in the fire.

Be still, and know that I am God: I will be exalted among the heathen, I will be exalted in the earth.

The LORD of hosts is with us; the God of Jacob is our refuge. Selah

By the end of the tribulation period, lasting a total of seven years (as implied in Dan, 9:27; Rev. 11:3, 13:5; etc), there will indeed be great desolation in the earth, with the lands and seas devastated and multitudes slain. "Therefore hath the curse devoured the earth, and they that dwell therein are desolate; therefore the inhabitants of the earth are burned, and few men left" (Isa. 24:6). In this same chapter, the prophet Isaiah gives further information concerning the awful changes on the earth during the tribulation. "The earth is utterly broken down, the earth is clean dissolved, the earth is moved exceedingly" (Isa. 24:19).

There have always been wars and rumors of wars somewhere on the earth (Matt. 24:6) practically every year since sin came into the world. Finally, all "the kings of the earth, and their armies" will have gathered together at Armageddon "to make war against [Christ] . . . and against his army" (Rev. 16:12–16, 19:19), but these will all be destroyed by the power of His mighty voice, and then all wars will cease for a thousand years. "He shall speak peace unto the heathen: and his dominion shall be from sea even to sea, and from the river even to the ends of the earth" (Zech, 9:10). Swords will be converted to plowshares, and "they shall not hurt nor destroy in all my holy mountain: for the earth shall be full of the knowledge of the LORD, as the waters cover the sea" (Isa. 11:9).

With such glorious prospects before them, the suffering remnant during the Tribulation can be comforted in their fiery trials. The same is true in any age, of course. No matter how traumatic the suffering or heavy the burden, the Holy Spirit exhorts us to "be still, and know that I am God."

When the Children of Israel had Pharaoh's army pursuing them, and the Red Sea confronting them, Moses could say to them with complete confidence; "Fear ye not, stand still, and see the salvation of the LORD" (Exod. 14:13). When the people of Judah in Hezekiah's day were desperately hoping that Egypt would help them against the powerful and cruel Assyrian invaders, God's counsel through the prophet was not to trust in human deliverance, but to rely on God: "Their strength is to sit still" (Isa. 30:7). He said; "In quietness and confidence shall be your strength" (Isa. 30:15).

Today also, as the perilous times of the last days (2 Tim. 3:1) press hard upon us, "we may boldly say, The Lord is my helper, and I will not fear what man shall do unto me" (Heb. 13:6).

During the kingdom age following the tribulation, the Lord will indeed "be exalted in the earth." The Father has said to the Son: "I shall give thee the (nations) for thine inheritance, and the uttermost parts of the earth for thy possession" (Ps. 2:8). "The LORD, shall be king over all the earth; in that day shall there be one LORD, and His name one" (Zech. 14:9). "Of the increase of his government . . . there shall be no end" (Isa. 9:7). The prayers of God's people through the centuries will finally be answered. His kingdom will come and His will shall be done on earth as it is in heaven.

The Psalmist appropriately closes this great psalm of the coming kingdom with the same testimony as in verse 7. "The LORD of hosts is with us; The God of Jacob is our refuge."

No matter where or when, the Lord is with us. In this age, in fact, He actually indwells us! "Your body is the temple of the Holy Ghost, which is in you, which ye have of God" (1 Cor. 6:19).

In fact, that is His very name — Emmanuel ("God with us" — Matt. 1:23)! "Selah!" Therefore will not we fear.

Chapter 18

Confederacy against Israel

Psalm 83

T he 83rd psalm might well be considered one of the imprecatory psalms because of its prayers (by Asaph, the writer) to destroy the enemies of Israel (note especially verses 9–17). However, on closer examination, it also seems to contain significant prophetic implications for the latter days.

The conflict described in the psalm, while stated in terms of nations contemporary with ancient Israel, would actually have to take place in the distant future. This is indicated by its last two verses, which say that the ultimate defeat of the nations attacking Israel will result in their permanent recognition of the God of Israel as "the most high over all the earth." This certainly did not happen during the times of the original Psalmist, but it will indeed be fulfilled in the latter days.

Verses 1–5

Keep not thou silence, O God: hold not thy peace, and be not still, O God.

For lo, thine enemies make a tumult: and they that hate thee have lifted up the head.

They have taken crafty counsel against thy people, and consulted against thy hidden ones.

They have said, Come, and let us cut them off from being a nation; that the name of Israel may be no more in remembrance.

For they have consulted together with one consent: they are confederate against thee:

The focus of the psalm is clearly on Israel and her bitter enemies. The Psalmist, as Israel's spokesman, is earnestly praying for God to protect His people against what seems to be an overwhelming confederation of enemy nations surrounding them. There has never been such an occasion in the history of ancient Israel as depicted by this psalm, however, and this is another reason for seeking a prophetic interpretation. The "hidden ones" are hidden only in the sense that they are God's sheltered ones and He has promised to bless them.

It is indisputable that the situation described in these verses is very similar to that prevailing today in the Middle East. Although none of the nations named in the psalm exist today, at least under these names, the psalm almost reads like a modern news account of the current tension between Israel and her Arab neighbors.

No matter how many concessions Israel has made to their demands, these Muslim nations still continue to "make a tumult" against her very existence. Their oft-stated purpose is to "cut them off from being a nation: that the name of Israel may be no more in remembrance."

Note that they have "taken crafty counsel" and "consulted together with one consent," being "confederate against thee." But it is always dangerous to form a league of nations against God's nation, because God has made an irrevocable promise to Jacob (that is, Israel) that "the land whereon thou liest, to thee will I give it, and to thy seed . . and thou shalt spread abroad to the west, and to the east, and to the north, and to the south; and in thee and in thy seed shall all the families of the earth be blessed" (Gen. 28:13–14). The promise was given to Jacob (not Esau, or Edom), confirming that previously given to Isaac (not Ishmael or Midian) and before him to Abraham (not Lot).

The promise was unconditional, in the form of an *everlasting* covenant (note Ps. 105:6–11; Gen. 17:19, 48:4; etc). Thus, when these other descendants of Abraham (Ishmael, Midian, Esau, etc.) attempt to take the promised possession away from Israel, they are fighting against God himself, not just the children of Israel. "I will bless them that bless thee, and curse him that curseth thee," was God's promise to Abraham (Gen. 12:3), and so it has been all through history. God has often used other nations (often wicked nations) to punish Israel when they rebelled against God and His Word, but then blessed them again when they repented and returned to Him.

By far their most serious rebellion, however, was that of rejecting and crucifying their Messiah when He finally came into the world as promised by the prophets. For this great crime, the nation was scattered in a worldwide dispersion, where they would be forced to "abide many days without a king, and without a prince, and without a sacrifice, and without an image, and without an ephod, and without teraphim" (Hos. 3:4). This condition continued almost 2,000 years.

God's covenant, however, was everlasting, and for almost a century now, Israelites have been returning to their ancient land, even being officially recognized (in 1948) by other nations once again as the nation of Israel. Still they have not repented, and they still reject Jesus as their Messiah and still largely continue to reject God's laws. Nevertheless, God has started His work of restoring Israel to her Promised Land. "Thus saith the Lord God: I do not this for your sakes, O house of Israel, but for mine holy name's sake, which ye have profaned among the heathen, whither ye went. . . . For I will take you from among the heathen, and gather you out of all countries, and shall bring you into your own land" (Ezek. 36:22–24).

Nevertheless, they have returned to the land in unbelief and still today persist in rejecting their Messiah. Ezekiel compared their return and superficial restoration to a great army of skeletons with flesh beginning again to cover their bones, but with no spirit in them. "The bones came together, bone to his bone. . . . The sinews and the flesh came upon them, and the skin covered them above: but there was no breath in them" (Ezek. 37:7–8).

Therefore, they still must undergo severe judgment from God before they are fully restored. They are back in the Promised Land (or, at least part of it), but they do not yet possess God's Holy Spirit. All of this is the background for the events prophesied here in Psalm 83. Back in their land, yet surrounded by nations that hate them and have conspired to destroy them, the children of Israel are still unwilling to turn to the Lord Jesus Christ for deliverance (although they do not hesitate to call on the "Christian nations" of America and Europe to help defend them!).

Verses 6–12

The tabernacles of Edom, and the Ishmaelites; of Moab, and the Hagarenes;

Gebal, and Ammon, and Amalek, the Philistines with the inhabitants of Tyre;

Assur is also joined with them: they have holpen the children of Lot. Selah.

Do unto them as unto the Midianites, as to Sisera, as to Jabin, at the brook of Kison:

Which perished at En-dor: they became as dung for the earth.

Make their nobles like Oreb, and like Zeeb: yea, all their princes as Zebah, and Zalmunna:

Who said, Let us take to ourselves the houses of God in possession.

The nations named in these verses no longer exist by these names. Nevertheless, the context of the prophecy surely applies ultimately to the times near the end. The probable solution to this enigma is to recognize that these ancient peoples have gone through many changes over the centuries — wars, migrations, intermarriages, and other changes — so that the present inhabitants of the regions surrounding Israel are in varying degrees and mixtures, the descendants of these very nations that adjoined Israel in ancient times.

Edom, Moab, and Ammon, for example, were Israel's neighbors on the east and southeast, the area now occupied largely by the nation of Jordan. In fact, Amman, the capital of Jordan, seems even to perpetuate the ancient name, Ammon. The Philistines along the western seacoast adjacent to the southern part of Israel are now represented by the Palestinians. Tyre of the Phoenicians was north of Israel along the Mediterranean shores, in the area now known as Lebanon and essentially controlled by Syria. Assur was probably an Arabian tribe descended from Abraham and Keturah, as were the Midianites (Gen. 25:1–3). The Ishmaelites were also Arabs, descendants of Abraham and Hagar (Gen. 25:12–15). Gebal was an area between the Dead Sea and Edom. There is some uncertainty whether the Hagarenes were Arabians (descended from Hagar, like Ishmael) or Syrians. Possibly there were Hagarene tribes in both areas. The Amalekites had apparently dwelt (at least originally) in the Negev (that is, "south") wilderness area, just south of Israel.

Jabin and Sisera were Canaanites, whose capital had been Hazor (Judg. 4:2). They were slain when Deborah, with Barak, was judge of Israel. Zebah and Zalmunna, as well as Oreb and Zeeb, had been chieftains of the Midianites, all of whom were slain by Gideon (Judg. 7:25, 8:21). The Psalmist was beseeching the Lord to smite the nations besieging Israel with deadly force, just as He had done long before to the Canaanites and Midianites, in the days of Deborah and Gideon, respectively.

In terms of the prophetic future envisioned in the psalm, however, these nations surrounding Israel, either adjacent to Israel or very near to it, would currently have names like Jordan, Lebanon, Palestine, Syria, Iraq, and Arabia. They all bitterly hate Israel and want to destroy her completely, thus hoping to gain the entire region for the Arabs and Muslims.

Furthermore, they are not the only nations with such goals. Surrounding the small nations that more immediately encompass Israel is a group of larger nations that will also be seeking to invade and destroy Israel in the latter days. These are described in the famous Gog and Magog prophecy of Ezekiel 38 and 39.

In that passage, the nations going against Israel are "the land of Magog, the chief prince of Meshech and Tubal," plus "Persia, Ethiopia, and Libya with them . . . Gomer and all his bands; the house of Togarmah of the north quarters, and all his bands: and many people" (Ezek. 38:2–6).

This group of powerful nations, under a leader named Gog, will undertake to invade Israel, along with the smaller nations mentioned here in Psalm 83. "Thou shalt come up against my people of Israel, as a cloud to cover the land; it shall be in the latter days" (Ezek. 38:16). The leading nation in this confederacy is Magog, which almost certainly is now Russia, with its two strategic capitals, Meshech (Moscow) in the west and Tubal (Tobolsk) in the east.

Persia, of course, is modern Iran. Ethiopia, in biblical times, probably included Sudan on its south and west and Yemen, across the Red Sea in the east. Libya was essentially the same then as now. Gomer and Togarmah are less easily identified, but both seem originally to have settled in Asia Minor. Their names may be preserved in the Crimea (and possibly Germany) and Turkestan (possibly including Armenia), respectively.

Taken as a whole, the nations listed in Ezekiel 38 seem today to be either Muslim nations (like those in Ps. 83) or heavily impacted by Communism, or both. All seem strongly motivated either by hatred of Israel or materialistic covetousness. It is not too far-fetched to foresee a soon-coming time when all of them will organize together to invade and try to completely destroy God's chosen nation of Israel, taking all her land and other riches for themselves.

Verses 13–18

O my God, make them like a wheel: as the stubble before the wind.

As the fire burneth a wood, and as the flame setteth the mountains on fire;

So persecute them with thy tempest, and make them afraid with thy storm.

Fill their faces with shame; that they may seek thy name, O LORD.

Let them be confounded and troubled for ever; yea, let them be put to shame, and perish:

That men may know that thou, whose name alone is JEHOVAH, art the most high over all the earth.

The last six verses of this psalm consist of a final urgent prayer to God, beseeching Him to deliver Israel and punish her enemies. The prayer requests of the Psalmist are violently imprecatory, as well as picturesque in their metaphors, and even prophetic in their anticipations.

First, he prays that God will make these nations "like a wheel" and as "stubble before the wind." The Hebrew word used here is not the usual word for "wheel," and is evidently intended to mean a rapidly spinning "wheel" of "stubble before the wind" — that is, a whirlwind stirring up dirt and stubble, then soon dying away into oblivion.

He wants them to be like mountain brush destroyed by a firestorm or as ships torn apart in a great tempest at sea. All these prayers of vengeance may seem unspiritual for a man of God, but they are nevertheless inspired by the Spirit of God, and God will eventually answer them in a most spectacular way. But again we must go to Ezekiel 38 and 39, in the account of the sudden invasion of Israel by Gog and all the nations under his command, in order to see the prophesied answer to these prayers.

"In that day there shall be a great shaking in the land of Israel," says the prophet (Ezek. 38:19). There will be "an overflowing rain, and great hailstones, fire, and brimstone" (Ezek. 38:22). "And I will send a fire on Magog, and among them that dwell carelessly in the isles" (Ezek. 39:6).

The judgment will not only fall on the invading armies, but on those directing them at home and offshore in the sea. "The fishes of the sea . . . and all the men that are upon the face of the earth, shall shake at my presence" (Ezek. 38:20).

As far as the invasion forces themselves are concerned, five-sixths of them will perish. "Behold, I am against thee, O Gog . . . and I will turn thee back, and leave but the sixth part of thee. . . . Thou shalt fall upon the mountains of Israel, thou, and all thy bands, and the people that is with thee" (Ezek. 39:1–4).

The end result of these terrible disasters sent by God will be that all these nations "will seek thy name, O LORD" (verse 16). That is, those that survive among their national leaders will acknowledge that the judgments have come from God and that they brought them on themselves by going against God's chosen nation.

This is also the testimony of the Ezekiel prophecy. "Thus will I magnify myself; and I will be known in the eyes of many nations . . . that I am the Lord" (Ezek. 38:23). The leaders of Israel will also acknowledge that their deliverance has come from God. "So the house of Israel shall know that I am the LORD their God from that day and forward" (Ezek. 39:22).

The Psalmist closes with a similar summary. "That men may know that thou, whose name alone is JEHOVAH, art the most high over all the earth" (verse 18). The emphasis on this redemptive name of God is so strong here that the King James translators elected not to render it in the usual way as "the LORD," but to leave it untranslated as "JEHOVAH," the only place in the Psalms, and one of only four places in the Bible, where they did this.

We need to remember in this connection that JEHOVAH in the Old Testament is Jesus (meaning "Jehovah saves") in the New Testament. Thus, the nations of Psalm 83 and Ezekiel 38 will, in this still-future time, finally come to realize — at least in their minds — that the Lord Jesus Christ is truly the Messiah and the Son of God. This will not yet be true of the other nations of the world, however, and Israel must yet face great persecution arising from that source, but that is another subject.

Chapter 19

Thy Kingdom Come

Psalms 95–100

T his sextet of stirring psalms, all of anonymous human authorship, seem to comprise one unit of praise, tied together by an intriguing structure indicated by certain key phrases in their respective opening verses. Note the following:

Psalm 95:1	"Oh come let us sing unto the LORD."
Psalm 96:1	"Oh sing unto the LORD a new song."
Psalm 97:1	"The LORD reigneth; let the earth rejoice."
Psalm 98:1	"O sing unto the LORD a new song."
Psalm 99:1	"The LORD reigneth, let the people tremble."
Psalm 100:1	"Make a joyful noise unto the LORD."

Then, when we look into the themes of the six psalms, we note that all seem to focus on the Lord as the great King and Judge of all the earth, looking forward to His coming millennial kingdom, when the age-long prayers of God's people will finally be answered: "Thy Kingdom come. Thy will be done in earth, as it is in heaven" (Matt. 6:10).

Psalm 95:3	"For the LORD is a great God, and a great King above all gods."
Psalm 96:10	"Say among the heathen that the LORD reigneth . . . He shall judge the people righteously."
Psalm 97:9	"For thou, LORD, art high above all the earth: thou art exalted far above all gods."
Psalm 98:6	"With trumpets and sound of cornets make a joyful noise before the LORD, the King."

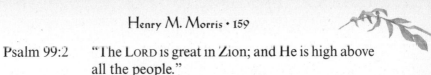

Psalm 99:2   "The LORD is great in Zion; and He is high above all the people."

Psalm 100:3   "Know ye that the LORD he is God; it is he that hath made us, and not we ourselves."

Although these beautiful psalms have been of immediate blessing to the people of God in every generation, it would seem that they are best understood in the context of the future thousand-year reign of Christ on earth (Rev. 20:2–6). The unknown Psalmist, from that perspective, notes that God was first our Creator, then our Savior, then the fulfillment of His promised coming as Judge, and finally His reign as the great King of all creation.

Psalm 95 (verses 1–11)

O come, let us sing unto the LORD: let us make a joyful noise to the rock of our salvation.

Let us come before his presence with thanksgiving, and make a joyful noise unto him with psalms.

For the LORD is a great God, and a great King above all gods.

In his hand are the deep places of the earth: the strength of the hills is his also.

The sea is his, and he made it, and his hands formed the dry land.

O come, let us worship and bow down: let us kneel before the LORD our maker.

For he is our God: and we are the people of his pasture, and the sheep of his hand. To day if ye will hear his voice,

Harden not your heart, as in the provocation, and as in the day of temptation in the wilderness.

When your fathers tempted me, proved me, and saw my work.

Forty years long was I grieved with this generation, and said, It is a people that do err in their heart, and they have not known my ways:

Unto whom I sware in my wrath that they should not enter into my rest.

The fact of His special creation of all things is stressed in verse 5. "The sea is his, and he made it: and his hands formed the dry land." An even greater work of creation is echoed in the last psalm of the sextet. "It is he that hath made us, and not we ourselves" (Ps. 100:3). Also note Psalm 96:5, "The LORD made the heavens."

There are other ties between Psalm 95 and 100. The first verses of the two psalms exhort His people to "make a joyful noise unto the LORD" (Ps. 100:1). "Let us make a joyful noise to the rock of our salvation" (Ps. 95:1). Note also Psalm 95:2 and 98:4, 6. Actually the exhortation to "make a joyful noise" is one word in the Hebrew (*ruwa*), and is most commonly rendered simply as "shout."

The exhortation to "come before his presence with thanksgiving" (Ps. 95:2) is answered by "come before his presence with singing" and "enter into his gates with thanksgiving" in Psalm 100:2, 4.

Finally Psalm 95:7 says that "He is our God, and we are the people of his pasture, and the sheep of his hand." Then Psalm 100:3 echoes back: "We are his people, and the sheep of his pasture."

Not only is God the Creator of all things, He is also the sustainer. "In his hand are the deep places of the earth: the strength of the hills is his also" (Ps. 95:4).

Even though the earth is under God's curse because of sin, He sustains it so that His great plan of salvation can be worked out for His people. In the first verse of this sextet of verses, He is even called "the rock of our salvation" (Ps. 95:1).

In the context of these psalms, the work of Christ in providing salvation has also been completed, so that His people are exhorted to "shew forth his salvation from day to day" (Ps. 96:2), because "He preserveth the souls of his saints" (Ps. 97:10). In the millennial setting of these psalms, it will have been literally true that "all the ends of the earth have seen the salvation of our God" (Ps. 98:3). "The LORD hath made known his salvation: his righteousness hath he openly shewed in the sight of the heathen" (Ps. 98:2).

It may be especially — and beautifully — significant that the Hebrew word for "salvation" in these verses is *yeshua*, which is the very name given to the Son of God in His human incarnation — that is "Jesus." In fact, it is not unreasonable to substitute "Jesus" for "salvation" in the above verses. In that coming day, it will be true to say that "all the ends of the earth have seen Jesus," for "the LORD hath made known his Jesus."

However, the last four verses of Psalm 95 look back to the failures of Israel in the days of Moses, and then in the days of the apostles, perhaps as a warning to those who will be born during the millennial age, and therefore still in the flesh, living on the earth. In spite of the personal presence of Christ on the earth, and all the other blessings of the kingdom age, these people will still be sinners by nature and will still need to be redeemed through faith in Christ. Accordingly, the warning in verses 7–11 of Psalm 95 constitute a sober warning against backsliding, just as they have been to believers in every generation since they were written.

The importance of the warning is further pointed up by its inclusion in the New Testament. Verses 7–11 of Psalm 95 are quoted almost verbatim in Hebrews 3:7–11, then stressed again in Hebrews 3:15–18 and Hebrews 4:5–7.

These verses in the psalm hearken back to the days when the Children of Israel, newly set free from their terrible bondage in Egypt, instead of rejoicing in the Lord and giving glad obedience to His commandments and the leadership of Moses, murmured and argued again and again. Finally, at Kadesh-Barnea, when the ten spies counseled against going on into Canaan, God committed them all to 40 years of wandering in the wilderness, until all the men of 20 years old or more would die (see Num. 14:22–39).

Unto these men, God had said: "I sware in my wrath that they should not enter into my rest" (verse 11). The "rest" of which He spoke was the anticipated victory over the Canaanite tribes to be followed by Israel living peacefully and righteously in the Promised Land.

Although the second generation of men *did* enter Canaan and conquer most of the tribes living there, they were never able to remain at peace because they disobeyed God in not *completing* the work of conquest. Thus, "the word preached did not profit them, not being mixed with faith in them that heard it" (Heb. 4:2). Throughout the ensuing centuries, these words and their exposition in Hebrews 4 have served as a warning to God's people against incomplete obedience.

Even more specifically, they will be a warning to men and women in the millennial age, which ostensibly should be a thousand years of spiritual "rest" for the world and all its inhabitants.

But there is no real "rest" for any men or women — whether in the Mosaic age, the church age, or the millennial age — until that person has received the Lord Jesus as the Christ, the Savior, and the King of his life. This will be as true in the coming kingdom age as it is in this present age. "Come unto me," He said, "and ye shall find rest unto your souls" (Matt. 11:28–29).

Psalm 96 (verses 1–13)

O sing unto the LORD a new song: sing unto the LORD, all the earth.

Sing unto the LORD, bless his name: shew forth his salvation from day to day.

Declare his glory among the heathen, his wonders among all people.

For the LORD is great, and greatly to be praised: he is to be feared above all gods.

For all the gods of the nations are idols: but the LORD made the heavens.

Honour and majesty are before him: strength and beauty are in his sanctuary.

Give unto the LORD, O ye kindreds of the people, give unto the Lord glory and strength.

Give unto the LORD the glory due unto his name, bring an offering, and come into his courts.

O worship the LORD in the beauty of holiness: fear before him, all the earth.

Say among the heathen that the LORD reigneth: the world also shall be established that it shall not be moved:

He shall judge the people righteously.

Let the heavens rejoice, and let the earth be glad, let the sea roar, and the fulness thereof.

Let the field be joyful, and all that is therein: then shall all the trees of the wood rejoice

Before the LORD: for he cometh, for he cometh to judge the earth: he shall judge the world with righteousness, and the people with his truth.

This beautiful psalm is essentially an exhortation by the Psalmist to praise the Lord, in anticipation of that great coming age when He shall come back to the world He had created and finally establish a reign of righteousness which would include all nations of the earth. The events inaugurating this kingdom age will indeed call for a "new song" (verse 1) to be sung throughout "all the earth." The deliverance of the remnant of the faithful from the intolerable reign of the beast (Antichrist) at the end of the great Tribulation (Rev. 19:20–21) will surely cause them to "shew forth his salvation from day to day" and to declare "his wonders among all people" (verses 2–3).

The whole remaining world population (at least at the beginning of the millennial age) will finally acknowledge that the God of the Bible is the one true God of creation and salvation. "All the gods of the nations" — whether handmade images or humanistic philosophies (e.g., evolutionism) or any other icon of life — are nothing but "idols" (that is, "empty vanities"). What a tragic mistake it is, with eternally sad consequences, for anyone to center his faith and life around anything or anyone other than the one God who "made the heavens" (verse 5) and who has become incarnate in Jesus Christ and then died and rose again in order to provide forgiveness and salvation for all who trust Him.

Note that "nations" (verse 5) and "heathen" (verses 3, 10) are translations of the same Hebrew word (also frequently translated "Gentiles"). Although Israel is God's chosen nation and will be fully recognized as such during the kingdom age, surviving remnants of other nations of the world (the Gentiles, or heathen nations) will also, in that age, acknowledge Jehovah as Creator and Jesus Christ as Savior and King.

With one accord, all will "say among the heathen that the LORD reigneth" (verse 10) and that "He shall judge the people righteously." (Note also verse 13, as well as Ps. 97:8, 98:9, and 99:4, as additional affirmations of the righteousness of His judgments when He comes to govern the earth.)

Even nature itself will seem to be rejoicing, after the traumatic natural upheavals of the tribulation period. The "heavens rejoice" and "the earth [is] glad," the sea roars its approval, "the field (is) joyful" and even "the trees . . . rejoice" (verses 11–12). The prophet Isaiah received a similar vision: "The wilderness and the solitary place shall be glad for them; and the desert shall rejoice, and blossom as the rose . . . for in the wilderness shall waters break out, and streams in the desert" (Isa. 35:1–6).

The continuing presence of "the sea" (verse 11) provides an incidental proof that all of this will be taking place on the present earth, for in the new earth, there will be "no more sea" (Rev. 21:1). However, much of what applies in the millennial age will also prevail in the eternal ages on the new earth, and so can be considered as at least a type, or foregleam, of the glories of *that* age. This present earth and atmosphere will be completely purged at the end of the millennium (2 Pet. 3:10; Rev. 20:11), and then renovated as the "new heaven and new earth." This is at least anticipated in verse 10. "The world also shall be established that it shall not be moved." However, this truth also applies to the millennial period, in the sense that there shall be no more earthquakes such as had devastated the earth in the tribulation period.

The glorious summation of all these glorious prospects is centered on this great promise. "The LORD . . . cometh, for he cometh to judge the earth: he shall judge the world with righteousness, and the people with his truth" (verse 13).

Psalm 97 (verses 1–12)

The LORD reigneth; let the earth rejoice; let the multitude of isles be glad thereof.

Clouds and darkness are round about him: righteousness and judgment are the habitation of his throne.

A fire goeth before him, and burneth up his enemies round about.

His lightnings enlightened the world: the earth saw, and trembled.

The hills melted like wax at the presence of the LORD, at the presence of the Lord of the whole earth.

The heavens declare his righteousness, and all the people see his glory.

Confounded be all they that serve graven images, that boast themselves of idols: worship him, all ye gods.

Zion heard, and was glad; and the daughters of Judah rejoiced because of thy judgments, O LORD.

For thou, LORD, art high above all the earth: thou art exalted far above all gods.

Ye that love the LORD, hate evil: he preserveth the souls of his saints; he delivereth them out of the hand of the wicked.

Light is sown for the righteous, and gladness for the upright in heart.

Rejoice in the LORD, ye righteous; and give thanks at the remembrance of his holiness.

The first verses of Psalm 97 continue in the same vein of joy as Psalm 96. There, however, it is as though the witness is recalling the traumatic physical calamities that God had just visited upon the earth in the tribulation period. There will have been widespread lethal fires on the earth (Rev. 8:7–9, 16:8–9; Joel 1:15–20; etc), lightnings (Rev. 8:5, 11:19, 16:18, etc.) and melting hills (Isa. 24:19).

Finally, at the climactic end of the great tribulation, the Lord would descend to earth from heaven and it would then be true that "all the people see his glory" (verse 6). "Immediately after the tribulation of those days . . . shall all the tribes of the earth mourn, and they shall see the Son of man coming in the clouds of heaven with power and great glory" (Matt. 24:29–30). "Behold, he cometh with clouds, and every eye shall see him" (Rev. 1:7).

Furthermore, the tribulation judgments will have resulted in the final judgment on all the false gods and their images — especially the great image of the beast that all people had been commanded to worship (Rev. 13:13–15). Once and for all, it had been made clear to all that the true God is "exalted far above all gods" (verse 9) and that even these false "gods" (that is, the rebellious angels that had followed Satan and passed themselves off as the host of heaven, various gods and goddesses) were commanded to "worship him, all ye gods" (verse 7). In that great day, "at the name of Jesus every knee should bow, of things in heaven, and things in earth, and things under the earth; And that every tongue should confess that Jesus Christ is Lord, to the glory of God the Father" (Phil. 2:10–11).

It is also wonderful to note that, even during all the fearful days of the great Tribulation, the Lord "preserveth the souls of his saints; he delivereth them out of the hand of the wicked. Light is sown for the righteous, and gladness for the upright in heart" (verses 10–11). Though many of these will be martyred, the Lord still preserves their souls! All who know and love the Lord, can indeed "rejoice in the LORD," and "give thanks at the remembrance of his holiness" (verse 12).

Psalm 98 (verses 1–9)

O sing unto the LORD a new song: for he hath done marvelous things: his right hand, and his holy arm, hath gotten him the victory.

The LORD hath made known his salvation. His righteousness hath he openly shewed in the sight of the heathen.

He hath remembered his mercy and his truth toward the house of Israel: all the ends of the earth have seen the salvation of our God.

Make a joyful noise unto the LORD, all the earth: make a loud noise, and rejoice, and sing praise.

Sing unto the LORD with the harp: with the harp, and the voice of a psalm.

With trumpets and sound of cornet make a joyful noise before the LORD, the King.

Let the sea roar, and the fulness thereof; the world, and they that dwell therein.

Let the floods clap their hands: let the hills be joyful together

Before the LORD; for he cometh to judge the earth: with righteousness shall he judge the world, and the people with equity.

Psalm 98 is the only psalm in the entire Book of Psalms that is headed with the simple, seemingly redundant, superscription, "A Psalm." The reason for the title is not clear, although possibly it is to call special attention to verse 5, the central verse of the psalm: "Sing unto the LORD with . . . the voice of a psalm." This is the only verse in the Hebrew of the

Old Testament that has the words "a psalm" in the actual text of a biblical passage. Evidently this "new song" (verse 1), telling of God's great work in cleansing the earth and establishing His millennial kingdom, was to be a beautiful melody sung to the accompaniment of a harp (verse 5), then followed with a loud song ("joyful noise") accompanied by trumpets and cornet (verse 6).

However, the "psalm" of verse 5 is actually a slightly different Hebrew word than in the psalm's title. It can also be rendered as "melody." The fact that this melody is actually to be a psalm (probably this very psalm) is possibly the reason for the unusual title, which otherwise would seem unnecessary.

Obviously this psalm is — like Psalm 96 — a song of joy and triumph. The two are surely written by the same (though anonymous) author. This fact is indicated by comparing Psalm 96:1 and 96:13 with Psalm 98:1 and 98:9 (the first and last verses in the two psalms). Similarly, verses 7 and 8, like verses 11 and 12 of Psalm 96, speak of the joyful testimony of the creation itself.

Verse 8 — "Let the floods clap their hands" — warrants a special clarification. In the Old Testament, the phrase "clap their hands" does not indicate applause for a performance, as it does in our present society. The Hebrew word for "clap" is usually rendered "smite" or "strike," and the practice was used as a gesture of triumph over an enemy that had been "smitten" in combat. Here it would suggest the exultation of the natural world, long groaning in travail (Rom. 8:22) that had, along with redeemed Israel, been delivered in considerable measure from its bondage under God's primeval curse on the ground (Gen. 3:17).

Israel, of course, will also have been set free to serve again as God's elect nation during the kingdom age, and "all the ends of the earth (will) have seen the salvation of our God" (verse 3).

Psalm 99 (verses 1–9)

The LORD reigneth, let the people tremble: he sitteth between the cherubims; let the earth be moved.

The LORD is great in Zion; and he is high above all the people.

Let them praise thy great and terrible name; for it is holy.

The king's strength also loveth judgment; thou dost establish equity, thou executest judgment and righteousness in Jacob.

Exalt ye the LORD our God, and worship at his footstool; for he is holy.

Moses and Aaron among his priests, and Samuel among them that call upon his name; they called upon the LORD, and he answered them.

He spake unto them in the cloudy pillar: they kept his testimonies, and the ordinance that he gave them.

Thou answeredst them, O LORD our God: thou wast a God that forgavest them, though thou tookest vengeance of their inventions.

Exalt the LORD our God, and worship at His holy hill; for the LORD our God is holy.

This psalm begins with the same words as Psalm 97: "The LORD reigneth." But then there is a sober difference. The response to this proclamation in Psalm 97 is: "Let the earth rejoice." Here, however, is: "Let the people tremble." The personal reign of Christ over the earth during the millennial age will be one of social righteousness and peace and prosperity, and naturally it will mostly be a time of rejoicing.

At the same time, it will still be necessary for God to judge sin. Although there will be a relatively small earthly population at the beginning of the millennium (note Isa. 24:6), the population will soon grow almost explosively. With an ideal environment and climate, no war or crime, and medical research thriving, people will live to great ages and no doubt produce large families.

However, they will still have the same inherited sin nature that we have today and can become inwardly rebellious even if restrained from outward evil. They will still need to be saved the same way people are today — by repentance and personal faith in Christ as Savior and Lord, on the basis of His sacrificial death and resurrection. If they don't do this, they will be judged. "The child shall die an hundred years old; but the sinner being an hundred years old shall be accursed" (Isa. 65:20).

Especially as the centuries roll on, and the past ages of the world become more and more dim in memory, this judgmental aspect of the millennial period will have to be exercised more frequently by the great Judge. Even so, He "dost establish equity . . . and righteousness in Jacob" (verse 4).

The psalm seems to tell us that, when He is thus acting in judgment, He is sitting "between the cherubims" (verse 1), "high above all the people" (verse 2), on His "holy hill" (verse 9) "great in Zion" (verse 2).

Also there is the command to "worship at his footstool" (verse 5). What is to be understood by God's "footstool"? This unusual concept is perhaps clarified by Isaiah 66:1: "Thus saith the LORD, The heaven is my throne, and the earth is my footstool."

In Scripture, the mighty cherubims, highest of all the angelic hierarchy, are always seen in the presence of God (Gen. 3:24; Ezek. 10:20; Rev. 4:6–8). Two golden cherubims were placed in the wilderness tabernacle (Exod. 25:18–22) to overshadow the mercy seat where God could come to communicate with His people. We remember also that whenever God has actually appeared to His people, it was in the person of God the Son (John 1:18). That must mean that when God has appeared to man in the midst of the golden cherubims, that appearance was also in the person of the Son.

The Lord Jesus Christ must therefore be the one who is the subject of this psalm, judging the people from His high throne. "For the Father judgeth no man, but hath committed all judgment unto the Son" (John 5:22).

First of all, however, before any future judgments, there will be the rapture and resurrection of the believers of this age (1 Thess. 4:13–17), although this has probably been preceded by the resurrection and rapture of Old Testament believers just after Christ's resurrection (Matt. 27:52–53). The first judgment after this great future resurrection will be the judgment of believers at the judgment seat of Christ (2 Cor. 5:10), followed by the judgment of the living Gentiles still on earth at the close of the great Tribulation (Matt. 25:31–46). At this judgment, Christ will "sit upon the throne of His glory" (Matt. 25:31), which probably will not be the same throne as His judgment seat. The first will be somewhere high in the air, the second on the earth, most likely on the earthly Mount Zion in Jerusalem.

Then follows the great millennial period, during which time the previously resurrected believers — presumably both pre-Calvary and post-Calvary believers — will share judgment duties with their Lord. "And I saw thrones, and they sat upon them, and judgment was given unto them." And who are "they"? "Blessed and holy is he that hath part in the first resurrection . . . they shall be priests of God and of Christ, and shall reign with him a thousand years." (Rev. 20:4–6). "Do ye not know that the saints shall judge the world?" (1 Cor. 6:2).

And just where will *our* judgment thrones be? We shall be with Christ, for when we are caught up to meet Him *in the air*, then "shall we ever be with the Lord" (1 Thess. 4:17). At present, He has gone to "prepare a place" for us (John 14:2) in the heavenly city, which is thereafter to be identified with "the bride, the Lamb's wife . . . that great city, the holy Jerusalem, descending out of heaven from God" (Rev. 21:9–10).

However, that great city cannot descend from the heavens until after the last great judgment of all the unsaved of the ages (note Rev. 20:11–21:2). That judgment will not take place until the final satanic rebellion at the end of the thousand-year kingdom age on the present earth has been put down, and "the earth and the heaven fled away" (Rev. 20:11). Note the command of the Lord Jesus here in Psalm 99:1

to "let the earth be moved," as "the people tremble."

All of these considerations lead to the inference (and it is only that, for the Scriptures never say so explicitly) that Christ and His saints will be in the heavenly city during the kingdom age, whence they can as necessary descend to earth for their governing responsibilities. That city will have come from the heaven of heavens down to the "air" (1 Thess. 4:17), that is, the atmospheric heaven, at the time of Christ's return, where it will apparently remain as a great terrestrial satellite until time to descend to the new earth after the last judgment.

The Psalmist prophet then, in his vision of these great future events, sees Moses and Aaron and Samuel — and possibly other Old Testament saints — there with the Lord in the holy hill of heavenly Zion. This leads him to recall (and us as well, for we also shall see them there) God's marvelous works back in the earthly days of these great men of God.

God — that is, the Lord Jesus Christ — is the same God for us "today," as He was for them "yesterday" and will be for all His saints "for ever" (Heb. 13:8). Thus, it is fitting for us today, as it was for them back then and as it shall be for God's people in the ages to come, to "exalt the LORD our God, and worship at his holy hill, for the LORD our God is holy" (verse 9).

Psalm 100 (verses 1–5)
A Psalm of Praise

Make a joyful noise unto the LORD, all ye lands.

Serve the LORD with gladness: come before his presence with singing.

Know ye that the LORD he is God: it is he that hath made us, and not we ourselves; we are his people, and the sheep of his pasture.

Enter into his gates with thanksgiving, and into his courts with praise: be thankful unto him, and bless his name.

For the LORD is good; his mercy is everlasting; and his truth endureth to all generations.

Psalm 100 — "Old Hundredth," our forefathers called it — has been appropriate for believers in every age, but it becomes most meaningful of all when we visualize our singing it with all the saints in the coming millennial age. It is the only psalm with the superscription "A Psalm of Praise," and it is indeed just that. Almost all the psalms include notes of sadness or conflict, but in this psalm, there is nothing but praise. It is a fitting climax and conclusion to the sextet of triumph psalms discussed in this chapter. Actually, the word "praise" in the title is the same as "thanksgiving" (verse 4), and this thought is also a clear note in the psalm.

The opening exhortation to "make a joyful noise" is directed not just to Israel, but to "all ye lands." In the great kingdom age, all people will (at least at the beginning of the age) "serve the Lord with gladness." At the judgment seat of Christ, each believer will have been rewarded with appropriate responsibilities according to His previous service for Christ, and then will have the joy of serving Him in happy, fruitful ministries in all the eternal ages to come (Rev. 22:3).

If there had ever been any question about the existence and identity of God in the period between the time this psalm was written and the time of its ultimate fulfillment in the kingdom age, there will never be any further doubt when that day comes. All will learn and know that Jehovah (that is Jesus the Savior) is the God of creation (John 1:3). Not only has He created us, but we are His special "workmanship, created in Christ Jesus unto good works" (Eph. 2:10), and these will we do throughout eternity!

Modern humanistic evolutionists have the absurd notion that "we ourselves" have made us into whatever we are, but about all that we have done is to resist the Lord as He tries to make us what He wants us to be. Current naturalistic theories suppose that "nature" somehow made us from literally nothing by chance and natural selection into human beings, after which we ourselves have evolved ourselves upward into our present state of supposedly high development.

But this idea is pure speculation, without an iota of scientific proof. God in Christ made us in His own image and has also paid the price to save us from sin and then lead us as His sheep to the pastures where we can grow into what He would have us be.

As we "enter into His gates" in the holy city, we fulfill the spiritual type He was presenting when He called himself both the "good shepherd" and "the door of the sheepfold" (John 10:7, 11). "I am the door," He said, "by me if any man enter in, he shall be saved, and go in and out, and find pasture" (John 10:9).

Indeed, "the Lord is good," and everything He made was "very good" (Gen. 1:31). When we finally enter into the pearly gates of the heavenly Jerusalem, we shall thank and praise and serve Him forever. Our God is a God of unending mercy (Ps. 103:17), giving us unending life. His truth also is everlasting and we shall spend eternity learning more and more of His truth both from His inspired Word (which is forever settled in heaven — Ps. 119:89) and in His infinite creation.

Part IV

Scientific Foregleams
in the Psalms

Chapter 20

Man and the Universe

Psalm 8

One of the greatest concerns of scientists and philosophers throughout the ages has been that of the nature and meaning of the physical universe and, in particular, the role of man in the universe. The Psalms often deal with this theme and, of course, ascribe it all to God. For example, the 8th Psalm begins and ends with the great testimony of praise: "O LORD our Lord [two names of God, Jehovah, our Adonai], how excellent is thy name in all the earth!" The dual name suggests that God is both Father and Son, and the occasion for praise is that God has come to earth as Son of Man as well as Son of God.

The Vastness of the Heavens
Verses 1–4

O LORD our Lord, how excellent is thy name in all the earth! Who hast set thy glory above the heavens.

Out of the mouth of babes and sucklings hast thou ordained strength because of thine enemies, that thou mightest still the enemy and the avenger.

When I consider thy heavens, the work of thy fingers, the moon and the stars, which thou hast ordained;

What is man, that thou art mindful of him? and the son of man, that thou visitest him?

The Book of Psalms, as we have noted before, is primarily a book of praise, and these praises often center upon the vast expanses of the heavens and upon the one who could create such an infinite, intricate cosmos. And, of course, no matter how great may be the universe, the glory of God is far above the glory of the heavens. The cause must be greater than the effect! The Creator is above the creation.

Furthermore, there are other components of the creation which even themselves are greater than the physical cosmos. Those who can praise God for His excellent name are greater. Those who can praise God in true sincerity (babes and sucklings) are greater even than those who can praise in eloquence. Such praise is "perfected praise" (see the quotation from verse 2 in Matt. 21:16 and the commentary in Matt. 11:25).

We do not yet know what purpose God may have for the stars of heaven. The nearest star is 30 trillion miles away from the earth, and it is futile to hope that men in this lifetime will ever be able to travel to the stars in spaceships. The heavens are "thy heavens;" "the heavens are the LORD's: but the earth hath he given to the children of men" (Ps. 115:16). One important purpose for the visible stars, at least, is to serve "for signs, and for seasons, and for days, and for years" (Gen. 1:14).

However, man has corrupted the meaning and purpose of the stars in two ways. In one, he has assumed the stars have direct influence over human lives and had developed a monstrous system of pagan astrology. In the other, as his concept of the vastness of space has increased, he has assumed that man is of no importance; the earth is merely a speck of dust in an infinite evolving universe, and man is an accidental bit of organic scum on the dust particle.

This 20th-century question was raised in essence long ago by the Psalmist. How could the God who created the mighty heavens possibly be interested in man?

In the very question, however, divine inspiration impelled the Psalmist to anticipate God's ultimate testimony to the importance of the earth and of man's life on earth — namely, that He, himself, would become man on earth. Not only does he ask, "What is man?" but also, "What is the son of man, that thou visitest him?" The verb, "visit," is the same as "number" or "acknowledge." In some unique way, the "son of man" is acknowledged or counted, by God on behalf of "man," of whom He is still "mindful."

This is the first time in Scripture when the term "son of man" is used, but it is far from the last! The Lord Jesus applied it to himself no less than 80 times, beginning with Matthew 8:20 ("the Son of man hath not where to lay his head"). This passage (verses 4–6) is quoted in the New Testament (. 2:6–8; 1 Cor. 15:27) and applied to Christ, so there is no doubt that the primary meaning is messianic and prophetic.

Far from being of no importance, the earth and man are so central in God's purposes that God had from eternity planned to come to earth and become a man himself, in the person of His Son. Furthermore, when the earth is finally purged and made new, the Lord Jesus will dwell here on this earth forever (Rev. 21:1–3, 22–27). There is no other star or planet in the universe whose importance to God is comparable to that of the earth.

Even man in the strict biological sense is infinitely more complex than the stars, of course. It is absurd to belittle man simply because of his size. Although a star is big, it is very simple, composed mostly of hydrogen and helium. The measure of significance in the universe is not size but order and complexity, and the human brain is by far the most complex aggregation of matter in the universe, so far as science can determine. In the strictly physical sense, the earth is the most complex aggregation of inanimate matter about which we know in the universe, and it is uniquely designed as man's home.

Lower than the Angels
Verse 5

For thou hast made him a little lower than the angels, and hast crowned him with glory and honour.

In amplifying the question, "What is man?" the Psalmist notes that he has been made "lower than the angels." Evolutionists believe man is merely an animal that has evolved "higher than the apes," but such a notion is absurd. Never has any creature been found, or any fossil been found of any animal which is partially man and partially ape (or part man and part anything else), although many fossils of both apes and men have been discovered. There is no scientific evidence whatever that man was not created as man, in the image of God, exactly as the Bible says (Gen. 1:27).

In what sense is man "lower than the angels"? Angels are "spirits" not subject to the limitations of gravitational and electromagnetic forces, whereas man *has* a spirit, bound within a body which is "earthy." Angels are "ministers of God," and "excel in strength" (Ps. 103:20–21), but they are also "ministering spirits, sent forth to minister for them who shall be heirs of salvation" (Heb. 1:14). Under the curse, man goes through physical death, and, in fact, it was for "the suffering of death" that Christ, as Son of Man, was made lower than the angels (Heb. 2:9). But man can also receive salvation, a privilege which is denied the fallen angels (2 Pet. 2:4; Judg. 6).

The phrase, of course, applies especially to Christ as *the* Son of Man. Jesus, as Son of Man, must take on flesh and blood, not "the nature of angels" (Heb. 2:14, 16), in order to die and to arise and to restore man's lost dominion. He who was the eternal Word must become flesh (John 1:14); He who was equal with God must become a bond servant (Phil. 2:7). Actually, the phrase, "a little lower than the angels," could also carry the meaning "for a little time [that is, 33 years] lower than the angels."

The word "angels" in verse 5 is not the usual word for "angels," but rather is *elohim*, the most frequent name of God, also occasionally rendered "gods." That here it really means angels, however, is evident from its New Testament quotation (Heb. 2:7). The use of this word here clearly suggests that the fallen angels are in view, those that are worshiped as "gods" in connection with the astrological religions of the heathen who worship "the moon and the stars which thou hast ordained." Christ, as Son of Man, was lower even than these!

But because He died and thereby conquered death, He is to be crowned with glory and honor. Those also who suffer with Him will be "found unto praise and honour and glory at the appearing of Jesus Christ" (1 Pet. 1:7).

Man's Dominion
Verses 6–8

Thou madest him to have dominion over the works of thy hands; thou hast put all things under his feet:

All sheep and oxen, yea, and the beasts of the field;

The fowl of the air, and the fish of the sea, and whatsoever passeth through the paths of the seas.

Man, created in God's image, was given dominion over all the works of God's hands, including especially the animal kingdom. The reference even to those deep-sea animals that "pass through the paths of the seas" long ago inspired the great Christian hydrographer and scientist Matthew Maury to find and chart these subterranean pathways, and he has for over a century been honored by mariners as the "pathfinder of the seas."

Although man was given this dominion (Gen. 1:26–28), he has never exercised it fully or faithfully, and since the flood there has actually been enmity between man and the animals (Gen. 9:2–5). This dominion and harmony will someday be fully restored (Isa. 11:6–9; Hos. 2:18), but only after Christ returns.

When Jesus Christ came as the Son of Man, He occasionally did manifest His authority over the animal kingdom (Matt. 17:27), as well as the physical creation (Mark 4:41), but He had come to bear and remove the Curse on the earth and so was "obedient unto death" (Phil. 2:7–11). Therefore, although God had "put all things under his feet" (verse 6), nevertheless, "now we see not yet all things put under him" (Heb. 2:8).

The Son of Man Acknowledged
Verse 9

O Lord our Lord, how excellent is thy name in all the earth!

At this point in Psalm 8, between verses 8 and 9, there is a great parenthesis. Although God had given man dominion over the earth, he had failed. Before the Son of Man could be "acknowledged" (verse 4) as having regained this dominion and having thereby inherited the promises, He must pay the price to redeem it.

In this parenthesis, therefore, we must insert Hebrews 2:8–9: "Thou hast put all things in subjection under his feet. For in that he put all in subjection under him, he left nothing that is not put under him. But now we see not yet all things put under him. But we see Jesus, who was made a little lower than the angels for the suffering of death, crowned with glory and honour; that he by the grace of God should taste death for every man."

It is only after the substitutionary death of the Son of Man, followed by His victorious resurrection and His coronation at the second coming, that He will indeed reign over all the earth.

Then will he surely be acknowledged as King of kings and Lord of lords. Then will it finally be fitting to exclaim with the Psalmist, "O Lord, our Lord [Jehovah, our Adonai], how excellent is thy name in all the earth!"

Chapter 21

Revelation in Science and Scripture

Psalm 19

One of the grandest objects of praise to God is that of His marvelous creation, and this theme, as noted before, is prominent in the psalms. As the Psalmists sing of the wonders and beauties of the physical universe, they necessarily deal with many of the same phenomena which are the objects of study in modern science. It is significant that as they do, their poetic expressions are always remarkably in accord with the most modern scientific descriptions of the same phenomena. Often, in fact, their insights anticipate modern science by thousands of years. One of the most remarkable of the psalms with such features is Psalm 19.

The Space-Mass-Time Universe
Verses 1–2

The heavens declare the glory of God; and the firmament sheweth his handywork.

Day unto day uttereth speech, and night unto night sheweth knowledge.

The 19th psalm is divided into two main parts — the first six verses, discussing God's revelation through His created world, and the last eight verses, stressing His even greater revelation through His written Word. It begins by calling attention to the physical universe, verse one stating the testimony of space, and verse two, that of time.

Each of these two verses uses the structure of Hebrew poetic parallelism to emphasize its theme. In verse one, the terms "heavens" and "firmament" are synonymous (note Gen. 1:8 — "God called the firmament Heaven"), and both mean essentially what we mean by our modern scientific term, *space*. Thus, the vast reaches of space everywhere provide the backdrop, as it were, for God to "show forth his power and his work." Everywhere throughout the infinite universe occur phenomena declaring His omnipotence and His orderliness, "the glory of God," and his *handywork.*"

Similarly, verse two speaks of *time*, during which ("Day after day" and "night after night") the phenomena in space perpetually yield information in unending communication between the Creator and His creation. Thus, everywhere in space occur phenomena, energized and ordered, transmitting information eternally through time.

Modern science recognizes the universe to be a *continuum* of space, time and energy (or Information), and so does this ancient Psalm! Everything that happens in space and time (call it an "event," a "process," "system," or whatever) involves "power" doing "work" and "communication" transmitting "knowledge."

The Standard of Measure
Verses 3–4

There is no speech nor language, where their voice is not heard.

Their line is gone out through all the earth, and their words to the end of the world. In them hath he set a tabernacle for the sun.

This marvelous universe is always teaching people of all nations about God. Although there is neither audible voice nor written message, the lesson is freely available in all times and places. "The *invisible* things are clearly seen!" (Rom. 1:20), and the inaudible words are plainly heard, so that men are "without excuse" if they fail to heed. By the simple, universal experience of cause-and-effect ("every effect must have an adequate cause"), the universe teaches about the great First Cause. The cause of boundless space and endless time must be infinite and eternal; the cause of universal power and complex order must be omnipotent and omniscient; the communicator of needed knowledge to personal beings must be personal and gracious. Therefore, the God of creation is an infinite, eternal, omnipotent, omniscient, personal, gracious being!

This universal testimony is itself the divine standard which measures human response. The Psalmist calls it the surveyor's "line" which goes out to "measure" the hearts of men through all the earth. That is, the manner in which a person responds to the witness of God in creation measures the very nature of his heart-attitude toward God, himself. The apostle Paul, answering his own rhetorical question ("But I say, have they not heard?"), quotes this very verse (see Rom. 10:13–18) to prove that all men have access to the knowledge of the true God, merely through observing His creation.

The great indictment, however, is that, although "the heavens declare the glory of God," all men "come short of the glory of God" (Rom. 3:23). The "line" has "gone out" to measure them but they have not measured up. They have all "changed the glory of the incorruptible God" into a form suitable to human conceit rather than to the divine standard, and thus "God also gave them up" (Rom. 1:23–24).

The Testimony of the Sun
Verses 5–6

Which is as a bridegroom coming out of his chamber, and rejoiceth as a strong man to run a race.

His going forth is from the end of the heaven, and his circuit unto the ends of it: and there is nothing hid from the heat thereof.

The greatest of the works of God in the physical creation, as far as the earth is concerned, is the sun. "In them" (that is, in space and time) God has established a "tent" for the sun. The sun provides all the energy for all the earth's processes, doing so through its continual "going forth." This phrase does not refer mainly to the sun's daily orbit, but is a translation of a Hebrew word (used also in Mic. 5:2; Deut. 8:3; and Ps. 65:8) which speaks of something which goes forth from the object itself.

The reference clearly is to the sun's radiant energy, going forth from its surface as a result of unknown reactions in its depths. A part of that energy reaches the earth, where it is converted through various processes into the chemical energy of its biosphere, the electrical and kinetic energies of its atmosphere, the hydraulic energy of its rains and rivers, and all the other energy resources on which the earth subsists.

Not only does the sun's radiation energize the earth, but all the rest of the solar system. In fact, as the sun moves in a gigantic orbit through the Milky Way Galaxy (an orbit that would require 230 million years for one circuit, at a speed of 600,000 miles per hour), and the galaxy moves in an unknown path relative to the other galaxies of space, its circuit seems truly to be from one end of the heavens to the other. As its radiant energy continually goes forth, it is literally true that "there is nothing hid from the heat thereof."

As far as the earth is concerned, this physical "light of the world" provides energy for all its work, especially for the maintenance of life on its surface. These processes, drawing on the solar heat energy, must obey the laws of thermodynamics ("heat power"). It is providential, however, (and perhaps ironic, as well) that, just as God's revelation in creation both illumines and judges the human heart, so the sun both energizes and disintegrates physical and biological systems on earth. The first law of thermodynamics is the law of conservation of energy, reflecting the completion and sustenance of God's finished work of creation. The second law is the law of increasing non-availability of energy, reflecting the curse on God's creation because of man's sin.

Both laws seem to be specially implemented by the sun. The environmental radiations cause somatic mutations, leading to the aging and death of individual organisms, and also genetic mutations, leading to the deterioration and extinction of species. Storms, erosion, rusting, and most other decay mechanisms are triggered by solar energy. And yet the sun's energy continually replenishes the earth's deteriorating energy resources. "There is nothing hid from the heat thereof."

The sun is also a beautiful type of the Lord Jesus Christ, the spiritual "light of the world" (John 8:12). The heavens declare the glory of God, and He is the very "out-raying of the glory of God" (Heb. 1:3) "upholding all things by the word of his power." He is the Creator of all things and therefore all created things reflect His handiwork. The sun, in its daily triumph over the darkness, emerging as a great bridegroom racing forth to rescue the darkened world and claim it as its own, continually renews God's promise of a heavenly Bridegroom who will someday save and cleanse His earthly bride from the curse of death and darkness.

The Written Word
Verses 7–14

The law of the LORD is perfect, converting the soul: the testimony of the LORD is sure, making wise the simple.

The statutes of the LORD are right, rejoicing the heart: the commandment of the LORD is pure, enlightening the eyes.

The fear of the LORD is clean, enduring for ever: the judgments of the LORD are true and righteous altogether.

More to be desired are they than gold, yea, than much fine gold: sweeter also than honey and the honeycomb.

Moreover by them is thy servant warned: and in keeping of them there is great reward.

Who can understand his errors? Cleanse thou me from secret faults.

Keep back thy servant also from presumptuous sins; let them not have dominion over me: then shall I be upright, and I shall be innocent from the great transgression.

Let the words of my mouth, and the meditation of my heart, be acceptable in thy sight, O LORD, my strength, and my redeemer.

In spite of the tremendous witness concerning God and His grace and power plainly revealed in the created cosmos, men everywhere mistake or distort or reject its message. The testimony is there, so that men are without excuse; but the testimony is not received, so that they are also without salvation.

The *world* of the Lord is imperfect in its bondage to the curse, thus condemning the souls of men, but the *Word* of the Lord is perfect, converting their souls. What natural revelation only promises, written revelation accomplishes! ". . . the holy scriptures, which are able to make thee wise unto salvation through faith which is in Christ Jesus" (2 Tim. 3:15). They bring not only conversion, but also wisdom and joy, illumination, endurance, and righteousness. When the creation was completed, it was all "very good," but it has since been corrupted by sin and the curse. The written Word, however, despite all the attempts of men and devils to corrupt and destroy it, remains "living and powerful," the "incorruptible seed," the "words which will not pass away" (Hebrews 4:12; I Peter 1:23; Matthew 24:35). The Scriptures are perfect and sure, right and pure, clean and true.

These very verses in Psalm 19 bespeak its divine origin by their modern perspective on scientific truth. It is important to understand the witness of God in creation, but far more important to understand the Word!

In verses 7–9, there is a remarkable eighteen-fold testimony of the nature and power of the Holy Scriptures. Note the following outline:

The Written Word of the Lord

What It Is	What It Does	Why It Can
Law (i.e., torah)	Converts	Perfect
Testimony	Instructs	Sure
Statutes (or "precepts")	Rejoices	Right
Commandment	Enlightens	Pure
Fear	Endures	Clean
Judgments	Makes Righteous	True

David had only a small part of the complete Scriptures in his day, and yet he could make such statements concerning them. Far more was available to the apostle Paul when he said: "All Scripture is given by inspiration of God, and is profitable for doctrine, for reproof, for correction, for instruction in righteousness: That the man of God may be perfect; throughly furnished unto all good works" (2 Tim. 3:16–17).

Thus, combining the testimonies of David and Paul, "The law of the LORD is perfect . . . that the man of God may be perfect!" The man who knows the Scriptures is wealthier than the richest man on earth, because they are more to be desired than much fine gold. The most exquisite pleasures of life are nothing in comparison, for God's Word is sweeter than honey!

The Scriptures provide all necessary warning, lest we suffer loss and all necessary instruction, that we might earn great rewards. They impel us to seek cleansing even from sins of ignorance ("secret faults"), as well as to pray for strength against yielding to willful and presumptuous sins, or even the "great transgression" of final rejection of the Word of God itself. "Let them not have dominion over me," he prays, and the answer comes: "For sin shall not have dominion over you: for ye are not under the law, but under grace" (Rom. 6:14).

The final verse is a beautiful prayer, recognizing the necessary relation between the thoughts of our hearts and the words on our lips (compare Rom. 10:9–10; Col. 3:16; 1 Pet. 3:15; etc.). If the Word of God is the center of both, then both will indeed be acceptable to the One who will be both Redeemer and strong refuge to our souls.

Chapter 22

King at the Flood

Psalm 29

The 29th Psalm is often known as the "Psalm of the Voice of the Lord," because of the seven-times repeated occurrence of this phrase in its verses. Other than this rather obvious characteristic, however, the exact interpretation of the psalm has often been confusing to commentators. They have usually explained it as a poetic description by David of a great storm blowing inland from the Mediterranean Sea, but the details of this interpretation seem obscure, to say the least.

The real key to its meaning, however, is found in verse 10: "The Lord sitteth upon the flood." There are ten Hebrew words translated "flood" in the Old Testament, but the word here is *mabbul*, a word used uniquely to refer to the worldwide cataclysm in the days of Noah. In fact, this is the only place in the Bible where this word is used except in the story of the great flood in Genesis 6–9, where it is always used. Therefore, it is certain that the writer of Psalm 29 was speaking of that great cataclysmic storm, and no other.

Probably, as David was sitting at his upper palace window one day, gazing with awe at a great storm of wind and rain blowing in from the sea, raging from Hermon and Lebanon in the north to Kadesh in the south, he felt himself translated in the Spirit backwards in time to that great cataclysm of the past. In his vision, he saw and recorded these tremendous events accompanying the great flood.

Sons of the Mighty
Verses 1–2

Give unto the LORD, O ye mighty, give unto the LORD glory and strength.

Give unto the LORD the glory due unto his name; worship the LORD in the beauty of holiness.

The psalm opens with a scene in heaven picturing a mighty host around God's throne. The leader of the host calls out a great exhortation to "give unto the LORD glory and strength," addressing his appeal to "ye mighty." The original word is a compound, *bene elim*, "sons of the mighty." It is also used in Psalm 89:6 in a similar setting: "For who in the heaven can be compared unto the LORD? Who among the sons of the mighty can be likened unto the LORD?" Here the expression is *bene el*. Both, of course, are practically identical with *bene elohim*, translated "sons of God" in Genesis 6:1 and 4.

Thus, it becomes clear that the scene depicts the angelic "sons of God," who had been faithful to God at the time of the great flood, praising Him for His mighty victory over those rebellious sons of the mighty one. Through the vehicle of demon-possession, the rebellious angels had gained control of the bodies of both the sons and daughters of the sinful men of the primeval world, developing their progeny into evil giants who brought great violence on the earth. Such illicit possession of the bodies of human beings and attempted corruption of all human flesh had finally led God to bring that great judgment on the earth in the days of Noah (Gen. 6:1–13). The worship of the faithful angels takes place in the beautiful temple of God in heaven ("the beauty of holiness [the sanctuary]"), immediately following God's victory over the wicked angels and their human instruments.

The Voice of the Lord

The first two verses of the psalm are an exhortation to praise. The remainder of the psalm contains the response of praise, as the heavenly host recounts the judgments of the Lord in the great flood, culminating in victory over the wicked ones.

Seven times, the "voice of the Lord" speaks, each time resulting in mighty works in the earth. It is an interesting comparison to note that in the Genesis record of the flood there are exactly seven times when God spoke to Noah (Gen. 6:13, 7:1, 8:15, 9:1, 8, 12, and 17). In each case, however, though the scene was one of judgment, God's word to Noah was one of grace. Likewise, in a future time of worldwide judgment, there will again be a seven-fold voice from heaven: ". . . and when he cried, seven thunders uttered their voices" (Rev. 10:3). The message of the seven thunders is evidently also one of grace in the midst of judgment, but the precise message is not yet revealed (Rev. 10:1–7).

That there is a biblical connection between the seven thunders in Revelation and the seven voices of the Lord in Psalm 29 as indicated by the thunder accompanying the first of these:

Verse 3

The voice of the LORD is upon the waters: the God of glory thundereth: the LORD is upon many waters.

This was no doubt the first time the angry sound of thunder had ever echoed in God's beautiful world. There had never been a rainstorm before (Gen. 2:5), but suddenly "many waters" poured down from the "waters above the firmament" (Gen. 1:7) above the heavens and up from the great deep (Gen. 7:11–12).

Verse 4

The voice of the LORD is powerful; the voice of the LORD is full of majesty.

Tremendous reservoirs of energy were unleashed as the fountains of the great deep burst open and the giant floodgates in the skies released their torrents. These energies soon would devastate and level the globe.

The Hebrew word for "majesty" is the same as "honor," and the testimony is one of God's reaffirmed sovereignty. Satan, through his host of fallen spirits, with a multitude of corrupt men and women whose bodies they had possessed, and the race of giants they had fathered, had filled the earth with violent wickedness, but the longsuffering of God had finally been exhausted and the judgment had come.

Verses 5–6

The voice of the LORD breaketh the cedars; yea, the LORD breaketh the cedars of Lebanon.

He maketh them also to skip like a calf; Lebanon and Sirion like a young unicorn.

The mighty trees of the verdant antediluvian forests (which, in his vision, could only be described by David as like the cedars of Lebanon) were broken and uprooted by the rushing waters. With the vegetation all eventually washed away in great mats, the fields and hills were bare and easily eroded. Further, the erupting fountains of the deep had been followed by tremendous earthquakes and landslides; the mountains (like

David's Hermon and Sirion) were skipping like a calf and a young "unicorn" (or wild bull).

Verse 7

> The voice of the LORD divideth the flames of fire.

The Hebrew for "divideth" is actually "digs out." The picture is one of fiery lavas and burning vapors emerging from the depths. The rocks of the earth bear abundant witness to the vast amounts of igneous rocks that were laid down during the year of the flood.

Verse 8

> The voice of the LORD shaketh the wilderness; the LORD shaketh the wilderness of Kadesh.

After the overwhelming waters had uprooted the forests and eroded the hills, after the great earth movements and igneous flows had restructured the earth's crust, and then after new continents had arisen from the depths and the waters had retreated into new basins (Ps. 104:8–9), the land surfaces had become utterly barren. It was a wilderness, and David could think of no more apt comparison than to call it the desolate wilderness of Kadesh. But then the wilderness began to *shake*! The original language is graphic, describing a female in travail about to give birth to her young. It is the same word as "calve" in verse 9, and is often translated by "travail" or a similar term. The figure of speech depicts the barren wilderness as ready to bring forth its grass and trees again, the powerful voice of the Lord bringing new life to a dead world.

Verse 9

> The voice of the LORD maketh the hinds to calve, and discovereth the forests: and in his temple doth every one speak of his glory.

This final word from heaven enabled the land animal population, represented only by two survivors of each kind, to multiply rapidly to replenish the earth. Simultaneously, the quivering ground brought forth great trees once again, as the voice of the Lord "discovereth" (literally, "draws out") the forests.

"And in his temple doth everyone speak of his glory" (literally, "answer 'glory!' "). The old world was buried and the new world born despite the concerted rebellion of the legions of Satan and the world of mankind. The mere *voice* of the Lord was greater than all! And this was sufficient to warrant the great shout of "Glory!" from the heavenly host.

Strength for His People
Verses 10–11

The LORD sitteth upon the flood; yea, the LORD sitteth King for ever.

The LORD will give strength unto his people; the Lord will bless his people with peace.

Psalm 29 begins with a two-verse prologue introducing the angels of heaven, and finally concludes with a two-verse epilogue, giving their last chorus of praise and victory. The seven verses between record the seven-times sounded "voice of the Lord" and the global renovations proceeding therefrom.

In the epilogue, the angelic climactic chorus sounds forth: "The LORD sitteth upon the flood; yea, the LORD sitteth king forever" (verse 10). The word "sitteth" means literally "sits still." All the violence stirred up by men and devils could be quelled merely by God's spoken word; He did not even need to arise from His throne! The devastating cataclysm which destroyed the world of the antediluvians left God still seated calmly as the eternal King. His majesty unruffled, His throne secure against the wiles of Lucifer (Isa. 14:12–15). The Lord omnipotent reigneth!

And so the final verse of the psalm is a word of comfort and encouragement to all those of His creatures who trust Him. No matter what future attacks may be made against God's people by man or demon, "the LORD will give strength unto his people." Even in the future fiery judgment of the world, God is as able to keep His people through the fire as He was through the flood. "The LORD will bless his people with peace."

Several later psalms also refer back to the great flood. See the discussions, for example, in Psalm 46 in chapter 17, Psalm 74 in chapter 45, and, especially Psalm 104 in chapter 26.

The mighty waters, the great earth-shakings, the fiery lavas, the uprooted forests — these provide the true cause and explanation of the vast sedimentary rockbeds and fossil graveyards comprising the earth's crust all over the world. But the ultimate cause of these was the powerful voice of the Lord speaking judgment on the wickedness of the primeval world.

Chapter 23

Mighty Word of Creation

Psalm 33
Introduction

Psalm 33 is one of the only four anonymous psalms in Book I of the Psalms, the others being Psalms 1, 2, and 10. All the others (through Psalm 41) are attributed to David. Acts 4:25 attributes Psalm 2 to David, and it might seem appropriate that the 1st Psalm would have been David's as well. Psalm 10 seems clearly to be a continuation of Psalm 9, and Psalm 33 quite possibly ties in to Psalm 32. Also, Psalm 33 is attributed to David in the Septuagint Version. It is thus at least possible that David authored all the psalms of Book I, including this one.

The dominant theme of the 33rd psalm is the Word of the Lord, and it is appropriate that it contains 22 verses, corresponding to the number of letters in the Hebrew alphabet. Three tremendous statements are made concerning the Word. In verse 4, it is claimed that "the word of the Lord is right." According to verse 6, "By the word of the Lord were the heavens made, and all the host of them by the word of his mouth." Then, in verse 9 it says, "He spake, and it was done." God's Word, therefore, is *right* and *powerful* and *certain*!

In addition to a strong emphasis on the *Word* of God, Psalm 33 emphasizes the *works* of God. Its 22 verses divide naturally into four stanzas of four, five, six, and seven verses, respectively. Verses 1–4 contain an exhortation to praise the works of God; verses 5–9 constitute a testimony to God's work of creation; verses 10–15 are a testimony to God's work of providence; and verses 16–22 give a testimony to God's work of salvation.

Exhortation to Praise God's Works
Verses 1–4

Rejoice in the LORD, O ye righteous: for praise is comely for the upright.

Praise the LORD with harp: sing unto him with the psaltery and an instrument of ten strings.

Sing unto him a new song; play skillfully with a loud noise.

For the word of the LORD is right; and all his works are done in truth.

Verse 1 begins with a command which echoes the last verse of Psalm 32, exhorting the righteous to rejoice and praise the Lord, for praise (not boasting!) is comely for the one who has received the Lord's righteousness. The second and third verses call for praise in song accompanied by those who can play "skillfully with a loud noise" (not just noisily!). Two musical instruments are specifically mentioned, the "harp" (probably the four-stringed lyre) and the "psaltery . . . an instrument of ten strings." To these today could no doubt be added the many-stringed piano as well as other instruments (see Ps. 150).

The exhortation, furthermore, is to sing a *new* song, one with a glorious theme not before sung in the psalms. For the first time, the grand work of fiat creation is to be extolled, giving honor to the Creator. This is the first of six "new songs" in the Book of Psalms (the others are in Ps. 40:3, 96:1, 98:1, 144:9, and 149:1).

The reason for such rejoicing and praise and singing is given, finally, in verse 4. "For the word of the LORD is right; and all his works are done in truth." What a testimony! "I esteem all thy precepts concerning all things to be right" (Ps. 119:128). His works are done, literally, in "steadfastness." They will stand forever because they are true. Whether or not we understand, we can have absolute confidence that whatever God says is right and whatever He does will stand, for the simple reason that He is God.

God's Work of Creation
Verses 5–9

He loveth righteousness and judgment: the earth is full of the goodness of the LORD.

By the word of the LORD were the heavens made; and all the host of them by the breath of his mouth.

He gathereth the waters of the sea together as an heap: he layeth up the depth in storehouses.

Let all the earth fear the LORD: let all the inhabitants of the world stand in awe of him.

For he spake, and it was done; he commanded, and it stood fast.

In these verses is found perhaps the strongest affirmation of fiat creation in the Bible. After an introductory acknowledgment that the entire earth manifests God's goodness (literally "mercy"), as well as the righteousness and judgment which His nature loves, the Psalmist harks back to the record of its very creation, when God created it with these purposes in His heart.

Note that it was not just by the Lord, but by the *Word* of the Lord that the heavens were made. This, of course, is a reference back to the account of creation in Genesis 1, in which there are no less than 17 references to God speaking. It further anticipates the manifestation of God in and to His creation, under the name of The Word (John 1:1–3) by whom all things were made and who became flesh, as the incarnate Son of God. In the New Testament, of course, Jesus Christ is clearly recognized as the Creator (Col. 1:16; Heb. 1:2; Eph. 3:9). Reference to the Word of God as the one by whom the heavens and earth were originally made is also found in 2 Peter 3:5 and Hebrews 1:3.

The "*heavens*" constitute the space component of the space-mass-time universe, and the "host of them" include both the stars (Jer. 33:22) and the angels (2 Chron. 18:18), both of which are *in* the heavens. All were made by the "breath of his mouth," but this phrase might very well be translated the "spirit of his mouth" (the Hebrew *ruach* is translated either "wind," or "breath," or "spirit" depending on context), thus reflecting the work of the Spirit as described in Genesis 1:2.

Verse 7 is a reference to the "deep" of Genesis 1:2 (same word as "depth") and the "gathering together of the waters" is a reference both to the waters under and over the firmament (Gen. 1:6–8) and the gathering of the waters under the firmament into "seas" (Gen. 1:9–10). These were laid up in "storehouses," to provide the antediluvian hydrologic cycle and the wonderful climatic environment prepared originally by God for the created world. In another sense, these waters were also stored up to serve as waters of judgment in the great flood (2 Pet. 3:6) when the "fountains" of this "great deep" were broken up (Gen. 7:11). It was probably in reference to this event that the Psalmist in verse 8 exhorted the inhabitants of the earth to fear and stand in awe of the Lord.

Finally, verse 9 says, literally, "For he spake, and it *was*; he commanded, and it *stood*." There was no process of creation, no time involved. God's Word is omnipotent, and when He speaks in creative power, the result is instantaneous. There is obviously no possibility of "evolution" in such an act of fiat creation. The entities created by God were created complete and mature and functioning right from the start. "For he commanded and they were created. He hath also stablished them for ever and ever" (Ps. 148:5–6).

God's Work of Providence
Verses 10–15

The LORD bringeth the counsel of the heathen to nought: he maketh the devices of the people of none effect.

The counsel of the LORD standeth for ever, the thoughts of his heart to all generations.

Blessed is the nation whose God is the LORD; and the people whom he hath chosen for his own inheritance.

The LORD looketh from heaven; he beholdeth all the sons of men.

From the place of his habitation he looketh upon all the inhabitants of the earth.

He fashioneth their hearts alike; he considereth all their works.

The next six verses of Psalm 33 stress God's overruling sovereignty in the world He had created, especially among the nations that had been established after the flood. Though these nations had gone in their own ways, ignoring their maker, He was still in control and was working especially through His chosen nation. Verses 10 and 11 contrast the "counsel of the nations" (that is their doctrines and philosophy) which is brought to nought, with the "counsel of the LORD" which stands forever. The "devices of the people" will be made of no effect, but "the thoughts" (same word as "devices") of God's heart will endure to all generations. All of man's vaunted knowledge and wisdom are foolish and will come to nothing (1 Cor. 2:6, 3:19), and it is therefore futile for us to spend years being educated in this wisdom rather than in the true wisdom of God according to the Scriptures.

Verses 12–15 give assurance that God indeed is in control. He "beholds all," according to verse 13; He "fashions all" and "understands all" in verse 15. He is thus omnipresent, omnipotent, and omniscient. In sovereign grace, therefore, He "chooses" His own (verse 12). Even though He chose a particular nation, however, He still deals with all the nations. The Noahic covenant (Gen. 9:6, 9) is still in effect (Rom. 13:1; Acts 17:26), and God still rules the nations through His divinely established institution of human government.

God's Work of Salvation
Verses 16–22

There is no king saved by the multitude of an host: a mighty man is not delivered by much strength.

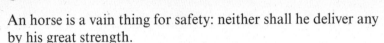

An horse is a vain thing for safety: neither shall he deliver any by his great strength.

Behold, the eye of the LORD is upon them that fear him, upon them that hope in his mercy;

To deliver their soul from death, and to keep them alive in famine.

Our soul waiteth for the LORD; he is our help and our shield.

For our heart shall rejoice in him, because we have trusted in his holy name.

Let thy mercy, O LORD, be upon us, according as we hope in thee.

The final section of Psalm 33 extols the third of God's great works, that of salvation, or deliverance. First, the Psalmist in verses 16 and 17 stresses that real salvation cannot be found in those things to which most men look. It is not to be found in the "multitude of an host," that is, not by *military power*. Neither is it in "much strength," or *manpower*. Also, a horse is "a vain thing for safety" (literally, "salvation"), so it is not in *horsepower*.

Salvation is only in the Lord and His power! "The eye of the LORD is upon them that fear him" (verse 18). The "eyes of the LORD" symbolize the care and protection of the Lord. They are "upon the righteous" (Ps. 34:15), and they "preserve knowledge" (Prov. 22:12). They are "in every place, beholding the evil and the good" (Prov. 15:3); and "all the goings" of man (Prov. 5:21). They "run to and fro throughout the whole earth, to shew himself strong in the behalf of them whose heart is perfect toward him" (2 Chron. 16:9).

God's great deliverance is received by those who "hope in his mercy" — that is who believe in His grace. To these, He supplies all the material needs of life (verse 19), as well as guidance ("help") and protection ("shield") to those who "wait for the LORD" (verse 20). Furthermore, true joy in salvation is shared by all who trust in His name (verse 21).

In verse 5, it was noted that the entire earth, as created, was "full of the goodness of the LORD." The word "goodness" is the same word as "mercy" in verses 18 and 22, often translated "loving-kindness." The "goodness" with which the beautiful earth was clothed when God pronounced it "very good" (Gen. 1:31) is also "upon us, according as we hope in thee." That "hope" (verses 18, 22) is merely confident faith in God's Word. And since the Word of the Lord is right and powerful and sure, our hope in Him is secure forever!

Chapter 24

The Days of Our Years

Psalm 90

The 90th Psalm is probably the oldest of all the psalms. According to the received text, David is recognized as author of 75 of the psalms, Asaph as author of 12, and Ethan and Heman of 1 each. No definite author is listed for 60 of them, although it is probable that David wrote many of these. This 90th psalm, however, is ascribed to Moses, the man of God. (Because of similarity in phraseology, it is quite possible that Moses also wrote Psalm 91.) It is placed as the opening chapter in Book IV of the psalms (the Book of Psalms is divided into five books, beginning with Psalms 1, 42, 73, 90, and 107, respectively).

The Everlasting God
Verses 1–4

Lord, thou hast been our dwelling place in all generations.

Before the mountains were brought forth, or ever thou hadst formed the earth and the world, even from everlasting to everlasting, thou art God.

Thou turnest man to destruction; and sayest, Return, ye children of men.

For a thousand years in thy sight are but as yesterday when it is past, and as a watch in the night.

The setting seems to be at the entrance to the Promised Land towards the very end of Moses' life. The end of his writings had been "the blessing, wherewith Moses the man of God blessed the children of Israel before his death" (Deut. 33:1). Then, perhaps, followed this psalm, "a prayer of Moses the man of God" (Ps. 90, superscript). Moses had studied the record of all the patriarchs, from Adam through Jacob, and had edited and recorded them in final form in the Book of Genesis, and no doubt they had made a profound impression on him. Then he had recorded all of God's dealings with himself and the Children of Israel, both in Egypt and in the wilderness, and he was keenly aware of the unity and comprehensiveness of God's plan in history for mankind everywhere in all ages. It is this big picture which dominates the 90th psalm.

And what a picture! Wherever God was, that's where home was! Whether in the Garden of Eden, in the violent world of the antediluvians, in the ark during the great flood, in a tent in the land of Canaan, in bondage in Egypt, or following the cloud in the wilderness, Jehovah, himself, had always been their abiding place. In this life, the people of God are pilgrims and have no certain dwelling place, for they seek a city with foundations, whose builder and maker is God (Heb. 11:8–14).

Moses, recalling how God had "formed the earth and the world" (that is, the basic elements of the ground and also the beautiful inhabitable cosmos made from those elements), stressed that God existed prior to all *creation*. Only in the Bible do we find such a revelation of God's eternal pre-existence. All other religious "Scriptures" begin with eternal matter in some form, and thus do not attempt to explain real creation. The true God, however, was before all things. The Creator, of course, is none other than Christ himself — the "Alpha and Omega" (Rev. 1:8).

After the creation came the Fall, and then the Curse. Moses recalls this sad event as well: "Thou turnest man to destruction [literally 'crumbling' — that is, the 'dust' of Gen. 3:19]: and sayest, Return, ye children of men [or, literally 'Adam']." Though God had formed all things, even the human body, from the dust of the earth, they would all eventually return back to the dust. This principle of "crumbling" is now known to be so universally true as to be recognized scientifically as the *law* of increasing entropy, or disorder — one of the two basic laws of science.

For a long time after the Curse, however, men continued to live almost a thousand years before dying. The average age of the antediluvian patriarchs (excluding Enoch, who did not die at all) was 912 years, and one of them (Methuselah) lived 969 years. But their days had been almost forgotten by the time of Moses' generation. Even a man who could live a thousand years would be forgotten soon after he was gone. And in God's sight, such a tremendous span of time (as humans measure time) would be trivial indeed. Life spans had greatly deteriorated after the flood, so that Moses, at age 120 years, was 60 years older than any of his contemporaries. All of those who would have been older than 60 years of age had died in the wilderness (see Num. 14:29, 34 and Deut. 34:7). Because of all this, Moses was profoundly impressed with the ephemeral nature of

human longevity in contrast to God's timelessness.

Men today casually discuss geological dates in terms of millions and billions of years, but this is mere evolutionary vacuity. Such dates are meaningless in terms of man's experience. He can barely recall events of his own earlier years, and historical data of only two millennia ago are regarded as *ancient* history. The human mind cannot begin to comprehend the concept of a million or a billion years.

This verse (Ps. 90:4) has often been combined with 2 Peter 3:8 by modern commentators, and then both used to justify the notion that the six days of creation in Genesis correspond to the evolutionary ages of geology. Such strained exegesis is contradicted by the contexts of both verses, and there is no good evidence that Peter was even referring to Moses' statement at all. In Psalm 90, Moses is contrasting the brevity of man's life — even those antediluvian men who lived almost a thousand years — with the changeless and ageless Creator.

Finite, Mortal Man
Verses 5–11

Thou carriest them away as with a flood; they are as a sleep: in the morning they are like grass which groweth up.

In the morning it flourisheth, and groweth up; in the evening it is cut down, and withereth.

For we are consumed by thine anger, and by thy wrath are we troubled.

Thou hast set our iniquities before thee, our secret sins in the light of thy countenance.

For all our days are passed away in thy wrath; we spend our years as a tale that is told.

The days of our years are threescore years and ten; and if by reason of strength they be fourscore years, yet is their strength labour and sorrow; for it is soon cut off, and we fly away.

Who knoweth the power of thine anger? Even according to thy fear, so is thy wrath.

This contrast is further stressed in the next section of the psalm. The span of human life is first likened to the debris carried away by a flood (probably the antediluvians carried off by the great Noahic deluge along with the massive plant and animal remains now preserved as fossils in the sedimentary rocks), then to a dream in a single night's sleep, and then to the grass that grows and soon withers. Indeed, "all flesh is like grass" (Isa. 40:6–8; 1 Pet. 1:24; Ps. 103:14, 16), ever since the curse came on the world.

The problem is not biological, but theological. Gerontologists will never reverse the process of aging and death by scientific research, though they may be able to retard it slightly. As long as there is sin, there will be death "for we are consumed by thine anger." There are two aspects to sin, "iniquities" — that is, overt acts of sin — and "secret sins" — that is, the sin-nature which impels us to sin even when we are not consciously sinning. Both aspects are exposed "in the light of thy countenance."

Every babe entering the world inherits such a nature, and thus "*all* our days" are spent in the presence of God's wrath. Consequently, in contrast to God's unending life and to His original purpose for man's life, "we spend our years as a sigh." In the Authorized Version, the rendering is "tale that is told," but the word is, simply, "sigh," very brief and conscious of futility. As James says, "For what is your life? It is even a vapour, that appeareth for a little time, and then vanisheth away," (James 4:14). As Paul says, "For the creature was made subject to vanity [that is, 'futility']" (Rom. 8:20).

Then, in the midst of these melancholy thoughts, Moses pens his classic lament: "The days of our years are threescore years and ten." Though Moses himself was 120 years old, and though he had been contemplating the golden age of the past when men lived a thousand years, all others of his own people were only 60 years of age or younger. He knew the normal life span could never again greatly exceed 70 years, as long as the present world order prevailed. Under some conditions, men might live to be 80 years of age or a little older, but such old age would involve little but "labour and sorrow," exactly as God had told Adam himself (Gen. 3:17, 19). Very soon, at best, the body would be "cut off," and the spirit would "fly away."

Men fear growing old and dying, and do all they can to avoid or delay it, often complaining against God because of it, forgetting that it all results from God's curse on sin. The great power of God's wrath and anger, though not recognized or understood by lost men, is ample reason to fear the Lord, and men should be instructed by the very fact of the mysterious and unnatural brevity of their own lives to seek God's forgiveness and guidance.

True Wisdom and Salvation
Verses 12–17

So teach us to number our days, that we may apply our hearts unto wisdom.

Return, O LORD, how long? And let it repent thee concerning thy servants.

O satisfy us early with thy mercy; that we may rejoice and be glad all our days.

Make us glad according to the days wherein thou hast afflicted us, and the years wherein we have seen evil.

Let thy work appear unto thy servants, and thy glory unto their children.

And let the beauty of the LORD our God be upon us: and establish thou the work of our hands upon us; yea, the work of our hands establish thou it.

The remaining verses of Psalm 90 constitute a prayer for God's complete salvation. Man is helpless and dying, but God is mighty and eternal. Only He can grant true wisdom and endless life. Since our days are few, and since even those few days are passed in the presence of God's wrath and are full of labor and sorrow, we need to "number our days in order to acquire a heart of wisdom." As already acknowledged, the number of the days of man's years corresponds only to 70 years, and probably not more than 50 years (18,000 days) of these can be used for productive work for God. How urgent, therefore, to use each of these days effectively.

O that they were wise, that they understood this, that they would consider their latter end! (Deut. 32:29).

See then that ye walk circumspectly, not as fools, but as wise, Redeeming the time because the days are evil (Eph. 5:15–16).

True wisdom is found only in God, himself, as well as true salvation from life's futility. "But of him are ye in Christ Jesus, who of God is made unto us wisdom, and righteousness, and sanctification, and redemption" (1 Cor. 1:30).

At the time God pronounced the Curse, He also made the first promise of a coming Savior who would make all things right again (Gen. 3:15).

But the ages have passed, and the Curse seems more bitter than ever. Moses cries out: "How long, O LORD?" The promise had seemed long delayed even to Moses. In our day, the promised deliverance from the Curse has been delayed yet another 3,000 years, but the apostle Peter reminds us that the "long-suffering of our Lord is salvation" (2 Pet. 3:15).

Moses climaxes his prayer with seven specific requests to the Lord, which we could well make our own in these latter days:

1. "Let it repent thee concerning thy servants." As Paul says, "The earnest expectation of the [creation] waiteth for the manifestation of the

sons of God. . . . We ourselves groan within ourselves, waiting for the adoption, to wit, the redemption of our body" (Rom. 8:19–23).

2. "O satisfy us early [i.e., 'in the morning'] with thy mercy; that we may rejoice and be glad all our days." Salvation and true happiness are gifts of God's grace, but those who receive it early may pass all their days — even though man's days are days of sorrow under God's curse — as days of joy, "as sorrowful, yet always rejoicing" (2 Cor. 6:10).

3. "Make us glad according to the days wherein thou hast afflicted us, and the years wherein we have seen evil." In verse 4 ("a thousand years are as yesterday"), verse 9 ("our days are passed away in thy wrath . . . our years as a sigh"), and verse 10 ("the days of our years . . . are labour and sorrow"), man's days and years are brought together. Days stretch into years and years into thousands of years, and yet God still delays. Some day, however, He will come, and "Our light affliction, which is but for a moment, worketh for us a far more exceeding and eternal weight of glory" (2 Cor. 4:17).

4. "Let thy work appear unto thy servants." If only we could understand the world and man as God sees them, what a transformation it would make in our lives. Indeed, his servants redeemed from sin themselves constitute the greatest of the mighty works of God (Eph. 2:10).

5. "And thy glory unto their children." Even more important than to understand the work of God is to comprehend the glory of God. When we see Him as He is, we shall finally become *like* He is (1 John 3:2).

6. "Let the beauty of the LORD our God [i.e., 'Jehovah our Elohim'] be upon us." When His "workmanship" (literally, His "poem," His great masterwork — Eph. 2:10) is complete in us, we — like His completed physical creation — will be "very good" (Gen. 1:31). Three of the great names of God appear in this psalm — *Elohim* (verse 2), *Jehovah* (verse 3), and then *Jehovah our Elohim* in the final verse. As all the fullness of God dwells bodily in Christ (Col. 2:9), so all His love and beauty shall become ours through Christ.

7. "And establish thou the work of our hands upon us." In this life it is vital first that we recognize *God's* work (verse 16) and, then, that He order and establish *our* work. It must be in this order, of course. "Work out your own salvation with fear and trembling. For it is God which worketh in you both to will and to do of his good pleasure" (Phil. 2:12–13).

Therefore, although we must in this present age live under the curse, with its bondage to sin and death, we can — like Moses — look by faith into the Promised Land across the Jordan, and thereby live by faith victoriously, even in this present world.

Chapter 25

Angels and Dragons

Psalm 91
Background

The 91st psalm is certainly one of the mountain-peak chapters of the Bible, speaking to both heart and mind, and assuring the godly believer of God's blessing and protection under all circumstances. Not even the fiery dragon can prevail against God's almighty angels! Psalm 91 has the unique distinction of having been quoted (really misquoted!) by none other than Satan himself when he was tempting Christ, suggesting that this is really a section of Scripture that gives Satan intense concern and which he would like most to destroy if possible.

No author is listed for this psalm, but it is at least plausible that it may originally have come from Moses. The preceding psalm (90) has always been attributed to Moses, and there are certain common themes and terms in the two psalms as well as indications that the miraculous deliverance of the Israelites from Egypt was in the mind of the author as he wrote.

The first verse of Psalm 90, for example, speaks of the Lord as our "dwelling place." The same Hebrew word is used in Psalm 91:9, speaking of making the Lord our "habitation." The brevity of human life is stressed in Psalm 90, and then Psalm 91 assures the trusting believer "long life," probably meaning eternal life. The references to deliverance from armies and plagues in Psalm 91 are most understandable in light of God's power as shown against the Egyptians. Although it is not possible to say for certain that Moses wrote the psalm, it at least makes it beautifully understandable to regard it as Moses' own *personal* testimony, supplementing his psalm for the nation as a whole, so to speak, in Psalm 90. Even if this is true, of course, it can likewise be appropriated as the personal experience and testimony of any believer.

Invitation to Trust the Lord

Psalm 91 seems to be divided into four main sections, as follows:

1. Verse 1 is an invitation and testimony from a witness, perhaps the Holy Spirit, himself; spoken in the third person, offering God's salvation to that one who will trust Him.
2. Verse 2 is the acceptance of that invitation and a statement of faith by the responding believer (Moses originally, perhaps).
3. Verses 3 through 13, the bulk of the psalm, is the testimony of assurance and guidance given to the new convert, again in the third person.
4. Verses 14 through 16 are a confirming promise from God, himself, given in the first person directly to the believer, assuring him of the validity of the great promises made by the Witness in verses 1 and 3–13, and then extending them even more.

Verse 1

He that dwelleth in the secret place of the most High shall abide under the shadow of the Almighty.

The first section, consisting of one verse only, is a beautiful promise which draws the listener directly to the heart of God. "He that sits down [literal meaning of 'dwelleth' here] in the secret place of the most High [Hebrew *Elyon*] shall pass the night under the shadow of the Almighty [Hebrew *Shaddai*]." God is introduced under two of His less-used names, both of which stress His ability to protect and sustain the believer. The "Most High" is over all. The "Almighty" is under all, providing sustenance and support (the word *Shaddai* is derived from the Hebrew *shad*, meaning "breast.").

The "secret place" is actually the "hiding place." The picture is of one finding rest and protection and nourishment in God's bosom like a helpless child, during the dark and dangerous night of life in a world under Satan's control. It is the same word as in Psalm 119:114: "Thou art my hiding place and my shield." Therefore, as the apostle Paul says, "Set your affection on things above, not on things on the earth. For ye are dead, and your life is hid with Christ in God" (Col. 3:2–3).

Acceptance of the Lord
Verse 2

I will say of the LORD, he is my refuge and my fortress: my God; in him will I trust.

Such a wonderful promise should certainly not be refused. Accordingly, the believer does respond, accepting the gracious invitation: "I will say of the LORD [Hebrew *Jehovah*], he is my refuge and my fortress: my God [Hebrew *Elohim*]; in him will I trust."

Two little-used names of God were used in the first verse, but the two most-used names appear in the second verse. God is all, and in all, and it takes many names to adequately describe His attributes, many figures of speech to describe His relation to the believer. The figure of the refuge and fortress would certainly be meaningful to Moses. In his last word to the tribes, he had told them: "The eternal God is thy refuge and underneath are the everlasting arms" (Deut. 33:27). Though neither the Children of Israel in the wilderness nor the Christian pilgrim in this age could ever dwell securely in a literal fortress, the Lord himself surrounds them, that "we might have a strong consolation, who have fled for refuge to lay hold upon the hope set before us: which hope we have as an anchor of the soul, both sure and steadfast" (Heb. 6:18–19). With such promises as surety, the seeking soul can sit down in confident faith. "In him will I trust!"

The Promise of Divine Protection
Verses 3–13

Surely he shall deliver thee from the snare of the fowler, and from the noisome pestilence.

He shall cover thee with his feathers, and under his wings shalt thou trust: his truth shall be thy shield and buckler.

Thou shalt not be afraid for the terror by night; nor for the arrow that flieth by day;

Nor for the pestilence that walketh in darkness; nor for the destruction that wasteth at noonday.

A thousand shall fall at thy side, and ten thousand at thy right hand; but it shall not come nigh thee.

Only with thine eyes shalt thou behold and see the reward of the wicked.

Because thou hast made the LORD, which is my refuge, even the most High, thy habitation;

There shall no evil befall thee, neither shall any plague come nigh thy dwelling.

For he shall give his angels charge over thee, to keep thee in all thy ways.

They shall bear thee up in their hands, lest thou dash thy foot against a stone.

Thou shalt tread upon the lion and adder: the young lion and the dragon shalt thou trample under feet.

Again the divine witness speaks, giving assurance of all needed protection and guidance to the new believer in verses 3 through 13. The figures seem often directly taken from the actual experiences of Moses and the Children of Israel in Egypt and the wilderness, where they were not symbols at all, but real dangers!

They had been like helpless chicks, but He had said, "Ye have seen what I did unto the Egyptians and how I bare you on eagles' wings, and brought you unto myself" (Exod. 19:4). Note also Deuteronomy 32:9–13, etc. So He promises: "He shall deliver thee from the snare of the fowler and the deadly pestilence." He also had said to Moses, "If thou wilt . . . keep all his statutes, I will put none of these diseases upon thee which I have brought upon the Egyptians; for I am the LORD that healeth thee" (Exod. 15:26).

Continuing with the figure of the great eagle, "He shall cover thee with his feathers, and under his wings shalt thou trust." But then appears an important clarification. This is no mere sentimentalism, as is true of so much "deeper-life" teaching. "His truth shall be thy shield and buckler!" This implies that Satan's lies will be his greatest weapons against the believer. He is the great deceiver, and his primeval humanistic lie persuading man to think he is able to play God is still his most effective tool.

But God's promises are inscripturated promises, and it is the written Word that still provides the Christian's defense, just as it was when Christ himself defeated Satan who had misquoted this very psalm (see below). "I have given them thy word," Jesus said. "Sanctify them through thy truth; thy word is truth" (John 17:14–17). "Stand therefore, having your loins girt about with truth . . . Above all, taking the shield of faith, wherewith ye shall be able to quench all the fiery darts of the wicked" (Eph. 6:14–16).

In verse 5 is promised courage both day and night, against the daytime arrows of the enemy and the unknown dangers of the night. To the Children of Israel, "The LORD went before them by day in a pillar of a cloud, to lead them the way; and by night in a pillar of fire, to give them light; to go by day and night" (Exod. 13:21). Neither midnight pestilence nor noonday attack could harm them (verse 6). "A thousand shall fall at thy side, and ten thousand at thy right hand; but it shall not come nigh thee" (verse 7). The armies of Moses had experienced this very thing in reverse when they had rebelled against God. "How should one chase a thousand, and two put ten thousand to flight, except their Rock had sold them, and the LORD had shut them up?" (Deut. 32:30). But

God is an impregnable refuge and fortress to His trusting ones!

"Only with thine eyes shalt thou behold and see the reward of the wicked" (verse 8). This also had been their experience. "And Moses said unto the people, Fear ye not, stand still, and see the salvation of the LORD. . . . And Israel saw that great work which the LORD did upon the Egyptians: and the people feared the LORD" (Exod. 14:13–31). "And to you who are troubled, rest with us, when the Lord Jesus shall be revealed from heaven with his mighty angels; In flaming fire taking vengeance on them that know not God, and that obey not the gospel of our Lord Jesus Christ" (2 Thess. 1:7–8). The mighty plagues and miracles by which God routed the ancient Egyptians are firmly anchored as facts of history, regardless of the skepticism of modern scientists. The very existence of Israel is proof of God's power to preserve His own.

In verse 9, there is a brief parenthesis, reminding the believer again just why God will bless him so. "Because thou hast made [referring back to his confession of faith in verse 2] the LORD 'My refuge' [quoting what he had said], the most High thy dwelling place." How infinite are the resources of the man who truly trusts God!

Continuing his assurances, the witness promises: "There shall no evil befall thee, neither shall any plague come nigh thy dwelling." Because, of course, that dwelling place is God himself! In Egypt, during the awful plagues on the Egyptians, neither the flies nor the murrain, nor the boils, nor the hail, nor the thick darkness, nor the death angel entered the dwellings or fields of the Children of Israel (Exod. 8:22, 9:6, 11, 26, 10:23, 11:7).

But how is it that the Lord places such marvelous protection around His people? It is through His mighty angels!

"For he shall give his angels charge over thee, to keep thee in all thy ways. They shall bear thee up in their hands, lest thou dash thy foot against a stone" (verses 11–12).

There does exist "an innumerable company of angels" (Heb. 12:22), that "excel in strength" (Ps. 103:20), whose very purpose is "to minister for them who shall be heirs of salvation" (Heb. 1:14). "The angel of the Lord encampeth round about them that fear him, and delivereth them" (Ps. 34:7).

There is no ground for presumption in all these glorious promises, of course. Such angelic protection is conditioned on our making the Most High our habitation and making His truth our shield and buckler. There is no safer place in the cosmos than in the center of God's will as recognized through faith in His word, but there is darkness and pestilence and fearfulness outside.

And when it is time for the believer finally to enter into the light of

God's personal presence (not just the *shadow* of the Almighty!), then these very angels will accompany him through the valley of death and translate him in his spiritual body through the heavens to Christ's throne (Luke 16:22; 2 Cor. 5:8).

These verses (Ps. 91:11–12) are the verses which Satan used unsuccessfully in trying to persuade Christ to cast himself down from the pinnacle of the temple (Matt. 4:5–7; Luke 4:9–12). But the great deceiver, true to his character, misquoted and distorted God's words, just as he had done long before with Eve. This time, he omitted the key words "in all thy ways." Angels would indeed keep Him "in all thy ways," but Christ's ways were not Satan's ways! His answer, "Thou shalt not tempt the Lord thy God," shows that faith in God's promise is no ground for presumption and boastful display.

So will angels today "keep" us in all our ways, but these ways must please the Lord. "In all thy ways acknowledge him, and he shall direct thy paths" (Prov. 3:6).

The next verse (13) climaxes this section, and indicates why Satan desired so urgently to destroy Christ with his temptation. "Thou shalt tread upon the lion and adder: the young lion and dragon shalt thou trample under feet." This also is a promise for protection against the most dangerous animals — even dragons. This word (Hebrew *tannin*) actually means "dragon," not "snake," as is evident from its other occurrences. It most likely refers to some extinct reptile such as the dinosaur, which had no doubt survived the flood long enough to be well known to the ancient world. Other references to dragons in the Bible and in ancient traditions all over the world, as well as to *behemoth* and *leviathan* (see, especially, Job 40 and 41), and also to the dinosaur pictographs made by early tribesmen, all confirm the implication (evolutionists' claims notwithstanding) that men and dinosaurs once lived contemporaneously.

In any case, the terminology here evidently goes beyond the actual trampling and slaying of lions and reptilian monsters. Genesis 3:15, the great promise of a future crushing of Satan, that old serpent, by the "seed of the woman," was probably in Moses' mind as he penned these words. These are, perhaps, among Moses' last words, just as Genesis was the first book he had compiled and recorded, and such a thought would be most appropriate at this point. Not only would the Lord protect his people against all their enemies, He would eventually destroy the greatest enemy of all — that old Serpent, the roaring lion, the great dragon, the one who had opposed God and His plan through the ages. And in anticipation of that great victory, we can, through His power, defeat the enemy in his temporal attacks against us even now. "And the God of peace shall bruise Satan under your feet shortly" (Rom. 16:20).

God's Personal Assurance
Verses 14–16

Because he hath set his love upon me, therefore will I deliver him: I will set him on high, because he hath known my name.

He shall call upon me, and I will answer him: I will be with him in trouble; I will deliver him, and honor him.

With long life will I satisfy him, and shew him my salvation.

In the final section of this great psalm, verses 14–16, God speaks directly to the believer, confirming the promises of the witness in the preceding verses. This is the explicit answer to the believer's confession of faith in verse 2.

"Because he hath set his love upon me, therefore will I deliver him; I will set him on high, because he hath known my name." Deliverance in response to real love— exaltation because of true knowledge! Moses had good reason to recognize the value of knowing God's holy name, because he had been introduced to Him under never-to-be-forgotten circumstances in the wilderness (Exod. 3:14–15).

Thus, not only does God assure the believer of physical deliverance, as had already been promised by the witness, but of glorification in heaven! In verse 15, He makes four more amazing promises: (1) the promise of answered prayer; (2) the promise of the presence of God himself, not of the protecting angels alone; (3) the promise to arm him, evidently with divine armor (this is a better translation than "deliver" in the King James Version: there are three different Hebrew words all translated "deliver" in this psalm, in verses 3, 14, and 15); (4) the promise finally to honor him. It is a testimony of amazing grace that the God of all holiness should save a sinner, but that He should honor him is yet more amazing!

In the very last verse is the climax of all that has gone before. "With long life will I satisfy him." The phrase "long life" is really "length of days," and the context indicates the meaning really to be forever. It is, in fact, so translated in Psalm 23:6 — "I will dwell in the house of the LORD for ever." The believer is promised everlasting life as the satisfaction of his trust in God. Then, lastly, ". . . and shew him my salvation." God's great salvation for lost men has cost the shed blood of His own Son, so it is infinitely great, and He will show it to us in eternity. "That in the ages to come He might show the exceeding riches of his grace in his kindness toward us through Christ Jesus" (Eph. 2:7).

Chapter 26

Earth's Primeval Ages

Psalm 104

The 104th Psalm is one of the most important chapters in the Bible dealing with the early history of the world. It first sets forth some of the amazing truths concerning the very first events of creation week, then discusses the gap in history caused by the great flood, and finally the events establishing the post-flood world.

The Beginning of Creation
Verses 1–3

Bless the LORD, O my soul, O LORD my God, thou art very great; thou art clothed with honour and majesty:

Who coverest thyself with light as with a garment: who stretchest out the heavens like a curtain:

Who layeth the beams of his chambers in the waters: who maketh the clouds his chariot: who walketh upon the wings of the wind:

The psalm opens with the same exhortation with which the previous psalm had closed: "Bless the LORD, O my soul." As the writer — presumably David, who had also written Psalm 103 — began to catch a glimpse of the magnificent vision God was about to give him, he had to break out in an excited exclamation of praise, "O LORD my God, thou art very great; thou art clothed with honour and majesty." The glory of God was breaking in on his soul just as it had broken in on the universe in the beginning of the creation.

Now, the very first thing that happened in this created universe was the entrance of God himself into it, in the very act of creating it. This is the testimony of verse 2, "Who coverest [literally 'arrayest'] thyself with light as with a garment." He had been from eternity covered with honor and majesty, but now also clothed himself with the actual physical light which He created.

God, ever since, has been "dwelling in the light which no man can approach unto" (1 Tim. 6:16). The basic energy of matter and all phenomena in the physical universe is light energy. Indeed, "God is light" (1 John 1:5). Associated with God's light, radiating out from His presence in space and time, were the very space and time ("heaven" and "beginning") which He concurrently created (Gen. 1:1). He "stretchest out the heavens like a curtain." Verse 3 then alludes to the construction of God's actual "dwelling" in these heavens. Somewhere — no man knows where — is an actual location in the universe where God dwells in light. It is "far above all heavens" (Eph. 4:10) — beyond the atmospheric and sidereal heavens, but, nevertheless, somewhere in the universal "heaven" or "space," and it is there that God's essential glory is centered.

According to this passage, there are actual "chambers" (literally "upper chambers") erected upon "beams," all surrounded by mighty "waters." Furthermore, it is said that God rides upon a heavenly "chariot" composed of great clouds, probably clouds of intense glory, and that He "rides on the wings" of the wind (or, perhaps, the "Spirit," since "wind" and "spirit" are both translations of the Hebrew *ruach*).

The obvious question is whether these beams and chambers and waters and clouds are meant to be understood in their literal sense or, if not, exactly what they do symbolize. Similar figures are used to describe the environs of God's presence in other parts of Scripture (Ezek. 1:4, 24; Rev. 22:1; etc.).

A cardinal rule in Bible hermeneutics is to take any passage primarily in the sense intended by the writer (both human and divine), as determined from both its immediate context and the context of other related parts of Scripture. Normally, a passage would be taken literally unless a literal sense is not possible. When figures are used, it should be expected that the meaning of the figures is clarified elsewhere, since the purpose of the writer is communication, not confusion.

Since no explanation is offered here, we should conclude either that the description is literal, or else that the reality of the scene is so indescribable that man can only comprehend it in terms of an actual throne room where God dwells in His glory. In any case, the message clearly comes through that God's presence occupies a specific location somewhere in His created universe. The Lord Jesus Christ, at His ascension, was in a literal body when a literal "cloud" received Him in sight of His disciples.

He then ascended on into the distant heaven of God's dwelling where He "sat down" on the right hand of the Father (Mark 16:19; Col. 3:1; etc.).

On the other hand, the fact that God does have an upper chamber in the heavens where His presence is centered does not contradict the even greater fact of His omnipresence. Thus, in another sense, the entire cosmos is His dwelling place, and His glory can be especially illustrated to man in the heavens stretching over the earth like a curtain arrayed in light diffused around it from the sun and stars, and acting through the waters and winds and fires that sustain life on the earth.

Creation of the Angels
Verses 4–5

Who maketh his angels spirits; his ministers a flaming fire:

Who laid the foundations of the earth, that it should not be removed for ever.

According to the record here in Psalm 104, the next act after the creation of the space-time cosmos and the establishment of God's light-arrayed throne therein was the creation of the angels. "He maketh his angels spirits, and his ministers a flame of fire."

Some writers, knowing that the word "angel" means "messenger" in the Hebrew, and "spirit" is the same as "wind," have rendered this passage somewhat as follows: "He makes the wind his messenger and the fire his servant." This cannot be the full meaning, however, since the New Testament quotes this verse in such a way that it could only mean *angels* (see Heb. 1:7). Angels are mighty spirit beings, and they were evidently created right at this time.

This remarkable verse seems also to state that these servants of God are actually also composed of flaming fire, in addition to being spirits. This concept is beyond our naturalistic comprehension, but that is no reason for us to reject or spiritualize it prematurely. We do not know the nature of angels. Man was made of the natural chemical elements ("dust of the earth"), and is, therefore, subject to the electromagnetic and gravitational forces which control these elements. Angels have the remarkable ability to assume the *appearance* of men, including the actual biological and material substance (note Gen. 18:8), but they are normally invisible spirits, though quite real. They can "fly swiftly" (Dan. 9:21) from God's throne to earth when so commanded and are not limited by gravity or other natural forces. They are often, in Scripture, associated directly with the stars of heaven — which, of course, are orbs of flaming fire — and it may be that the essential structure of their "bodies" is analogous to that of the stars. In any case, they are often closely associated in the Bible with an appearance of fire (Gen. 3:24; 2 Thess. 1:7–8; etc.).

People often think that angels must have existed in some fourth dimensional state long before this present world was made. Indeed, they were certainly present before the earth received its *foundations*. Angels are seen as singing together and shouting for joy when God laid the earth's foundations (Job 38:4–7). Also, here in Psalm 104, verse 5 speaks of God laying the foundations of the earth right after He made the angels in verse 4. (In this verse, however, a better translation might be "He established the habitation of the earth" — that is, its position as a distinct body in space.)

On the other hand, the basic stuff of the physical space-mass-time cosmos must have been made before God made the angels, since angels exist in the cosmos. Furthermore, they were created specifically to minister to people (Heb. 1:14), and people live in the cosmos. The "earth" of Genesis 1:1 was originally "without form" (Gen. 1:2), so that it did not assume a definite shape or location until the Spirit of God began to "move in the presence of the waters." As the earth became spherical (as the force of gravity was activated) and energized when God called for "light," as recorded in Genesis 1:3 (and the electromagnetic force system began to function), it was still essentially a vast solution — or suspension — of elements in a mighty matrix of waters (note 2 Pet. 3:5). Not until the third day did solid earth material begin to appear in and above the waters. It is probably this series of divine acts that are referred to as "laying the foundations of the earth."

In any case, it is important to note that this foundation (or habitation) of the earth will not be removed forever. God had an eternal purpose for the earth when He created it, and though it would have to undergo a mighty cataclysm of water one day, and eventually an even greater cataclysm of fire (2 Pet. 3:10), it would be renewed in each case. Eventually, God, himself, would establish His eternal dwelling place on the renewed and perfected earth (Rev. 21:1–3).

The Coming of the Deluge
Verses 6–9

Thou coveredst it with the deep as with a garment: the waters stood above the mountains.

At thy rebuke they fled; at the voice of thy thunder they hasted away.

They go up by the mountains; they go down by the valleys unto the place which thou hast founded for them.

Thou hast set a bound that they may not pass over; that they turn not again to cover the earth."

Verses 6 through 9 of Psalm 104 obviously refer to the great deluge. Not until the very end of the psalm, however, is mention made of the effect of sin on the earth. The primary purpose of this psalm is simply to describe the mighty creative and providential acts of God in relation to the earth. Therefore, the narrative jumps directly from the act which called the earth out of the water to that which again plunged it beneath the waters.

"Thou coverest it with the deep as with a garment." This statement notes the contrast between God covering (literally "arraying") himself with light as with a garment, and his covering (literally "hiding" — a different Hebrew word) the earth as with a garment. One was for display of glory, the other for covering its shame.

"The waters stood above the mountains" (see Gen. 7:19–20), so the whole earth was inundated. The mountains so mentioned were the gentle mountains of the antediluvian topography; the next verse describes the uplift of the great and rugged mountains of the present world.

Verse 8 speaks of a gigantic earth movement which terminated the universal flood. The eruption of the "fountains of the great deep" and the pouring of huge torrents of rain on the earth from "the windows of heaven" (Gen. 7:11) had left great empty caverns in the earth's crust and piled tremendous beds of sediments in all the antediluvian seas, leaving the crust in a state of complex stress. Eventually, great faults and earth movements began to develop. The American Standard Version renders this verse accurately as follows: "The mountains rose, the valleys sank down." Great continental uplifts took place, with corresponding sinking of the basins. A great storm of wind (Gen. 8:1) and lightning and thunder (verse 7), none of which had ever been experienced by the earth before the flood, triggered the mighty orogenies.

Verse 9 then refers to God's promise to Noah never again to send the flood to destroy the earth (Gen. 9:11). Job 26:10 also refers to this promise: "He hath compassed the waters with bounds, until the day and night come to an end." The isostatic equilibrium is now sufficiently established so that the seabed can never rise against sufficiently to plunge waters over the mountains. Also, the waters remaining in the heavens and below the ground are no longer present in such quantities as to make possible a worldwide flood.

The World after the Flood

The last part of the 104th Psalm describes God's providential arrangements for the animals and men in the vastly changed post-flood world. Verses 10–15 speak of His provision of food and drink; verses 16–18 tell of His arrangements for dwelling-places; verses 19–23 describe His plans for their activities; verses 24–30 summarize His universal, providential care of all His creatures; and verses 31–35 constitute a statement of the divine purpose in creation and providence, with man's acceptable response in praise.

Verses 10–13

He sendeth the springs into the valleys, which run among the hills.

They give drink to every beast of the field: the wild asses quench their thirst.

By them shall the fowls of the heaven have their habitation, which sing among the branches.

He watereth the hills from his chambers: the earth is satisfied with the fruit of thy works.

The immediate need after the flood, for both men and animals, was survival. The world had been literally devastated by the great cataclysm and now would have to be repopulated under much harsher environmental conditions than had prevailed in the original creation. The first need was for a new water supply system. The waters of the flood were laden with debris and all kinds of sediments and dissolved chemicals, not to mention carcasses of dead animals and people drowned in the flood.

The deposited sand and mud, however, formed ideal filtration systems for purifying the waters. Accordingly, although most of the waters flowed into the newly formed ocean basins, scouring out drainageways and even canyons in the process, many of the waters percolated into the ground to form great subterranean waterways. At intervals these emerged as springs of pure water, thence forming permanent rivers in the new valleys. This provision is summarized in verse 10: "He sendeth the springs into the valleys, which run among the hills."

From the network of streams, "every beast of the field" would receive drink. Trees would thrive by them, in which the birds could live. The water table sustaining the streams would likewise support a covering of grasses and herbs, providing food for both the cattle and for man himself,

who would once again be able to till the ground and raise his crops.

Once the waters of the flood had drained into these underground aquifers, however, they would have to be maintained.

The antediluvian hydrologic cycle was evidently subterranean in nature, but the eruption of the fountains of the great deep had destroyed this mechanism. A new system would have to be instituted to water the earth, and this would have to be an atmospheric mechanism. "He watereth the hills from his [upper] chambers: the earth is satisfied with the fruit of thy works" (verse 13). There had been no rain in the primeval economy (Gen. 2:5) because of the worldwide equable warm temperatures maintained by the "waters above the firmament," but these were all precipitated at the flood. With worldwide temperature differentials now established, soon the present global atmospheric circulation was functioning and the remarkable atmospheric heat engine and water cycle were operating.

Provision of Food and Shelter
Verses 14–28

He causeth the grass to grow for the cattle, and herb for the service of man: that he may bring forth food out of the earth;

And wine that maketh glad the heart of man, and oil to make his face to shine, and bread which strengtheneth man's heart.

The trees of the Lord are full of sap; the cedars of Lebanon, which he hath planted;

Where the birds make their nests: as for the stork, the fir trees are her house.

The high hills are a refuge for the wild goats; and the rocks for the conies.

He appointed the moon for seasons: the sun knoweth his going down.

Thou makest darkness, and it is night: wherein all the beasts of the forest do creep forth.

The young lions roar after their prey, and seek their meat from God.

The sun ariseth, they gather themselves together, and lay them down in their dens.

Man goeth forth unto his work and to his labour until the evening.

O LORD, how manifold are thy works! In wisdom hast thou made them all: the earth is full of thy riches.

So is this great and wide sea, wherein are things creeping innumerable, both small and great beasts.

There go the ships: there is that leviathan, whom thou hast made to play therein.

These wait all upon thee; that thou mayest give them their meat in due season.

That thou givest them they gather: thou openest thine hand, they are filled with good.

Not only did the underground water table, the springs and rivers, and the intermittent rains make the lands green again, but they produced luscious fruits (symbolized by the vine and olive tree, producing fresh wine and oil) for man's happiness, and corn and wheat to produce bread for man's strength. God was also concerned about the animals. They had been preserved on Noah's ark, and were even included in the post-flood Noahic covenant (Gen. 9:9–10).

There is no doubt that God cares for all His creatures; not even a bird dies without His notice, according to the Lord Jesus (Matt. 10:29). Verses 16 through 23 of this psalm describe specifically God's provision for habitation and occupation of the animals after the flood.

First, there is mention of the growth of mighty forests, where the birds could dwell, then of high mountains and rocky terrains for certain animals which might otherwise be defenseless. Neither of these environments was suitable for human dwellings.

The day-night cycle established at creation had not been affected by the flood, as the sun and moon continued their appointed functions relative to the earth. God had made a specific promise to Noah after the flood that this would be so as long as the earth endured (Gen. 8:22). Man would labor to produce his own food during the day, while the carnivorous animals were resting in their lairs. The beasts of the forests, in turn, would go forth to seek their own prey at night. These are obviously general provisions, rather than inviolable laws.

The reference in verse 21 to lions seeking prey and God providing it for them indicates that the Edenic provision of only the "green herb" for animal food (Gen. 1:30) had been changed at the flood, at least for some animals. Similarly, man was, for the first time after the flood, permitted to eat meat (Gen. 9:3). The much harsher post-flood environment evidently dictated such provisions, both for the sake of maintaining appropriate ecological balances in nature, and also for providing the needed proteins for man and those animals that required them. This was because the herbs growing from the redeposited and minerally impoverished soils would no longer be able to provide them in adequate abundance and variety.

The Psalmist at this point (verse 24) interjects a doxology in gratitude for God's power and wisdom in designing and making such wonderful provisions for the post-flood world, even through the cataclysmic destruction of another system.

The next two verses shift from the animals on land and in the air to those in that "great and wide sea." This graphic phrase emphasizes the much more extensive oceans that were formed after the flood by the retreating waters. All the waters once above the firmament and in the great deep below the crust were now in "this great and wide sea." As the land is full of God's riches (literally "acquisitions" — verse 24), so the sea also houses innumerable other living creatures. The "creeping things" are especially mentioned, no doubt the marine invertebrates of all kinds and sizes which live deep under the surface.

On the surface of the ocean, along with the ships of man's commerce, occasionally appear great monsters of the deep, to whom the wide ocean is a playground. The mysterious *leviathan* is mentioned here (also in Ps. 74:14; Job 41:1; and Isa. 27:1). This was evidently some great marine reptile (not a crocodile, as some commentators say, since the descriptions of this animal in no way fit any crocodile or whale, nor does it fit any such ordinary modern animal. He is also described in these passages as a fire-breathing dragon, and as a great sea serpent. It seems likely that such animals are now extinct, but the great marine sedimentary beds deposited by the flood have yielded fossils of plesiosaurs or other marine reptiles which would well fit the description.

Verses 27 and 28 summarize the marvelous plans and provisions God has made for every single animal He created. Although "they gather" their food, it is really God who gives it to them. When their Maker opens His hand, they are "filled with good." And, as the Lord Jesus said to His followers, "ye are of more value than many sparrows" (Luke 12:7) in the care of a loving Heavenly Father.

The Problem of Suffering and Death
Verses 29–30

Thou hidest thy face, they are troubled: thou takest away their breath, they die, and return to their dust.

Thou sendest forth thy spirit, they are created: and thou renewest the face of the earth.

It is true, both in the animal kingdom and in human life, that although God has made provision for life, the world is still under the bondage of struggle and death. The effects of man's sin and God's curse (Gen. 3:17–19) still shackle the whole creation. The flood itself had constituted the greatest visitation of death on both human and animal realms the world has ever seen.

Verses 29 and 30 refer to this aspect of nature and, probably, in a specific sense, to the flood and its effects. When God, as it were, "hides His face" from His creatures, the divine power which sustains the life of the world (Acts 17:27–28) is cut off, and they are "troubled." Then their "breath" (or "spirit") departs and their bodies disintegrate to the elements from which they had been formed.

But, though individuals — both animals and men — die, yet life continues! Verse 30 is a remarkable testimony that God actually *creates* each new "spirit" by His own Spirit. This is primarily a reference to the "breath of life" which has been shared by both animals and men ever since the special creation of the entity of the *nephesh*, the "living creature" or "living soul," on the fifth day of creation (Gen. 1:21). In one sense, this breath or spirit is applied individually at each birth by that same Creator. The exact nature of the "breath of life" is still completely inexplicable to the biologist, no matter how much he knows about the breathing apparatus and the blood circulation system which utilizes and maintains it.

This passage, therefore, does not refer to an actual new special creation of the animals after the flood, as some have interpreted it. The Genesis record is plain in teaching that all present land animals are descendants of those that survived the flood in the ark (Gen. 7:21–22, 8:17, 19, 9:9–10, 16).

Praise to God for His Goodness
Verses 31–35

The glory of the LORD shall endure for ever: the LORD shall rejoice in his works.

He looketh on the earth, and it trembleth: he toucheth the hills, and they smoke.

I will sing unto the LORD as long as I live: I will sing praise to my God while I have my being.

My meditation of him shall be sweet: I will be glad in the LORD.

Let the sinners be consumed out of the earth, and let the wicked be no more. Bless thou the LORD, O my soul. Praise ye the LORD.

Our response to these wonderful provisions of God should, obviously, be like that of the Psalmist in the last verses of this psalm, a grateful testimony that "The glory of the LORD shall endure forever." Despite the global rebellion of wicked men and angels that caused God to send the flood, He was not about to be, nor will He ever be, dethroned!

During the flood, it is significant that God wished to preserve each animal "kind," as well as mankind. Though we may not yet understand exactly why He created so many different creatures, yet He did so, if for no other reason, than that it gave Him joy to do so. "The LORD shall rejoice in his works" (verse 31). If there was joy in His creating and preserving life, however, how much greater will be His joy in seeing the love of redeemed sinners, a joy that led Him even to endure the cross (Heb. 12:2).

The writer of the psalm (presumably David), in his glorious vision, now seeing before his enraptured eyes the awesome landscapes of the post-flood world, noted one other feature accompanying the rising mountains and reviving plant and animal kingdoms. Though the earth would never suffer such a worldwide hydraulic upheaval again, there was still much evidence in the earth of awesome power able to unleash local convulsions in testimony of God's continuing power to judge the world. The earth was still quaking and many hills still smoking (verse 32).

There was much "residual catastrophism" for many centuries after the flood (earth movements, volcanic activity, local floods, encroaching ice sheets, etc.), and in fact, such activities have never altogether ceased. God's goodness is wonderfully evident everywhere in nature, but so are His power and judgment. Also, though God has promised no more worldwide hydraulic cataclysms, the continuing tectonic and volcanic activity should serve to remind man of the coming judgment by a global fire (2 Pet. 3:10).

As the Psalmist concludes his narrative, he is constrained by what He has seen in the creative and catastrophic works of God to give his own personal testimony in response. "I will sing unto the LORD as long as I live. I will sing praise to my God while I have my being. My meditation of him shall be sweet. I will be glad in the LORD!"

Great numbers of men and women today are likewise finding within themselves a great heart of thanksgiving and joy in the Lord as they have come to recognize in a new way the reality of God's creation and sovereign control over this world which has seemed to ignore Him for so long.

As the sinners once were purged from the earth by the great waters which stood over the mountains, so once again will "the sinners be consumed out of the earth," and then will "the wicked be no more." God's perfect creation will be renewed forever, and therein will all His glorious purposes be fulfilled.

But then, in one final Amen, he added a great plea to all who might read it: "Praise ye the LORD!" Here is the first time this phrase (equivalent to one combined work in the Hebrew — hallelujah) occurs in the Book of Psalms. It also is the concluding word for Psalm 105, as well as the first and last word of Psalm 106, which is the final psalm in Book IV of the Book of Psalms. It then occurs as the initial and final admonition for each of the last five psalms in the entire Book of Psalms. Occurring 22 times altogether in the Book of Psalms, it could be considered as a theme phrase for the entire book, or at least the last third of the book.

It occurs *first*, however, here at the end of this wonderful 104th psalm. This is a natural and appropriate conclusion to any study of the glorious works of God. Hallelujah!

Chapter 27

Fearfully and Wonderfully Made

Psalm 139

This familiar psalm was written by King David, after many years of fellowship with the God who had made and called him, and then guided and protected him through all kinds of circumstances and in every kind of experience. The psalm has 24 verses, and these divide evenly into four stanzas of six verses each. The first six verses deal with God's omniscience; the second stanza emphasizes God's omnipresence; the theme of verses 13 through 18 is that of God's omnipotence; and the last stanza stresses what might be called God's omnipurity. These four themes might be expressed this way: (1) "God knows everything about me;" (2) "God sees everything around me;" (3) "God does everything for me;" (4) "God judges everything in me."

The psalm is intensely personal, written as a prayer of David to his Lord. He uses the first person pronouns ("I," "me," "my," etc.) no less than 48 times in these 24 verses. In speaking to God, he uses the second person ("thou," "thee," "thine," etc.) 28 times, and, in addition, he cries "O Lord," three times, and "O God" three times.

David's experiences, of course, parallel in many respects those of every other believer, so that we could all well appropriate both his testimonies and his prayers as our own. No doubt, in fact, this is exactly what the Holy Spirit intended us to do, at least with many of the psalms, and this is why He included them in the Holy Scriptures which He inspired. Psalm 139 is an especially thrilling example of a psalm of great blessing and encouragement, as well as being an exhortation, to the Christian today.

The Omniscience of God
Verses 1–6

O LORD, thou hast searched me, and known me.

Thou knowest my downsitting and mine uprising, thou understandest my thought afar off.

Thou compassest my path and my lying down, and art acquainted with all my ways.

For there is not a word in my tongue, but, lo, O LORD, thou knowest it altogether.

Thou hast beset me behind and before, and laid thine hand upon me.

Such knowledge is too wonderful for me; it is high, I cannot attain unto it.

David exhausts every superlative in describing how God knows absolutely everything there is to know about him — more, even, than he knew about himself. And if God knew one person so intimately, He would also know everything about every other person as well. Since human beings are the most complex systems in the universe, it follows that God knows everything about all less complex systems, too. In short, He is omniscient!

"O LORD, thou hast searched me and known me. Thou knowest my downsitting and mine uprising; thou understandest my thought afar off." Not only does the Lord know everything we do, He also understands everything we think. Nor is He like some human mentalist, who supposedly can read the minds of people near him. God knows our thoughts no matter where we are, and even before they enter our own minds. That is why He can say: "Your Father knoweth what things ye have need of, before ye ask him" (Matt. 6:8).

"Thou compasseth my path and my lying down, and art acquainted with all my ways." Whether rising or walking or sitting or lying down, the Lord is fully aware, moment by moment, of everything in which we are involved. The path we follow is all explored for us ahead of time because God has, as it were, "sifted" (a more precise meaning than "compassed") it out with His divine sieve, removing any insuperable obstacles or unavoidable pitfalls before we travel it.

"For there is not a word in my tongue, but, lo, O LORD, thou knowest it altogether." If God anticipates even our very thoughts, it is no very great thing if He hears all our words. But words affect other people, and therefore Jesus said, "But I say unto you, That every idle word that men shall speak, they shall give account thereof in the day of judgment. For by thy words thou shalt be justified, and by thy words thou shalt be condemned" (Matt. 12:36–37).

"Thou hast beset me behind and before, and laid thine hand upon me." God knows what lies ahead of us, and what has happened in our wake after us, and has His guiding and constraining hand upon us each present moment. Future, past, and present are alike in His understanding, since He is the Creator even of time itself — therefore, controlling all that can ever happen during time.

David concludes this stanza by confessing: "Such knowledge is too wonderful for me: it is high, I cannot attain unto it." How many people have engaged in endless and pointless controversy over the wonders of God's foreknowledge and election in relation to man's freedom and responsibility! We should remember that "as the heavens are higher than the earth, so are my ways higher than your ways, and my thoughts than your thoughts" (Isa. 55:9). We can rejoice in the assurance of God's foreordaining efforts on our behalf, as the Psalmist does here, but we cannot comprehend them. Such knowledge is too wonderful for our minds, and we cannot attain unto it.

God's Omnipresence
Verses 7–12

Whither shall I go from thy spirit? Or whither shall I flee from thy presence?

If I ascend up into heaven, thou art there: if I make my bed in hell, behold, thou art there.

If I take the wings of the morning, and dwell in the uttermost parts of the sea;

Even there shall thy hand lead me, and thy right hand shall hold me.

If I say, Surely the darkness shall cover me; even the night shall be light about me.

Yea, the darkness hideth not from thee; but the night shineth as the day: the darkness and the light are both alike to thee.

It does seem a little easier for us to grasp the concept of space than of time, and we are thus a little more comfortable with the fact that God is everywhere in space than we are in contemplating the divine contemporaneity of all events in time. In any case, David proceeds in the next stanza of the psalm to discuss the impossibility of going anywhere to escape the presence of God.

"Whither shall I go from thy spirit? Or whither shall I flee from thy presence?" These parallel questions are obviously rhetorical. The Holy Spirit is omnipresent. "Do not I fill heaven and earth? saith the LORD" (Jer. 23:24). Even if it were humanly possible to build a spaceship to carry us out to the very end of space, or a tunneling projectile to convey us to the center of the earth, God would be awaiting us there. As David expressed it: "If I ascend up into heaven, thou art there: if I make my bed in hell, behold thou art there."

"If I take the wings of the morning, and dwell in the uttermost parts of the sea. . . ." The "wings of the morning" refers to the east, the "uttermost parts of the [Mediterranean] sea" to the west. Whether up to heaven or down to hell, whether infinitely east or infinitely west — wherever one could conceive of ever going or being — "even there shall thy hand lead me, and thy right hand shall hold me."

One can never be hidden from God's all-seeing eye. "If I say, Surely the darkness shall cover me; even the night shall be light about me." After all, God is light, and "the light shineth in darkness" (John 1:5). "Yea, the darkness hideth not from thee; but the night shineth as the day: the darkness and the light are both alike to thee." "He revealeth the deep and secret things: he knoweth what is in the darkness, and the light dwelleth with him" (Dan. 2:22). Indeed, "all things are naked and opened unto the eyes of Him with whom we have to do" (Heb. 4:13).

The Creation of the Human Body
Verses 13–18

For thou hast possessed my reins: thou hast covered me in my mother's womb.

I will praise thee; for I am fearfully and wonderfully made: marvellous are thy works; and that my soul knoweth right well.

My substance was not hid from thee, when I was made in secret, and curiously wrought in the lowest parts of the earth.

Thine eyes did see my substance, yet being unperfect; and in thy book all my members were written, which in continuance were fashioned, when as yet there was none of them.

How precious also are thy thoughts unto me, O God! How great is the sum of them!

If I should count them, they are more in number than the sand:
when I awake, I am still with thee.

Verses 13 through 18 stress the omnipotence of God, focusing especially on His creation of the human body and its ability for reproduction
and multiplication. Man's body is, by far, the most complex and intri-
cately designed system in the universe. The absurd notion that such a
marvelous organism could have developed slowly over the ages by ran-
dom processes of evolution is a graphic commentary on man's desire to
escape from God at all costs.

To the one whose heart and mind are open to God, his own body is
a continual witness to the power and wisdom of God. "For thou hast
possessed my reins [that is, literally, 'my kidneys,' stressing both the in-
most emotions and also the marvelous physiologic provision for daily re-
newal and cleansing of the body]: thou hast covered me in my mother's
womb." The word "covered" is the same as "shielded," and refers to the
amazingly efficient design of a protective chamber in which the fragile
embryonic body can develop, cushioned hydraulically from injury, yet
continuously sustained and fed through the mother's body.

"I will praise thee: for I am fearfully and wonderfully made: marvelous are thy works: and that my soul knoweth right well." The "works" of
God are a testimony to His power. In fact, modern science equates the
accomplishment of the work required to produce any system or to maintain any process with the expenditure of energy, and, therefore, with the
continual availability of power, and this must ultimately be the omnipotence of God himself. But mere power is not sufficient — there must also
be "information," to direct the application of the power in producing complex systems. Higher organisms, especially man, could never be produced
by the simple availability of raw energy from the sun or any other source.
It must be *directed* energy, guided by an information program containing
all the specifications on how to proceed.

And this is exactly of what the Psalmist speaks. When he considers
the production of his body, he marvels that he is so "wonderfully" made.
The word actually is "differently," stressing the amazing fact that each
individual is quite unique and distinct from all others, in spite of his development by a process common to all.

Next comes a marvelous verse, long anticipating modern science.
"My substance was not hid from thee, when I was made in secret, and
curiously wrought in the lowest parts of the earth." There is a somewhat
parallel passage in Ecclesiastes 11:5: "As thou knowest not what is the
way of the spirit, nor how the bones do grow in the womb of her that is
with child: even so thou knowest not the works of God who maketh all."

The word "substance" could well be rendered "frame," and refers to the complete structure of the adult person. The full-grown body had actually been planned, designed, and programmed when it was not even large enough to be visible, in the "unseen parts of the earth." The mysterious process was one of "embroidering" (the literal meaning of the striking phrase "curiously wrought" is "embroidered"). It is as though a form were being sewed onto an intricate and beautiful pattern already laid out. This is an accurate description of the remarkable process of embryonic growth as delineated by modern molecular biology. The pattern in the DNA molecule is an intricate double-helical structure, which serves as a template for specifying and building up, cell by cell, the final adult body. It is an amazing process, which modern geneticists are only beginning to understand, but it was outlined here in Scripture almost three thousand years before it began to be understood at all.

"Thine eyes did see my substance yet being unperfect." The latter phrase ("substance yet being unperfect") is actually one word, meaning "embryo." "In thy book all my members were written, which in continuance were fashioned when as yet there was none of them." The word "continuance" is the Hebrew word "days" and the word "fashioned" is "formed" — the same word used in the account of man's creation, when God "formed" man of the dust of the earth. The phrase "my members" is not in the original. Thus, the meaning of this verse is somewhat as follows: "All the events of my days have been formed and written down in thy book before I was ever conceived."

That is, not only has God designed all things in space, He has planned all events in time. We indeed are fearfully and wonderfully made! No wonder the Psalmist exclaims: "How precious also are thy thoughts unto me, O God! How great is the sum of them!" By God's omniscience were all things planned and by His omnipotence were all His plans implemented, under the all-seeing eye of His omnipresence.

And since God knows our thoughts (verse 2), we should desire to know His thoughts. They are "precious" and "great in sum." It is significant that this was the purpose of the truly great scientists such as Isaac Newton — that is, to "think God's thoughts after him." So, likewise, it should be our desire to "bring into captivity every thought to the obedience of Christ" (2 Cor. 10:5). There is no danger that such concentration of our thoughts on His thoughts (and these, of course, are available to us both in His Word and in His world) would ever be limited or circumscribed. "If I should count them, they are more in number than the sand: when I awake, I am still with thee."

The Holiness of God
Verses 19–24

Surely thou wilt slay the wicked, O God: depart from me therefore, ye bloody men.

For they speak against thee wickedly, and thine enemies take thy name in vain.

Do not I hate them, O LORD, that hate thee? And am not I grieved with those that rise up against thee?

I hate them with perfect hatred: I count them mine enemies.

Search me, O God, and know my heart: try me, and know my thoughts:

And see if there be any wicked way in me, and lead me in the way everlasting.

Now some might conclude that since God had planned everything long before it happened, those deeds which are evil were also planned and thus will be excused by God. But not only is God perfect in knowledge and power and present everywhere in space and time, He is also perfect in holiness. He can, therefore, by no means condone wickedness forever. "Surely thou wilt slay the wicked, O God: depart from me therefore, ye bloody men ['or men of blood']." These final six verses of Psalm 139 emphasize God's omnipurity and His demand for His people to separate from all ungodliness and from all ungodly associations.

"For they speak against thee wickedly and thine enemies take thy name in vain." The very essence of wickedness is to speak against God and His Word, or to treat them with lightness. This attitude is the precursor of all other sins. It is presumptuous to question any of the attributes of God's sovereignty, such as those emphasized in this very psalm. But, it is even greater presumption to use God's sovereignty, as some do, to excuse sin. Even though in our finite minds we cannot understand how to reconcile God's sovereignty with man's responsibility (as verse 6 indicates, "such knowledge is too wonderful for me"), they are both absolutely real and true. We can rejoice, as David did, in the glories of His never-failing guidance and presence and power, and yet tremble at the reality of His judgment.

"Do not I hate them, O LORD, that hate thee? And am not I grieved with those that rise up against thee?" The latter expression is, literally, "I loathe them!" The believer must not only put away sin in his own life, but must discern and hate sin as God does.

But how is this attitude to be reconciled with Christ's command to "love your enemies" (Matt. 5:44)? The next verse even says: "I hate them with perfect hatred: I count them mine enemies."

There can be no contradiction in God's Word, of course. We are to love *our* enemies, but hate *His* enemies! And we are to hate them with *perfect* hatred — that is, we must hate sin as God does and seek to think His thoughts on *this* matter, also. But just as there is a glorious paradox in the relation between God's sovereignty and man's freedom, so there is a similar grand paradox between God's perfect hatred of wicked men and His perfect love of redeemed men. Believers likewise are to exhibit both perfect hatred and "perfect love, which casteth out fear" (1 John 4:18). Furthermore, even a perfect hatred of those who "hate thee" (verse 21) can never contradict God's sacrificial love for lost men. "But God commendeth his love toward us, in that, while we were yet sinners, Christ died for us" (Rom. 5:8).

The psalm closes with one of the greatest prayers of the Bible. The natural response of one who has caught a glimpse of God's glory and majesty, as David had done in this psalm, is to become acutely aware of his own sinfulness and to seek forgiveness and cleansing. When righteous Job saw the Lord, he cried out, "I abhor myself, and repent in dust and ashes" (Job 42:6).

The same is true with David. Having meditated on God's omniscience, experienced His omnipresence, marveled at His omnipotence, and realized His perfect holiness, he could only pray, "Search me, O God, and know my heart; try me, and know my thoughts."

But the prayer had already been answered! In verse 1 he had testified "thou hast searched me" and in verse 2, he had acknowledged "thou understandest my thought afar off."

"And see if there be any wicked way in me, and lead me in the way everlasting." In verse 3, David had also recognized that "thou art acquainted with all my ways." The intent of the prayer obviously was not merely to urge God to search his mind and heart and to examine his ways, because he well knew that God had already done all this. Like all the rest of his psalm, this really is an expression of his desire to know the mind of God himself — to know even his *own* heart as God knows it.

And when we can finally understand as God understands, thinking His thoughts after Him, not only about His great creation, but even about our own sinfulness and need of His salvation, then He truly is leading us in the way everlasting.

Part V

The Songs of Degrees and the Christian Life

Chapter 28

The Cry for Salvation

I mmediately after Psalm 119, the longest chapter in the Bible, is found a series of 15 remarkable short psalms known as the Songs of Degrees. Each one has that phrase in its traditional title, but there has been much difference of opinion among Bible scholars as to its exact significance. The middle one (Psalm 127) is entitled "A Song of Degrees for Solomon"; two in the first half (122 and 124) and two in the second half (131 and 133) are each entitled "A Song of Degrees of David." The remaining ten (five in the first half and five in the second half) are entirely anonymous, each being called simply, "A Song of Degrees."

The word translated "degrees" is the Hebrew *maalah*, often translated "steps," "stairs," etc. It means literally "going up to a higher place." Most authorities believe these psalms were sung by the Children of Israel as they traveled from their homes to Jerusalem for the annual ascent up to the higher elevations on which the holy city was built.

The themes do seem appropriate for such a use, proceeding as they do from the great cry of spiritual need in Psalm 120 up to the joyful note of blessing and unity on Zion and in the temple, the themes of Psalms 133 and 134. But there is also an obvious spiritual parallel in the journey of a believer through life, from the time of the conviction of sin and his cry for salvation until his final exaltation in glory. The psalms may thus also be regarded as depicting 15 stages in a spiritual "pilgrim's progress." This concept is somewhat similar to the concept of the 22 chapters in the believer's diary as suggested in our exposition of Psalm 119 in chapter 14.

Possible Background and Authorship

Even assuming that these psalms were indeed sung by pilgrims on the way to Jerusalem, that does not mean they were originally composed or compiled for this purpose. Except for the four psalms attributed to

David and one possibly authored by Solomon, no one really knows why, when, or by whom they were written.

One very plausible suggestion, however, supported by certain circumstantial evidences, is that they could be attributed to the great king Hezekiah, commemorating his recovery from a fatal sickness and the deliverance of Judah and Jerusalem from the armies of the Assyrians. The story of the deliverance and healing was apparently originally reported by the prophet Isaiah (Isa. 36–38), and it was later incorporated almost verbatim into the historical books (2 Kings 18–20), a remarkable fact which perhaps indicated the importance attributed to the event by the Jewish scribes who later brought together the two Books of Kings.

It will be recalled that Sennacherib's host had invaded Judah and laid siege to Jerusalem. The leader of the host, Rabshakeh, had made a series of blasphemous threats against Hezekiah and the Jews, and Hezekiah had desperately prayed to God for deliverance. God had heard his prayer and saved Jerusalem by a mighty miracle. Soon after that, Hezekiah experienced another miracle. He was about to die, but again prayed to the Lord for deliverance, and God answered through Isaiah once again.

> Then came the word of the LORD to Isaiah, saying, Go, and say to Hezekiah, Thus saith the LORD, the God of David thy father, I have heard thy prayer, I have seen thy tears: behold, I will add unto thy days fifteen years. And I will deliver thee and this city out of the hand of the king of Assyria: and I will defend this city. And this shall be a sign unto thee from the LORD, that the LORD will do this thing that he hath spoken; Behold, I will bring again the shadow of the degrees, which is gone down in the sundial of Ahaz, ten degrees backward. So the sun returned ten degrees, by which degrees it was gone down (Isa. 38:4–8).

The "degrees" by which the sun's shadow returned on the dial is the same word as is used in "Songs of Degrees." The "ten degrees" were the sign that Hezekiah's life would be miraculously extended by "15 years." The suggestion has been made, therefore, that Hezekiah composed 10 psalms, 1 for each degree, and that he added 4 more unpublished psalms of David's plus the 1 "for Solomon," possibly also written by David, to make a total of 15, 1 for each year of his prolonged life.

Immediately after the miracle, in fact, Hezekiah had composed one psalm of thanksgiving (Isa. 38:19–20), which ended with this promise: "The living, the living, he shall praise thee, as I do this day: the father to the children shall make known the truth. The LORD was ready to save me: therefore we will sing my songs to the stringed instruments all the days of our life in the house of the LORD."

These "songs to the stringed instruments" (one word in the Hebrew, *neginoth*) may thus have been these 15 songs of degrees, just as "all the days of our life" were his 15 years. An additional reason why Hezekiah and his descendants, "the father to the children," regarded this miracle as so important is the fact that he actually had no children at this time! God's great promise to David (2 Sam. 7:13) would have failed had Hezekiah died at this time, since his first son was not born until three years after his healing (2 Kings 21:1).

Theme of the Songs

The most obvious theme of the 15 psalms is what has been called "the hope of Israel," the great plan and promises associated with Israel and Jerusalem in the economy of God. This theme dominates most of these 15 psalms and is assumed in the others (note, for example, 121:4, 122:1–6, 125:1–2, 126:1, 128:5–6, 129:5, 130:7–8, 131:3, 132:13, 133:3, 134:3, etc.).

Certain numerical features may also be noted: The word "Israel" occurs seven times in these songs, the word "Zion" occurs seven times and the words "Jacob" and "Jerusalem" together occur a total of seven times.

Although God's relation to Israel is the primary theme of these psalms, we have already noted that a broader theme may well be that of the spiritual pilgrimage of a believer through life. The theme of deliverance from enemies, as experienced by Hezekiah, also recurs frequently, giving support to the idea of his original authorship, as does the frequent mention of God's promise of the seed to David and the blessing of children in general.

Crying for Salvation
Psalm 120
Verses 1–7

In my distress I cried unto the LORD, and he heard me.

Deliver my soul, O LORD, from lying lips, and from a deceitful tongue.

What shall be given unto thee? Or what shall be done unto thee, thou false tongue?

Sharp arrows of the mighty, with coals of juniper.

Woe is me, that I sojourn in Mesech, that I dwell in the tents of Kedar!

My soul hath long dwelt with him that hateth peace.

I am for peace: but when I speak, they are for war.

The songs of the degrees begin with a cry of distress to the Lord, calling for deliverance from "lying lips" and the deceitful and false tongue, lips that hate peace and desire war. One can almost hear the insolent harangue of Rabshakeh and Hezekiah's desperate plea to God for deliverance.

The reference in verse 5 to dwelling in Mesech and Kedar is rather cryptic, since Mesech was in the far north and Kedar probably south in the Arabian Desert. Mesech (same as Meshech) was originally one of Noah's grandsons, whose descendants traveled north from Babel, and eventually into what is now Russia, their name still reflected in the names Moscow and Muscovite. Kedar was a son of Ishmael (Gen. 25:13), and one of the ancestors of the Arabs. There is perhaps a prophetic note here, since both the Russians and Arabs were to be particular enemies of Israel in the latter days.

More likely, the lament is a figure of speech for living far from home in an enemy land. Spiritually, it would answer to one of God's elect under conviction of sin but still living in the ungodly world ruled by the great adversary, the father of all lying lips and deceitful tongues. "My soul hath long dwelt with him that hateth peace" (verse 6). The only answer to the need of an unsaved soul is the Lord, and finally he seeks and finds the God of peace. "In my distress I cried unto the LORD, and he heard me. Deliver my soul, O LORD" (verses 1, 2). An experience such as this has been shared by every redeemed soul; the Lord always hears and delivers all who call on Him in repentance and faith.

Chapter 29

Assurance of Salvation

Psalm 121
Verses 1–8

I will lift up mine eyes unto the hills, from whence cometh my help.

My help cometh from the LORD, which made heaven and earth.

He will not suffer thy foot to be moved: he that keepeth thee will not slumber.

Behold, he that keepeth Israel shall neither slumber nor sleep.

The LORD is thy keeper: the LORD is thy shade upon thy right hand.

The sun shall not smite thee by day, nor the moon by night.

The LORD shall preserve thee from all evil: he shall preserve thy soul.

The LORD shall preserve thy going out and thy coming in from this time forth, and even for evermore.

The first verse of Psalm 121 is often misquoted because of a poor choice of punctuation (the original Hebrew was not punctuated but was interpreted according to context). A proper reading would be as follows: "Shall I lift up mine eyes unto the hills? From whence cometh my help?" Then the question is answered. "My help cometh from the Lord, which made heaven and earth."

There is nothing in the hills that could provide help to a needy soul, as the usual punctuation might suggest. As a matter of fact, the prophets were frequently called on by God to condemn and destroy the "high places," where the people were continually being tempted to lapse into idolatry and worship the host of heaven. God had commanded through Moses, "Ye shall utterly destroy all the places, wherein the nations which ye shall possess served their gods, upon the high mountains, and upon the hills, and under every green tree" (Deut. 12:2).

There is a perverseness in man which makes him desire to "worship and serve the [creation] more than the Creator" (Rom. 1:25), to be nature-worshipers, and worshipers of the personified forces of nature. The entire system of paganism, and its modern counterpart, evolutionism, is based on such worship. But nature in itself is without power to save. No wonder Jeremiah cried, "Truly in vain is salvation hoped for from the hills, and from the multitude of mountains: truly in the LORD our God is the salvation of Israel" (Jer. 3:23).

The Psalmist was not looking to the hills for help! He was calling on the One who had made heaven and earth. The seeking sinner of the first Song of Degrees thus becomes the secure believer of the second song. The lesson in type is most appropriate today, for the worship of nature in one form or another abounds as never before in history. True salvation can only be found by calling on the great Creator of the universe. He alone is able to save, but He is indeed able to save to the uttermost all who call on Him (Heb. 7:25). And that Creator, of course, is none other than Jesus Christ! He has made everything in heaven and earth as God (Col. 1:16) and has been given all power in heaven and earth as man (Matt. 28:18).

Then follows one of the most remarkable testimonies of assurance and security for the believer to be found anywhere in Scripture. The word "keep" (also translated "keeper" and "preserve") occurs no less than six times in five verses (3, 4, 5, 7, and 8). "The LORD is thy keeper." Whether day or night is immaterial, because "He that keepeth thee" will neither slumber nor sleep. Whether attacked by evil men or evil circumstances does not matter, because "The LORD shall preserve thee from all evil." Though the whole world may lie in the wicked one, yet "He that is begotten of God keepeth himself, and that wicked one toucheth him not" (1 John 5:18). Furthermore, "He shall preserve thy soul." The Father will answer the Son's prayer: "Holy Father, keep through thine own name those whom that hast given me" (John 17:11). "The LORD is thy defense [same word as 'shade'] upon thy right hand" (verse 5). "No man is able to pluck them out of my father's hand" (John 10:29).

Then in a final all-comprehensive promise, He assures the believer He will preserve him in every circumstance of this life, whether "going out or coming in," and then in heaven "even for evermore." The soul that cried to the Lord for help has put his trust in the great Creator, who also is the Savior, and has thus found a secure salvation and everlasting life.

Chapter 30

Fellowship in God's House

Psalm 122
Verses 1–9

I was glad when they said unto me, Let us go into the house of the LORD.

Our feet shall stand within thy gates, O Jerusalem.

Jerusalem is builded as a city that is compact together:

Whither the tribes go up, the tribes of the LORD, unto the testimony of Israel, to give thanks unto the name of the LORD.

For there are set thrones of judgment, the thrones of the house of David.

Pray for the peace of Jerusalem: they shall prosper that love thee.

Peace be within thy walls, and prosperity within thy palaces.

For my brethren and companions' sakes, I will now say, Peace be within thee.

Because of the house of the LORD our God I will seek thy good.

Immediately after receiving salvation and the assurance of salvation, the most important step for a new believer to take next is to unite with the Lord's people in the institution established for that very purpose, a local church. It is appropriate that the next "degree" is Psalm 122, which has the theme of fellowship in God's house. "I was glad when they said unto me, Let us go into the house of the LORD" (verse 1).

Just as "Hezekiah went up into the house of the LORD, and spread it

· 233 ·

before the LORD" (Isa. 37:14), when he prayed for Jerusalem's deliverance, and just as the "tribes go up, the tribes of the LORD, unto the testimony of Israel, to give thanks unto the name of the LORD" (verse 4), so believers today should go to "the house of God, which is the church of the living God, the pillar and ground of the truth" (1 Tim. 3:15). The widespread practice of believers today — neglecting the church, established by Christ for the fellowship and growth of His followers, is unfortunate and unscriptural.

The theme of the national hope of Israel itself is dominant in this psalm, however. Not only the ancient pilgrims but also the future regathered and redeemed Israelites will "stand within thy gates, O Jerusalem," where will be "set thrones of judgment, the thrones of the house of David" (verses 2 and 5 also Isa. 9:6–7; Ezek. 34:23–24, 37:21–25; Luke 1:32, 22:29–30). "Pray for the peace of Jerusalem" (verse 6). Jerusalem ("the city of peace") has seldom known real peace throughout its long history, but in that coming day, this prayer will be answered. "For out of Zion shall go forth the law, and the word of the LORD from Jerusalem. And He shall judge among the nations, and shall rebuke many people . . . nation shall not lift up sword against nation, neither shall they learn war any more" (Isa. 2:3–4).

Though the primary reference is to Jerusalem and its temple, it is certainly appropriate in this present age to heed its spiritual lesson relative to the heavenly Jerusalem in its present local manifestation, namely, the church of the Lord Jesus. "For my brethren and companions' sakes, I will now say, Peace be within thee. Because of the house of the LORD our God I will seek thy good" (verses 8–9).

The above discussion in no way seeks to minimize the tremendous contribution of many of the interdenominational ministries and parachurch organizations today. They often provide needed specialized services and strategic missionary outreaches which no local church could accomplish. To the extent that they are sound in doctrine and practice, they should be considered as cooperating with, and extending the ministries of, local churches in areas and ways that would not be reached otherwise. Nevertheless, they cannot take the place of the church, and each believer, even if he is working in some specialized ministry of this sort, needs also to be associated with the fellowship of believers in a biblically sound local church.

Chapter 31

Fervent Prayer

Psalm 123
Verses 1–4

Unto thee lift I up mine eyes, O Thou that dwellest in the heavens.

Behold, as the eyes of servants look unto the hand of their masters, and as the eyes of a maiden unto the hand of her mistress, so our eyes wait upon the LORD our God, until that he have mercy upon us.

Have mercy upon us, O LORD, have mercy upon us: for we are exceedingly filled with contempt.

Our soul is exceedingly filled with the scorning of those that are at ease, and with the contempt of the proud.

The 123rd Psalm contains only four verses, but its theme is all-important. The sinner must call upon God for salvation (Ps. 121), but the believer must then continue to call upon God for deliverance from every enemy and for the supply of every need. Though he has been delivered from this present evil world (Gal. 1:4) as far as his eternal destiny is concerned, he is still very much in the world physically.

Just as for his salvation, his daily help must come from the God of creation. "Unto thee lift I up mine eyes, O Thou that dwellest in the heavens" (verse 1). There is no more a question of whether he should lift up his eyes to the hills (Ps. 121:1), for he knows there is no help from any source but the God of heaven. The believer should very early acquire the practice of daily seeking the will and the mercy of the Lord, looking unto Jesus only (Heb. 12:2). He is our master; we are His servants. Therefore, "our eyes wait upon the LORD our God." Three times the Psalmist cries for God's mercy. We must never think we deserve God's favor; it is always by His grace.

The godly man, truly trusting in God alone, will always be the object of contempt and scorning from those who are proud of their own accomplishments and at ease in the present world. It was true with godly King Hezekiah enduring the blasphemous scorn of Rabshakeh and Sennacherib. But God delivered him in answer to believing prayer, and will do the same for His people in any age.

The widespread contempt for God's Word — and therefore for God's people who believe and seek to obey God's Word — is becoming more and more blatant everywhere, even in "Christian" America. This attitude is predicted to "grow worse and worse" (2 Tim. 3:13) as the day of the Lord nears. Many Christians are inclined to compromise their biblical convictions in order to mitigate the contempt of the world, but this is a grievous mistake. Instead, we are commanded to "continue," knowing that "all Scripture is given by inspiration of God" (2 Tim. 3:14, 16). God's Word will stand forever, and we must stand by it.

Chapter 32

Answered Prayer

Psalm 124
Verses 1–8

If it had not been the LORD who was on our side, now may Israel say;

If it had not been the LORD who was on our side, when men rose up against us:

Then they had swallowed us up quick, when their wrath was kindled against us:

Then the waters had overwhelmed us, the stream had gone over our soul:

Then the proud waters had gone over our soul.

Blessed be the LORD, who hath not given us as a prey to their teeth.

Our soul is escaped as a bird out of the snare of the fowlers: the snare is broken, and we are escaped.

Our help is in the name of the LORD, who made heaven and earth.

Psalm 123 records the desperate prayer of a believer in danger from the ungodly; Psalm 124 is his testimony of answered prayer. The one follows the other as surely as day follows night, because the Lord is on *our* side, not *their* side!

The "little flock" of God (Luke 12:32) has but "little strength" (Rev. 3:8) of its own, compared to the tremendous resources of the world's political and educational establishments. But these overwhelming odds merely give God a chance to "shew himself strong in the behalf of them whose heart is perfect toward him" (2 Chron. 16:9).

But we must never make the mistake of relying on some other defense or some other power, because these will inevitably fail. They themselves are part of the world system and so cannot long prevail in a fight against it! "If it had not been the LORD who was on our side, when men rose up against us: then they had swallowed us up quick when their wrath was kindled against us" (verses 2–3). The proud waters would have overwhelmed our souls, but, "When the enemy shall come in like a flood, the Spirit of the LORD shall lift up a standard against him" (Isa. 59:19). We are like birds ensnared in a trap devised by the deceivers in the world system, but the Lord will not allow His own to become a prey to such as these. He will, in good time, make a way to escape, and the snare is broken. Even as the Psalmist had recognized when he first sought salvation, he returns again to the same Savior for every deliverance, to the God who created all things and who therefore controls all things. "My help cometh from the LORD, which made heaven and earth" (Ps. 121:2, 124:8).

Chapter 33

Faith and Rest

Psalm 125
Verses 1–5

They that trust in the LORD shall be as mount Zion, which cannot be removed, but abideth forever.

As the mountains are round about Jerusalem, so the LORD is round about his people from henceforth even for ever.

For the rod of the wicked shall not rest upon the lot of the righteous; lest the righteous put forth their hands unto iniquity.

Do good, O LORD, unto those that be good, and to them that are upright in their hearts.

As for such as turn aside unto their crooked ways, the LORD shall lead them forth with the workers of iniquity: but peace shall be upon Israel.

As one grows older in the Lord, experiencing time after time His mercies and answers to prayer, he becomes stronger in faith, no longer fearful when trials and adversities abound. Having seen God often turn defeat into victory, and darkness into light, the believer is increasingly confident that "the LORD is round about his people from henceforth even for ever" (verse 2). "And we know that all things work together for good to them that love God" (Rom. 8:28).

The 125th psalm thus speaks of settled trust in God, with perfect peace for those whose minds are stayed on Him (Isa. 26:3). "They that trust in the LORD shall be as mount Zion, which cannot be removed, but abideth for ever" (verse 1), and "peace shall be upon Israel" (verse 5).

There is also recognition that, though the wicked may sometimes appear to prosper in this world, eventually "the LORD shall lead them forth" into judgment. Furthermore, "the rod of the wicked shall not rest upon the lot of the righteous." That is, the wicked shall not be able to govern the actions of the righteous. His "sceptre" shall not rule over that possession which has been given to the righteous. No matter how strong the pressure, God "will make a way to escape, that ye may be able to bear it" (1 Cor. 10:13). Indeed, the Lord will "do good unto those that be good, and to them that are upright in their hearts" (verse 4).

Chapter 34

Sowing and Reaping

Psalm 126
Verses 1–6

When the LORD turned again the captivity of Zion, we were like them that dream.

Then was our mouth filled with laughter, and our tongue with singing: then said they among the heathen, The LORD has done great things for them.

The LORD hath done great things for us; whereof we are glad.

Turn again our captivity, O LORD, as the streams in the south.

They that sow in tears shall reap in joy.

He that goeth forth and weepeth, bearing precious seed, shall doubtless come again with rejoicing, bringing his sheaves with him.

The first verse of this beautiful psalm refers to the "captivity of Zion," and thus offers one of the main reasons why many commentators believe the "Songs of Degrees" were written after the return from the Babylonian captivity. As already noted, however, four of them are attributed to David and one to Solomon, and there is much internal evidence that they were written or gathered originally by King Hezekiah. Even Psalm 126 easily yields to that interpretation, with the "captivity" a very apt term for the long siege of Sennacherib. The sudden miraculous deliverance from that captivity would indeed have generated exactly such joyful laughter and singing in the city of Zion as the psalm describes. Note how naturally the words fit this great occasion: "When the LORD turned again [literally 'converted'] the captivity of Zion, we were like them that dream. Then was our mouth filled with laughter, and our tongue with singing: then said they among the heathen, the LORD hath done great things for them."

This was indeed the reaction of the heathen, according to 2 Chronicles 32:23. "And many brought gifts unto the LORD to Jerusalem, and presents to Hezekiah king of Judah: so that he was magnified in the sight of all nations from thenceforth."

In the spiritual analogue, of course, this "conversion" from captivity must refer to the miracle of salvation and regeneration. How often have these words been appropriated by believers to their own experiences? "The LORD *hath* done great things for us; whereof we are glad!" The new surge of living water through a believer's life (John 7:38) when he is set free from his bondage to the old life of sin and death is like the dry watercourses in the southern wilderness (the "south," the *Negev*) suddenly bursting with streams of water after long-awaited rains.

Hezekiah had "wept sore" before the Lord (Isa. 38:3) when praying for healing from his fatal sickness. When the Lord heard and healed him, having seen his tears (Isa. 38:5), Hezekiah composed his psalm of thanksgiving, and vowed to sing before the Lord all the days of his life. He had sown in tears, but reaped in joy, and this was the result of a special experience subsequent to his even greater experience of victory over Sennacherib.

The Psalmist compares such experiences to the difficult labor of seed-sowing. Because of sin, the ground is cursed, and man must eat his bread in the sweat of his face (Gen. 3:17) and in sorrow, all the days of his life. To accomplish the work of maintaining physical life and the even more difficult work of bringing spiritual life to those dead in sins, blood and sweat and tears are often required. Even the Lord Jesus, like Hezekiah, "in the days of his flesh . . . offered up prayers and supplications with strong crying and tears unto him that was able to save him from death" (Heb. 5:7).

Hezekiah needed to live in order to have the son God had promised, and God saw his earnest tears and answered his prayer. The sowing of seed was applied in the New Testament by the Lord Jesus to the work of spreading the Word of God (Luke 8:11), in His great parable of the sower. Psalm 126 thus, in retrospect, becomes a beautiful picture and promise of fruitful witnessing. "He that goeth forth and weepeth, bearing precious seed, shall doubtless come again with rejoicing, bringing his sheaves with him" (verse 6).

No seed is so precious as the Word (Psalm 19:10, 119:72), and no joy so great as that of bringing forth spiritual life as fruit from sowing the

Word. This is an important part of the life of a believer — both sowing and reaping. The sowing must be both individually compassionate, as was that of Christ (Mark 6:34) and yet also cast abroad as widely as possible, for all need it. "Cast thy bread upon the waters: for thou shalt find it after many days. . . . He that observeth the wind shall not sow; and he that regardeth the clouds shall not reap. . . . In the morning sow thy seed, and in the evening withhold not thine hand: for thou knowest not whether shall prosper, either this or that, or whether they both shall be alike good" (Eccles. 11:1–6).

There are tears involved in the sowing, but the promise of joy in the reaping. "And he that reapeth receiveth wages, and gathereth fruit unto life eternal: that both he that soweth and he that reapeth may rejoice together" (John 4:36).

Chapter 35

Children in the Lord

Psalm 127
Verses 1–5

Except the LORD build the house, they labour in vain that build it: except the LORD keep the city, the watchman waketh but in vain.

It is vain for you to rise up early, to sit up late, to eat the bread of sorrows: for so he giveth his beloved sleep.

Lo, children are an heritage of the LORD: and the fruit of the womb is his reward.

As arrows are in the hand of a mighty man; so are children of the youth.

Happy is the man that hath his quiver full of them: they shall not be ashamed, but they shall speak with the enemies in the gate.

Psalm 126 contains the promise of a fruitful harvest following industrious and difficult sowing. Psalm 127 is an actual testimony of the harvest and its blessings, no longer described figuratively as a field of grain, but as a fruitful home, with an abundance of children.

These children may well be either actual physical progeny or spiritual children in the Lord. God's first command to mankind was to "Be fruitful and multiply" (Gen. 1:28). This command was repeated after the flood (Gen. 9:1) and has never been withdrawn, even in the prophetic context of a latter-day supposed population explosion. Godly parents especially should pray and work to have large families, so that they can "bring them up in the nurture and admonition of the Lord" (Eph. 6:4), thereby multiplying not only their descendants but also their own ministry and witness.

The Scriptures often teach that children in a home constitute a sign of God's favor (e.g., Deut. 28:1–4), though, of course, this is not necessarily a universal principle. This 127th Psalm occupies the central position in the Songs of Degrees, and the middle verse of this central psalm is the strongest testimony to this effect to be found in the Bible. "Lo, children are an heritage of the LORD: and the fruit of the womb is his reward" (verse 3). Then the next verse, which is actually the middle verse of the entire 15-psalm assemblage, emphasizes this truth by another figure: "As arrows are in the hand of a mighty man; so are children of the youth."

One can almost see Hezekiah wistfully penning these words, perhaps copying from an old psalm written for Solomon (who, with his thousand wives and concubines, probably had as many children as any man in history) and hoping that God would be willing to give him at least one son in his old age! As we have noted, his son and successor, Manasseh, was not born until three years after his miraculous healing (2 Kings 20:6, 21:1).

"Happy is the man that hath his quiver full of them." Continuing with the figure of children as weapons, it is stressed that having *many* children — enough to fill the "quiver" — is good. Especially those who were children of the youth will be grown and vigorous men when their father is growing too old for effective combat in the battle against the enemy in the gate, whether that enemy is an actual physical combatant or the great enemy of the souls of men.

It should always be remembered, however, that such blessings in the home and in the nation do not come automatically just because there are many children or many citizens. "Except the LORD build the house, they labour in vain that build it: except the LORD keep the city, the watchman waketh but in vain" (verse 1). No amount of effort or scheming or fretting will accomplish the work — whether that work be a home, a church, a college, a city, or a nation. If it is the Lord's work, then it's the *Lord's* work, and He will see it through according to His own good will.

Though the Curse is still on the earth, and it is man's province to eat his bread in sorrow (Gen. 3:17), Christ has redeemed us from the Curse of the Law (Gal. 3:13). He giveth His beloved sleep instead of fear, rest instead of labor, joy in place of sorrow.

All of these wonderful blessings apply to physical children and, yet much more, to spiritual children, fruit not of the womb, but of the Word. Whether or not God chooses to bless one of His children with a mate and family, every believer has the privilege of sowing the good seed, and thus producing spiritual children. Happy, indeed is the Christian whose quiver is full of them.

Chapter 36

Fruitfulness and Godly Maturity

Psalm 128
Verses 1–6

Blessed is every one that feareth the LORD; that walketh in his ways.

For thou shalt eat the labour of thine hands: happy shalt thou be, and it shall be well with thee.

Thy wife shall be as a fruitful vine by the sides of thine house: thy children like olive plants round about thy table.

Behold, that thus shall the man be blessed that feareth the LORD.

The LORD shall bless thee out of Zion: and thou shalt see the good of Jerusalem all the days of thy life.

Yea, thou shalt see thy children's children, and peace upon Israel.

Psalm 128 continues the theme of Psalm 127, speaking of the blessings of a house built by the Lord, with a God-fearing father walking in the will of the Lord (verse 1). Such a man, God promises (in both verse 1 and verse 4), will be blessed with a fruitful wife and sturdy children, strong and durable as the olive plant (verse 3).

Not only would there be many children born (the theme of Ps. 127), but these children would be a joy in the home, especially in the blessed times of fellowship around the family table, and they in turn would then beget children of their own, bringing still more blessing to the family circle.

There need be no concern that such a large family would be too expensive to feed, for "thou shalt eat the labour of thine hands; happy shalt thou be, and it shall be well with thee" (verse 2).

These are wonderful promises, and many, many godly families can testify to its literal fulfillment in their own experiences. On the other hand, there have undoubtedly been many families of equal spirituality who have, in one way or another, failed as yet to experience their literal fulfillment. That is, some men of great godliness (e.g., the apostle Paul) never even acquired a wife at all. There were no doubt some godly families carried into captivity from Jerusalem during the time of Nebuchadnezzar and who, therefore, did not really "see the good of Jerusalem all the days of thy life" (verse 5). Many similar families have experienced sickness, tragedy, and heartbreak in their children, and some have, through no fault of their own, been childless.

Thus, the main thrust of these promises (though often fulfilled literally as evidence of God's genuine concern for His divine institution of the human family) must be in its spiritual principles. Every man who truly fears the Lord and walks in his ways will see the birth and growth of many spiritual children. (Even if not in this life, he will see them in the new "Jerusalem all the days of thy [eternal] life.") Just as literal children are begotten from a fruitful wife, so are spiritual sons begotten with the Word of truth (James 1:18) from the fruitful ground of honest and good hearts (Luke 8:15). It is, in fact, God who gives the increase. "The LORD shall bless thee out of Zion" (verse 5), and such a man will even have the joy of seeing his spiritual grandchildren to many generations, after the Lord's return, when there will be everlasting "peace upon Israel" (verse 6).

Chapter 37

Lifelong Preservation

Psalm 129
Verses 1–8

Many a time have they afflicted me from my youth, may Israel now say:

Many a time have they afflicted me from my youth: yet they have not prevailed against me.

The plowers plowed upon my back: they made long their furrows.

The LORD is righteous: He hath cut asunder the cords of the wicked.

Let them all be confounded and turned back that hate Zion.

Let them be as the grass upon the housetops, which withereth afore it groweth up:

Wherewith the mower filleth not his hand; nor he that bindeth sheaves his bosom.

Neither do they which go by say, the blessing of the LORD be upon you: we bless you in the name of the LORD.

As the mature believer continues to witness for the Lord through the years, he will encounter opposition and persecution, sometimes open and violent, more commonly covert and insidious. Looking back over the years he can testify: "Many a time have they afflicted me from my youth, yet they have not prevailed against me" (verses 1–2). Sometimes he had been, as it were, cut deeply, like a plow furrowing the ground, or restrained, as one bound with cords, but the Lord will always eventually heal the wounds and break the chains, either in this life or the life to come.

Not only is the righteous man protected but, eventually, the wicked man is judged, because "the LORD is righteous" (verse 4). The great host of those who "hate Zion" have, one by one, been "confounded and turned back" (verse 5). In contrast to the true believer, whose roots are deep and whose branches are fruitful (as in Ps. 127 and 128), the wicked are like grass attempting to grow on a housetop. Where there can be no roots, there will be no harvest. The one who sows good seed on good ground will bring many sheaves (Ps. 126:6).

Though such haters of Zion may for a while be much esteemed by the world, eventually all will recognize them for what they are. Those who "go by," observing their eternal barrenness, will see that God's blessing is not on them, and so will not *ask* God's blessing on them (verse 8). "And they shall go forth, and look upon the carcasses of the men that have transgressed against me: for their worm shall not die, neither shall their fire be quenched; and they shall be an abhorring onto all flesh" (Isa. 66:24).

Chapter 38

Longing for His Coming

Psalm 130
Verses 1–8

Out of the depths have I cried unto thee, O Lord.

Lord, hear my voice: let thine ears be attentive to the voice of my supplications.

If thou, Lord, shouldest mark iniquities, O Lord, who shall stand?

But there is forgiveness with thee, that thou mayest be feared.

I wait for the Lord, my soul doth wait, and in his word do I hope.

My soul waiteth for the Lord more than they that watch for the morning: I say, more than they that watch for the morning.

Let Israel hope in the Lord: for with the Lord there is mercy, and with him is plenteous redemption.

And he shall redeem Israel from all his iniquities.

The subject seems suddenly to change in the 130th psalm. Instead of primary attention directed to his family or to his opponents, the believer now is thinking only of his own relation to the Lord, and of his desire to be with Him. He has been through deep waters, perhaps fallen into some sin of which he is deeply ashamed. The sense of the Lord's blessing and fellowship, which had been his portion for so long, had been withdrawn, and he was under great conviction.

Every Christian has been through such an experience, and the waters can indeed be very deep, until repentance and confession lead to the

Lord's return in blessing once again. "If we say that we have no sin, we deceive ourselves, and the truth is not in us. If we confess our sins, He is faithful and just to forgive us our sins, and to cleanse us from all unrighteousness" (1 John 1:8–9).

A real believer, of course, will be chastened of the Lord when he sins (Heb. 12:5–11) and does not confess and forsake his sin. He does well to take the course described here by the Psalmist: "Out of the depths have I cried unto thee, O LORD [Jehovah], Lord, [Adonai], hear my voice: let thine ears be attentive to the voice of my supplications. If thou, Lord [Jehovah], shouldest mark iniquities, O Lord [Adonai], who shall stand? But there is forgiveness with thee, that thou mayest be feared" (verses 1–4).

The alternating use of the two divine names (*Jehovah* and *Adonai*) is striking. The same sequence occurs in verses 5 and 6 again. It is as though the Psalmist were, in his anxious search for cleansing, invoking every attribute of the divine name. He does, indeed, find forgiveness, as did David (Ps. 32, 51, and 143), and as all do even today, who come to the Lord Jesus in sincere confession and trust.

Verses 5 and 6 are two of the most beautiful expressions of faith in the Lord's coming to be found in Scripture. "I wait for the LORD, my soul doth wait, and in His word do I hope. My soul waiteth for the Lord more than they that watch for the morning." The primary thought, of course, is that of longing for the light of God's presence and the joy of His salvation after the dark night of conviction and chastisement experienced because of sin in his life as a believer. The expression "wait for" could as well be rendered "expect." One has the right to *expect* forgiveness and cleansing from the Lord when he has met the condition of repentance and confession, because this is God's promise. "In His *word* do I hope!" It is significant that this is one of only two explicit references to the word of God in all the 15 psalms of degrees, in striking contrast to the 176 references to it in the great psalm which immediately precedes them (the other is in Ps. 132:12).

The repetition of the phrase "they that watch for the morning" (verse 6) indicates particular significance to the concept of watching for the Lord. This is an important admonition, apparently, just as it was important for the temple night watchman to watch intently for the first sign of dawn in the eastern sky, as he called out the hours through the night (see Isa. 21:11–12).

Though the primary reference is to waiting for the Lord's forgiveness and restoration, this is only a type of the complete deliverance of the believer from the very presence of sin when the Lord returns to bring salvation to all the earth. The stress on watching for the Lord in this psalm certainly justifies our making this secondary application, especially in light

252 · Treasures in the Psalms

of the frequent New Testament exhortations to watch for His coming (e.g., Heb. 9:28; 2 Tim. 4:8; Matt. 24:42; Luke 21:36). "Watch ye therefore: for ye know not when the master of the house cometh, at even, or at midnight, or at the cockcrowing, or in the morning: Lest coming suddenly he find you sleeping. And what I say unto you I say unto all, Watch" (Mark 13:35–37).

In the spiritual analogue which we have been following in these Songs of Degrees, it is appropriate that this great theme (both of increased dependence on the Lord's forgiving mercy and of watching for His imminent coming) should be introduced toward the end of the believer's stay on earth. The older one grows in the Lord, the more conscious he becomes of his own unworthiness and the more anxious he becomes to see His Savior. "For with the LORD there is mercy, and with him is plenteous redemption" (verse 7). Finally, at His second coming, there will be full blessing also for the redeemed of the chosen people, as well as for all true believers everywhere. "And so all Israel shall be saved: as it is written, There shall come out of Sion the Deliverer, and shall turn away ungodliness from Jacob" (Rom. 11:26). "And he shall redeem Israel from all his iniquities" (verse 8).

Chapter 39

Hope in the Lord

Psalm 131
Verses 1–3

LORD, my heart is not haughty, nor mine eyes lofty: neither do I exercise myself in great matters, or in things too high for me.

Surely I have behaved and quieted myself, as a child that is weaned of his mother: my soul is even as a weaned child.

Let Israel hope in the LORD from henceforth and for ever.

This brief psalm, only three verses long, speaks particularly of the believer's settled conviction of God's sovereignty in all things and his complete confidence in God's goodness. Such an assurance represents the testimony of long experience in the Lord and long delight in His word.

"Lord, my heart is not haughty, nor mine eyes lofty." There is no longer room for personal pride when one finally becomes persuaded that only God is lofty. "Neither do I exercise myself in great matters, or in things too high for me" (verse 1). How many and how endless — how inconclusive — have been the controversies over predestination and free will, over divine sovereignty and human responsibility. The Scriptures teach that both are true, but men try to argue one or the other, believing they can rationalize one in terms of the other, or the other in terms of the one. But such infinite comprehension is possible only for the infinite God, and the heart confirms what the Scriptures teach, that man is free and responsible while God is simultaneously sovereign and all-predestinating. Our finite minds cannot resolve such an infinite paradox, but we don't have to do so. Such "things are too high for me." "Such knowledge is too wonderful for me; it is high, I cannot attain unto it" (Ps. 139:6).

The counsels of God need not be explained to the believer, because he knows that whatever God does is good, by definition. Like a weaned child, he is mature enough to make his choices, but innocent enough to trust his parents.

God's promises are unchangeable and His power to implement them irresistible. Therefore, we may "hope in the LORD from henceforth and for ever" (verse 3). Happy is the mature believer in Christ who has come to such a settled faith.

Chapter 40

Praying for the Kingdom

Psalm 132
Verses 1–18

Lord, remember David, and all his afflictions:

How he sware unto the Lord, and vowed unto the mighty God of Jacob;

Surely I will not come into the tabernacle of my house, nor go up into my bed;

I will not give sleep to mine eyes, or slumber to mine eyelids,

Until I find out a place for the Lord, a habitation for the mighty God of Jacob.

Lo, we heard of it at Ephratah: we found it in the fields of the wood.

We will go into his tabernacles: we will worship at his footstool.

Arise, O Lord, into thy rest; thou, and the ark of thy strength.

Let thy priests be clothed with righteousness; and let thy saints shout for joy.

For thy servant David's sake turn not away the face of thine anointed.

The Lord hath sworn in truth unto David; he will not turn from it; Of the fruit of thy body will I set upon thy throne.

If thy children will keep my covenant and my testimony that I shall teach them, their children shall also sit upon thy throne for evermore.

For the LORD hath chosen Zion; he hath desired it for his habitation.

This is my rest for ever: here will I dwell; for I have desired it.

I will abundantly bless her provision: I will satisfy her poor with bread.

I will also clothe her priests with salvation: and her saints shall shout aloud for joy.

There will I make the horn of David to bud: I have ordained a lamp for mine anointed.

His enemies will I clothe with shame: but upon himself shall his crown flourish.

Not only does the strong Christian desire to see the Lord, but he also desires to see the accomplishment of God's purposes on earth. It is one thing to desire the Lord's return in order to be delivered from our troubles; it is another to desire to see His will done on earth as it is in heaven, simply because we love Him and His will! It is an indication of yet greater maturity of faith and love when we come to desire the fulfillment of His promises and His great purposes on the earth, not for our own comfort and joy, but for *His* glory!

This is the underlying theme of Psalm 132, which is the longest of the Songs of Degrees. The Psalmist is especially concerned with the promises that God had made to David concerning the coming messianic kingdom. If Hezekiah was the author or compiler of these Songs, as we have inferred, it reflects his own concern lest he die before he had a son who would be able to continue the line of descent specified in the promises. In answer to Hezekiah's prayer, God had assured him: "For I will defend this city, to save it, for mine own sake, and for my servant David's sake" (2 Kings 19:34, 20:6). This language is very similar to that of the prayer in verse 10: "For thy servant David's sake turn not away the face of thine anointed." It is, of course, especially significant that the word "anointed" (Hebrew *Messiah* = Christ) is used here and also in verse 17: "There will I make the horn of David to bud: I have ordained a lamp for mine anointed [i.e., 'Christ']."

The Psalmist rehearses the background of God's promise to David, urging God to remember David's desire to build God a house, and God's responding promise to build David's house. It might seem almost presumptuous for a believer to "remind" God of His promises, but as a matter of fact, God seems to delight in this. There are many such prayers recorded in the psalms (e.g., Ps. 119:49) and in the prophets (e.g., Jer. 14:21). Hezekiah himself had called on God to remember (Isa. 38:3). It almost seems as though God frequently waits until His people are earnest enough to study His Word and to call upon Him to fulfill His Word, before He acts on it.

The exact breakdown of Psalm 132 into its component parts is difficult, with much difference of opinion among commentators. The following appears the most plausible outline in the context of the inferred Hezekian origin of the Songs of Degrees.

Verses 1–2	Prayer of Hezekiah
Verses 3–5	Prayer of David as quoted by Hezekiah
Verses 6–10	Continued prayer of Hezekiah
Verses 11–18	Response of God to David as confirmed to Hezekiah

Twice (verses 2 and 5), God is called "the Mighty One of Jacob." This is a very unusual name for God, occurring elsewhere only in Isaiah 49:26 and Isaiah 60:16 (Isaiah, of course, being a contemporary of Hezekiah) and in Genesis 49:24 (from which it no doubt was derived), where it was first used in connection with Jacob's dying blessing on his sons. The Psalmist, in using such a name, stressed that God's promises applied not only to Judah, but to all Israel, and that His might was ample to accomplish them.

Verse 6 is particularly difficult: "Lo, we heard of it at Ephratah: we found it in the fields of the wood." Ephratah is the ancient name of Bethlehem (where God's "anointed" one was born, a term applying both to David and to Christ). By Hebrew parallelism, the "fields of the wood" is probably either synonymous or directly related. Many have identified it with Kirjath-jearim, where the ark was kept for a while, but this identification seems nebulous (even though *jearim* means "woods"). Since the psalm is both prophetic and messianic, it may well be a prophecy of the coming of the anointed One to His people. The people of Israel first "heard" of His birth while in the fields near Bethlehem (Luke 2:8, 15, 16), and they "found" His "habitation," not in the mighty temple, but in a lowly manger. One can almost hear the Judaean shepherds saying, "We will go into his tabernacles: we will worship at his footstool" (verse 7).

The Psalmist, no doubt, looked far beyond His humble birth to His glorious reign: "Arise, O LORD, into thy rest; thou and the ark of thy strength. Let thy priests be clothed with righteousness; and let thy saints shout for joy" (verses 8, 9).

The answer to this prayer is found in God's response: "For the LORD hath chosen Zion; he hath desired it for his habitation. This is my rest for ever: here will I dwell. . . . I will also clothe her priests with salvation; and her saints shall shout aloud for joy" (verses 13–16). "Behold, the tabernacle of God is with men, and he will dwell with them" (Rev. 21:3). "[He] hath made us kings and priests unto God and his Father; to him be glory and dominion for ever and ever" (Rev. 1:6).

The basis of God's coming glorious kingdom, centered in the New Jerusalem but extending throughout the universe, is the coming of His anointed into the world, to redeem and reclaim the world from the enemy. His "priests" can be "clothed with righteousness" (Rev. 19:8) because they have been first "clothed with salvation" (Isa. 61:10). On the other hand, "His enemies will I clothe with shame" (verse 18).

He will surely "ordain a lamp for mine anointed" (verse 17). "They need no candle, neither light of the sun (Rev. 22:5). The Lamb is the light thereof" (Rev. 21:23).

This glorious future eternal kingdom can well occupy the thoughts and prayers of the people of God — all the more as they continue to grow in both physical and spiritual maturity. But this will not be because of selfish desires for peace and everlasting personal joys, but because we seek to desire that which God desires. And this, indeed, is why He created and redeemed His people, that He might have eternal fellowship with them in the New Jerusalem. "This is my rest for ever: here will I dwell; for I have desired it. I will abundantly bless her provision: I will satisfy her poor with bread" (verses 14–15).

Chapter 41

End of the Journey

Psalm 133
Verses 1–3

Behold, how good and how pleasant it is for brethren to dwell together in unity!

It is like the precious ointment upon the head, that ran down upon the beard, even Aaron's beard: that went down to the skirts of his garments;

As the dew of Hermon, and as the dew that descended upon the mountains of Zion: for there the LORD commanded the blessing, even life for evermore.

In their long, upward trek to Jerusalem for the annual feasts, the pilgrims eagerly looked forward to the end of the journey. When they finally arrived, there would be great rejoicing and a wonderful spirit of unity with all the people of God who had converged on the city.

Just so will there be rejoicing and oneness when "we shall all be changed, In a moment, in the twinkling of an eye, at the last trump" (1 Cor. 15:51–52). Since we will be with the Lord himself, we shall all become one in Him. "Till we all come in the unity of the faith, and of the knowledge of the Son of God, unto a perfect man, unto the measure of the stature of the fullness of Christ" (Eph. 4:13).

Then will finally be fulfilled completely the prophecy of verse 1: "Behold, how good and how pleasant it is for brethren to dwell together in unity." In type, it *should* be descriptive of each local congregation of believers, for they are "brethren," but in practice it is seldom found.

This beautiful unity is illustrated by a remarkable simile, being compared to the fragrant anointing oil for the high priest, covering his head, his beard, and down over the skirts of his garments. Oil is well-known in Scripture as a symbol of God's Spirit, so in this case it speaks especially of unity produced by the Holy Spirit — "the unity of the Spirit in the bond of peace" (Eph. 4:3). The only two occurrences of the word "unity" in the New Testament are these that have just been cited (Eph. 4:3 and 13), both fitting well the symbology of Psalm 133. There needs to be unity of both "the faith" and "the Spirit," "speaking the truth in love" (Eph. 4:15).

A like simile is used in the third verse. This pervasive unity is also compared to the dew on Mount Hermon and Mount Zion. As the anointing oil "descended on Aaron" from his head to his beard to his skirts, so the dew "descended" on Hermon and then "descended" on Zion. Thus, as the pilgrims had ascended to Jerusalem, so a spirit of unity had descended on them when they arrived. Just so, after we are "caught up together with them in the clouds, to meet the Lord in the air" (1 Thess. 4:17), we shall soon see "that great city, the holy Jerusalem, descending out of heaven from God" (Rev. 21:10).

Mount Hermon is far in the north and is very lofty. Mount Zion is in the south and is much lower in elevation. Yet the same dew covered both, symbolizing the eventual unification of the northern and southern kingdoms and the pervasive presence of the Lord in all His people, no matter how exalted or how lowly.

The end of the journey for every believer is finally on Mount Zion. "But ye are come unto mount Sion, and unto the city of the living God, the heavenly Jerusalem" (Heb. 12:22). There will then be no more divisions or dissensions, "for there the Lord commanded the blessing, even life for evermore" (verse 3).

Chapter 42

Eternal Blessing

Psalm 134
Verses 1–3

Behold, bless ye the LORD, all ye servants of the LORD, which by night stand in the house of the LORD.

Lift up your hands in the sanctuary, and bless the LORD.

The LORD that made heaven and earth bless thee out of Zion.

T he last of the Songs of Degrees is also the shortest, but comprises in type the longest period of time, with its end in eternity. After the journey's end in glory, then must follow nothing but goodness forever — blessing from the Lord *to* His people and a blessing of the Lord in praise *by* His people.

These eternal praises were pictured in type by those in the temple who were responsible for its care and services during the night, indicating that God is particularly pleased with those whose hearts continue to praise Him even in the darkness. "It is a good thing to give thanks unto the LORD, and to sing praises unto thy name, O Most High: To shew forth thy lovingkindness in the morning, and thy faithfulness every night" (Ps. 92:1–2). It was at midnight in the Philippian prison that "Paul and Silas prayed, and sang praises unto God"(Acts 16:25), an event which led to a miraculously timed earthquake and the salvation of the keeper of the prison and his family.

In the New Jerusalem, of course, there will be "no night there" (Rev. 22:5), as well as "no more death, neither sorrow, nor crying" (Rev. 21:4). Nevertheless, those who have learned to praise God even during times of sorrow and crying and death will be all the more able in eternity to "shew forth the praises of him who hath called you out of darkness into his

262 · Treasures in the Psalms

marvelous light" (1 Pet. 2:9). The possible implication of verse 2 is that it will be such as these who will be closest of all to the Lord's personal presence in eternity. "Lift up your hands in the sanctuary, and bless the LORD" (verse 2).

The final note of the Songs of Degrees is a beautiful invocation, looking back to the creation and forward to the consummation, recognizing God alone as the author of all blessing. He made all things in heaven and earth, and finally will reconcile all things in heaven and earth (Col. 1:20). With His throne in the New Zion (Rev. 22:1), there shall be "no more curse" (Rev. 22:3), only blessing forevermore! "The LORD that made heaven and earth bless thee out of Zion" (verse 3).

Part VI

Psalms of Comfort and Guidance (The Maschil Psalms)

Chapter 43

The Blessing of Sins Forgiven

Psalm 32

There are 13 psalms given the special name of Maschil, from a Hebrew word interpreted by some scholars as "instruction," and by others as "contemplation" or "meditation." Probably it encompasses both, so that they could be called "Devotional Didactic Psalms," providing instruction in many key aspects of a believer's experience, yet always in a context of spiritual encouragement and guidance.

One of the 13 psalms designated in their superscripts as Maschil is Psalm 42. However, Psalm 43 is obviously a continuation of Psalm 42, so it properly should be included, making a total of 14 Maschil psalms. Interestingly, these 14 (2 x 7) psalms contain a total of 287 (41 x 7) verses.

There are five authors associated with these 14 psalms, and they also show an interesting pattern.

Psalm 32	Book I	David
Psalms 42–45	Book II	Sons of Korah
Psalms 52–55	Book II	David
Psalms 74, 78	Book III	Asaph
Psalm 88	Book III	Heman the Ezrahite
Psalm 89	Book III	Ethan the Ezrahite
Psalm 142	Book V	David

That is, note that the first and last of the Maschil psalms were written by David, as well as the middle four.

More important than any such structural features, of course, are the lessons to be learned from these didactic poems, written by various human authors, but all inspired by the Spirit of God, for the instruction of believers in every age. In this section, we shall look at some of these vital lessons.

As far as the authors are concerned, David is well known as the author not only of six of these Maschil psalms, but of at least half of the entire Book of Psalms. The sons of Korah were Levites and descendants of Korah, who had perished after his attempted rebellion against Moses (Num. 16:32), along with two leaders of the tribe of Reuben, Dathan, and Abiram, and their families. At least some of the sons of Korah did not perish with Korah, however (Num. 26:9–11), presumably because they obeyed Moses' command to separate themselves from their father before the judgment of God fell on Korah and the rest of his family (Num. 16:25–27).

These surviving sons of Korah continued in their duties as Levites and eventually became, under David, honored servants and musicians for the tabernacle and temple services.

Asaph was also a Levite and was considered an outstanding musician in the time of David. His descendants continued to serve as temple musicians for centuries (note Neh. 7:44). Heman and Ethan, on the other hand, are said to be Ezrahites, a tribal name possibly indicating descent from Zerah, of the tribe of Judah. Both were considered very wise men (1 Kings 4:31). They are indicated in 1 Chronicles 2:6 to have been brothers, and also to have been grandsons of Judah. However, there are several men with the name Ethan and Heman mentioned in the Bible, and Ethan at least must have been a contemporary of David, since he mentioned David by name in the psalm he wrote (Psalm 89:3, 20, 35, 49). Furthermore, 1 Chronicles 15:17 and 19 mentions "the singers, Heman, Asaph, and Ethan," as Levites playing on cymbals when David moved the ark back to Jerusalem. Thus, the precise authorship of at least these two psalms (88 and 89) is somewhat uncertain.

However, the exact human authorship is not as important as the messages in the psalms, for all of the psalms ultimately came from the divine author, the Holy Spirit. The result is, as we shall see, that there are many instructional blessings there and we shall now seek to learn some of them.

In Psalm 32, the first of the Maschil, or devotional didactic, psalms, it is fitting that the Holy Spirit, speaking through David and his experience, should teach us the vital importance of having our sins forgiven if we desire to have a right relationship with God. There is nothing more important to a person than this, whether that person is still unsaved or is a backslidden believer. "For if the word spoken by angels was stedfast, and every transgression and disobedience received a just recompence of reward; How shall we escape, if we neglect so great salvation?" (Heb. 2:2).

David knew from grievous experience, the deep despondency of soul when he realized that he had deeply offended God by his terrible sin of adultery and indirect murder, causing God's enemies to blaspheme His holy name because of what he had done. But then he also knew the deep joy when he received forgiveness, and he wrote about it in this heart-searching psalm.

Verses 1–2

Blessed is he whose transgression is forgiven, whose sin is covered.

Blessed is the man unto whom the LORD imputeth not iniquity, and in whose spirit there is no guile.

This is the second of six psalms that begin with the word "Blessed" (the others are Ps. 1, 41, 112, 119 and 128). It is the word that begins the entire Book of Psalms, and certainly sets an appropriate tone for the book. "*Blessed*" is commonly understood to mean "happy," but the word implies a stronger feeling than just outward happiness — something like "having abundant blessing with deep joy."

Such blessing comes to one who knows his forgiveness is real and lasting once his sin has been "covered." The meaning of the Hebrew verb (*kacah*) is indicated the first time it is used, when it is said, "all the high hills . . . and the mountains were covered" by the waters of the flood (Gen. 7:19–20). Not only so, but "the LORD imputeth not iniquity" to the man so blessed. That is, God no longer counts it against him.

For this to be so, that man must exercise true faith in God as his Savior from sin. This is indicated the first time that word is used, when Abram "believed in the LORD, and he counted it to him for righteousness" (Gen. 15:6). Paul quotes these two passages as he elaborates the great principle of justification by faith. "To him that worketh not, but believeth on him that justifieth the ungodly, his faith is counted for righteousness. Even as David also describeth the blessedness of the man, unto whom God imputeth righteousness without works, Saying, Blessed are they whose iniquities are forgiven, and whose sins are covered. Blessed is the man to whom the Lord will not impute sin" (Rom. 4:5–7).

But how is it that mere faith can be sufficient to transfer the guilt of sin away from a sinner and replace it with the blessedness of imputed righteousness? Everyone has faith in something or other — even atheists! But saving faith must be placed in the only one who can forgive sins and save souls — that is, our great Creator and Savior. From our post-Calvary perspective, we know that this is none other than the Lord Jesus Christ, and we know that He can save because He alone could have paid the price for our forgiveness and redemption. "For he hath made him to be sin for us, who knew no sin; that we might be made the righteousness of God in him" (2 Cor. 5:21). God in Christ "bare our sins in His own body on the tree, that we, being dead to sins, should live unto righteousness." (1 Pet. 2:24).

David could hardly have had the knowledge that we now have about the person and work of the Lord Jesus Christ in paying the price for our forgiveness. However, he manifested the same kind of faith in what he did know about the grace and love of His Creator, believing that God would someday send a Savior who would, indeed, take away his sins. He had even written prophetically about God's Son (see the exposition of Ps. 2 in chapter 3), concluding his psalm with the promise: "Blessed are all they that put their trust in him" (Ps. 2:12).

And there could be no equivocation in that faith! "Blessed is the man . . . in whose spirit there is no guile." One does not exercise a saving faith in Christ when he offers to believe on Christ provided he can still believe in evolution or can still continue his drinking practices or any other conditions whatever. He must come in true repentance as a guilty sinner — in fact as one "dead in trespasses and sins" (Eph. 2:1). A dead man does not make conditions before he will consent to being given new life! He must put his whole trust in the only one who can save him and give true forgiveness. And that is what David did!

Verses 3–4

When I kept silence, my bones waxed old through my roaring all the day long.

For day and night thy hand was heavy upon me: my moisture was turned into the drought of summer. Selah.

But before David finally confessed his sin and trusted in God's forgiveness, he experienced the heavy hand of God's convicting Spirit. David's external silence was accompanied by inward roaring! This is the same word as used for the roaring of a lion or that of a raging sea. It was causing his very bones to "wax old" — that is, to waste away. A guilty conscience can, indeed, cause physical deterioration.

Note also, in passing, that David used the same word as he described the future sufferings of Christ on the cross: "My God, my God . . . why art thou so far from helping me, and from the words of my roaring?" (Ps. 22:1). Unfortunately, most modern translations (as is often their wont) have tried to dilute this passage by translating "roaring" as "groaning."

But Christ was not groaning! He bore his agonies in silence. "As a sheep before her shearers is dumb, so he openeth not his mouth" (Isa. 53:7). Like David, His bones were roaring, not (like David) with the weight of His own sins, for He was the spotless Lamb of God (1 Pet. 1:19), but with the crushing burden of David's sins, and our sins, and the sins of the whole world. He — and He alone — paid the awful price for the sin of the world, so that we, like Abraham and like David, could be justified by faith.

David was already a believer, but believers can also sin grievously, and he felt that God's "hand was heavy upon me." In a similar psalm, he had written, "For thine arrows stick fast in me, and thy hand presseth me sore. There is no soundness in my flesh because of thine anger: neither is there any rest in my bones because of my sin" (Ps. 38:2–3).

The Lord had chosen David and had loved him dearly and used him mightily, but now he had sinned grievously. He had not lost his salvation, but had surely lost "the joy of his salvation" (Ps. 51:12), and God must chasten him. "For whom the Lord loveth he chasteneth, and scourgeth every son whom he receiveth" (Heb. 12:6).

Verse 5

"I acknowledged my sin unto thee, and mine iniquity have I not hid. I said, I will confess my transgressions unto the LORD; and thou forgavest the iniquity of my sin. Selah."

The day came when God sent the prophet Nathan to David to make him see the tragedy of his sin and its consequences. David finally saw clearly what he had to do. "And David said unto Nathan, I have sinned against the LORD. And Nathan said unto David, the LORD also hath put away thy sin; thou shalt not die" (2 Sam. 12:13). In the 51st psalm, David described in more detail his prayer to God. "For I acknowledge my transgressions: and my sin is ever before me. Against thee, thee only, have I sinned, and done this evil in thy sight" (Ps. 51:3–4).

And God forgave him! He had sinned against Uriah and Bathsheba, but all sin is ultimately and most basically against the God who created us. Other people are affected too, by our sins. As Nathan said, "By this deed thou hast given great occasion to the enemies of the LORD to blaspheme" (2 Sam. 12:14). Nevertheless, God forgave him.

Because of what Christ has done; "If we confess our sins, he is faithful and just to forgive us our sins, and to cleanse us from all unrighteousness" (1 John 1:9). David's experience of forgiveness and restoration of joy and great blessing has been repeated in the testimonies of many, many others through the years.

Nevertheless, even though sin can be forgiven and the joy of salvation restored, it can still have sad consequences here on earth. David's son from this adultery died (2 Sam. 12:14–18), along with other tragic results (2 Sam. 12:10–12). No sin — not even confessed and forgiven sin — should ever be taken lightly.

Then after David wrote of his forgiveness, he interjected the special word "*Selah.*" The same word is also inserted after verses 4 and 7. Altogether, it occurs 73 times in the psalms, plus three times in Habakkuk. It appears to be the imperative of the Hebrew verb *salah*, which means "to rest." It seems to mean something like "pause and reflect on the thought just mentioned," and the happy awareness of forgiven sin is surely worth reflecting on!

Verses 6–7

For this shall every one that is godly pray unto thee in a time when thou mayest be found; surely in the floods of great waters they shall not come nigh unto him.

Thou art my hiding place, thou shalt preserve me from trouble; Thou shalt compass me about with songs of deliverance. Selah.

God is easily "found" when a believer repents and confesses his sin. God only "hides" from him when he tries to hide or excuse his sin. "Behold, the LORD's hand is not shortened, that it cannot save; neither his ear heavy, that it cannot hear: But your iniquities have separated between you and your God, and your sins have hid his face from you, that he will not hear" (Isa. 59:1–2).

And when that believer is truly restored and living in the will of God, there is no safer or happier place in the world. "For the eyes of the Lord are over the righteous, and his ears are open unto their prayers" (1 Pet. 3:12).

Verses 8–11

I will instruct thee and teach thee in the way which thou shalt go: I will guide thee with mine eye.

Be ye not as the horse, or as the mule, which have no understanding; whose mouth must be held in by bit and bridle, lest they come near unto thee.

Many sorrows shall be to the wicked; but he that trusteth in the LORD, mercy shall compass him about.

Be glad in the LORD, and rejoice, ye righteous: and shout for joy, all ye that are upright in heart.

After the last "*Selah*," (verse 7, it seems that God responds to David's faith (and to ours) in the next two verses, promising to give the wisdom and direction we need in order to know and follow His will. We need to keep our eyes upon Him, so that He can guide us with His "eye," just as a mother can correct and direct her children just by looking at them. We need constantly to be "looking unto Jesus, the author and finisher of our faith" (Heb. 12:2), so He can "direct thy paths" (Prov. 3:6), and "teach thee in the way which thou shalt go."

All too often, however, we — like the horse and mule — don't want to go where He would lead us, preferring (like sheep — Isa. 53:6) to "go astray" or else to insist stubbornly to stay just where we are. It is not that such animals have no brains, but only that they don't "understand" the purpose that the Lord — and their human masters — have for them. And so they must then be forcibly constrained, to obey, just as the Lord must all too often have to deal with us. If not strongly constrained, they also might "come near" us, with intent to kick or bite. In like fashion, believers sometimes lash out at God, blaming Him for difficulties and testings. But God's loving admonition is: "Don't act like mules." Remember Romans 8:28 and remember that God has assured His children that even though "no chastening for the present seemeth to be joyous, but grievous: nevertheless afterward it yieldeth the peaceable fruit of righteousness unto them which are exercised thereby" (Heb. 12:11).

The "wicked," on the other hand, have no such assurance. One should also remember that the most wicked act of all is to reject or ignore God's loving gift of salvation through Jesus Christ. "The wicked shall be turned into hell, *and* all the nations that forget God (Ps. 9:17; note that the conjunction "and" is not in the original). "He that believeth not is condemned already, because he hath not believed in the name of the only begotten Son of God" (John 3:18). On the other hand, God's lovingkindness (same word as "mercy" in the original) always surrounds him, even during times of suffering and sorrow.

Therefore, the believer is indeed "blessed." He should always "be glad" and "rejoice." Rejoice in the Lord alway:" said the apostle Paul, "and again I say, Rejoice" (Phil. 4:4). Sorrows will often come in a world hostile to the Christian mission, but we can be, like Paul, "as sorrowful, yet always rejoicing" (2 Cor. 6:10). Our sins are forgiven, our future is secure, and God loves us! No wonder Christians can sing for joy. The Hebrew word (*ranan*) is sometimes translated "shout for joy," sometimes "sing for joy." Whether a believer expresses joy by singing or by shouting or both is a matter of temperament. Either is acceptable to the Lord if it is genuine joy in the Lord.

Chapter 44

The Strange Silence of God

Psalms 42 and 43

The 42nd psalm is the first of the four Maschil (or "instructional") psalms written for the sons of Korah. The theme of the first Maschil (Ps. 32) was the blessedness of repented, confessed, and forgiven sin. The devotional lesson, around which Psalm 42 is centered, is the longing of the heart for restored fellowship with God in a time when, for reasons unknown, God seems strangely distant and unconcerned.

Verses 1–5

As the hart panteth after the water brooks, so panteth my soul after thee, O God.

My soul thirsteth for God, for the living God: when shall I come and appear before God?

My tears have been my meat day and night, while they continually say unto me, Where is thy God?

When I remember these things, I pour out my soul in me; for I had gone with the multitude, I went with them to the house of God, with the voice of joy and praise, with a multitude that kept holyday.

Why art thou cast down, O my soul? And why art thou disquieted in me? hope thou in God: for I shall yet praise him for the help of his countenance.

Here is the heart cry of a true believer in "the living God" (verse 2), who had faithfully worshiped and served and loved God, but who has

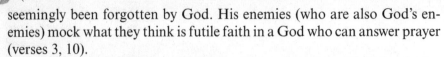

seemingly been forgotten by God. His enemies (who are also God's enemies) mock what they think is futile faith in a God who can answer prayer (verses 3, 10).

Many others, before and since, have had similar experiences. The verses of this psalm almost seem to come from the lips of the ancient patriarch Job, the most righteous man on earth in his day, yet suddenly forsaken by God and soon ridiculed and berated by friends and enemies alike. Like the Psalmist, he also cried out for an opportunity to "come and appear before God" (see Job 23:3–9).

Or one might think of the future martyrs under the altar, crying out to God, "How long, O Lord" (Rev. 6:10). There were also all the great "heroes of faith" whose testimonies are enshrined in Hebrews 11, who "all, having obtained a good report through faith, received not the promise" (Heb. 11:39).

Indeed, most true Christians over the centuries have experienced, like Job, such trials of faith, when — for reasons not known — God seems to have forgotten them, while sinners mocked. Like the hart, thirsty for water, who finds the brook all dried up, for reasons he didn't cause and doesn't understand, such a saint might be tempted to complain or renounce his calling as he searched for the water of life to soothe the thirst of his soul.

But like Job, if he is genuine, he will never lose his faith. He may cry out: "Why?" But his cry should not be one that questions God. He should not ask God why he is being treated unfairly. Rather, he must question his own doubts. "Why art thou cast down, O my soul?" God has reasons which we, like Job, may not be able to understand now, but we can always trust Him to do right by those for whom He sacrificed His own Son.

When the "why?" questions intrude and God remains strangely silent, we must simply say with our Psalmist: "Hope thou in God." In His own good time, "I shall yet praise him for the help of his countenance."

Verses 6–11

O my God, my soul is cast down within me: therefore will I remember thee from the land of Jordan, and of the Hermonites, from the hill Mizar.

Deep calleth unto deep at the noise of thy waterspouts: all thy waves and thy billows are gone over me.

Yet the LORD will command his lovingkindness in the daytime, and in the night his song shall be with me, and my prayer unto the God of my life.

I will say unto God my rock, Why hast thou forgotten me? Why go I mourning because of the oppression of the enemy?

As with a sword in my bones, mine enemies reproach me; while they say daily unto me, Where is thy God?

Why art thou cast down, O my soul? And why art thou disquieted within me? hope thou in God: for I shall yet praise him, who is the health of my countenance, and my God.

The first "stanza" of Psalm 42 ends with the same words as the second stanza (verses 5 and 11), the Psalmist still exhorting his disquieted soul to hold fast to his hope in God.

His soul has again been "cast down," almost to the very depths. It seemed that he was, as it were, engulfed in the violence of an oceanic tornado. The word translated "waterspouts" is applied to any vertical column of water, and is rendered "waterfalls" in some translations. The remarkable phrase "deep calleth unto deep" seems, however, to refer to a thunderous cyclonic water column extending from the oceanic "deep" all the way up into the cloudy "deep" of the heavens, generating mighty waves and billows on the deep sea.

Yet, even in such tumultuous circumstances the believer can pray to "the God of my life," confident of His grace and mercy day after day confident even of His songs in the night. "He hath said, I will never leave thee nor forsake thee" (Heb. 13:5), so He is there, whether or not we can feel His presence. We can believe, even when we cannot see or hear or sense Him at the time.

In such times of testing, we can make ourselves remember the earlier times of blessing — like the lofty heights of Mount Hermon or the cool flowing waters of Jordan or even the little pleasures of Mizar (probably a small hill near Jerusalem).

True witnessing Christians inevitably have enemies, and sometimes their words of ridicule and rejection cut like "a sword in my bones" — especially when they deny the very God whom we trust. Nevertheless, God is "my rock," so "why go I mourning"; how can I allow myself to think he has forgotten me? So again the Psalmist questions himself, not God: "Why art thou cast down, O my soul?" he asks. "Hope thou in God."

Psalm 43

Psalm 43 is included in this chapter because it is so closely and clearly tied to Psalm 42. Most authorities seem to think that it was originally a part of Psalm 42 but that somehow, for reasons unknown, was separated from it by some ancient scribe.

More likely, however, it was intended from the beginning to be a separate psalm, though it obviously continues the same theme and was almost certainly written by the same author. The latter, whoever he may have been, specifically tied it to his previous psalm by using the same closing verse with which he had closed each of the two stanzas in Psalm 42. Also, note how verse 2 is essentially the same as Psalm 42:9.

Verses 1–5

Judge me, O God, and plead my cause against an ungodly nation: O deliver me from the deceitful and unjust man.

For thou art the God of my strength: why dost thou cast me off? Why go I mourning because of the oppression of the enemy?

O send out thy light and thy truth: let them lead me; let them bring me unto thy holy hill, and to thy tabernacles.

Then will I go unto the altar of God, unto God my exceeding joy: yea, upon the harp will I praise thee, O God my God.

Why art thou cast down, o my soul? And why art thou disquieted within me? hope in God: for I shall yet praise him, who is the health of my countenance, and my God.

We can note just in passing how neatly symmetrical the three stanzas are when the two psalms are grouped together.

Psalm 42:1–5	Five verses
Psalm 42:6–11	Six verses
Psalm 43:1–5	Five verses

Each of the three stanzas ends with the same introspective challenge, and this challenge — to both the Psalmist and to us — is surely the key message in both psalms.

Quite possibly, Psalm 43 was written at some later date than Psalm 42, which is most likely the reason why they are separated. In the interim, the writer had meditated further on the situation and, although God still had not "delivered him from the deceitful and unjust men" who were seeking to destroy his faith, he was growing in his understanding of God and His ways. He was learning better how to pray, and where to look for answers.

"O send out thy light and thy truth: let them lead me." This had become his prayer, and this should be the burden of our own prayers when men are opposing our stand for the Lord and God seems strangely silent.

As a matter of fact, God has already sent out His light and His truth, so that we need not walk in darkness or stumble along in ignorance. "Thy word is a lamp unto my feet, and a light unto my path. . . . The entrance of thy words giveth light" (Ps. 119:105 and 130). "Thy word is truth" (John 17:17). "Thy word is true from the beginning" (Ps. 119:160). We have the Word of God, which contains all the light and truth we shall ever need for any situation.

And it does say that, when God does not seem to answer, even when, so far as we can understand, there is nothing we have done to cause His silence, we need simply to follow His Word, as well as we can, and continue in prayerful faith. "Let them that suffer according to the will of God commit the keeping of their souls to him in well doing, as unto a faithful Creator" (1 Pet. 4:19).

We must not complain and we must not question God. Instead, we question ourselves. "Why art thou cast down, O my soul?" Then we answer our own question. "Hope thou in God." Let the light and the truth in His Word be our guide.

Chapter 45

Psalm of the Martyrs

Psalm 44

I t seems impossible to assign this psalm to any specific period of Israel's history, though it begins with a stirring testimony to God's hand in the initial establishment of Israel in the Promised Land. It has essentially the same superscription as Psalm 42, but in its scope it applies to an entire people rather than to an individual. It is entirely a prayer to God, thanking Him for past victories on their behalf (verses 1–8) then expressing bewilderment at their current sufferings despite their continuing faithfulness to His name (verses 9–22), then finally pleading with Him once again to make His power known on behalf of His people (verses 23–26).

Since it cannot be identified with any particular time in history, it seems likely that God intended it for appropriation by His faithful martyrs in any age. This interpretation is strengthened by the fact that the apostle Paul applied one of its key verses (verse 22) to the suffering Christians of the first century (Rom. 8:36).

Verses 1–8

We have heard with our ears, O God, our fathers have told us, what work thou didst in their days, in the times of old.

How thou didst drive out the heathen with thy hand, and plantedst them: how thou didst afflict the people, and cast them out.

For they got not the land in possession by their own sword, neither did their own arm save them; but thy right hand, and thine arm, and the light of thy countenance, because thou hadst a favour unto them.

Thou art my king, O God: command deliverances for Jacob.

Through thee will we push down our enemies: through thy name will we tread them under that rise up against us.

For I will not trust in my bow, neither shall my sword save me.

But thou hast saved us from our enemies, and hast put them to shame that hated us.

In God we boast all the day long, and praise thy name for ever. Selah."

This first section of the psalm (call it the first stanza) is a strong testimony to the power of God, bringing victory after victory to His people over nations mightier than they. "If God be for us, who can be against us?" (Rom. 8:31).

God indeed has performed great and mighty acts on behalf of His people "in the times of old," and we have the sure testimony of these today in the inspired record of the Scriptures, not merely in what "our fathers have told us." As far as the Children of Israel were concerned, they got their "land in possession" not by their own power or wisdom but only because God had "a favour unto them" — that is, by the sovereign grace and strength of their Creator.

This was the testimony of the unknown Psalmist and his people in the first three verses of his psalm. Perhaps this all contributed to just a hint of presumption, that God's special favor would automatically continue in the future as it had in the past. "Through thee will we push down our enemies: through thy name will we tread them under that rise up against us." Their confidence was completely in the Lord, of course, not in their own strength. It is only "in God we boast all the day long."

Nevertheless, they were boasting. It is good to have strong faith in God, but sometimes faith can become presumption. Furthermore, it is often God's will to allow His children to experience suffering and defeat, as well as prosperity and victory. "For unto you it is given in the behalf of Christ, not only to believe on him, but also to suffer for his sake" (Phil. 1:29), said Paul, concerning the sufferings of himself and his fellow believers. For "tribulation worketh patience; and patience, experience: and experience, hope." (Rom. 5:3–4).

That would be the experience of the Psalmist and his people. And over the centuries it has been the experience of many other faithful believers, both individuals and churches and entire populations of Christians. That is the theme of the next eight verses of the psalm. The first stanza ends with a reflective "Selah."

Verses 9–22

But thou hast cast us off, and put us to shame; and goest not forth with our armies.

Thou makest us to turn back from the enemy: and they which hate us spoil for themselves.

Thou hast given us like sheep appointed for meat; and hast scattered us among the heathen.

Thou sellest thy people for nought, and dost not increase thy wealth by their price.

Thou makest us a reproach to our neighbors, a scorn and a derision to them that are round about us.

Thou makest us a byword among the heathen, a shaking of the head among the people.

My confusion is continually before me, and the shame of my face hath covered me,

For the voice of him that reproacheth and blasphemeth; by reason of the enemy and avenger.

All this is come upon us; yet have we not forgotten thee, neither have we dealt falsely in thy covenant.

Our heart is not turned back, neither have our steps declined from thy way;

Though thou hast sore broken us in the place of dragons, and covered us with the shadow of death.

If we have forgotten the name of our God, or stretched out our hands to a strange god;

Shall not God search this out? For he knoweth the secrets of the heart.

Yea, for thy sake are we killed all the day long: we are counted as sheep for the slaughter.

At first it seems from the context that the Psalmist is still speaking of the Jewish nation, once in such favor with God and reaching a great pinnacle of prosperity and influence under David and Solomon, but then later cast off and put to shame and scattered among the heathen (verses

9–11). Indeed such a development had been prophesied long before by Moses. "And thou shalt become an astonishment, a proverb, and a byword among all nations whither the Lord shall lead thee" (Deut. 28:37; compare verse 14 above).

The problem with this interpretation, however, is that the Mosaic prophecy was in a context of God's judgment on an apostate nation. The immediately preceding verse had said that in their scattering among other nations, they would "serve other gods, wood and stone" (Deut. 28:36). In this psalm, on the other hand, the people are faithful even under their sufferings. "All this is come upon us, yet have we not forgotten thee. . . . Our heart is not turned back" (verses 17–18).

Could it be that the psalm is focusing on only the remnant of faithful Israelites rather than on the whole nation? There were many caught up in the Babylonian exile, for example, who were grieved with the sins of the nation and were themselves true to the Lord, such as Daniel. But that could hardly be the meaning, since the natural tone of the psalm indicates the writer is speaking of the nation as a whole. Furthermore, even righteous Daniel identified himself with the sins of the nation, saying, "We have sinned" (Dan. 9:5). There is no hint in the psalm of sin or judgment being the cause of their sufferings or abandonment by God.

We are left with the conclusion that the Psalmist must be writing prophetically of every body of believers that would some day be called on to suffer for Christ's sake. Many, indeed, would be the times in future history when the fires of persecution would sweep over the people of God. These would not suffer because of their disobedience and rebellion against God, but because of their faithful obedience and testimony to His Son, witnessing of His atoning death and bodily resurrection.

First there was the persecution of the apostles and their early converts under Herod and then under Nero and the Romans. In fact, all the Apostles (save John) and multitudes of others were actually put to death for their faithfulness to the Lord. The many waves of persecution in the next three centuries under the Romans were soon followed by the deadly Moslem invasions. Then there were the slaughters of the Albigenses and the Waldensians and the Huguenots and others who sought to uphold the biblical Christian faith during the times of apostasy by the dominant church. Modern times have seen wholesale persecutions of Christians in fascist and communist nations, not to mention that of the Christian enclaves in Islamic and pagan cultures.

Believers in all such times and places could surely have recited the verses of this psalm in poignant cries to the God who seemed to have forgotten them. In fact, the apostle Paul confirmed that this was its fitting application when he recited the climactic verse of this section of the psalm as descriptive of the experiences of the early Christians. "As it is written, For thy sake we are killed all the day long: we are accounted as sheep for the slaughter" (Rom. 8:36).

Verses 23–26

Awake, why sleepest thou, O Lord? Arise, cast us not off forever.

Wherefore hidest thou thy face, and forgettest our affliction and our oppression?

For our soul is bowed down to the dust: our belly cleaveth unto the earth.

Arise for our help, and redeem us for thy mercies' sale.

The Lord never forgets His people, of course, though He may allow them to witness by their suffering, as well as by their preaching. The final four verses of the psalm seem to be a desperate and climactic prayer for God to "arise" for His people, as He had done in earlier times.

But there is no assurance in the psalm itself that He will do so. The final cry of the suffering people is a plea for redemption and mercy. "Arise for our help, and redeem us for thy mercies' sake,"

The fact is, of course, that God does hear and does care; He is our Redeemer, and He is plenteous in mercy. And He will answer their prayer in abundance of blessing, but it may not be in this present time. "For our light affliction, which is but for a moment, worketh for us a far more exceeding and eternal weight of glory" (2 Cor. 4:17). "The sufferings of this present time are not worthy to be compared with the glory which shall be revealed in us" (Rom. 8:18). "Beloved, think it not strange concerning the fiery trial which is to try you. . . . But rejoice, inasmuch as ye are partakers of Christ's sufferings, that, when his glory shall be revealed, ye may be glad also with exceeding joy" (1 Pet. 4:12–13).

Remember the promise of the Lord Jesus Christ. "And shall not God avenge his own elect, which cry day and night unto him, though he bear long with them? I tell you that he will avenge them speedily. Nevertheless when the Son of man cometh, shall he find faith on the earth?" (Luke 18:7–8). Whatever trials the Lord may allow to fall on His people, they must simply continue to believe and serve and pray, even until death, or until He comes again.

"Be patient therefore, brethren, unto the coming of the Lord. . . . Behold, we count them happy which endure. Ye have heard of the patience of Job, and have seen the end of the Lord, that the Lord is very pitiful, and of tender mercy" (James 5:7–11).

Chapter 46

The Glorious Coming of the King

Psalm 45

P salm 45 is the final "Maschil" psalm for the sons of Korah (following Ps. 42, 43, and 44), and it is fitting that its theme of triumph follows the cries of the suffering people of God in Psalm 44. The return of King Messiah is so prominent in this psalm that it is often (and properly) considered one of the messianic psalms. We include it here as a key "Maschil" devotional lesson for God's people, since this is where it has been placed in God's Word.

Verses 1–2

My heart is inditing a good matter: I speak of the things which I have made touching the king: my tongue is the pen of a ready writer.

Thou art fairer than the children of men: grace is poured into thy lips: therefore God hath blessed thee for ever.

The superscript to the psalm indicates that it is also "A Song of Loves." It speaks not only of the King's triumph, but also of His bride, whose beauty appropriately fits His glory. Although the setting may be in analogy to a royal wedding on earth, the language clearly goes far beyond any such earthly ceremony. It can only be properly understood in terms of Christ, the royal bridegroom, being wedded to his espoused Bride, the people redeemed by Him out of earthly bondage.

The Psalmist speaks of "inditing" a good matter. The word is used only this once in Scripture, and Hebrew scholars say its root meaning is to "gush forth," like an overflowing fountain. His heart is overflowing with his testimony about the King, and he asserts in effect, that, like David, "the Spirit of the LORD spake by me, and his word was in my tongue" (2 Sam. 23:2).

Speaking to the King, he exclaims: "Thou art fairer than the children of men." No mere sinful man ever appeared like this man. He was not just a son of man, He was *the* Son of Man, and the Psalmist possibly was seeing Him in vision as John did on the Isle of Patmos (Rev. 1:13–16), in His glorified body.

Not only His appearance, but also His words are glorious, as "grace is poured into thy lips." Even while on earth, his enemies had testified: "Never man spake like this man" (John 7:46). Now, because of His perfections, this King is not to reign just for a time; instead, "God hath blessed thee forever." In a similar prophetical marriage setting, it is said that "His mouth is most sweet: yea, he is altogether lovely" (Song of Sol. 5:16). He is without "spot, or wrinkle or any such thing" (Eph. 5:27), and His bride must be likewise prepared.

Verses 3–5

Gird thy sword upon thy thigh, O most mighty, with thy glory and thy majesty.

And in thy majesty ride prosperously because of truth and meekness and righteousness; and thy right hand shall teach thee terrible things.

Thine arrows are sharp in the heart of the king's enemies; whereby the people fall under thee.

Before the wedding, however, the King must triumph over all His enemies, and the Bride also must be made ready. The next three verses of the psalm speak of His riding forth to battle. He is addressed as "most mighty," or literally as "O Mighty One." He is, in fact, none less than "the Mighty God" (Isa. 9:6).

So in all the regalia of divine majesty, the King proceeds to ride forth in the cause of truth and meekness and righteousness, doing battle with the forces of deceit and pride and wickedness, all of which are implicit in their leader, Satan, who is the father of lies, the proud rebel who would dethrone God, and a murderer from the beginning. But the Mighty One can defeat the wicked one, and all his minions, both human and demonic.

This great battle is described further in Revelation 19:11–16: "And I saw heaven opened, and behold a white horse; and he that sat upon him was called Faithful and True, and in righteousness he doth judge and make war. . . . And out of his mouth goeth a sharp sword, that with it he should smite the nations . . . and he hath . . . on his thigh a name written, KING OF KINGS, AND LORD OF LORDS."

The sword on his thigh becomes a sharp sword going out of His mouth. Replacing it on his thigh is the mighty Name above every name, to which every knee shall one day bow and confess His Deity (Phil. 2:10). Satan will be cast into the bottomless pit, the beast and the false prophet into the lake of fire, and all their followers will be "slain with the sword of him that sat upon the horse, which sword proceeded out of his mouth" (Rev. 19:21). As Martin Luther sang: "One little word shall fell him."

Verses 6–8

Thy throne, O God, is for ever and ever: the sceptre of thy kingdom is a right sceptre.

Thou lovest righteousness, and hatest wickedness: therefore God, thy God, hath anointed thee with the oil of gladness above thy fellows.

All thy garments smell of myrrh, and aloes, and cassia, out of the ivory palaces, whereby they have made thee glad.

The grace in His lips (verse 2) had become the lethal sword from His mouth, and all the rebellious nations ("the people" of verse 5 could probably be read as "the peoples") had been put down. His eternal kingdom had been established, forever secure against the forces of evil.

In verse 2 it was noted that God had blessed Him forever; now finally His throne will have also been established forever. "Of His kingdom there shall be no end" (Luke 1:33). And note also that the Psalmist addresses the King as God. "Thy throne, O God, is for ever and ever."

Yet, in the next verse, he recognizes that the King has been anointed by God. "O God, thy God hath anointed thee with the oil of gladness above thy fellows." The King, who is God, has been anointed by His God to be King over all kings. He is King of kings and Lord of lords. He is a man, yet fairer than all the sons of men. The scepter of His kingdom is a "right sceptre" — that is, a sceptre of righteousness, for He loves righteousness and hates wickedness. He is the perfect man — man as God had created man to be — but He is also God, the God/man.

Here is the great mystery of the incarnation. God has become man, yet remains God, and there is communication between God the Father and God the Son. A similar conversation appears in Psalm 2:7–8: "The

LORD hath said unto me, Thou art my Son; this day have I begotten thee. Ask of me, and I shall give thee . . . the uttermost parts of the earth for thy possession." Also in Psalm 110:1–2: "The LORD said unto my Lord, Sit thou at my right hand, until I make thine enemies thy footstool. The LORD shall send the rod of thy strength out of Zion: rule thou in the midst of thine enemies."

The righteous King is the "anointed" king, anointed by God with the oil of gladness. This further identifies the King as Messiah, or Christ — the Hebrew and Greek terms both meaning "The Anointed." This identification is confirmed also in the New Testament, where verses 6 and 7 are quoted and applied to Christ. "But unto the Son, he saith, Thy throne, O God, is for ever and ever: a sceptre of righteousness is the sceptre of thy kingdom. Thou hast loved righteousness, and hated iniquity; therefore God, even thy God, hath anointed thee with the oil of gladness above thy fellows" (Heb. 1:8–9).

The "oil of gladness" probably refers to the holy anointing oil ordained by God for the anointing of His priests (Exod. 30:22–25). It was composed by a mixture of myrrh, cinnamon, calamus, and cassia in olive oil in amounts prescribed by God. The same phrase ("oil of gladness") is rendered "oil of joy" in Isaiah 61:3, which is another beautiful messianic passage, speaking of the future kingdom ministry of Messiah. "To appoint unto them that mourn in Zion, to give unto them beauty for ashes, the oil of joy for mourning, the garment of praise for the spirit of heaviness, that they might be called trees of righteousness, the planting of the LORD, that he might be glorified."

His garments are also anointed with a sweet-smelling perfume compounded of myrrh and aloes and cassia, all of which were costly spices from plants of the Middle East. It is worth noting also that myrrh, with frankincense, was presented to Him at His human birth (Matt. 2:11); myrrh, with wine, was offered to Him on His cross (Mark 15:23); and myrrh, again with aloes, was used on Him at His burial (John 19:39).

But the gladness and the joy were necessarily preceded by the suffering (Heb. 12:2). Psalm 45 is a psalm of His glorification and triumphant joy, but the myrrh interjects just a brief reminder that His human life, death, and burial were essential accomplishments that led to the great victory.

In the heavenly city where He will eventually take His bride, there are many mansions prepared by Him (John 14:2). The wonderfully scented garments have been prepared amidst these palaces, all glittering white like polished ivory.

The word "whereby" has been translated as "stringed instruments" in Psalm 150:4. The meaning of the passage is somewhat uncertain, but perhaps the thought is that beautiful music as well as beautiful garments and pleasant aromas emanate from these resplendent ivory mansions, and all of this will contribute to the gladness of the King and His bride.

Verses 9–12

King's daughters were among thy honourable women; upon thy right hand did stand the queen in gold of Ophir.

Hearken, O daughter, and consider, and incline thine ear; forget also thine own people, and thy father's house;

So shall the King greatly desire thy beauty: for he is thy Lord; and worship thou him.

And the daughter of Tyre shall be there with a gift; even the rich among the people shall intreat thy favor.

The royal wedding will take place once the enemy is completely defeated and cast into eternal exile. In the New Testament, the triumphant King is also identified as the Lamb, who has taken "away the sin of the world" (John 1:29). "Let us be glad and rejoice . . . for the marriage of the Lamb is come, and his wife hath made herself ready" (Rev. 19:7). After accompanying the Lamb in His great victory, His bride, first being clothed in fine linen ("the righteousness of saints — Rev. 19:8), will then assume her role as His queen and will be arrayed "in gold of Ophir." Although the exact location of the ancient region of Ophir is still unknown, the quality and quantity of its gold was fabulous in the ancient world. Perhaps its mines will be rediscovered and new veins mined in the coming millennial age.

The queen was the Bride who has now become the wife of the King. But who are those "honorable women" who attend her, who have themselves been daughters of kings? Each is urged to "forget thine own people, and thy father's house." This specification fits those who have left the world to follow the Lord. "If any man come to me," Jesus said, "and hate not his father, and mother, and wife, and children, and brethren, and sisters, yea, and his own life also, he cannot be my disciple. And whosoever doth not bear his cross, and come after me, cannot be my disciple." (Luke 14:26–27).

Thus, the queen seems to represent the corporate body of believers, everywhere in every age, who have followed their Lord, while her "daughters" would be all the individual believers, "daughters of the church," so to speak, the true church being the bride of Christ (note John 3:29, 35; 2 Cor. 11:2; Rev. 21:9).

But the Bride is not only His queen, but also is the servant of the King. Hence the admonition "He is thy Lord, and worship thou him." In the eternal ages, centered in the holy city, "His servants shall serve him" (Rev. 22:3). It will be glorious, joyful service, of course, but we can never forget that He is our loving Lord. He will always love us because He died to save us. "The King shall greatly desire thy beauty," for He himself has made us beautiful in His sight, our garments washed and "made white in the blood of the Lamb" (Rev. 7:14).

"The daughter of Tyre," representing all "the rich among the people" will be there with an expensive gift, hoping thereby to "intreat the favor" of the Bride and her King. But it is too late for that, because she is not included among the "kings' daughters" who constitute the Bride. And besides, none can purchase His favor with a "gift," no matter how costly.

Tyre, the chief city of the Phoenician empire along with Sidon, was geographically very near to Israel, but never was subjugated by it, as were the Canaanite nations. Its seafaring trade made it exceedingly prosperous, but it was a pagan and licentious nation. One of its queenly daughters was the notorious Jezebel, daughter of the king of Sidon (1 Kings 16:31) and its king was so wicked that he became actually the possession of Satan (note Ezek. 28:12–19). Ancient Tyre was eventually completely destroyed, so that no "daughter of Tyre" could actually be present at this great future wedding of the Lamb/King and His spiritual Bride. The figure here most likely represents not only Tyre but also all the Gentile nations and their people who have developed their own systems of works-religion, seeking unsuccessfully to buy their way into the favor of "the gods."

Verses 13–17

The King's daughter is all glorious within: her clothing is of wrought gold.

She shall be brought unto the King in raiment of needlework: the virgins her companions that follow her shall be brought unto thee.

With gladness and rejoicing shall they be brought: they shall enter into the King's palace.

Instead of thy fathers shall be thy children, whom thou mayest make princes in all the earth.

I will make thy name to be remembered in all generations: therefore shall the people praise thee for ever and ever.

The last five verses of the psalm are difficult to understand in detail, since the psalm, as a whole is so rich in symbolism. It is probably significant that both the queen and the King's daughter are arrayed in gold, and that both the King's daughter and her virgin companions are to be brought to the King's presence in His palace — presumably one of His ivory palaces. And all will contribute to His rejoicing. In fact, it was "for the joy that was set before him" that He endured the cross (Heb. 12:2).

Even if we are not quite sure just who are those represented by the kings' daughters, the honorable women, the King's daughter, her virgin companions, and even the queen herself, they all are brought to the great King in the beautiful mansions — prepared for them by the King (John 14:2). They all will gratefully accept His glad welcome as He says, "Enter thou into the joy of thy Lord" (Matt. 25:21).

"Blessed are they which are called unto the marriage supper of the Lamb" (Rev. 19:9). Just as God, when He had formed Eve from Adam's side, "brought her unto the man" (Gen. 2:22), so God now had brought the Bride to the King. And just as Adam had said, "This is now bone of my bones, and flesh of my flesh" (Gen. 2:23), Jesus had promised, "I will . . . receive you unto myself; that where I am, there ye may be also" (John 14:3).

Having come to the marriage and participated joyfully in the marriage supper, all of these then will go forth as "thy children," assigned to render service as "princes in all the earth." They will have been made "kings and priests unto God and his Father" as "judgment was given unto them" (Rev. 1:6, 20:4).

Even the ancient fathers, from Adam on to the last person redeemed before Christ's coming, will be there among the rejoicing throngs around His throne. As his spiritual children they will be sent out as His princes to serve Him throughout His universal dominion.

As the Psalmist is about to conclude His inspired prophecy, God speaks directly of His Son, the great King. "I will make thy name to be remembered in all generations." An unknown scribe in a small nation wrote this down 2,500 to 3,000 years ago, yet it has been gloriously fulfilled in all the ages since, and will never be forgotten. As the Psalmist responds, "The people shall praise thee for ever and ever," he ends his prophecy.

God has blessed Him forever (verse 2), and has established His throne forever (verse 6). Therefore His people will praise His name forever. His words have been confirmed in every generation since, and will continue to be fulfilled in all the ages to come, world without end. Amen.

Chapter 47

Other Maschil Psalms

The first five of the Maschil psalms have been explored in some detail. Each has a vital message to convey. As noted in our preliminary discussion of these psalms, the term "Maschil" means something like "devotional instruction" or "meditative teaching."

What seems to be the dominant theme of this sort in each individual psalm has been indicated in the respective chapter titles. Thus, Psalm 32 dealt with "The Blessing of Sins Forgiven." Chapter 44, covering both Psalms 42 and 43 was called "The Strange Silence of God." Psalm 44 was denoted as "The Psalm of the Martyrs," and Psalm 45 has the theme of "The Glorious Coming of the King."

The other nine Maschil psalms also have vital themes, but we shall not discuss them in the same detail as the first five. Along with the key "meditative teaching" of each, we can at least point out certain significant verses as we survey them in order.

Psalm 52

The next four of the Maschil psalms — 52, 53, 54, and 55 — were all written by David. According to its superscript, Psalm 52 was written by David after Doeg the Edomite betrayed the priest Ahimelech and then slew all the priests of the Lord at Nob (see 1 Sam. 21:7, 22:9–19), while David was hiding from Saul in the cave Adullam.

The theme of the psalm is the certainty of eventual judgment on the wicked. Doeg, though an Edomite, had become prosperous in the service of Saul, but cared nothing for the God of Israel. When Saul's servants refused to obey Saul's command to slay the priests, Doeg quite willingly took on the commission to kill these defenseless servants of God. No wonder David wrote, under God's inspiration: "Thou lovest all devouring words, O thou deceitful tongue. God shall likewise destroy thee for ever, he shall take away, and pluck thee out of thy dwelling place, and root thee out of the land of the living. Selah" (verses 4–5).

What a warning to those who deliberately and knowingly dishonor their Creator! "Lo, this is the man that made not God his strength . . . and strengthened himself in his wickedness" (verse 7).

Psalm 53

This psalm is practically identical with Psalm 14, both stressing the utter folly of atheism. It is significant that Psalm 14 was not named as a Maschil psalm, whereas its duplicate, Psalm 53, is so identified. One might suggest that this repetition is itself the special lesson — namely, that God regards atheism, with its equivalent philosophies such as humanism, pantheism, and others, as the very pinnacle of foolishness.

Paul quotes portions of the psalm in Romans 3:10–12, still further emphasizing this truth that "the fool hath said in his heart, There is no God" (verse 1). He developed the theme still further in Romans 1:21–25: "When they knew God, they glorified him not as God, neither were thankful; but became vain in their imaginations, and their foolish heart was darkened. Professing themselves to be wise, they became fools. . . . Who changed the truth of God into a lie, and worshipped and served the creature more than the Creator."

Psalm 54

The superscript to Psalm 54 indicates that David wrote it as a result of the inhospitality of the inhabitants of the wilderness of Ziph, south of Israel, as he was fleeing from Saul (see 1 Sam. 23:19–24, 26:1–2). It is both a prayer for help against those who persecute believers and a testimony of confidence that God will indeed deliver them.

Many of the older theologians believed that, in this psalm, David had become a type of Christ, so that the psalm was really messianic in its fuller meaning. That is, it reveals the unspoken thoughts, words, and prayers of the Lord Jesus, as He suffered for us at the hand of God's enemies, but was finally delivered by God after He had "freely sacrificed" (verse 6) His life to save the lost. Such an interpretation actually does fit the words of the psalm, and it could well be that this was indeed the ultimate meaning woven into it by the Spirit's inspiration.

Psalm 55

These four Davidic Maschils culminate in this one, which is longer by one verse than the other three combined. All have similar themes — suffering and oppression causing great stress and anxiety, but nevertheless bearable in view of God's holy purposes and ultimate sure deliverance.

290 · Treasures in the Psalms

Usually, the immediate cause of David's suffering seems to involve human opponents of David's. In Psalm 52 it was Doeg's betrayal and Saul's pursuit of David, whereas in Psalm 53 it was the people of Ziph aiding Saul against David.

In this psalm, it seems to be the treachery of his one-time friend Ahithophel that grieves David. Ahithophel had been David's counselor (1 Chron. 27:33, 2 Sam. 16:23), but later became one of Absalom's conspirators against David (2 Sam. 15:31). But as in the other three psalms, there is also an underlying messianic prophetic theme, with David's suffering and betrayal prefiguring those of Christ. In the later case, of course, Judas Iscariot is the betraying friend. "We took sweet counsel together," Jesus could have said, "and walked into the house of God in company" (verse 14). "He hath put forth his hands against such as be at peace with him: he hath broken his covenant. The words of his mouth were smoother than butter, but war was in his heart" (verses 20–21).

These could certainly have been thoughts concerning Ahithophel's treason, but they are even more fitting as the unspoken words Jesus could have uttered in His heart about His disciple Judas, the betrayer.

Many of the saints of God over the centuries have experienced similar "oppression of the wicked" (verse 3) as they have tried to serve God. Some have, like Jesus, been betrayed by erstwhile friends, and this is more painful than overt opposition by enemies. As David mourned: "For it was not an enemy that reproached me: then I could have borne it" (verse 12).

There seems also to be an anticipation of Jonah's experience (Jon. 1:1–17) here. "And I said, Oh that I had wings like a dove! for then would I fly away, and be at rest" (verse 6). Jonah, whose very name means "dove," tried to do just that, seeking to "wander far off, and remain in the wilderness" (verse 7). But as he fled on the ship, God sent a violent storm on the sea. One does not escape his problems or his God-sent responsibilities by fleeing from them! "I would hasten my escape from the windy storm and tempest" (verse 8) must have been Jonah's desperate thinking, as he urged the sailors to drown him in the sea.

But just as Noah's dove could find no rest on the stormy seas of the great flood until she returned to the ark (Gen. 8:9) so Jonah (that is, the "dove") that God had sent to Nineveh could not even escape God in the sea until he returned to the will of God.

So with David, and so with us. Instead of fleeing from God, David prayed. "As for me, I will call upon God; and the LORD shall save me" (verse 16). A significant "imprecatory" prayer is uttered in verse 9. "Destroy, O Lord, and divide their tongues." The word "divide" is the Hebrew *palag*, used elsewhere in Scripture only in Job 38:25 ("(God) hath divided a watercourse for the overflowing of waters") and in Genesis 10:25, with 1 Chronicles 1:19 ("in his days the earth was divided").

The patriarch Peleg was actually named after this division, apparently right after the dispersion at Babel, when the primeval nations were divided by the confusion of tongues. Thus, David was praying for an analogous division of the tongues in the counseling of those who were counseling Absalom in his rebellion against his father. That is exactly what happened, in answer to David's prayer (2 Sam. 16:20, 17:7, 14, 23).

The psalm concludes with this very wise counsel: "Cast thy burden upon the LORD, and he shall sustain thee: he shall never suffer the righteous to be moved. But thou, O God, shalt bring them down into the pit of destruction [that is Sheol, or Hades]: bloody and deceitful men shall not live out half their days; but I will trust in thee" (verses 22 and 23).

The Hebrew word here for "burden" is used only here and actually means "gift," reminding us that "unto you it is given in the behalf of Christ, not only to believe on him, but also to suffer for his sake" (Phil. 1:29). Then, as we trust Him, He will "sustain us" — or, literally, "hold us erect."

Psalm 74

The next two Maschil psalms in order are Psalm 74 and Psalm 78. Asaph, one of David's prominent musicians, wrote both these. As in so many of the psalms, Asaph is concerned with the apparent prominence and prosperity of the wicked, especially with their blasphemous contempt for the worship of God. The first 11 verses of Psalm 74 contain this lamentation.

The response beginning at verse 12, however, is different from other psalms in that it focuses on God's great works in controlling His great creation. He is able, therefore, to answer the prayers of His creatures. Indeed, "God is my king of old, working salvation in the midst of the earth" (verse 12).

In support of this assertion, the Psalmist recalls the events of the great flood over a thousand years earlier. God had "divided the sea by his strength" (verse 13), when "all the fountains of the great deep [were] broken up" (Gen. 7:11). Further, He broke "the heads of the dragons in the waters," thereby "providing meat to the people inhabiting the wilderness" (verses 13–14). In the antediluvian world, the early seas were rich with swarms of fishes and other marine animals, in answer to God's command: "Let the waters bring forth abundantly." Among these were the "great whales . . . which the waters brought forth abundantly" (Gen. 1:20–21).

The Hebrew word here in Genesis for "whales" is the same word (*tannim*) normally translated "dragons," including the "dragons in the waters" of Psalm 74:13. These particular animals are the same as the "leviathan" of the next verse. That "leviathan" was a species of "dragon" is confirmed in Isaiah 27:1, which speaks of "Leviathan that crooked serpent . . . the dragon that is in the sea." The description of a leviathan is given in some detail by God in Job 41, and it is evident that it is some kind of extinct sea monster, like nothing now known in the present oceans. The many other references in the Bible to "dragons" would indicate that it is a sort of generic name for various kinds of fierce reptiles, some small but some huge, some on land, some in the sea, with the leviathan being a great sea dragon. In fact, all the biblical references to dragons compare very well to what we know about the extinct animals that, since Darwin's time, have been called dinosaurs.

These great marine reptiles, possibly plesiosaurs or some similar species, were numerous in the world before the flood, but their numbers were severely curtailed by the violent upheavals of the ocean bottoms that initiated the flood. Their flesh then became food for the fish and other sea creatures that were able to survive these upheavals. These are likely what is meant by "the people inhabiting the wilderness" (verse 14). The word "people" is sometimes used for animals (Prov. 30:25).

Then, after the flood, there were for a time many "mighty rivers," draining the waters of the flood back into the deepened ocean basins when the mountains were uplifted (note Ps. 104:6–9). But eventually God "driedst up mighty rivers," (verse 15) so that their remnants in the present age are, in every case, much smaller than they were when they scoured out the great canyons and laid down the thick alluvium beds in their flood plains.

God also "prepared the light and the sun," day and night, summer and winter, to be stabilized at uniform rates after the flood, to endure "as long as the earth remaineth" (Gen. 8:22). Note, by the way, that "the light" and "the sun" are not synonymous terms. Light existed before the sun was created to give out light. "God is light," and the future holy city will have "no need of the sun" for "the Lamb is the light thereof" (Rev. 21:23). God also "set all the borders of the earth" (verse 17) after the flood, establishing the continental landmasses and the ocean basins which they border, in essentially their present positions.

In view of God's great power, as well as His great love for His redeemed people, it is surely appropriate for those people to pray to their Creator/Redeemer whenever they are being oppressed. God can surely hear and answer, but it will be always in accord only with His own good and acceptable will.

Psalm 78

The 78th Psalm has the distinction of being the second longest of all the 150 psalms in the Book of Psalms. Its 72 verses are second only to the

176 verses of Psalm 119. Its obvious theme is a retelling of Israel's history in poetic form, with special emphasis on their deliverance from Egypt, their times in the wilderness, and then their conquest of Canaan, eventually establishing David as the king of Israel. The purpose of the writer Asaph was to encourage the people to "set their hope in God, and not forget the works of God, but keep his commandments" (verse 7).

He reminded the people that their fathers had often murmured against God and even rebelled against Him, but that again and again He had forgiven them and continued to care for them. "He, being full of compassion, forgave their iniquity, and destroyed them not" (verse 38). Asaph apparently wrote during the time of David, hoping their future history under David and the kingdom would be happier than in the past. Sadly, however, it was not to be. They would forget David, as they had forgotten Moses and Joshua, and soon the kingdom would be divided and eventually the people sent into exile.

Nevertheless, the history was true, and God was still the same. The final verse of the psalm reaffirms "the integrity of his heart, and . . . the skillfulness of his hands" (verse 72). God's truth abideth still.

A few incidental points touched on by Asaph might be noted. Over a millennium after the dispersion of the nations at Babel, Egypt was still recognized as the land of Ham (verse 51). God was recognized by Asaph as "the LORD" (verse 4), as "their rock" and "their redeemer" (verse 35), as "the Holy One of Israel" (verse 41), and as "the most high God" (verse 56). He also knew that the earth had been "established for ever" by God (verse 69), and that God's purposes could never be defeated.

Psalm 88

This Maschil, written by Heman the Ezrahite, is a unique psalm of lament — unique in that its complaints are never softened with any note of hope, as is true in all the other psalms of sadness. The "instructional" aspect of this Maschil is to show that even godly believers can be brought into deep despondency at times. There is never cause for spiritual pride or presumption in a Christian. Heman was apparently reputed to be a man of wisdom (1 Kings 4:31), but whether this might have led to pride and a resultant fall would be speculative. In any case, he does direct his prayer to "the God of my salvation," praying "day and night," so he does have faith and hope, even though he does not express it.

There is also a real possibility that the psalm is intended at least in part as a messianic prophecy, simulating the thoughts of the suffering Savior. This interpretation may give new insights into the heart and life of Christ. For example, at the height of his despair, the suffering one asks, "Why hidest thou thy face from me?" (verse 14), immediately causing one to think of Christ crying from the cross. "Why hast thou forsaken me?" (Matt. 27:46). Then in the next verse he remembers that "I am afflicted and ready to die from my youth up" (verse 15). The four gospels are mostly silent about the early years, when Jesus was a youth, but the Psalmist, perhaps speaking for the Lord on the cross, indicates that he was rejected and opposed even in his early years.

Once the suffering was complete, however, and the sin-debt completely paid, fellowship with His father was fully restored. The same would be true of Heman, of course, and of Job, and of the saints of every generation, when God's purpose in the testing has been accomplished.

"Shall thy lovingkindness be declared in the grave? or thy faithfulness in destruction?" (verse 11). In this verse, "the grave" is Sheol and "destruction" is Abaddon, both names denoting the prison of the dead deep in the earth. The answer of course, is "Thou wilt not leave my soul in hell [i.e., Sheol]" (Ps. 16:10). This promise was specifically fulfilled in the resurrection of Christ, but the principle is valid for every true believer, "for he hath said, I will never leave thee, nor forsake thee" (Heb. 13:5).

Psalm 89

Ethan, the author of Psalm 89, was very likely the brother of Heman (1 Kings 4:31). Both were Ezrahites, probably descended from Zerah, of the tribe of Judah, and both considered wise men. His Psalm 89 was, unlike that of his brother, excitingly positive, a fit response to the negative outlook of Heman in Psalm 88. After Psalms 119 and 78, it is the third longest psalm, with its 52 verses. It begins with the exulting assertion: "I will sing of the mercies of the Lord for ever" (verse 1), and closes with the doxology that ends Book II of the psalms: "Blessed be the LORD for evermore. Amen and Amen" (verse 52).

Verses 2–4 quote the Lord himself, reiterating his everlasting covenant with David, to be fulfilled in its fullest sense in the Messiah's coming kingdom. Then, the Psalmist shows that the setting is actually at God's throne in the heavens, "in the congregation of the saints" (verse 5) — that is, in the presence of His angels. "For who in the heaven can be compared unto the LORD? who among the sons of the mighty can be likened unto the LORD?" (verse 6). The phrase "sons of the mighty" is, in Hebrew, *Bar elim,* or "sons of God," referring to the angels.

The time is in the future when Christ returns after defeating Satan and the armies of his minions on earth. "Thou hast broken Rahab in pieces . . . scattered thine enemies" (verse 10). Rahab, meaning "the proud one" is a reference to Satan.

"The north and the south thou hast created them" (verse 12). Such directions are really meaningful only on a spherical planet with a polar axis of rotation, all created by God on the first day of creation when He established the cycle of day and night.

God again speaks in verses 19–37, this time clearly in messianic terms. Speaking of David's kingdom, He promises "His seed also will I make to endure forever, and his throne as the days of heaven" (verse 29). Note also that the sun and moon, like David's throne, will endure eternally. "His seed shall endure for ever, and his throne as the sun before me. It shall be established for ever as the moon, and as a faithful witness in heaven. Selah" (verses 36–37).

In the remaining verses, however, he seems to revert to a complaint almost like that of his brother Heman in Psalm 88, noting that these glorious promises are not being fulfilled now.

No, and not yet either, 3,000 years later! But they will be, in God's own perfect time. In the meantime, "Blessed be the LORD for evermore. Amen and Amen" (verse 52).

Psalm 142

The last of the Maschil psalms, like the first (Ps. 32), was written by David. The superscript says that it was written while he was in the cave Adullam (1 Sam. 22:1), hiding from Saul, who was bent on killing him. It had been written, therefore, long before David's affair with Bathsheba, and thus before Psalm 32. For some reason, however, it was not included in the first collection of David's psalms (that is, in Book I), but finally was incorporated in Book V.

Under the circumstances, it is not surprising that it is a psalm of anxiety, calling out for God's intervention. One of David's most familiar verses in this vein, has often been appreciated by missionaries on behalf of their unreached multitudes in the difficult places: "I looked on my right hand, and beheld, but there was no man that would know me: refuge failed me; no man cared for my soul" (verse 4).

David was eventually delivered, of course, and went on to become Israel's greatest king, as well as the one whose throne would belong to his "seed," the Lord Jesus Christ, forever.

Part VII

The Book-End Psalms

Chapter 48

Betrayal and Victory

Psalm 41

A s discussed in chapter 1, the Book of Psalms is organized in terms of five books, or collections of psalms. There has never been a generally accepted explanation for this division, or why certain psalms were placed in each collection. It may have been simply a matter of human convenience at the time — first one collection was "published," later another, and so on, like a series of anthologies in modern times.

Even so, the writing of each psalm was divinely inspired, as are all the other books of the Bible, and individual verses are frequently quoted in the New Testament (often even by Christ), so that God evidently at least *approved* of the resulting collections. It is certainly possible also that the particular book divisions and arrangements were themselves also divinely inspired, whether or not we can yet discern God's purposes involved.

If that is so, one could easily further assume that the first and last psalm in each book both had some particular significance with relation to these purposes — that is, the two "book-ends" of each book. It is surely significant, for example, that each of the five books *ends* with a grand doxology, involving a special "blessing" of the Lord by the psalm writer.

That is why we shall now take a closer look in this section of our study at these great "book-end" psalms of the five books. They are all beautiful and very meaningful psalms, well worthy of close analysis. In Book I, these are Psalm 1 and Psalm 41. Psalm 1 has already been studied (chapter 2), so we shall proceed to look at Psalm 41.

Verses 1–3

Blessed is he that considereth the poor; the Lord will deliver him in time of trouble.

The LORD will preserve him and keep him alive; and he shall be blessed upon the earth: and thou wilt not deliver him into the will of his enemies.

The LORD will strengthen him upon the bed of languishing: thou wilt make all his bed in his sickness.

It is interesting that the first verses of each of the two "book-end" psalms of Book I begin with the pronouncement "Blessed. . . ." There are only five other psalms in the whole Book of Psalms that begin thus (Ps. 32, 112, 119, 128, and 144), and it is worth noting in passing what these seven descriptions of the "blessed" one (that is the seven opening "beatitudes" in the Psalms tell us.

Blessed is the man that walketh not in the counsel of the ungodly (Ps. 1:1)

Blessed is he whose transgression is forgiven, whose sin is covered (Ps. 32:1).

Blessed is he that considereth the poor (Ps. 41:1).

Blessed is the man that feareth the LORD, that delighteth greatly in his commandments (Ps. 112:1).

Blessed are the undefiled in the way, who walk in the law of the LORD (Ps. 119:1).

Blessed is every one that feareth the LORD; that walketh in his ways (Ps. 128:1).

Blessed be the LORD my strength (Ps. 144:1).

All of these except the seventh (which fittingly blesses — or praises — God for His many blessings to man) could be seen as a sort of running commentary on the blessed man of Psalm 1:1. Surely there are countless blessings for those who walk in the ways of God instead of the counsel of the ungodly.

In a very real sense, Psalm 41, while growing out of David's experiences, is ultimately a messianic psalm. Verse 9 of the psalm was actually quoted by the Lord Jesus as prophetic of His own betrayal by Judas (see John 13:18).

The Lord did, again and again, "deliver" David "in time of trouble" (verse 1), and "keep him alive" (verse 2), as Saul and many others sought to slay him. But this also was true of the Lord Jesus, until His work was finally accomplished on the cross. As we examine the verses of this psalm, we will be thinking especially of their fulfillment in Christ.

In His human incarnation, the Lord indeed was "poor," and His needs were largely met by others. Once he left His childhood home with Joseph and Mary, He was a "homeless" man. On one occasion, He said, "The foxes have holes, and the birds of the air have nests; but the Son of man hath not where to lay his head" (Matt. 8:20). Indeed, "though he was rich, yet for your sakes he became poor, that ye through his poverty might be rich" (2 Cor. 8:9). Finally, when He died on the cross, His only possessions were the garments He was wearing, and the soldiers took all of them. No wonder David (and Christ) could say: "Blessed be he that considereth the poor."

"The LORD will preserve him, and keep him alive" (verse 2). How gloriously has this promise been fulfilled in Christ! In His resurrection glory, He would say to John and to us: "I am he that liveth, and was dead; and, behold, I am alive for evermore. Amen; and have the keys of hell and of death" (Rev. 1:18). Now, "because I live," He had said to His followers, "ye shall live also" (John 14:19).

But what is meant by the "bed of languishing" and the "bed in his sickness" in verse 3? Jesus constantly was coming in contact with sick people, including those with the highly contagious and dreaded disease of leprosy. Yet, instead of being infected by them, He went about "healing all manner of sickness and all manner of disease among the people" (Matt. 4:23). Instead of transmitting their diseases to Him, "as many as touched him were made whole" (Mark 6:56), and He transmitted His divine health to them.

The word translated "languishing" in verse 3 is translated "sorrowful" the only other time it is used (Job 6:7), and the word translated "sickness" is translated "grief" on several occasions. Jesus was indeed, "a man of sorrows, and acquainted with grief" (Isa. 53:3). Thus, "we have not an high priest which cannot be touched with the feeling of our infirmities." Like those whose sorrow and grief He shared as He went about healing them in Galilee long ago, we may "come boldly unto the throne of grace, that we may obtain mercy, and find grace to help in time of need" (Heb. 4:15–16).

Verses 4–5

I said, LORD, be merciful unto me: heal my soul; for I have sinned against thee.

Mine enemies speak evil of me, When shall he die, and his name perish?

David, of course, could surely confess to the Lord that "I have sinned against thee" (note especially Ps. 51:4) and then plead for mercy. But how could such a statement apply to Christ, if this is, indeed, a messianic psalm?

Christ's enemies did "speak evil" of Him repeatedly, accusing Him of Sabbath-breaking (John 5:18), gluttony and wine-bibbing (Luke 7:34), and even of blasphemy (John 10:33). But these were all false accusations, for He "did no sin" (1 Pet. 2:22). He "was in all points tempted like as we are, yet without sin" (Heb. 4:15).

All this is gloriously true; nevertheless He became the very greatest of all sinners — in fact, He became Sin itself! God the Father even had to forsake His own Son (Matt. 27:46), because "He hath made him to be sin for us, who knew no sin" (2 Cor. 5:21). Not just a sinner, but *SIN*! And this was all *for us*! He "bare our sins in his own body on the tree" (1 Pet. 2:24). "He is the propitiation for our sins; and not for ours only, but also for the sins of the whole world" (1 John 2:2).

Once the penalty for all our sins was fully paid, His Father finally could answer His prayer for mercy and healing. "For he hath not despised nor abhorred the affliction of the afflicted; neither hath he hid his face from him; but when he cried unto him, he heard" (Ps. 22:24). Though He must die for sin, and be buried, He could say prophetically: "My flesh also shall rest in hope. For thou wilt not leave my soul in hell; neither wilt thou suffer thine holy one to see corruption" (Ps. 16:9–10; Acts 2:27). "I waited patiently for the LORD, and he inclined unto me, and heard my cry. He brought me up also out of an horrible pit . . . and established my goings" (Ps. 40:1–2).

Verses 6–9

And if he come to see me, he speaketh vanity: his heart gathereth iniquity to itself: when he goeth abroad, he telleth it.

All that hate me whisper together against me: against me do they devise my hurt.

An evil disease, say they, cleaveth fast unto him: and now that he lieth he shall rise up no more.

Yea, mine own familiar friend, in whom I trusted, which did eat of my bread, hath lifted up his heel against me.

The Lord here (through David) is speaking of His enemies (verse 5), especially thinking of His false friend, Judas Iscariot, who would soon betray Him to His enemies. These external "enemies" (verse 5) — political and religious enemies, who were seeking His life — became personalized in "mine enemy" (verse 11). A supposed friend who is really a secret enemy is more grievous to one's heart than a horde of impersonal external enemies.

Note how these verses probe deeply and perfectly into the thoughts and acts of Judas, climaxing on the night he betrayed Christ to those external enemies seeking Christ's death. "If he come to see me, he speaketh vanity." Turn to the record of Judas coming to Him in Gethsemane. "And immediately, while he yet spake, cometh Judas. . . . And as soon as he was come, he goeth straightway to him, and saith, Master, master; and kissed him" (Mark 14:43–45). Vain speech indeed!

Before that, of course, "his heart" — that is, the wicked heart of Judas — had gathered iniquity to itself, to such an extent that "Satan entered into him. Then said Jesus unto him, That thou doest, do quickly." Thereupon, Judas "went immediately out: and it was night" (John 13:27–30).

Judas quickly "goeth abroad" and "telleth it" (verse 6) to the priests waiting with their band of soldiers ready to arrest Jesus at night and away from the crowds, as soon as Judas would come to lead them to Him. There they would all "whisper together against me" to "devise my hurt" (verse 7).

And what excuse could they give for such an evil plan? The "evil disease" (verse 8) which is mentioned by them was not a deadly illness of some kind, unless they were thinking of it as a spiritual sickness from their perspective. The word translated "disease" is so translated only this one time in the Bible, but it does occur frequently and is rendered in many different ways — most frequently simply as "thing."

This "thing" the Lord Jesus was teaching was God's wonderful plan for His people, but to the politico-religious establishment, it was an "evil thing." For it would destroy their whole corrupt system if the people accepted it, so they felt they must finally rid themselves of this danger once and for all. If they could once get Him out of the way, executed as a criminal, then He and His teaching would "rise up no more."

And their whole plot depended upon getting one of His friends to betray Him in some quiet place in the dark of night. That would be Judas. "Yea, mine one familiar friend." When Judas kissed Him in the garden, Jesus even greeted him as "Friend" (Matt. 26:50).

This verse 9, which so clearly identifies Psalm 41 as messianic, was actually quoted by Christ at the Last Supper. Speaking to His disciples, He said, "I know whom I have chosen: but that the scripture might be fulfilled, he that eateth bread with me hath lifted up his heel against me" (John 13:18).

Then, at the supper, when Jesus had told His disciples that one of them would betray Him, He answered their troubled inquiry by saying:

"He it is, to whom I shall give a sop, when I have dipped it. And when He had dipped the sop, He gave it to Judas Iscariot" (John 13:26). This gesture — dipping a piece of bread in the bowl and giving it to a guest at the meal — was considered in that day as a special token of friendship. But Judas took it as the indication that Jesus knew about his imminent betrayal of that friendship, so he had best carry it out quickly.

Verses 10–12

But thou, O Lord, be merciful unto me, and raise me up, that I may requite them.

By this I know that thou favourest me, because mine enemy doth not triumph over me.

And as for me, thou upholdest me in mine integrity, and settest me before thy face for ever.

But the Lord Jesus, still in His humanity and intensely aware of the cruel suffering and death awaiting Him, could still confidently and trustingly call on His Father for mercy and ultimate victory. Even though He must die, He could pray to His Father: "Raise me up that I may requite them . . . [that] mine enemy [Judas, of course, but ultimately Satan, who had entered into Judas] doeth not triumph over me" (verses 10–11).

And just *how* would He requite them? "O Jerusalem, Jerusalem . . . how often would I have gathered thy children together . . . and ye would not! Behold, your house is left unto your desolate" (Matt. 23:37–38). Judas, in particular, grief-stricken over what he had done, "went and hanged himself" (Matt. 27:5). And the great enemy, Satan, the instigator of the entire evil plot, had defeated himself. He programmed Christ's agonizing death, but it was only that "through death (Christ) might destroy him that had the power of death, that is, the devil; And deliver them who through fear of death were all their lifetime subject to bondage" (Heb. 2:14–15). Eventually "the devil that deceived them (shall be) cast into the lake of fire and brimstone . . . and shall be tormented day and night for ever and ever" (Rev. 20:10). Thus, will be the end of those who betray their great Creator and gracious Redeemer.

As for Christ himself, not only would God raise Him up from death, but also He would be restored to His presence, "before thy face for ever" (verse 12). "In thy presence is fullness of joy, at thy right hand there are pleasures for evermore" (Ps. 16:11). "For the joy that was set before him (he) endured the cross, despising the shame, and is set down at the right hand of the throne of God" (Heb. 12:2).

Verse 13

Blessed be the LORD God of Israel from everlasting and to everlasting. Amen, and amen.

This final verse of Psalm 41 is the first of the five great doxologies that close the five book divisions of Psalms. Although the Lord is the "God of Israel," He is also the one true God of creation and salvation for the entire cosmos, for He had no beginning and no ending. God in Christ is the Creator and sustainer of everything (Col. 1:16–17), and we can trust Him fully and bless His name forever.

Chapter 49

Christ and the Coming Kingdom

Psalm 72

Book I of the psalms contains 41 psalms, bounded by Psalm 1 and Psalm 41. All but three were written by David (see chapter 1). In fact, it is possible that *all* were written by David. Thus, Book I is clearly a collection of Davidic psalms, possibly arranged for "publication" by David himself.

Book II continues to be predominantly Davidic in authorship, with 18 of its 31 psalms written by him. Seven were either written by, or for, the sons of Korah, who were prominent in the music ministry during David's reign. One was written by Asaph, who was also an important musician during David's reign. Four have unknown authors, while the last was written either *by* Solomon or (more likely) *for* Solomon, by David. One might surmise from these statistics that Book II was also collected and arranged by David, near the very end of his reign, after he had designated Solomon as heir to his throne.

This collection begins with Psalm 42, one of the Maschil psalms, which has already been discussed in chapter 44. This is the first of the ten psalms inscribed as "For the Sons of Korah" — seven in Book II, three in Book III. (It is probable that Psalm 43 also should be included in this listing, because of its similarity to Psalm 42, as discussed in chapter 44.) It seems at least possible that David wrote these 10 (or 11) psalms with the purpose of having them used in the musical worship provided by the Sons of Korah.

The first "book-end psalm" of Book II is, therefore, Psalm 42, with its plaintive theme of God's strange silence. The last "book-end," on the other hand, is Psalm 72, with its exultation over the glorious future reign of God's chosen king. This psalm is headed by the superscript "A Psalm for Solomon," and probably was written by David, for it closes with these words: "The prayers of David the son of Jesse are ended" (verse 20). Some newer translations render the title as "A Psalm *of* Solomon" (either preposition could be correct), but the context is best understood as written by Solomon's father for Solomon.

Assuming this to be the case, David surely wrote it with God's great promises concerning both Solomon and the still greater "Son of David" (that is, the future King Messiah) in mind, as he had received them from God through the prophet Nathan, and as recorded in 2 Samuel 7:12–16.

Because of this great theme, Psalm 72 is usually considered as a messianic psalm, even though it is never directly cited as such in the New Testament. Its promises were not, and indeed *could not*, have been fulfilled in Solomon. These promises clearly point to the glorious future millennial reign of Christ when He comes again to set up His earthly kingdom of peace and righteousness on earth.

Verses 1–6

Give the king thy judgments, O God, and thy righteousness unto the king's son.

He shall judge thy people with righteousness, and thy poor with judgment.

The mountains shall bring peace to the people, and the little hills, by righteousness.

He shall judge the poor of the people, he shall save the children of the needy, and shall break in pieces the oppression.

They shall fear thee as long as the sun and moon endure, throughout all generations.

He shall come down like rain upon the mown grass: as showers that water the earth.

Psalm 72 is essentially a prayer offered by David, the king, about to turn the kingdom over to Solomon, the king's son. He prays for himself first, that his "judgments," or decisions, might be God's decisions, desiring most of all (as should we, always) that he would be sensitive and obedient to the will of God. Having decided that Solomon would inherit the throne, David then prayed that Solomon as king would reflect and apply God's righteousness in his reign. God had chosen Solomon to be king (1 Chron. 22:9), and David had promised Bathsheba (Solomon's mother) that this would be done (1 Kings 1:17), and so it was.

God did bless and prosper Solomon's reign in many marvelous ways, at least in its earlier years. But David's prayer was — no doubt by divine inspiration — directed more particularly to his distant greater son, the Lord Jesus, who will eventually fulfill all the prophetic promises expressed in his prayer. As the angel Gabriel told Mary, His mother, "The Lord God shall give unto him the throne of his father David: And he shall reign over the house of Jacob forever, and of his kingdom there shall be no end" (Luke 1:32–33). This promise of an eternal, righteous kingdom is confirmed several times in this great psalm (verses 5, 7, 17, and 19).

But we must await its establishment until the return of Christ, when He shall finally put down all rebellion and wickedness and set up His great millennial kingdom over all the earth. At that time, "The kingdoms of this world (will) become the kingdoms of our Lord, and of his Christ; and he shall reign for ever and ever" (Rev. 11:15).

The first stage of this eternal kingdom, however, will last one thousand years, and natural-born men and women will be its subjects. The glorified saints of earlier ages will participate with Christ in the governing of this kingdom. "They shall be priests of God and of Christ, and shall reign with him a thousand years" (Rev. 20:6).

It is *this* period, with Christ reigning in righteousness over a world where some sin still exists in the hearts of natural men and women, that is especially in view in this "kingdom psalm." The high and rugged "mountains" will become "little hills" (note Isa. 40:4) and even the gentle and pleasant topography of the millennial world will speak of peace and righteousness (verse 3). At least in the early centuries of this period, there will be little overt sin, and any such outbreak will be put down quickly (verse 4).

Verses 7–15

In his days shall the righteous flourish; and abundance of peace so long as the moon endureth.

He shall have dominion also from sea to sea, and from the river to the ends of the earth.

They that dwell in the wilderness shall bow before him; and his enemies shall lick the dust.

The kingdom of Tarshish and of the isles shall bring presents: the kings of Sheba and Seba shall offer gifts.

Yea, all kings shall fall down before him: all nations shall serve him.

For he shall deliver the needy when he crieth: the poor also, and him that hath no helper.

He shall spare the poor and needy, and shall save the souls of the needy.

He shall redeem their soul from deceit and violence: and precious shall their blood be in his sight.

And he shall live, and to him shall be given of the gold of Sheba: prayer also shall be made for him continually; and daily shall he be praised.

These verses continue describing the righteous reign of Christ in the millennium. It is obvious that not all of this was accomplished during Solomon's reign, but it *will* be done when that greater Son of David comes to rule the earth. Then "shall the righteous flourish; and abundance of peace" (verse 7). "Thy King . . . shall speak peace unto the (nations): and his dominion shall be from sea even to sea, and from the river even to the ends of the earth" (Zech. 9:9–10). In that great prophetic passage, the prophet Zechariah, many centuries after David, actually appropriated David's words in verse 8.

The two "seas" mentioned in this verse may have been the Mediterranean and the Dead Sea, and the "river" may have been the Euphrates (these were boundaries associated with God's ancient promise to Abraham — Gen. 15:18), but the "dominion" will actually be global, "unto the ends of the earth."

Likewise, the kingdoms mentioned — Tarshish, Sheba, and Seba — were nations distant from Israel in David's world, but they no longer exist today, so they must represent in his prophetic vision all the distant lands of "the whole earth" (verse 19). "All nations shall serve him" (verse 11). The Father had promised his Son "the uttermost parts of the earth for thy possession" (Ps. 2:8).

There will still be human death in that age, because there will still be sin, but even "the child shall die an hundred years old . . . the sinner being an hundred years old shall be accursed" (Isa. 65:20). "His enemies shall lick the dust" (verse 9).

But "He shall live" (verse 15), for "death hath no more dominion over him" (Rom. 6:9). In this age, Christ is "despised and rejected of men" (Isa. 53:3) but in that wonderful age, "daily shall he be praised."

Verses 16–20

There shall be an handful of corn in the earth upon the top of the mountains; the fruit thereof shall shake like Lebanon: and they of the city shall flourish like grass of the earth.

His name shall endure for ever: his name shall be continued as long as the sun: and men shall be blessed in him: all nations shall call him blessed.

Blessed be the LORD God, the God of Israel, who only doeth wondrous things.

And blessed be his glorious name for ever: and let the whole earth be filled with his glory. Amen, and amen.

The prayers of David, the son of Jesse are ended.

The "handful of corn . . . upon the top of the mountains" surely refers to more than the physical grain, though this no doubt will also be produced abundantly in the millennium, not only in earth's fertile valleys and plains but even on the mountaintops. However, the reference to "the city" in verse 16 must, it would seem, refer to Jerusalem, for if any other city were in view, it surely would be named. Thus, the small handful of corn which soon becomes tall stalks waving in the mountaintop winds like the great cedars of Lebanon and then eventually spreads and flourishes over the earth like grass, must refer to the inhabitants of Jerusalem — that is, the people of Israel.

At the close of the tribulation period, followed by Christ's judgment of the nations (Matt. 24:29–31, 25:31–46), there will be "few men left" (Isa. 24:6) adjudged worthy to enter the kingdom age while still in natural human flesh. These will, of course, include the believing remnant in Israel, all of whom will have been saved when they recognize and receive the Lord Jesus as their Messiah and Savior (Zech. 12:10; Rom. 11:26).

This remnant will presumably, therefore, constitute the "handful of corn," in their city on the "top of the mountains" — that is, Mount Zion — which in that day will be "beautiful for situation, the joy of the whole earth . . . on the sides of the north, the city of the great King" (Ps. 48:2).

Israel has actually been symbolized occasionally in the Bible by corn (e.g., Amos 9:9 — "as corn sifted in a sieve"), and this handful of corn will rapidly multiply into a great nation, the leading nation on earth during the Millennium. "It shall come to pass in the last days that the mountain of the LORD's house shall be established in the top of the mountains, and shall be exalted above the hills; and all nations shall flow unto it" (Isa. 2:2).

And note how this prophecy also fits beautifully the King, the great Son of David. He said, "Except a corn of wheat fall into the ground and die, it abideth alone: but if it die, it bringeth forth much fruit" (John 12:24). Not only a handful of corn but even just one corn of wheat, once buried, under the right conditions, may proliferate into a great field of wheat on the top of the mountains. Such has been the result of the death, burial, and resurrection of "the great King."

Furthermore, His kingdom "shall endure for ever" (verse 17), and "shall be continued as long as the sun." Verse 7 had said that "in his days shall the righteous flourish . . . so long as the moon endureth." Verse 5 promised that the Lord would be feared "as long as the sun and moon endure, throughout all generations."

And how long shall the sun and moon endure? Modern evolutionary astronomers to the contrary notwithstanding, God "hath also stablished them for ever and ever" (Ps. 148:3, 6). At the end of the Millennium, the earth and heavens will be drastically renovated (2 Pet. 3:10), but then will be remade into "new heavens and a new earth" (2 Pet. 3:13), which, like the stars (Dan. 12:3), will never pass away.

Christ's great thousand-year kingdom of peace and righteousness on earth — still harboring sin and death among its proliferating Gentile populations — will similarly be translated ultimately into the eternal kingdom centered in the New Jerusalem. This kingdom will then last forever and in it there will be no sin, and no more curse because of sin, and thus no more death (Rev. 21:4, 27, 22:3–5).

Then follows the great doxology that closes Book II of the psalms: "Blessed be his glorious name for ever: and let the whole earth be filled with his glory!" David had ended his first collection in Book I with a doxology (Ps. 41:13), perhaps thinking that it might be the only collection he would ever publish and that a doxology would be the most appropriate way to finish. Whether this was exactly what happened or not, this precedent has been followed in the subsequent books, including this second collection (presumably) of David's.

As a postscript, David then wrote the following emotion-laden addendum: "The prayers of David the son of Jesse are ended." Not David, the eminent king of Israel, or David, the mighty warrior or great poet, but just David the son of Jesse. Assuming David was writing this as part of his investiture of Solomon as king, shortly before he died, this psalm could indeed be considered his swan song, and he remembered and honored his father. The other 18 psalms of David presumably had been written earlier but for some reason either forgotten or lost until their rediscovery by later compilers after David's death. See chapters 44–46.

In any case, this 72nd psalm — the last before his death, except possibly for a brief testimony in 2 Samuel 23:1–7 — is a unique tribute by David to the promised Messiah and a marvelous prophetic word-picture of the still-coming kingdom age that the Messiah (that is, Christ) will bring.

Chapter 50

Temporal Prosperity or Everlasting Life

Psalms 73 and 89

B ook III of the psalms was probably compiled by Asaph after David's death. Asaph had been one of David's chief musicians, quite possibly in charge of all the others, and had been honored by David in having one of his own psalms (Ps. 50) included in David's second compilation (note 1 Chron. 16:5).

The first 11 psalms in Book III had been written by Asaph himself, with 1 each by David, Heman, and Ethan, plus 3 written "for the sons of Korah." Heman, Ethan, and the sons of Korah had also been among David's musicians, so it is possible they also may have worked with Asaph in arranging Book III.

The two "book-end" psalms of Book III are Psalm 73 (by Asaph) and Psalm 89 (by Ethan). The latter was also one of the Maschil psalms and was discussed briefly in chapter 47, so only a few further comments will be appended to this chapter. We now shall look more closely at Psalm 73, a psalm seeming to contain Asaph's own personal testimony as he introduced Book III.

Psalm 73
Verses 1–5

Truly God is good to Israel, even to such as are of a clean heart.

But as for me, my feet were almost gone; my steps had well nigh slipped.

For I was envious at the foolish, when I saw the prosperity of the wicked.

For there are no bands in their death: but their strength is firm.

They are not in trouble as other men: neither are they plagued like other men.

Asaph had apparently been raised to be a God-fearing young man and had tried to live a godly life in accordance with the laws of God (see verse 13). He was well aware of God's past blessings on Israel (verse 1) and on such men as David, and for a time had sought to channel his own life in ways pleasing to the Lord.

But then — like many other young men in every generation — he had observed the apparently good life of prosperity and pleasure being enjoyed by many ungodly men, and he allowed envy to tempt him to follow their ways. David had warned his people against this very danger: "Fret not thyself because of evil doers, neither be thou envious against the workers of iniquity. . . . A little that a righteous man hath is better than the riches of many wicked" (Ps. 37:1–16).

Nevertheless, Asaph began to drift away from the Lord, backsliding so far that his "feet were almost gone" (verse 2). He had observed worldly men prospering throughout their whole lives and even dying without any "bands" (verse 4). This word ("bands") is used only this once in the Old Testament and is of uncertain connotation; it probably suggests that these men seemed to live and die without any regrets, their "strength" still "firm." To all appearances, their skeptical attitude toward God and His commandments had helped them rather than hindered them, and all this had generated both doubt toward God and envy of the ungodly in Asaph.

Verses 6–11

Therefore pride compassest them about as a chain; violence covereth them as a garment.

Their eyes stand out with fatness: they have more than heart could wish.

They are corrupt, and speak wickedly concerning oppression: they speak loftily.

They set their mouth against the heavens, and their tongue walketh through the earth.

Therefore, his people return hither: and waters of a full cup are wrung out to them.

And they say, How doth God know? and is there knowledge in the Most High?

It does seem, in our day as well as in Asaph's day, that at least most (though, happily, not all) of the rich and powerful, the leaders in science and education, the top political and military figures, the star entertainers and athletes, and the captains of industry in every nation, are ungodly and amoral. Indeed, the apostle Paul has confirmed that "not many wise men after the flesh, not many mighty, not many noble are called" (1 Cor. 1:26). James warned the wealthy capitalists of the last days that "your riches are corrupted," noting that "ye have lived in pleasure on the earth, and been wanton" (James 5:2–5). It is all too frequent that ordinary people tend to "idolize" such leaders and try to emulate them if they can. The verses cited above, indeed, sound very much up-to-date.

The more blatant among these prominent people speak blasphemously against the authority — and even the very existence — of God; and the news media, both the popular media and those that are more sophisticated, quickly circulate the arrogant words of their tongues of unbelief and ridicule throughout the earth.

Even many of God's people, like Asaph, are tempted to follow them, parroting their skepticism. "Does God really care about what we do and say? Even if He is real, He is far off in heaven, and can hardly be interested in what we are doing down here." So they rationalize.

Verses 12–17

Behold, these are the ungodly, who prosper in the world: they increase in riches.

Verily I have cleansed my heart in vain, and washed my hands in innocency.

For all the day long have I been plagued, and chastened every morning.

If I say, I will speak thus; behold, I should offend against the generation of thy children.

When I thought to know this, it was too painful for me,

Until I went into the sanctuary of God: then understood I their end.

In contrast to the apparent prosperity and superficial happiness of the ungodly, Asaph (and many other true children of God) have suffered in many ways and degrees and it has often seemed so unfair that they begin to wonder whether God really cares. Like Asaph, such a believer may think that "I have cleansed my heart in vain," (verse 13), and may be strongly tempted to walk in the "counsel of the ungodly" (Ps. 1:1).

Yet they hesitate because they are fearful to "offend against the generation of thy children" (verse 15). The true child of God, even though strongly tempted and starting to backslide, can never become comfortable in the way of the ungodly.

Consequently, the more Asaph sought to understand this anomalous situation — that is, God's apparent blessings on the ungodly and the sufferings of the righteous — the more "wearisome" or "painful" it became. But, before yielding completely, he decided to seek God's answer and went to the temple to pray.

And that, of course, made all the difference in the world! In the presence of God, He began to see all these circumstances in the light of eternity. This present life is not all there is, by any means. As Paul said, we must not "look at the things which are seen, but at the things which are not seen" (2 Cor. 4:18), for "the sufferings of this present time are not worthy to be compared with the glory which shall be revealed in us" (Rom. 8:18).

In Asaph's day, the temple in Jerusalem was "the sanctuary" where God would meet with His people. This was the house of prayer, and even though the ordinary believer could not see God personally, he did know that this was where God really came personally once each year to meet with their high priest. They could always at least sense His presence there, and thus could see things in right perspective if they truly wished to do so. Asaph did so, and he could say, "Then understood I their end" (verse 17).

In our day, we don't need to journey to a temple in Jerusalem or even to our own local church to find God's answer, for God has said; "Ye are the temple of the living God." God himself, in the person of the Holy Spirit, has come to live in our very bodies if we have trusted Christ as our Savior. "God hath said, I will dwell in them, and walk in them; and I will be their God, and they shall be my people" (2 Cor. 6:16). In His daily presence, and with the Holy Scriptures inspired by Him, we need never fret about temporal circumstances, because we know that "in the ages to come, he (will show) the exceeding riches of his grace in his kindness toward us through Christ Jesus" (Eph. 2:7). The wicked and ungodly may be in prosperity and prominence now, but this is only for a short season. As David had written, and Asaph no doubt remembered, "I have seen the wicked in great power, and spreading himself like a green bay tree. Yet he passed away, and, lo, he was not: yea, I sought him, but he could not be found" (Ps. 37:35–36).

Verses 18–22

Surely thou didst set them in slippery places: thou castedst them down into destruction.

How are they brought into desolation, as in a moment! They are utterly consumed with terrors.

As a dream when one awaketh: so, O Lord, when thou awakest, thou shalt despise their image.

Thus my heart was grieved, and I was pricked in my veins.

So foolish was I, and ignorant: I was as a beast before thee.

When we (like Asaph) come to understand the real relation between time and eternity, and between earthly and heavenly wisdom, and between the future destinies of those who ignore and those who believe and obey the Word of God, then we (like Asaph) will be grieved in our hearts and understand how foolish and ignorant we were in our doubts. As the rich man in Christ's parable, each of the ungodly will hear Him say, "Thou in thy lifetime receivedst thy good things, and likewise Lazarus evil things: but now he is comforted, and thou art tormented" (Luke 16:25).

God may *seem* now to be sleeping, but He really never sleeps (Ps. 121:4), and when He "awakes," He will "despise their image." The vaunted "self-image," which modern intellectuals think we should develop, and which can be seen in so many of the supposedly successful men and women of this present age, will soon be broken in pieces like Nebuchadnezzar's dream image (Dan. 2:34), and they will be cast "down into destruction" (verse 18).

Verses 23–28

Nevertheless I am continually with thee: thou hast holden me by my right hand.

Thou shalt guide me with thy counsel, and afterward receive me to glory.

Whom have I in heaven but thee? and there is none upon earth that I desire beside thee.

My flesh and my heart faileth: but God is the strength of my heart, and my portion for ever.

For lo, they that are far from thee shall perish: thou hast destroyed all them that go a whoring from thee.

But it is good for me to draw near to God: I have put my trust
in the Lord God, that I may declare all thy works.

In spite of his foolish doubts, Asaph could finally testify that God
had never abandoned him (verse 23). He has also assured us that if we are
truly His children by faith in Christ, "I will never leave thee, nor forsake
thee" (Heb. 13:5). And what a wonderful assurance is this: "Thou shalt
guide me with thy counsel" (and we now have the complete inscripturated
Word of God with which He can guide us) and "afterward receive me to
glory" (verse 24). All this, and heaven, too!

Furthermore, when we are received up into His glorious presence,
He will be our "portion for ever" (verse 26). And, like Asaph, we "have
put [our] trust in the Lord God" (that is, *Adonai Elohim*, the God of both
present guidance and all power), and can henceforth wholeheartedly "declare all thy works" (verse 28).

Psalm 89

The last psalm in Book III is Psalm 89, written by Ethan, another of
David's musicians. It is one of the Maschil psalms, and was discussed
briefly in chapter 47. It is a long psalm (the third longest of all) and so
will not be treated in full here. However, in addition to those portions
discussed in chapter 47, there are a few other passages that would be good
to discuss briefly in this section on the "book-end" psalms.

The very first verse of Psalm 89 ties in beautifully with the last verse
of Psalm 73. "I will sing of the mercies of the LORD for ever: with my
mouth will I make known thy faithfulness to all generations." Since Ethan
was living only during David's generation, the only way he could sing to
all generations must be either through this one psalm, or perhaps — more
literally — he will be able to continue to sing God's praises in eternity,
when the saints of every generation will be dwelling together with the
Lord. And that's a wonderful prospect for all of us to contemplate: we
ourselves can hear Ethan sing someday — as well as David and the other
singers from every age. God's faithfulness will He "establish in the very
heavens" (verse 2). We also can "praise thy wonders, O LORD: thy faithfulness also in the congregation of the saints" (verse 5). Verse 15 speaks of
the "joyful sound." This is only one word in the original, and it connotes
a victorious blowing of trumpets.

In view of the context in these verses — that is, the great assembly in
heaven with God, the holy angels, and the saints of all generations, this
may well refer to the great trumpet call in 1 Thessalonians 4:16 and 1
Corinthians 15:52, when "the trumpet shall sound, and the dead shall be
raised incorruptible, and we shall be changed."

That will indeed be a joyful sound! In that day, all "the people that know the joyful sound . . . shall walk, O LORD, in the light of thy countenance" (verse 15), and "we shall ever be with the Lord" (1 Thess. 4:17).

The future triumph and eternal glory described so joyfully in verses 1–37 (the term "for ever" is used seven times in this section and the term "all generations," or equivalent, at least three times) is terminated by a "Selah." This is then suddenly followed (verses 38–51) by a lamentation concerning the harsh circumstances in Israel preceding the coming glory times. "Thou hast made his glory to cease, and cast his throne down to the ground" (verse 44). Assuming this section also was written by Ethan, it was presumably prophetic of the coming times of captivity in Babylon, or even possibly the worldwide dispersion after Calvary.

But then comes the doxology completing Book III, possibly added by Asaph himself. "Blessed be the LORD for evermore. Amen, and Amen" (verse 52). This is the final double "Amen" in the Bible (see also the doxologies at the ends of Ps. 41 and 72).

Chapter 51

He Abideth Faithful

Psalm 106

Book IV of the psalms, like Book III, is a collection of psalms, from Psalm 90 through Psalm 106. Thus, these two psalms (90 and 106) are the two "book-end" psalms of Book IV. Psalm 90 has already been discussed in some detail in chapter 24, so we shall look primarily at Psalm 106 in this chapter.

There is very little indication as to who might have been the compiler of this book, although Asaph might be as good a guess as any. The psalms in this book clearly were collected after the time of David, though probably not long after. Solomon is another possibility. Two of the psalms are attributed to David and one to Moses, but the rest have no author listed.

As discussed in chapter 24, however, there is a good possibility that Moses also wrote Psalm 91 as well as Psalm 90. There is considerable similarity of words and themes in these two psalms.

There is also a reasonable possibility that David wrote more than just the two psalms attributed to him (Ps. 101 and 103). For example, Psalm 104 begins and ends with the same expression as at the beginning and end of Psalm 103 — that is, "Bless the LORD, O my soul." This particular expression occurs nowhere else in the psalms.

And then, note also that Psalms 105 and 106 both end with the same word (that is "Hallelujah" or "Praise ye the LORD") as at the very end of Psalm 104, the latter being the first occurrence of this important word in the entire Book of Psalms. All of this might suggest that David wrote the whole series of psalms, from Psalm 101 through Psalm 106 — that is, the last six psalms of Book IV. Psalm 102 (verses 25–27) and Psalm 103 (verses 14–17) have one important common feature: they both contrast the principle of decay in the created universe, including man, with the truth of God's unchanging nature.

Psalms 95–100 also seem to be a connected unit, as noted in chapter 19, although no author is listed for any of them. Although these authorship suggestions are speculative, it is probable that someone of David's time or soon afterwards did collect them and bring them together as a 17-psalm set, the same number as in Book III. In any case, the essential point is that all were soon recognized as inspired by God and adopted into the Old Testament canon.

Psalms 90 and 106 appropriately serve their purpose as "book-ends" of Book IV. Psalm 90 is the oldest of all the psalms, written by Moses, and in content extends all the way back to before the creation. Psalm 106, probably written by David, completes the review of the history of the people of God begun in Psalm 105, extending up to the recovery of the ark of the covenant from the Philistines by David.

Since Psalm 90 has been treated in chapter 24, we can proceed now to a study of Psalm 106. As noted above, this psalm seems to comprise a connected series with Psalms 104 and 105, all ending with "Hallelujah," and all dealing with God's providential care of His creation and His people despite their failures. Psalm 104 discusses the ancient world and its inhabitants, down to about the time of Abraham. Psalm 105 reviews the history of the chosen people from the time of Abraham down to their early experiences with Moses. Psalm 106 then reviews the times of Moses down into the times in Canaan under the judges and until the early period of David's reign. The repeated failures of God's people and their chastisements by God are rehearsed, but always God had remained faithful to His promises to Abraham, and the people were restored.

Verses 1–5

Praise ye the LORD. O give thanks unto the LORD; for he is good: for his mercy endureth forever.

Who can utter the mighty acts of the LORD? Who can shew forth his praise?

Blessed are they that keep judgment, and he that doeth righteousness at all times.

Remember me, O LORD, with the favour that there bearest unto thy people: O visit me with thy salvation.

That I may see the good of thy chosen, that I may rejoice in the gladness of thy nation, that I may glory with thine inheritance.

These opening verses of Psalm 106 are an exhortation and then a prayer (by David, probably) as an introduction to the writer's long retelling of Israel's failures and God's faithfulness. Truly "His mercy endureth for ever" (verse 1). As the apostle Paul affirmed many centuries later: "If we believe not, yet he abideth faithful: he cannot deny himself" (2 Tim. 2:13).

Assuming David to have been the writer, his prayer in verses 4 and 5 for favor to the people of his kingdom, for good to God's chosen nation and for the gladness of Israel as God's inheritance surely would have been very appropriate in the early days of David's reign.

Verses 6–15

We have sinned with our fathers, we have committed iniquity, we have done wickedly.

Our fathers understood not thy wonders in Egypt; they remembered not the multitude of thy mercies; but provoked him at the sea, even at the Red sea.

Nevertheless he saved them for his name's sake, that he might make his mighty power to be known.

He rebuked the Red sea also, and it was dried up: so he led them through the depths, as through the wilderness.

And he saved them from the hand of him that hated them, and redeemed them from the hand of the enemy:

And the waters covered their enemies: there was not one of them left.

Then believed they his words; they sang his praise.

They soon forgot his works; they waited not for his counsel.

But lusted exceedingly in the wilderness, and tempted God in the desert.

And he gave them their request, but sent leanness into their soul.

In these next ten verses, the writer laments the sad fact that even God's mighty miracles as they began their journey out of Egypt were accompanied by unbelief and wickedness on the part of many of the Israelites. And incidentally, the fact of the unique miracle of the parting of the waters at the Red Sea (Exod. 14:13–31) is reaffirmed here, despite the skepticism of those modern liberal theologians who have tried to explain it away.

In fact, this great miracle is affirmed at least ten more times in accounts by people other than Moses — that is, by Rahab (Josh. 2:10); by Joshua (Josh. 4:23, 24:7); by Ezra (Neh. 9:11); by Asaph, and two other unnamed Psalmists (Ps. 78:13, 66:6, 136:15); by Isaiah (Isa. 43:16, 51:10), by Stephen (Acts 7:36); by Paul (1 Cor. 10:1), and by the writer of Hebrews (Heb. 11:29).

The uniquely mighty miracle of the Red Sea crossing was thus regarded throughout the history of Israel in both Old and New Testaments as a real event — in fact the very event which made Israel an independent nation as she escaped from her servitude in Egypt. Except for this tremendous miracle, Israel would have perished completely and there never would have been such a nation.

Nor can the Red Sea miracle be explained away as a purely natural phenomenon, such as wind blowing back the water in a shallow "Reed Sea" for a while. Moses' account says, "The waters were a wall unto them on their right hand, and on their left." The waters were deep enough that, when they returned after the Children of Israel had completed their own crossing, the waters "covered the chariots, and the horsemen, and all the host of Pharaoh that came into the sea after them" (Exod. 14:22–28).

The people believed and praised God for a brief time after their marvelous deliverance, but they were soon complaining again, even though the Lord had miraculously provided water, bread, and meat for them (Exod. 15:25, 16:13–14, and 17:6). As a result, God "gave them their request, but sent leanness into their soul" (verse 15), and eventually the men of that whole generation, after additional complaints and rebellions, were forced to wander for 40 years in the desert until all of the adult men (except Moses, Aaron, Joshua, and Caleb) had died. In fact, even Aaron and Moses, because of their failures in dealing with these rebellious complainers, also had to die before they reached the Promised Land. There is a sober warning for us today in this pungent verse 15. Concentration on physical and material needs rather than God's will may eventually result in an emaciated spirit and a withered soul in us as well

Verses 16–23

They envied Moses also in the camp, and Aaron the saint of the Lord.

The earth opened and swallowed up Dathan, and covered the company of Abiram.

And a fire was kindled in their company: the flame burned up the wicked.

They made a calf in Horeb, and worshipped the molten image.

Thus they changed their glory into the similitude of an ox that eateth grass.

They forgat God their saviour, which had done great things in Egypt;

Wondrous works in the land of Ham, and terrible things by the Red sea.

Therefore he said that he would destroy them, had not Moses his chosen stood before him in the breach, to turn away his wrath, lest he should destroy them.

These next eight verses recount two of the most flagrant offences committed in the wilderness against Moses' leadership, and thus also against God who had chosen Moses as their leader. The rebellion of Korah, Dathan, and Abiram, who had tried to organize a coup against Moses and Aaron (Num. 16) and the golden calf formed by Aaron to "depict" God (Exod. 32) while Moses was in the mountain receiving God's ten commandments, were almost incredible acts of insurrection against the God who had so marvelously delivered them from slavery in Egypt. The sin of Dathan and Abiram resulted in the death of all the rebels, some by being swallowed in an earth fissure, the others by fire. The golden calf incident almost resulted in the death of the entire nation had not Moses pled urgently with God for mercy. Even at that, about 3,000 men were slain for their participation in the abominations around the molten image.

God indeed is long-suffering, and His mercy endures forever, but the sins of ingratitude for what He has done and complaining about what He has not done are serious insults to a loving, gracious God. May He give us victory over such heinous sins today! The greatest of all insults to God, of course, is to reject or ignore the loving gift of His Son to die for our sins.

Note in passing the mention of Egypt as the land of "Ham" in verse 22. It was still recognized in David's time, 1,300 years or more after the great flood, that Noah's youngest son Ham had been the founder of the nation of Egypt, along with his own son Mizraim. (In fact, "Egypt" in the Old Testament is *Mizraim* in the Hebrew.) This in itself is a significant, though incidental, confirmation of the historical reality of Noah and his sons, as well as of the flood itself.

Verses 24—31

Yea, they despised the pleasant land, they believed not his word:

But murmured in their tents, and hearkened not unto the voice of the LORD.

Therefore he lifted up his hand against them, to overthrow them in the wilderness:

To overthrow their seed also among the nations, and to scatter them in the lands.

They joined themselves also to Baal-peor, and ate the sacrifices of the dead.

Thus they provoked him to anger with their inventions: and the plague brake in upon them.

Then stood up Phinehas, and executed judgment: and so the plague was stayed.

And that was counted unto him for righteousness unto all generations for evermore.

When the 12 spies returned from their mission into Canaan, Joshua and Caleb had reported enthusiastically of the "pleasant land" awaiting them. But the negative report of the other 10 caused the people to "despise" the land because of the giants there, and God sent them back into the wilderness for 40 years (see Num. 13–14).

Verse 27 speaks of the people actually being "scattered" in the lands. This judgment did not fall on them at that particular time, but Moses did prophesy that it would eventually happen if they continued in their fearful and rebellious behavior (see Deut. 28:15, 36, and 37).

Eventually, after their wilderness wanderings were nearly over, the men of the younger generation continued the rebellious ways of their fathers, even entering with the people of Moab into Baal worship on the mountain of Peor (Num. 23:28, 25:1–3). This flagrant act of disobedience and blasphemy so angered God that He sent a terrible plague among them, resulting in 24,000 dead (Num. 25:9; also see 1 Cor. 10:8). Phinehas, grandson of Aaron, finally took the lead in executing a prominent couple involved in a blatant case of Israelite-Midianite fornication. This seems to have been a symbolic act on the part of Phinehas, which served as an example to the host, and God honored Phinehas by assuring him that his seed would inherit the Aaronic priesthood from then on (Num. 25:6–13).

Verses 32–43

They angered him also at the waters of strife, so that it went ill with Moses for their sakes.

Because they provoked his spirit, so that he spake unadvisedly with his lips.

They did not destroy the nations, concerning whom the LORD commanded them:

But were mingled among the heathen, and learned their works.

And they served their idols: which were a snare unto them.

Yea, they sacrificed their sons and daughters unto devils,

And shed innocent blood, even the blood of their sons and of their daughters, whom they sacrificed unto the idols of Canaan: and the land was polluted with blood.

Thus were they defiled with their own works, and went a whoring with their own inventions.

Therefore was the wrath of the LORD kindled against his people, insomuch that he abhorred his own inheritance.

And he gave them into the hand of the heathen: and they that hated them ruled over them.

Their enemies also oppressed them, and they were brought into subjection under their hand.

Many times did he deliver them; but they provoked him with their counsel, and were brought low for their iniquity.

Next the Psalmist reminded them how their great leader, Moses, had been so provoked at the waters of Meribah, when the people complained once again, that he flared up in such anger and arrogance that the Lord had to punish even him (Num. 20:9–13) by not allowing him to enter the Promised Land.

Then after Moses and Aaron died, the Children of Israel did enter the land of Canaan and, under Joshua, conquered much of it. However, once Joshua died and then the chosen elders of that same generation, the people soon descended into more serious rebellion and sin than ever. This was the direct result of their incomplete obedience to God's order to destroy all the incurably wicked and idolatrous Canaanites. As they "mingled among the heathen and learned their works" (verse 35), instead of destroying them and their entire culture as God had commanded, they soon were ensnared in all their wicked ways themselves. The almost inevitable result of compromise, today as well as then, is that the children of God eventually take on the morals and practices of the children of evil.

Verses 37–43 comprise a capsule summary of the period of the judges, with its repeated cycles of apostasy, subjugation by Canaanite nations, repentance, deliverance, prosperity, and apostasy. Although not all details of their practices are given in the accounts in Judges, the record does say that they "served Baalim, and Ashtaroth, and the gods of Syria, and the gods of Zidon, and the gods of Moab, and the gods of the children of Ammon, and the gods of the Philistines" (Judg. 10:6). They could not have "served" all these pagan devil-gods without participating in all their evil rituals.

Nevertheless, God remained faithful to His covenant with Abraham, and when they repented and called on Him, "many times did he deliver them."

Verses 44–48

Nevertheless he regarded their affliction when he heard their cry.

And he remembered for them his covenant, and repented according to the multitude of his mercies.

He made them also to be pitied of all those that carried them captives.

Save us, O LORD our God, and gather us from among the heathen, to give thanks unto thy holy name, and to triumph in thy praise.

Blessed be the LORD God of Israel from everlasting to everlasting: and let all the people say, Amen. Praise ye the LORD.

The last two verses of Psalm 106 correspond to the last two verses of David's psalm recorded in 1 Chronicles 16:8–36. This fact strongly suggests that David was the author of Psalm 106. As noted earlier, this implication suggests in turn that Psalms 101–106 were all written by him.

The reference in verse 47 to being gathered from among the heathen does not apply, as some have suggested, to the return from the much later captivity in Babylon, but rather to the regathering of Israelites from the nearby lands of the Philistines, Moabites, Ammonites, and others that had been repeatedly at war with Israel, even up to the time of David.

The final verse, of course, is the beautiful doxology that closes Book IV of the psalms. In the first psalm of this Book, Moses had noted that God was eternal, "from everlasting to everlasting" (Ps. 90:2). Now, fittingly, the final psalm of the Book closes on the same note, "from everlasting to everlasting."

Chapter 52

The Redeemed of the Lord

Psalm 107

The last book of the psalms, Book V, begins with the beautiful Psalm 107, comprising in effect the combined testimony of all those men and women whose souls have been or will be redeemed from sin, despair, and death by the goodness of the Lord and His wonderful works on their behalf. "Let the redeemed of the LORD say so" (verse 2) is the great exhortation of the Psalmist to those who have experienced His redeeming mercy.

Verses 1–8

O give thanks unto the LORD, for he is good: for his mercy endureth for ever.

Let the redeemed of the LORD say so, whom he hath redeemed from the hand of the enemy;

And gathered them out of the lands, from the east, and from the west, from the north, and from the south.

They wandered in the wilderness in a solitary way; they found no city to dwell in.

Hungry and thirsty, their soul fainted in them.

Then they cried unto the LORD in their trouble, and he delivered them out of their distresses.

And he led them forth by the right way, that they might go to a city of habitation.

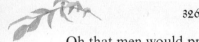

Oh that men would praise the LORD for his goodness, and for his wonderful works to the children of men!

The anonymous writer of Psalm 107 seemed to be trying consciously to tie his psalm back to the two psalms ending Book IV. Psalms 105, 106, and 107 each has in its opening verse the exhortation, "O give thanks unto the Lord." Also all three are somewhat structured around the history of God's dealings with His people. All three of these psalms are anonymous, as far as external identifications are concerned, whereas Psalms 105 and 108 — just before and after them — were both probably written by David.

In discussing Psalm 106, it was suggested, in fact, that all of these psalms quite possibly were of Davidic authorship. If so, Psalm 107 may well be from him, too. None of this is certain, of course, because the author(s) of these psalms (as well as the Holy Spirit who inspired them) chose for some reason to leave them unsigned.

In any case, whoever it was who organized Book V chose to start the collection with this hauntingly beautiful and joyful testimony of Psalm 107. Two other psalms in this collection, Psalm 118 and 136, both of which are also anonymous, begin with the same wonderful exhortation: "O give thanks unto the LORD, for he is good: for his mercy endureth for ever." And in all three cases, the verb "endureth" is not in the original Hebrew, but has been supplied (quite fittingly, of course) by the translators. It is as though the idea of "enduring" is redundant. God's goodness and mercy are, by definition, eternal, implicit in His very character.

The very fact that we who were utterly undeserving of His mercy have accepted the free gift of His mercy and grace will be in heaven forever is certain proof of that fact.

Verse 3, however, has led to various interpretations of the psalm. When, if ever, have His people been gathered together from foreign lands in all directions? The children of Israel came from Egypt in the west under Moses, and later from Babylon in the east under Ezra and Nehemiah, but not yet from either north or south. That is, at least, not until the modern era, when Jews have been migrating to the restored nation of Israel from all over the world.

This seems to indicate that the primary vision of the inspired psalm is prophetic, looking to the future, when such a gathering will indeed be literally fulfilled. Perhaps a secondary prophetic application will be, as many earlier expositors have understood it, in reference to the church age, when people of all nations and backgrounds will be gathering together in spirit to Christ, trusting Him for salvation and then "saying so" as "the redeemed of the LORD."

The modern return of the Jews to Israel may be a sort of precursive fulfillment of the prophecy but not the ultimate fulfillment, since modern Zionism is largely a secular and political movement — hardly involving "the redeemed of the LORD."

Thus, it would seem that the primary focus of the psalm is on the Jewish remnant returning to the Lord during the coming great Tribulation. "Alas! for that day is great, so that none is like it: it is even the time of Jacob's trouble; but he shall be saved out of it" (Jer. 30:7).

During the awful days of that period the world government and its head (called the beast, in the Book of Revelation) will seek to exterminate the Jews, as well as all true Christians — in fact, anyone who refuses to worship him and his image, in effect acknowledging Satan as the god of the whole world.

The testimonies in the psalm, although capable of being appropriated as needed by believers in any age, seem to be applicable especially to those suffering under the beast in the tribulation age, as they are trying to gather together from every land to meet the Lord Jesus Christ — the Jewish Messiah — returning in glory to Jerusalem at the end of that age. At that time, He will defeat the beast and all his armies, who have also gathered together from all nations toward Armageddon, not far from Jerusalem (note especially Zech. 12:9, 13:2, 14:3–4; Matt. 24:29–31; Rev. 19:11–16, 20, 20:2; Rom. 11:26–27).

Verses 3–31 of Psalm 107 seem then to be telling of four sets of experiences, corresponding to the four groups of believing Jews (possibly also including Gentile Christians) coming together from the four directions as mentioned in verse 3. Each of these sections ends with a testimony of deliverance and then the great exhortation "Oh that men would praise the LORD for his goodness, and for his wonderful works to the children of men" (verses 8, 15, 21, and 31).

On this assumption, verses 4–7 could give the testimony of those coming from the East. That, presumably, would include the believing (or seeking) Jews and others from Asia. Seeking to escape the minions of the beast government, they could find "no city to dwell in," and so "wandered in the wilderness" (verse 4). Like the ancient patriarchs, who "looked for a city which hath foundations, whose builder and maker is God" (Heb. 11:10), and like the apostle Paul, who could "have no certain dwellingplace" (1 Cor. 4:11), they followed God's leading in "the right way, that they might go to a city of habitation" (verse 7). This would bypass the beast's great capital at rebuilt Babylon (Rev. 17–18) and his armies also coming across the Euphrates and heading toward Israel.

Verses 9–15

For he satisfieth the longing soul, and filleth the hungry soul with goodness.

Such as sit in darkness and in the shadow of death, being bound in affliction and iron;

Because they rebelled against the words of God, and contemned the counsel of the most High:

Therefore he brought down their heart with labour; they fell down, and there was none to help.

Then they cried unto the LORD in their trouble, and he brought them out of their distresses.

He brought them out of darkness and the shadow of death, and brake their bonds in sunder.

Oh, that men would praise the LORD for his goodness, and for his wonderful works to the children of men!

Here is another group of people who finally had "cried unto the LORD" in their troubles (verse 13). They were, perhaps, coming from the west — that is, southern Europe, northern Africa, and probably the Americas. Many of these had apparently once been among the intellectuals who had "rebelled against the words of God" (verse 11), while still unwilling to bow to the beast, so God had allowed them to be imprisoned, awaiting execution. They were living "in the shadow of death, being bound in affliction and irons" (verse 10). However, as they repented and prayed for salvation, God had miraculously "brought them out of darkness and the shadow of death, and brake their bonds in sunder" (verse 14). When men finally do repent and believe on Christ, God indeed "satisfieth the longing soul, and filleth the hungry soul with goodness."

Verse 16–21

For he hath broken the gates of brass, and cut the bars of iron in sunder.

Fools because of their transgression, and because of their iniquities are afflicted.

Their soul abhorreth all manner of meat; and they draw near unto the gates of death.

Then they cry unto the LORD in their troubles, and he saveth them out of their distresses.

He sent his Word, and healed them, and delivered them from their destructions.

Oh that men would praise the LORD for his goodness, and for his wonderful works to the children of men!

Now the Psalmist seems to see in his vision a stream of refugees coming down from the north. These likewise had apparently been in prison but they also had "cried unto the LORD in their troubles," (verse 19), and "He sent his word" to them somehow, and they believed it, so He "healed them, and delivered them from their destructions" (verse 20).

As rapidly as they could get away from the broken gates and iron bars, they came streaming down from Russia and Scandinavia and other northern regions, heading towards Jerusalem, "prais(ing) the LORD for his goodness, and for his wonderful works to the children of men," as all the others were doing as they converged on the holy city.

But then there is an interesting variation, as the Psalmist looks toward the south. The Hebrew word translated "south" is so translated nowhere else, for it is the usual word for "sea." It occasionally is translated "west." The connection apparently is that due west of Jerusalem was the Mediterranean Sea and due south is the Red Sea.

Thus, verse 3 could be understood as saying that the people were being gathered from the east, the west, the north, and the "seas!" That is, some were coming by ship up the Red Sea, possibly from Australia or southern Africa, perhaps also some on the Mediterranean, maybe from America. In any case, they were being gathered by God and His angels (note Matt. 24:31) from all over the world.

Verses 22–31

And let them sacrifice the sacrifices of thanksgiving, and declare his works with rejoicing.

They that go down to the sea in ships, that do business in great waters;

These see the works of the LORD, and his wonders in the deep.

For he commandeth, and raiseth the stormy winds, which lifteth up the waves thereof.

They mount up to the heaven, they go down again to the depths: their soul is melted because of trouble.

They reel to and fro, and stagger like a drunken man, and are at their wits' end.

Then they cry unto the LORD in their trouble, and he bringeth them out of their distresses.

He maketh the storm a calm, so that the waves thereof are still.

Then are they glad because they be quiet, so he bringeth them unto their desired haven.

Oh that men would praise the LORD for his goodness, and for his wonderful works to the children of men!

If all of these migrations toward Jerusalem are actually taking place during the latter part of the tribulation, as we have inferred, the travelers will be seeking to escape the murderous claws of the beast. His agents, no doubt, will control all the airports and the major roadways, so they must flee mostly either on foot or riding on animals through the desert areas (verses 4-7) or else by private fishing or other boats on the open seas.

The verses in this section (verses 23–30) thus seem to be describing the great hardships and greater divine deliverance of those that "go down to the sea in ships" trying to reach "their desired haven" (verses 23, 30). Some might have stores of fuel to drive their craft; many others may have to rely on the wind and sails. All, no doubt, will encounter stormy seas along the way, and — except for the Lord — many would perish.

But as He does for those trekking through the wilderness, when they cry unto the Lord, He saves them, as He did long ago on the Sea of Galilee, saying, "Peace, be still" (Mark 4:39). "He maketh the storm a calm, so that the waves thereof are still" (verse 29), and then they joyfully "praise the LORD for his goodness, and for his wonderful works to the children of men" (verse 31 — also verses 8, 15, and 21).

The word "goodness" in these four verses is from the same Hebrew word (*chesed*) as translated "mercy" in the first verse of this psalm and "lovingkindness" in the last. The words "wonderful works" are only one word in the Hebrew (*pala*), sometimes translated "marvelous works," or even "miracles." "Praise the LORD" is often rendered "thank the LORD," depending on context. In each of the verses, the first "men" has been supplied by the translators, whereas the second is *Adam* in the Hebrew. Thus, a legitimate paraphrase of each of these four verses, in view of the context, might well be, "Oh, that everyone would thank the LORD for his great undeserved mercy, and for his marvelous works (in answer to fervent, believing, prayer) on behalf of these repentant and believing descendants of Adam."

Such an exhortation should be directed to each one of us as well, for we also (as believing children of God, in addition to being children of Adam, through faith in Christ) have experienced His great mercy and wonderful works.

Verses 32–38

Let them exalt him also in the congregation of the people, and praise him in the assembly of the elders.

He turneth rivers into a wilderness, and the watersprings into dry ground;

A fruitful land into barrenness, for the wickedness of them that dwell therein.

He turneth the wilderness into a standing water, and dry ground into watersprings.

And there he maketh the hungry to dwell, that they may prepare a city for habitation;

And sow the fields, and plant vineyards, which may yield fruits of increase.

He blesseth them also, so that they are multiplied greatly; and suffereth not their cattle to decrease.

As these pilgrims all converge on Jerusalem, we learn from later Scriptures, especially in Revelation, that the Lord will be descending in power and glory, defeating and destroying the beast and all the world's armies that also have been converging on Israel. This will mark the climactic termination of the period of great Tribulation.

In the meantime, throughout the Tribulation period, another great host had been assembled in heaven, composed of all the resurrected believers of all the ages prior to the Tribulation (1 Thess. 4:13–17). Leading their praises will be Christ himself, in the midst of the 24 elders of the redeemed people of God (Ps. 22:22, 25; Heb. 2:10–12; Rev. 4:4, 10–11).

It seems that the Psalmist's vision was momentarily transferred to the heavens, so that he could know that this "great cloud of witnesses" — "the general assembly and church of the firstborn . . . the spirits of just men made perfect" (Heb. 12:1–23), were also intensively concerned with these events on earth. So he cries out, "Let them exalt him also in the congregation of the people and praise him in the assembly of the elders" (verse 32).

Back on the earth, after all the ungodly have been purged out of it, and Satan bound in a deep prison (Rev. 20:1–3), the remnant that remains will become the pioneers of the millennial age. During the Tribulation the rivers and fountains had dried up from the 3+ year worldwide drought (Rev. 11:3, 6, 16:12; Joel 1:20), so "the fruitful land" had been "turned into barrenness, for the wickedness of them that dwell therein" (verse 34). But soon the period of judgment will pass and the thousand-year kingdom age will begin. Then "in the wilderness shall waters break out, and streams in the desert" (Isa. 35:6), and "there he maketh the hungry to dwell," and they will have prepared that "city for habitation" (verse 36) for which they had been longing (verse 7). They will "sow the fields, and plant vineyards" (verse 37) and soon "the desert shall rejoice, and blossom as the rose" (Isa. 35:1).

Verses 39–43

Again, they are minished and brought low through oppression, affliction, and sorrow.

He poureth contempt upon princes, and causeth them to wander in the wilderness, where there is no way.

Yet setteth he the poor on high from affliction, and maketh him families like a flock.

The righteous shall see it, and rejoice: and all iniquity shall stop her mouth.

Whoso is wise, and will observe these things, even they shall understand the lovingkindness of the LORD.

Although only a relatively small number of God-fearing people will survive the tribulation and enter the millennium (Isa. 24:6), conditions will be ideal in the world for the first time since Eden, and populations will rapidly multiply (verse 38). Unfortunately, men are still in the flesh, and as new generations are born and grow, memories may grow dim concerning God's great works of the past, and sin will again appear (verse 39). When Satan is once again allowed on earth to test the men and women of that highly privileged age, a great multitude of rebels will once again gather together to war against God and the reign of Christ in Jerusalem (Rev. 20:7–8).

This last rebellion, however, will mark the end of God's patience with natural men, and all unbelievers will quickly be brought to judgment and cast into hell (Rev. 20:11–15). Then, "the righteous shall see it, and rejoice, and all iniquity will stop her mouth" (verse 42). There will be no more sin and iniquity anywhere on earth, ever again! In the renovated earth, after this last judgment, the great Curse itself will have been removed (Rev. 22:3) and "there shall in no wise enter into it any thing that defileth" (Rev. 21:27).

This interpretation of Psalm 107, centering it particularly on the redeeming work of Christ during and after the great Tribulation, is admittedly unusual. It is still appropriate if one prefers to think of different parts of its testimonies as having *various applications* in individual lives, and in the history of Israel and the church. But it does seem that the only *consistently literal interpretation* of the whole psalm as a coherent unit must be one that is prophetic of the end times, developing in some such fashion as set forth herein.

In any case, the final wonderful verse of the psalm can surely be taken as a personal promise of the Lord to anyone who loves and follows His word in any age. "Whoso is wise, and will observe these things, even they shall understand the lovingkindness of the LORD." And if so, "let the redeemed of the LORD say so!"

Chapter 53

Praising the Lord Forever

Psalm 145

Psalm 145 is the closing "book-end" for Book V of the psalms. Except for the five-chapter epilogue (Ps. 146–150), it could be considered the closing book-end for the entire Book of Psalms, which had begun with Psalm 1 as the opening book-end. The 1st Psalm had set forth the contrast between those whose delight is in God's Word and those who prefer the counsel of the ungodly, a theme which continues to permeate all the later psalms until the last. Then the 145th Psalm in effect centers on the ultimate triumph of the righteous, and their resulting everlasting ministry of praising God.

Each of the five Books ends with a grand doxology. The first four doxologies are exhortations to bless the name of the Lord forever. Note the consistent theme in these.

> Psalm 41:13 — Blessed be the LORD God of Israel from everlasting and to everlasting. Amen, and amen.

> Psalm 72:19 — And blessed be his glorious name for ever: and let the whole earth be filled with his glory. Amen, and amen.

> Psalm 89:52 — Blessed be the LORD for evermore. Amen, and amen.

> Psalm 106:48 — Blessed be the LORD God of Israel from everlasting to everlasting: and let all the people say, Amen. Praise ye the LORD.

Then the final doxology, Psalm 145:21, becomes in effect a response to the four previous exhortations.

My mouth shall speak the praise of the LORD, and let all flesh bless his holy name for ever and ever.

There are, of course five other psalms after Psalm 145, and these are usually considered as part of Book V. However, the last verse of this group of psalms ends in a somewhat different vein, with no mention of "blessing" the Lord, as do all four of the others. Furthermore, each of the five closing psalms (146, 147, 148, 149, and 150) both begins and ends with the exhortation: "Hallelujah" — that is, "Praise ye the Lord."

The only other psalm with this distinctive feature is Psalm 106, the "book-end" psalm of Book IV.

All of this seems to suggest that the final five psalms should be considered as an epilogue to the entire Book of Psalms, constituting a great doxology in itself, a sort of Book VI as it were, with the over-arching theme of every segment of God's creation praising Him in eternity.

These five psalms will be treated under this assumption, in Part Nine, chapters 60 through 65, "The Praise Psalms of the Redeemed."

Considering, therefore, Psalm 145 as the "book-end" psalm of Book V, let us proceed to look at these 21 beautiful verses.

Verses 1–7

I will extol thee, my God, O king: and I will bless thy name for ever and ever.

Every day will I bless thee: and I will praise thy name for ever and ever.

Great is the LORD, and greatly to be praised: and his greatness is unsearchable.

One generation shall praise thy works to another, and shall declare thy mighty acts.

I will speak of the glorious honour of thy majesty, and of thy wondrous works.

And men shall speak of the might of thy terrible acts: and I will declare thy greatness.

They shall abundantly utter the memory of thy great goodness, and shall sing of thy righteousness.

The psalm has 21 verses, and these seem to fall more or less naturally into three stanzas of seven verses each. The first group features the testimony of men — both the psalm writer and those who read — to the greatness of the person and the works of their great Creator. The psalm is entitled "David's Psalm of Praise" and is the only psalm with such a title. Psalm 100, in the King James Bible, is titled "A Psalm of Praise," but here the Hebrew word is different, more commonly translated "Thanksgiving."

Furthermore, it is the final psalm attributed to David in the Book of Psalms. All five of the final psalms are anonymous, and this also is appropriate, since they represent the praise psalms of all the redeemed creation of God, both now and in the ages to come.

Note also that David begins this psalm with his own testimony: "I will bless thy name for ever and ever." He then concludes his psalm with his last exhortation to all others to do the same. "Let all flesh bless his holy name for ever and ever."

In extolling God's greatness, the Psalmist seems to exhaust his resources of language, for God's "greatness is unsearchable" (verse 3). This testimony is echoed by the apostle Paul when he says: "O the depth of the riches both of the wisdom and knowledge of God! How unsearchable are his judgments, and his ways past finding out!" (Rom. 11:33).

There is a fascinating prophecy in verse 4. "One generation shall praise thy works to another, and shall declare thy mighty acts." How could David know that this would happen? In any case, the prophecy has indeed been fulfilled, generation after generation after generation, ever since David wrote it down. From nation to nation, and year after year, "men shall speak of the might of thy terrible [that is, 'awesome'] acts" (verse 6). Furthermore, "they shall abundantly utter the memory of thy great goodness, and shall sing of thy righteousness" (verse 7). These prophecies are being fulfilled even today, 3,000 years later, in the congregations of thousands of churches, all over the world.

Verses 8–14

The LORD is gracious, and full of compassion; slow to anger, and of great mercy.

The LORD is good to all; and his tender mercies are over all his works.

All thy works shall praise thee, O LORD; and thy saints shall bless thee.

They shall speak of the glory of thy kingdom, and talk of thy power;

To make known to the sons of men his mighty acts, and the glorious majesty of his kingdom.

Thy kingdom is an everlasting kingdom, and thy dominion endureth throughout all generations.

The LORD upholdeth all that fall, and raiseth up all those that be bowed down.

The unsearchable greatness of God enables Him also to be "full of compassion" (verse 8) and "rich in mercy" (Eph. 2:4). All His "wondrous works" (verse 5) are accomplished and overshadowed by His "tender mercies" (verse 9).

That beautiful phrase ("tender mercies") is just one word in the Hebrew (*racham*) and is used no less than ten times in the psalms — first in Psalm 25:6 ("Remember, O LORD, thy tender mercies"), and last in this verse.

The prophetic theme of ongoing testimony continues in verses 10–12. "Thy saints shall bless thee. They shall speak of the glory of thy kingdom, and talk of thy power; To make known to the sons of men his mighty acts, and the glorious majesty of his kingdom."

And as the "saints" (that is, those who have been redeemed by faith in God's "great mercy" and "mighty acts") continue to witness to each generation, they not only speak of His tender mercies but also of "the glory . . . and the glorious majesty of his kingdom." Furthermore, their testimony is not only to the Children of Israel, but to "the sons of men" — that is, to men of every nation who will believe on the God of Israel, who was increasingly to be known as the Creator and Redeemer of all men everywhere.

Then, when David said, "Thy kingdom is an everlasting kingdom" (verse 13), he was thinking not only of his own immediate kingdom, but of the everlasting kingdom promised to his "seed." God had told David: "I will set up thy seed after thee . . . and I will stablish the throne of his kingdom for ever" (2 Sam. 7:12–13).

Then, many centuries later, God confirmed the promise through the prophet Isaiah, saying: "Of the increase of his government and peace there shall be no end, upon the throne of David, and upon his kingdom, to order it, and to establish it . . . for ever" (Isa. 9:7). After many further centuries, the angel Gabriel spoke to Mary, telling her of the imminent coming of the promised seed. "He shall be great, and shall be called the Son of the Highest: and the Lord God will give unto him the throne of his father David . . . and of his kingdom there shall be no end" (Luke 1:32–33). His kingdom, now in its spiritual phase only, will eventually be on earth as well and will last forever.

Between verses 13 and 14, there may be a fascinating omission. Psalm

145 is one of the acrostic psalms, except for this possible omission. That
is, each of the 21 verses of the psalm begins with the successive letters of
the Hebrew alphabet. Verse 1 begins with *aleph*, verse 2 with *beth*, verse 3
with *gimel*, and so on. However, the Hebrew alphabet has 22 letters, so
one letter is missing, and that letter is *nun*, the 14th letter.

Some ancient versions, however, do contain what could be the missing verse, which would read as follows: "Faithful is the LORD in all his
words, and holy in all his works." This would fit the context effectively.
On the other hand, it is hard to understand how the ancient Hebrew copy-
ists, who went to great lengths to insure accuracy as they copied the Scriptures, could have inadvertently omitted an entire verse, especially in what
was intended as an acrostic psalm. Perhaps a better suggestion is that
David may have omitted it intentionally, as a way of stressing the importance of verse 13, speaking of God's eternal kingdom — sort of a special
"Selah!" as it were.

Verses 15–21

The eyes of all wait upon thee; and thou givest them their meat
in due season.

Thou openest thine hand, and satisfiest the desire of every living thing.

The LORD is righteous in all his ways, and holy in all his works.

The LORD is nigh unto all them that call upon him, to all that
call upon him in truth.

He will fulfill the desire of them that fear him: he also will hear
their cry, and will save them.

The LORD preserveth all them that love him: but all the wicked
will he destroy.

My mouth shall speak the praise of the LORD: and let all flesh
bless his holy name for ever and ever.

It would be appropriate to consider verse 15 as an introduction to
the next six verses since the emphasis in these verses is of God's providential care of all His creation, especially of those who trust Him and who
share in the testimonies of the previous verses. God does care deeply about
all His creatures, not only men and women, but also "every living thing"
(verse 16). Not even a sparrow shall "fall on the ground without your
Father" (Matt. 10:29). In fact, verse 15 is essentially the same as Psalm

104:27, which reads: "These wait all upon thee; that thou mayest give them their meat in due season," speaking of all God's animals on both land and sea. This duplication is also an incidental confirmation of David's authorship of Psalm 104.

And as He deals with those in His own image, His ways sometimes seem hard to understand with our present limited knowledge. Nevertheless, we must not question Him, for He "is righteous in all his ways, and holy in all his works" (verse 17). What God does is right, by very definition. "For the word of the LORD is right; and all his works are done in truth" (Ps. 33:4).

We may not understand now but, as the old gospel song assures us, we shall understand it better by and by!

Even though God is so unimaginably great, He nevertheless "is nigh unto . . . all that call upon him in truth" (verse 18). To all who come to Him in repentance and faith, He "will hear their cry, and will save them" (verse 19). Although the Father's throne is in heaven, and the Son is at His right hand, He is nevertheless always present with His children through the indwelling Holy Spirit, at least ever since Christ went back to the Father (John 14:16–20). And, to top it all, "The LORD preserveth all them that love him" (verse 20). "The LORD shall preserve thy going out and thy coming in from this time forth, and even for evermore" (Ps. 121:8).

But, as God had warned in the last verse of the opening "book-end" psalm, "the way of the ungodly shall perish" (Ps. 1:6). Except for the doxology, He closes *this* psalm with the sober warning: "The wicked will he destroy" (verse 20).

Then comes the thrilling closing doxology of Book V. "My mouth shall speak the praise of the LORD: and let all flesh bless his holy name for ever and ever" (verse 21).

Part VIII

Psalms of Encouragement and Blessing

By Henry M. Morris III, D. Min.

Chapter 54

Confidence in God

Psalm 27

I n this section are included commentaries on several key psalms that
don't fit into the particular categories covered in other sections of the
book. However, they are all psalms that have been of special blessing,
comfort, and encouragement to God's people through all the centuries
since they were first written. The grouping may be somewhat arbitrary,
but all of these are wonderful psalms and certainly must not be omitted
from this treasury of great psalms.

This psalm, written by David, opens with a jubilant stanza of praise
for the confidence David has experienced in his life of conflict. The initial
praise is for God's "light, salvation, and strength."

Verse 1

The LORD is my light and my salvation; whom shall I fear? The
LORD is the strength of my life; of whom shall I be afraid?

These are familiar terms in the psalms, yet they are often glossed
over because of their familiarity. "Light" is, of course, most often associated with enlightenment and truth throughout the Word of God as well
as the psalms (Ps. 18:28, 36:9, 43:3). But it also indicates the provision of
"clarity" (Ps. 37:6, 38:10, 112:4) and "understanding" (Ps. 119:105,
119:130) and even "favor with God" (Ps. 4:6, 44:3, 89:15, 90:8). In this
opening song of joy of marvelous deliverance, the use here may very well
demand the broadest application possible. The Lord does provide "truth"
to us, whether in circumstantial need or as we search His word. He surely
grants "clarity" and "understanding" to us, and that is the primary ministry of the Holy Spirit on our behalf (John 16:13–15). And who can

ignore the "favor" we receive in our salvation (Eph. 2:8)?

The "salvation" of the psalms, although certainly applicable to the eternal salvation from sin which is the ultimate focus of the Word's message, is more often set in terms of a military rescue. God is said to be the "horn" of our salvation (Ps. 18:3), a "shield" (Ps. 18:35), the "rock" (Ps. 89:26), our "strength" (Ps. 140:7), as well as our "joy" (Ps. 51:12) and our "truth" (Ps. 69:13). And just as these similes draw a picture of "protection," so does the use of the phrase "strength of my life" in verse one. It is consistently used in the psalms of a "rock" or "fortress" that provides safety from enemy attack. All of these settings emphasize the "salvation" — the often sudden and unexpected rescue of God's people from sure defeat at the hands of an enemy.

Verses 2–3

When the wicked, even mine enemies and my foes, came upon me to eat up my flesh, they stumbled and fell.

Though an host should encamp against me, my heart shall not fear: though war should rise against me, in this will I be confident.

The wicked are ready to "eat up" the flesh of David. Whatever may be in view as the setting of this psalm, it surely warns of a catastrophic event. Often the use of this term in the Old Testament relates to the physical destruction of a people at the hands of a military conqueror (Num. 24:8; Ps. 53:1–5; Jer. 5:15; Mic. 5:6). In the New Testament, however, the emphasis seems to be on spiritual, mental, and character destruction (Gal. 5:15; 1 Cor. 3:3; 2 Cor. 12:20). Whether the application is physical or spiritual, the results are the same: the enemies "stumbled and fell."

Before the conflict ensues but after the strength of the enemy is known, the mature warrior of God is always intimidated by his own insufficiency. The short observation about the "host" surrounding and "war" rising recognizes that the confident child of God does not blithely enter into kingdom affairs in ignorance of the enemy nor of his own potential. Rather, "in this will I be confident." The emphasis is on the Christian's trust in the strength of his Savior, his rescuer. The bold warrior is bold because he is focused. Focused on "one thing have I desired of the Lord."

Verses 4–5

One thing have I desired of the Lord that will I seek after; that I may dwell in the house of the Lord all the days of my life, to behold the beauty of the Lord, and to inquire in his temple.

For in the time of trouble he shall hide me in his pavilion: in the secret of his tabernacle shall he hide me: he shall set me up upon a rock.

The intensity of the desire is singular. David will "seek after" a dwelling within the house of the Lord since he is absolutely confident that *there*, in God's dwelling place, is the security of his life and the surety of his purpose. It is *there* that David will find the "beauty of the LORD" and will be able to "inquire" for the necessary instructions. *There* in God's presence will "the beauty of the LORD our God be upon us" (Ps. 90:17) and *there* will wisdom dispense her "ways of pleasantness" (Prov. 3:17).

God's dwelling place is no longer confined to a tent or temple located within the borders of Israel, but is accessed through the indwelling of the Holy Spirit of God who has made the bodies of the saints His "temple" (1 Cor. 6:19). Today, the desperate saint need go no further than his own prayer closet to be in direct contact and under the sheltering "pavilion" in His "secret" tabernacle.

The descriptions of this dwelling place are all given in military terms in one form or another. David was a warrior. And, since the New Testament Christian is often compared to such a profession, it is certainly fitting that the Scriptures are replete with these portraits of protection and deliverance. The God of salvation and deliverance "hides" us from the eyes of the enemy. We are kept "as the apple of the eye . . . under the shadow of thy wings. From the wicked that oppress me, from my deadly enemies, who compass me about" (Ps. 17:8–9). We can never know the extent of God's protection in the spiritual realm, but we can be assured that He will hide us "from the secret counsel of the wicked: from the insurrection of the workers of iniquity" (Ps. 64:2). And even in the human realm, God will "hide them in the secret of thy presence from the pride of man: thou shalt keep them secretly in a pavilion from the strife of tongues" (Ps. 31:20).

Verse 6

And now shall mine head be lifted up above mine enemies round about me: therefore will I offer in his tabernacle sacrifices of joy; I will sing, yea, I will sing praises unto the LORD.

And now! Now is the victory song sung. Now is the sacrifice of joy offered. The battle is real, painful, often with terrible losses, but the victory is sweet. The release that we can know when we see God's victories in our lives should bring a "joy unspeakable and full of glory" (1 Pet. 1:8). The hallmarks of victory experiences during the time that we "work out

[our] salvation with fear and trembling" (Phil. 2:12) should be celebrated with a "sacrifice of praise" (Heb. 13:15). "Oh that men would praise the LORD for his goodness, and for his wonderful works to the children of men! And let them sacrifice the sacrifices of thanksgiving, and declare his works with rejoicing" (Ps. 107:21–22).

Verses 7–10

Hear, O LORD, when I cry with my voice: have mercy also upon me, and answer me.

When thou saidst, Seek ye my face; my heart said unto thee, Thy face, LORD, will I seek.

Hide not thy face far from me; put not thy servant away in anger: thou hast been my help; leave me not, neither forsake me, O God of my salvation.

When my father and my mother forsake me, then the LORD will take me up.

The message of the psalm shifts now to the prayer that David utters in his desperate hour of need. As such it stands as something of a model for the saint in trouble. The more famous "model" prayer taught by the Lord Jesus (Matt. 6:7–15) contains the request for protection, but is more broad as it encompasses the entire scope of heavenly address and petition. David's prayers were often more urgent, more intensely demanding for God to deliver or protect him from immediate circumstances that were threatening to "eat him up." This "model" provides a structure that seems to be followed in many of the prayers for help in "time of trouble."

Worthy of note is the *vocal* nature of this prayer. Although there is no requirement to pray out loud, there does seem to be a consistent pattern in those prayers that "cry out" for help in desperate times: the petitioner cries "with my voice" (Ps. 3:4, 27:7, 77:1, 142:1). Perhaps the need is so great that one forgets to be "formal" and just blurts out the need. Or perhaps, the urgency of the situation is so immediate that all concern for what others may think is obliterated. Or maybe, when we use our voice in our prayers more of our "being" is involved in the praying. Whatever the circumstances or reasons may be, the Scripture seems to bear out the need to vocalize our petitions. The widow who would not leave the judge alone (Luke 18:1–8) and the friend who pounded on the door for food at midnight (Luke 11:5–10) are two classic parables that encourage us to "insist" and to "persist" in our prayers before the Lord.

Not to be implied, however, is that mere "shouting" is sufficient to move the Lord to hear. Jesus warned against using "vain repetitions" and "much speaking" as a substitute for genuine petition (Matt. 6:7). We must "seek" Him with our "heart." There is something about the "urgent" nature of this kind of prayer that is like "thirsting" for the Lord's help "in a dry and thirsty land, where no water is" (Ps. 63:1). This kind of prayer reaches out with the soul to "desire thee in the night; yea, with my spirit within me will I seek thee early (Isa. 26:9). It is the "effectual *fervent* prayer of [the] righteous man that availeth much" (James 5:16).

Thanks be to our God that He will respond to the "seeking!" "Those that seek me early shall find me," Wisdom promises in Proverbs 8:17. "I will hearken unto you," the Lord says. "And ye shall seek me, and find me, when ye shall search for me with all your heart" (Jer. 29:12–13). Even when every resource we have at our disposal fails, even when those closest to us desert us, God promises, "Call unto me, and I will answer thee, and shew thee great and mighty things which thou knowest not" (Jer. 33:3).

Verses 11–12

Teach me thy way, O LORD, and lead me in a plain path, because of mine enemies.

Deliver me not over unto the will of mine enemies: for false witnesses are risen up against me, and such as breathe out cruelty.

The requests are simple: "teach, lead, and deliver" so that we will be able to get away from the "will" of our enemies and the "cruelty" of the plans of those who plot against us.

We need to be taught the "way" of God so that we can be led in a "plain path." God is petitioned to show us "thy ways, O LORD; teach me thy paths. Lead me in thy truth, and teach me" (Ps. 25:4–5), and to "walk in thy truth" (Ps. 86:11). The "truth" that is "thy Word" (John 17:17) is the basis upon which and by which the Holy Spirit will guide us "into all truth" (John 16:13). The prayer for deliverance must of necessity be a prayer in accordance with the revealed will of God — the written Word of God. God does not circumvent His Word, even for the sake of delivering His children. The Holy Spirit does not invent some new "truth" just to "help" one of God's erring children get out of a sin-produced jam. The deliverance will be in a "plain path." God will "lead them in paths that they have not known: I will make darkness light before them, and crooked things straight. These things will I do unto them, and not forsake them" (Isa. 42:16).

May our prayer contain the prayer of Psalm 143:10. "Teach me to do thy will; for thou art my God: thy spirit is good; lead me into the land of uprightness."

Verses 13–14

I had fainted, unless I had believed to see the goodness of the LORD in the land of the living.

Wait on the LORD: be of good courage, and he shall strengthen thine heart: wait, I say, on the LORD.

This closing comment by David is a magnificent testimony to his faith as well as a stable axiom for our own. God's promises are not just for the "by and by." They may well have an ultimate fulfillment that "the eye hath not seen, nor ear heard (1 Cor. 2:9), but all are focused on our welfare here and now. Even in the midst of the terrible destruction of Israel and the coming captivity, God told Israel, "I know the thoughts that I think toward you . . . thoughts of peace, and not of evil" (Jer. 29:11). Jesus tried to calm His frustrated followers and to direct them away from worry about the "things" of life (Matt. 6:25–34) where we are told not to worry about the "morrow" but to take courage from the evidence of the very grass and flowers of the field. For, "If God so clothe the grass of the field which today is, and to morrow is cast into the oven, shall he not much more clothe you, O ye of little faith?"

Paul's command to the Philippian church is sufficient to conclude this thought. "Be careful for nothing; but in every thing by prayer and supplication with thanksgiving let your requests be made known unto God. And the peace of God, which passeth all understanding, shall keep your hearts and minds through Christ Jesus" (Phil. 4:6–7).

Chapter 55

Divine Deliverance

Psalm 34

This is one of the nine alphabetical (or acrostic) psalms, the best known of which is Psalm 119. Our English language does not lend itself to represent the structure of these works, and we miss something of the beauty of the song in our translations. Nevertheless, the majesty of Psalm 34 is not lost. The title to the psalm notes that David was commemorating his escape from Abimelech (the title of Philistine kings — in this case, Achish, the King of Gath) as recorded in 1 Samuel 21:10–15. While little in the content of the psalm directly relates to the circumstances of David's specific experience in Gath, the Song of Praise (verses 1 through 10) and the Sermon of Instruction that follows (verses 11 through 22) are presented as the result of that harrowing experience.

Verses 1–3

I will bless the LORD at all times: his praise shall continually be in my mouth.

My soul shall make her boast in the LORD: the humble shall hear thereof, and be glad.

O magnify the LORD with me, and let us exalt his name together.

This is an open praise. David is not merely thanking God for His help, he is "bragging" about God to anybody who will listen. The "boast" that his "soul" is making is with his "mouth" in such a way that even the "humble" (Hebrew: *anav* = "poor") will know of his joy. The Hebrew word translated "boast" in this passage is the word *halal* from which Hallelujah is composed. Of the 165 times the word is used in the Old Testament, 117 of them are translated "praise," 14 are translated "glory," and 10 of them "boast."

We are drawn into this praise by the Psalmist and asked to "magnify the LORD" with him and to "exalt his name" with those praises. While the ideas of these words are transferred reasonably well in the English, there is something about the pictures implied in these praise terms that slips through our modern culture. "Magnify" (Hebrew: *gadal*) is an imperative verb that demand us to "make great", or elevate to "great importance" the memory of the Lord. "Bless the LORD, O my soul. O Lord my God, thou art very great; thou art clothed with honour and majesty" (Ps. 104:1). And, in similar emphasis, "exalt" (Hebrew: *ruwm*) demands that we "raise up" the very name of the Lord above all else. Isaiah bursts into praise at his under-standing of what God is going to do when He returns. "O LORD, thou art my God; I will exalt thee, I will praise thy name; for thou hast done won-derful things; thy counsels of old are faithfulness and truth" (Isa. 25:1).

Our church environment often connects the idea of praise with mu-sical episodes during our "worship" or with moments of "celebration" (clapping, vocal response, etc.). While these may contain elements of magnification or exaltation, they are not the fulfillment of the Psalmist's exhortation. The required response is an attitude change — a heart cor-rection and a mental focus. Mary, the gentle virgin girl, in response to Elisabeth's prophetic song said, "My soul doth magnify the Lord, and my spirit hath rejoiced in God my Saviour" (Luke 1:46–47). The people of Ephesus, when they heard of the debacle resulting from the attempt by the seven sons of Sceva to exorcise demons without authority from God, were afraid and "the name of the Lord was magnified. And many that believed came, and confessed, and shewed their deeds" (Acts 19:17–18)."

When we "magnify" and "exalt" the Lord and His name, our hearts are changed.

Verses 4–6

I sought the LORD, and he heard me, and delivered me from all my fears.

They looked unto him, and were lightened: and their faces were not ashamed.

This poor man cried, and the LORD heard him, and saved him out of all his troubles.

"Seeking" the Lord is a familiar theme throughout the prayers and songs of the psalms, and the phrase "seek the LORD" appears 26 times in the Old Testament. Always, with no exception, both the term and the phrase imply an intense focus, a singular purpose within the circumstance to find the Lord. There is not any ambivalence or half-hearted effort. "But if from thence thou shalt seek the LORD thy God, thou shalt find him, if thou seek him with all thy heart and with all thy soul" (Deut. 4:29. "Wherewithal shall a young man cleanse his way? by taking heed thereto according to thy word. With my whole heart have I sought thee; O let me not wander from they commandments" (Ps. 119:9–10). "Seek ye the LORD while he may be found, call ye upon him while he is near: Let the wicked forsake his way, and the unrighteous man his thoughts; and let him return unto the LORD, and he will have mercy upon him; and to our God, for he will abundantly pardon" (Isa. 55:6–7). If we are to find the Lord, we must seek him with the intensity and singularity of purpose represented in these passages.

Verses 7–9

The angel of the LORD encampeth round about them that fear him, and delivereth them.

O taste and see that the LORD is good: blessed is the man that trusteth in him.

O fear the LORD, ye his saints: for there is no want to them that fear him.

What marvelous promises are these! These are promises for today, not for the hereafter. We are protected. We are blessed. We are satisfied. Much of what God does for His precious saints is veiled in the Old Testament — often merely hinted at in poetic sections like the Psalms, or wrapped up in the principles contained in mighty miracles displayed in God's sovereign care for Israel. But the New Testament is replete with direct promises and insights. The first three chapters of Ephesians reveal the inexhaustible resources that we have at our disposal as the children of the king. Jesus promises that we need not worry about tomorrow or about our needs; the Heavenly Father already knows what we need and is anxious to give us "good gifts" (Matt. 7:7–11). Paul told the Philippian church that he knew that he could "do all things through Christ which strengtheneth me" (Phil. 4:13). He also understood that God "shall supply all your need according to his riches in glory by Christ Jesus (Phil. 4:19)."

But please notice: these promises are to those "that seek the LORD."

Verse 10

The young lions do lack, and suffer hunger: but they that seek the LORD shall not want any good thing.

After David's prayer of praise and thanksgiving, comes David's sermon of instruction and application.

Verses 11–15

Come, ye children, hearken unto me: I will teach you the fear of the LORD.

What man is he that desireth life, and loveth many days, that he may see good?

Keep thy tongue from evil, and thy lips from speaking guile.

Depart from evil, and do good: seek peace, and pursue it.

The eyes of the LORD are upon the righteous, and his ears are open unto their cry.

These opening verses of the instructional part of the psalm are quoted in 1 Peter 3:10–12, and could well be compared to the first stanza of Psalm 119.

Blessed are the undefiled in the way, who walk in the law of the LORD. Blessed are they that keep His testimonies, and that seek Him with the whole heart. They also do no iniquity: they walk in His ways. Thou hast commanded us to keep thy precepts diligently. O that my ways were directed to keep thy statutes! Then shall I not be ashamed, when I have respect unto all thy commandments. I will praise thee with uprightness of heart, when I shall have learned thy righteous judgments. I will keep thy statues: O forsake me not utterly (Ps. 119:1–8).

The message is plain. "The righteous LORD loveth righteousness; his countenance doth behold the upright" (Ps. 11:7). If we want to enjoy the blessings of our Creator, if we desire his fellowship and his hand on our efforts, if we are to maintain confidence in our relationship with the One in whom is "no darkness at all" (1 John 1:5), then we must "walk in the light, as he is in the light" (1 John 1:7).

This is such a simple concept, yet it is at the root of much of the conflict in the Christian life. So many people today appear to desire the approval of the world's philosophy or its adherents, attempting to compromise the clear messages of the Word of God with the views and lifestyles of the wicked.

Verse 16

The face of the LORD is against them that do evil, to cut off the remembrance of them from the earth.

Here is another clear, basic, often repeated message of Scripture. Why is it that many of God's people try to get around this fact? God does not tolerate evil. He does not approve nor overlook the deeds of wickedness. Although God demonstrated His incomprehensible and gracious love for us "while we were yet sinners" (Rom. 5:8), He is "not a God that hath pleasure in wickedness: neither shall evil dwell with thee. The foolish shall not stand in thy sight: thou hatest all workers of iniquity" (Ps. 5:4–5). We are never to think that God's love for the world extends beyond His provision through Jesus Christ on the Cross. Those who respond to His love are "created in righteousness and true holiness" (Eph. 4:24). Jesus said that those who do not accept His atonement and do not believe his word, "shall die in your sins" (John 8:24).

This is why the New Testament makes such a strong case for the *change* in the life of the believer. We are "new creations" (2 Cor. 5:17; Gal. 6:15) and are now a "new man" (Eph. 4:24; Col. 3:10). We are set free from sin (Rom. 6:6–7) and free from sin's law in our body (Rom. 8:2). Indeed, we are set at liberty, not only from the control of sin in our lives, but set free to perform the righteous works that God has decreed that we should do (Gal. 5:1, 13; Eph. 2:10). If we are God's chosen, we will live like God's chosen.

> Little children, let no man deceive you: he that doeth righteousness is righteous, even as he is righteous. He that committeth sin is of the devil; for the devil sinneth from the beginning. For this purpose the Son of God was manifested, that he might destroy the works of the devil. Whosoever is born of God doth not commit sin; for his seed remaineth in him: and he cannot sin, because he is born of God. In this the children of God are manifest, and the children of the devil: whosoever doeth not righteousness is not of God, neither he that loveth not his brother (1 John 3:7–10).

The close of the psalm emphasizes the contrast between the response of the Lord to those who are righteous and those who are evil. God *will* answer the prayer of the saint. God *will* deliver His children from their dilemmas. God *will* comfort those whose hearts are in tune with their need for God's help. But God *will* respond only in judgment to those who have set themselves against Him.

Verses 17–22

The righteous cry, and the LORD heareth, and delivereth them out of all their troubles.

The LORD is nigh unto them that are of a broken heart; and saveth such as be of a contrite spirit.

Many are the afflictions of the righteous; but the LORD delivereth him out of them all.

He keepeth all his bones: not one of them is broken.

Evil shall slay the wicked: and they that hate the righteous shall be desolate.

The LORD redeemeth the soul of his servants; and none of them that trust in him shall be desolate.

Like many other psalms, the message of this psalm also focuses prophetically on the one who was fully righteous, the Lord Jesus Christ. Although He was dying for sin, the executioners did not break any bones, as they were accustomed to do in such cases. Verse 20 is cited in John 19:36 as literally fulfilled in the crucifixion of Christ. He died before they could break any bones. The ultimate contrast, of course, is the closing comparison between the "redemption" of the righteous and the "slaying" and the "desolation" of the wicked.

One day this world and all that is in it will be "burned up" (2 Pet. 3:10) and the Lord of the universe will build a "new heavens and a new earth, wherein dwelleth righteousness" (2 Pet. 3:13). The One who saved us will "dwell" with us and be "with" us, ruling from a "new Jerusalem" (Rev. 21:2–3) in which no thing or being will enter that "defileth, neither whatsoever worketh abomination, or maketh a lie" (Rev. 21:27). All that is evil, all who are evil will be purged from this "new" world, and all that hurt and destroy will be removed from the very memory of those who are part of the redeemed (Isa. 11:9). We who own Jesus of Nazareth, the Son of God as our Savior and Lord now, will rest in the "peace that passeth understanding" (Phil. 4:7).

In that "real world" of eternity, prepared by our Lord Jesus, "God shall wipe away all tears from their eyes; and there shall be no more death, neither sorrow, nor crying, neither shall there be any more pain: for the former things are passed away" (Rev. 21: 4).

"Even so, come, Lord Jesus."

Chapter 56

Victory over the Wicked

Psalm 37

Certainly one of the more encouraging special blessings given in the psalmic literature is the promise that no matter how much the wicked seem to be succeeding over the efforts of the righteous, they will not win! The opening and closing verses of David's song recorded in Psalm 37 define the two great themes of this promise; the wicked will be destroyed and punished and the righteous will be victorious and rewarded.

Verses 1–2

Fret not thyself because of evildoers, neither be thou envious against the workers of iniquity.

For they shall soon be cut down like the grass, and wither as the green herb.

Verses 39–40

But the salvation of the righteous is of the LORD: he is their strength in the time of trouble.

And the LORD shall help them, and deliver them: he shall deliver them from the wicked, and save them, because they trust in him.

Sprinkled throughout this psalm are couplets that paint various contrasting pictures of these themes. This structure is always used with the purpose of providing the assurance of God's victory — not only in His eternal plan, but also in and through the lives of His precious saints.

Verses 9–11

For evildoers shall be cut off; but those that wait upon the LORD, they shall inherit the earth.

For yet a little while, and the wicked shall not be: yea, thou shalt diligently consider his place, and it shall not be.

But the meek shall inherit the earth; and shall delight themselves in the abundance of peace.

Verses 16–17

A little that a righteous man hath is better than the riches of many wicked.

For the arms of the wicked shall be broken: but the LORD upholdeth the righteous.

Verse 28

For the LORD loveth judgment, and foresaketh not his saints; they are preserved for ever: but the seed of the wicked shall be cut off.

Verses 37–38

Mark the perfect man, and behold the upright: for the end of that man is peace.

But the transgressors shall be destroyed together; the end of the wicked shall be cut off.

The continual message of these verses is that God will not forsake His beloved saints. They may *seem* to be forgotten for a season, but they are never out of the eye of Him who loves them. (See Ps. 33:18–19, 34:15; Job 36:7 and 1 Pet. 3:12 for parallel references.) God *is* protecting His beloved. God *does* have a plan in His sovereign and eternal mind. God *will* work all things "together for good, to them that love God, to them who are the called according to his purpose" (Rom. 8:28).

Frustration tends to come as the saints of God do battle with the forces of evil. We may be certain of the ultimate victory, but the pain and pressure of conflict is nonetheless real as the "devices" (Isa. 32:7) of the wicked take their toll in and among the people of God. It may indeed provide solace to know that the Lord will reduce the plans of the wicked to naught (Ps. 33:10), but while those plans are effective they do much hurt.

The psalm is focused on the solutions that will cure the "fretting" that comes in the heat of battle. Anger (Hebrew: *charah*) is a natural result of the hatred of those who would dare lift up their hand against the Lord of the universe. Envy (Hebrew: *qana*) is bound to explode from the heart of the righteous saint who loves the kingdom and is in anguish because of the success of the wicked. But "normal" reactions to the reality of the "struggle" against principalities and powers (Eph. 6:12) can never excuse *continued* anger and envy. If reactionary anger is not to become sin, it must not be allowed to continue (Eph. 4:26). If sin is not to control, it must not be allowed to reign (Rom. 6:12–14).

Several key actions are commanded in this psalm. These are those actions or activities (or perhaps they could be understood as *attitudes*) that are cited as *cures* for the "fret" and "envy" that *will* come and *may* dominate our lives whenever we stand for the great truths and purposes of the kingdom.

Verse 3

Trust in the LORD, and do good; so shalt thou dwell in the land, and verily thou shalt be fed.

Trust is the most basic of the characteristics of our relationship with the Lord and sets the foundation for all the rest. The Hebrew word carries the meaning of "confidence," or "boldness," and is often used in such a way that it would imply that we are to "gain support" and to "lean on" the one in whom we trust. The expanded definition of "trust" is contained in Proverbs 3:5–8:

Trust in the LORD with all thine heart; and lean not unto thine own understanding. In all thy ways acknowledge him, and he shall direct thy paths. Be not wise in thine own eyes: fear the LORD and depart from evil. It shall be health to thy navel, and marrow to thy bones.

But merely to have great confidence in the God of creation is not enough. We must "do good." The entire New Testament Book of James is devoted to this theme. "Faith without works is dead." (James 2:20). "Why call ye me Lord, Lord, and do not the things that I say," Jesus asked (Luke 6:46). "O that there were such an heart in them," God told Moses, "that they would fear me, and keep all my commandments always, that it might be well with them, and with their children for ever" (Deut. 5:29). If we would enjoy the blessings of God we must embrace the plan of God. If we are to expect the promise that we will "dwell" and will "be fed," then we must submit to the instructions of our Lord who told us to "seek ye first the kingdom of God, and his righteousness; and all these things shall be added unto you" (Matt. 6:33).

Verse 4

Delight thyself also in the LORD; and he shall give thee the desires of thine heart.

This beautiful promise and command insists that we "luxuriate" in our Lord. He is the Lord of inexhaustible riches (Phil. 4:19) and His inexpressible power is at work in His children (Eph. 3:20). Isaiah records God's rhetorical question: "Wherefore do ye spend money for that which is not bread? And your labour for that which satisfieth not? Hearken diligently unto me, and eat ye that which is good, and let your soul delight itself in fatness" (Isa. 55:2). God reminded Israel that the day was coming when she would "be delighted with the abundance of her glory" (Isa. 66:11). Jesus said, "how much more shall your Father which is in heaven give good gifts to them that ask him?" (Matt. 7:11).

When we trust the Lord to give us what we need as we "do good," is it any wonder that He who knows all and owns all will give us "the desires" of our heart? If my heart longs for the "kingdom of God and His righteousness," why should I marvel when the King of kings grants my desires? God hates the wicked and their efforts (Ps. 5:4–5). Why should I be surprised when He answers my prayer for their overthrow?

The key to this "effectual fervent prayer" (James 5:16) is a human heart that is in sync with the beat of the divine heart.

Verses 5–6

Commit thy way unto the LORD; trust also in him, and he shall bring it to pass.

And He shall bring forth thy righteousness as the light, and thy judgment as the noonday.

We are to know such a trust in the Lord that our life will be committed to Him. The unusual Hebrew word here translated "commit" (*galal*) is more often translated as "roll" on or with something. The picture of the word seems to imply such a unity with the one to whom he is committed that the committed one is bound up in the actions or activities of the thing or person committed to — we "roll on" or "roll with" the Lord in our "way."

Paul spends much of his letter to the Philippian church describing the interrelationship between the Creator Savior and the mind, heart, and lifestyle of the saint of God who has given his life over to God. "Being confident of this very thing," Paul says, "that he which has begun a good work in you will perform it until the day of Jesus Christ" (Phil. 1:6). To the believer Paul insists that we are to "work out your own salvation with fear and trembling. For it is God which worketh in you both to will and to do of his good pleasure" (Phil. 2:12–13). And while admitting that he had not yet "attained," he is so focused on the work of the kingdom that he is "forgetting those things which are behind, and reaching forth unto those things which are before, I press toward the mark for the prize of the high calling of God in Christ Jesus" (Phil. 3:13).

Verses 7–8

Rest in the LORD, and wait patiently for him: fret not thyself because of him who prospereth in his way, because of the man who bringeth wicked devices to pass.

Cease from anger, and forsake wrath: fret not thyself in any wise to do evil.

Once again, the warning and command for us is not to focus on the circumstances of the apparent success of the wicked person, philosophy, or condition. We are to *rest* in the *Lord*. The Hebrew word used here (*daman*) carries the sense of stunned silence. It is often translated as "silent," "cease" or "cut off." From the context of the psalm in which this command is set, we may understand that we are to be "stunned into silence" at what the Lord will do to the wicked who dare to set themselves up against the Lord's stewards.

Verses 12–15

The wicked plotteth against the just, and gnasheth upon him with his teeth.

The LORD shall laugh at him: for he seeth that his day is coming.

The wicked have drawn out the sword, and have bent their bow, to cast down the poor and needy, and to slay such as be of upright conversation.

Their sword shall enter in to their own heart, and their bows shall be broken.

Much may happen during the time that the Lord is "longsuffering to us-ward, not willing that any should perish, but that all should come to repentance" (2 Pet. 3:9). God's people "shall suffer persecution" (2 Tim. 3:12) if they will live for Him, but they will never be abandoned (Heb. 13:5).

Verses 18–22

The LORD knoweth the days of the upright: and their inheritance shall be forever.

They shall not be ashamed in the evil time: and in the days of famine they shall be satisfied.

But the wicked shall perish, and the enemies of the LORD shall be as the fat of lambs: they shall consume; into smoke shall they consume away.

The wicked borroweth, and payeth not again: but the righteous showeth mercy, and giveth.

For such as be blessed of him shall inherit the earth; and they that be cursed of him shall be cut off.

No matter what may happen in time and during the circumstances of this life, God has promised to bring such an ultimate righteous conclusion to the matter that we will be "stunned" by what He does. But there is also much more to the promise of this victory. We can be certain of His guidance, supply, and care during this life as well.

Verses 23–31

The steps of a good man are ordered by the LORD: and he delighteth in his way.

Though he fall, he shall not be utterly cast down: for the LORD upholdeth him with his hand.

I have been young, and now am old: yet have I not seen the righteous forsaken, nor his seed begging bread.

He is ever merciful, and lendeth; and his seed is blessed.

Depart from evil, and do good; and dwell for evermore.

For the LORD loveth judgment, and forsaketh not his saints; they are preserved for ever: but the seed of the wicked shall be cut off.

The righteous shall inherit the land and dwell therein for ever.

The mouth of the righteous speaketh wisdom, and his tongue talketh of judgment.

The law of his God is in his heart: none of his steps shall slide.

This continual promise of God's care of His holy ones does not vary through this psalm. There are two aspects of the theme, however. The ultimate fulfillment is yet future, in the concluding activity of a righteous Judge and Savior who will conquer all enemies and set up His eternal kingdom of righteousness (2 Pet. 3:10–13). But the everyday and ongoing fulfillment recognizes the reality of the onslaught of the evil one and his minions who would destroy both the Lord's people and the Lord's kingdom.

Verses 32–36

The wicked watcheth the righteous and seeketh to slay him.

The LORD will not leave him in his hand, nor condemn him when he is judged.

Wait on the LORD, and keep his way, and he shall exalt thee to inherit the land: when the wicked are cut off, thou shalt see it.

I have seen the wicked in great power, and spreading himself like a green bay tree.

Yet he passed away, and, lo, he was not: yea, I sought him, but he could not be found.

The last of the commands to action for the child of God in this psalm is to "wait" on the Lord. In spite of the apparent success of the wicked, we are to "wait on the LORD." Again the Hebrew word is unusual. The picture of the term *quvah* is used to describe the "binding together" of strings for a chord and to "collect" the water and dry land into separate areas on the third day of creation. It carries the idea of anticipation toward useful results. It does not mean to "hang around and wait." It does not imply useless boredom, waiting for something to happen. The essence of the term is to be alert, *watching* the events and activities of the Lord to react to His timing and His direction. Indeed, the word is translated "look" as often as any other term.

The great promise of "eagle's wings" given by Isaiah tells us that the source of our victory comes from the Lord alone. "He giveth power to the faint; and to them that have no might he increaseth strength. Even the youths shall faint and be weary, and the young men shall utterly fall: But they that wait upon the LORD shall renew their strength; they shall mount up with wings as eagles; they shall run, and not be weary; and they shall walk, and not faint" (Isa. 40:29–31).

The conclusion of this psalm is both sufficient and succinct.

Verses 37–40

Mark the perfect man, and behold the upright: for the end of that man is peace.

But the transgressors shall be destroyed together: the end of the wicked shall be cut off.

But the salvation of the righteous is of the LORD; he is their strength in the time of trouble.

And the LORD shall help them, and deliver them; he shall deliver them from the wicked, and save them, because they trust in him.

Chapter 57

Unfathomable Blessings

Psalm 103

This Davidic psalm is pure praise. It puts one in mind of the old hymn, "Count Your Blessings," wherein we are encouraged to count our blessings and "name them one by one." The Psalmist does that here, a list of the personal blessings he has known as one of God's redeemed, followed by a list of the broad blessings that encompass the children of God, and summarized by a list of the universal and foundational blessings upon which all of the kingdom may depend.

The song begins with a very personal command ("my soul" — verses 1–2). Then lists blessings that the reader should be aware of ("thine" and "thy" — verses 3–9). It continues with praise for joint awareness of God's forgiveness and mercy ("us" and "our" — verses 10–14). That is followed by a recognition of the broad application of God's care to all the redeemed ("them that fear him" — verses 15–19), and finally, a command to "his angels" and to "his works" to "bless the LORD."

Some have suggested that the psalm should be viewed as a three-tiered praise: Verses 1 through 9 speak of the *unlimited* blessings of the Lord to the saint. That is followed by an emphasis on the *unmerited* blessings of forgiveness and provisional care described in verses 10 through 15, summarized by the *unending* blessing and praise that is due the Lord throughout eternity in verses 16 through 22.

Others attempt to analyze the structure linguistically or grammatically, yet very few commentators agree on the structure. All agree, however, that the doctrines of forgiveness and mercy are the dominant themes in the praise.

This writer would prefer to remember the message by its major themes: forgiveness, salvation, mercy, and worship.

Verses 1–2

Bless the LORD, O my soul; and all that is within me, bless his holy name.

Bless the LORD, O my soul, and forget not all his benefits.

There are two main words used for "bless" in the Old Testament. The word in these opening verses, and the word that is always used in the phrase "bless the LORD," is the Hebrew, *barak*. Its primary meaning is "to kneel," and is most often translated "bless" in the sense of a "salute" or "praise" to the object of adoration. The emphasis in the Scriptures is always an honoring of God's great work in our lives. "Love the Lord thy God with all thy heart, and with all thy soul, and with all thy heart, and all thy mind, and with all thy strength" (Mark 12:30).

The great themes of this psalm are introduced initially as the inestimable personal gifts of grace that the believer has received at the hand of the Lord.

Verses 3–7

Who forgiveth all thine iniquities; who healeth all thy diseases;

Who redeemeth thy life from destruction; who crowneth thee with lovingkindness and tender mercies;

Who satisfieth thy mouth with good things; so that thy youth is renewed like the eagle's.

The LORD executeth righteousness and judgment for all that are oppressed.

He made known his ways unto Moses, his acts unto the children of Israel.

The intertwined gifts of forgiveness and salvation are introduced here as the foundation from which all the rest of God's lovingkindness and mercies flow. These eternal gifts are the result of the very nature of God himself: "The LORD, The LORD God, merciful and gracious, longsuffering, and abundant in goodness and truth, Keeping mercy for thousands, forgiving iniquity and transgression and sin, and that will by no means clear the guilty" (Exod. 34:6–7).

Forgiveness is the starting point, the platform from which salvation is launched. Were God not forgiving, none would stand before Him. His holiness can demand no less than total rightness. "Because it is written,

Be ye holy; for I am holy" (1 Pet. 1:16). It is very clear from the Word of God that no created being will ever stand before the Holy God without complete holiness. "Follow peace with all men, and holiness, without which, no man shall see the Lord" (Heb. 12:14). It is no wonder that David, and Paul, who quotes David, would say; "Blessed are they whose iniquities are forgiven, and whose sins are covered. Blessed is the man to whom the Lord will not impute sin (Rom. 4:7–8).

Surely the reader is aware of the phrase, "Christ died for our sins." But, perhaps that truth is so familiar that it is taken as a simple statement without awareness of what was accomplished by His death. Our forgiveness — the absolute eradication of both the *condition* of sinfulness and all the *deeds* of sinful behavior and thought — have been irrevocably removed from the very thought process of God. "I will forgive their iniquity, and I will remember their sin no more" (Jer. 31:34). "I have blotted out, as a thick cloud, thy transgressions, and, as a cloud, thy sins" (Isa. 44:22).

This is an unfathomable reality! God's holiness drives Him to punish sinful men "with everlasting destruction from the presence of the Lord, and from the glory of his power" (2 Thess. 1:9). He has provided an atonement, through Jesus Christ, by which "though your sins be as scarlet, they shall be white as snow; though they be red like crimson, they shall be as wool" (Isa. 1:18). "Thou hast in love to my soul delivered it from the pit of corruption: for thou hast cast all my sins behind thy back (Isa. 38:17).

But at what cost?

God cannot, merely because He is *love*, forgive sin. God's very nature abhors both the sinful condition and the sinner who dares to lift his heart to rebel against the authority of the Creator. "For thou art not a God that hath pleasure in wickedness: neither shall evil dwell with thee. The foolish shall not stand in thy sight: thou hatest all workers of iniquity (Ps. 5:4-5). He must "declare . . . at this time, his righteousness: that he might be just, and the justifier of him which believeth in Jesus" (Rom. 3:26). God *must* maintain His holiness. God *cannot* violate His nature. "Thou art of purer eyes than to behold evil, and canst not look on iniquity" (Hab. 1:13).

To forgive, God must maintain His holiness, mete out the punishment justly deserved on those who sin, and *then* make the sinner holy!

But the "wages of sin is death" (Rom. 6:23). And "all have sinned and come short of the glory of God" (Rom. 3:32). "There is none righteous, no not one. There is none that understandeth, there is none that seeketh after God" (Rom. 3:10–11). Whatever God must do, He must deal with a human race that is sinful, ignorant, and willfully avoiding

God. Man cannot redeem himself! We have "no hope, and [are] without God in the world" (Eph. 2:12).

It is to make possible the reconciliation of these humanly impossible and contradictory conditions that God the Father sent His only begotten son, Jesus the Christ, into the world.

> In this was manifested the love of God toward, us, because that God sent his only begotten Son into the world, that we might live through him. Herein is love, not that we loved God, but that he loved us, and sent his Son to be the propitiation for our sins (1 John 4:9–10).

> And he is the propitiation for our sins: and not for ours only, but also for the sins of the whole world (1 John 2:2).

> But God commendeth his love toward us, in that, while we were yet sinners, Christ died for us (Rom. 5:8).

> God was in Christ, reconciling the world unto himself, not imputing their trespasses unto them; and hath committed unto us the word of reconciliation. Now then we are ambassadors for Christ, as though God did beseech you by us: we pray you in Christ's stead, be ye reconciled to God. For he hath made him to be sin for us, who knew no sin, that we might be made the righteousness of God in him (2 Cor. 5:19–21).

We will never understand *all* that was done on our behalf. But this much is clear — we deserve nothing but the condemnation of a Holy God for both our inherited and our conscious sinfulness. God could only forgive us by transferring that sinfulness to one that did not deserve His condemnation, thereby maintaining God's own holiness and integrity. That recipient of our sins, the one who received God's wrath and judgment for our sins, was Jesus the Christ, God become flesh, that He might substitute himself for all of us. This done, God could justly offer pardon and reconciliation to those of the human race who would receive His pardon, and could make a "new man, which after God is created in righteousness and true holiness" (Eph. 4:24).

With forgiveness possible through the substitutionary death of God's Son, and individually appropriated by faith in the completed work of Christ, God can "save" us and make us "His child" (Gal. 4:5).

It is critical that the reader understands all that is spoken of by David in this psalm. We are so used to the Christian terms that we often read right over the familiar, and lose the majesty of the praise. Salvation is a work that only God performs, and can only be performed on those human beings who have heard of His gracious provision through Jesus Christ, who have believed that message, and who have placed their complete trust in what He alone has done on our behalf.

Perhaps it would be profitable to identify the main teaching on salvation as presented by the Scriptures.

Salvation, though undeserved, is granted freely to all that believe.

As many as received him, to them gave he power to become the sons of God, even to them that believe on his name: which were born, not of blood, nor of the will of the flesh, nor of the will of man, but of God (John 1:12–13).

For God so loved the world, that he gave his only begotten Son, that whosoever believeth in him should not perish, but have everlasting life (John 3:16).

He that believeth on the Son hath everlasting life; and he that believeth not the Son shall not see life; but the wrath of God abideth on him (John 3:36).

For by grace are ye saved through faith; and that not of yourselves: it is the gift of God: not of works, lest any man should boast (Eph. 2:8–9).

Salvation, once granted, is complete and eternal.

Verily, verily I say unto you, he that heareth my word, and believeth on him that sent me, hath everlasting life, and shall not come into condemnation; but is passed from death unto life (John 5:24).

My sheep hear my voice, and I know them, and they follow me: And I give unto them eternal life; and they shall never perish, neither shall any man pluck them out of my hand. My Father, which gave them me, is greater that all; and no man is able to pluck them out of my Father's hand (John 10:27–29).

I am the resurrection and the life: he that believeth in me, though he were dead, yet shall he live: And whosoever liveth and believeth in me shall never die. Believeth thou this? (John 11:25–26).

Ye are complete in him, which is the head of all principality and power (Col. 2:10).

Being confident of this very thing, that he which hath begun a good work in you will perform it until the day of Jesus Christ (Phil. 1:6).

Salvation, once implemented, provides all necessary spiritual power to live a godly life.

Therefore, if any man be in Christ, he is a new creature: old things are passed away; behold all things are become new (2 Cor. 5:17).

For we are his workmanship, created in Christ Jesus unto good works, which God hath before ordained that we should walk in them (Eph. 2:10).

According as his divine power hath given unto us all things that pertain unto life and godliness, through the knowledge of him that hath called us to glory and virtue: Whereby are given unto us exceeding great and precious promises: that by these ye might be partakers of the divine nature, having escaped the corruption that is in the world through lust (2 Pet. 1:3–4).

Salvation, once completely fulfilled in eternity, will totally bring the entire physical universe into conformity with God's holy will and nature.

Nevertheless, we, according to his promise, look for a new heavens and a new earth, wherein dwelleth righteousness (2 Pet. 3:13).

And I saw a great white throne, and him that sat on it, from whose face the earth and the heaven fled away; and there was found no place for them. And I saw the dead, small and great, stand before God; and the books were opened, and another book was opened, which is the book of life: and the dead were judged out of those things which were written in the books, according to their works. . . . And whosoever was not found written in the book of life was cast into the lake of fire (Rev. 20:11–15).

For our conversation is in heaven; from whence also we look for the Saviour, the Lord Jesus Christ: Who shall change our vile body, that it may be fashioned like unto his glorious body, according to the working whereby he is able even to subdue all things unto himself (Phil. 3:20–21).

Blessed be the God and Father of our Lord Jesus Christ, which according to his abundant mercy hath begotten us again unto a lively hope by the resurrection of Jesus Christ from the dead, To an inheritance incorruptible, and undefiled, and that fadeth not away, reserved in heaven for you, Who are kept by the power of God through faith unto salvation ready to be revealed in the last time (1 Pet. 1:3–5).

And I heard a great voice out of heaven saying, Behold, the tabernacle of God is with men, and he will dwell with them, and they shall be his people, and God himself shall be with them, and be their God. And God shall wipe away all tears from their eyes; and there shall be nor more death, neither sorrow, nor crying, neither shall there be any more pain: for the former things are passed away. And he that sat upon the throne said, Behold, I make all things new (Rev. 21:3–5).

Dear reader, while we share these profound thoughts together, do not pass over them with the gloss of haste or perfunctory acknowledgement. As you have read these words, if your heart and mind have been challenged with an awareness that you are not yet a participant in the grace of God, please, before you read another word, reach out with your heart and mind to the God who loves you, and ask Him for His gift of eternal life.

And dear brother in Christ, pause where we are now and give thanks to God "for His unspeakable gift."

All that has been dealt with heretofore is merely the beginning of the "blessings" from the Lord. Because of the complete substitutionary work of Jesus Christ on the cross, forgiveness is possible. It is granted out of the love of God in submission to the holiness of God. Once forgiveness has been received through faith, salvation is implemented, righteousness imputed, and a new spirit created "in righteousness and true holiness" (Eph. 4:24).

The resultant "blessings" flow from the new relationship with God. All that are listed by David in the opening verses: lovingkindness, good things, strength, judgment, knowledge of His ways — all are inherited from the same God who forgives and saves.

Blessed be the God and Father of our Lord Jesus Christ, who hath blessed us with all spiritual blessings in heavenly places in Christ: According as he hath chosen us in him before the foundation of the world, that we should be holy and without blame before him in love (Eph. 1:3–4).

Wherein he hath abounded toward us in all wisdom and prudence; having made known unto us the mystery of his will, According to his good pleasure which he hath purposed in himself (Eph. 1:8–9).

And this I pray, that your love may abound yet more and more in knowledge and in all judgment; That ye may approve things that are excellent; that ye may be sincere and without offence till the day of Christ; Being filled with the fruits of righteousness, which are by Jesus Christ, unto the glory and praise of God (Phil. 1:9–11).

For this cause we also, since the day we heard it, do not cease to pray for you, and to desire that ye might be filled with the knowledge of his will in all wisdom and spiritual understanding; That ye might walk worthy of the Lord unto all pleasing, being fruitful in every good work, and increasing in the knowledge of God; Strengthened with all might, according to his glorious power, unto all patience and longsuffering with joyfulness; giving thanks unto the Father, which hath made us meet to be partakers of the inheritance of the saints in light (Col. 1:9–12).

Having introduced his list of worshipful praises because of what he has known through the great forgiveness and salvation of God, David now begins to honor God for His mercy.

Verses 8–18

The LORD is merciful and gracious, slow to anger, and plenteous in mercy.

He will not always chide: neither will he keep his anger for ever.

He hath not dealt with us after our sins; nor rewarded us according to our iniquities.

For as the heaven is high above the earth, so great is his mercy toward them that fear him.

As far as the east is from the west, so far hath he removed our transgressions from us.

Like as a father pitieth his children, so the LORD pitieth them that fear him.

For he knoweth our frame; he remembereth that we are dust.

As for man, his days are as grass: as a flower of the field, so he flourisheth.

For the wind passeth over it, and it is gone; and the place thereof shall know it no more.

But the mercy of the LORD is from everlasting to everlasting upon them that fear him and his righteousness unto children's children;

To such as keep his covenant, and to those that remember his commandments to do them.

As will be further discussed in the chapter on Psalm 136, the theme of God's mercy is replete throughout all Scripture. "Mercy" is somewhat difficult to define, since "grace" is occasionally closely coupled with it. Most often, however, "mercy" can be understood as "judgment delayed" or "longsuffering in the face of deserved punishment" (note verse 10 of this psalm). This passage emphasizes the "mercy" of God as it is directed to those of the household of faith. There are frequent references to "those that fear him" and the recognition of "his children" and the relationship of "Father." Although the Bible does speak of God's mercy being exercised to all mankind (Matt. 5:45; Ps. 145:9, etc.), this psalm deals with God's actions and attitude toward the redeemed.

Central to this relationship is the ability of God to withdraw His just anger at the sins of His people. This is often seen during the history of the nation of Israel, but the principle is an eternal one. God's holiness is roiled when any man sins, but is tested most intimately when His own children, those to whom He has given His own divine nature, choose to sin.

And my people are bent to backsliding from me: though they called them to the most High, none at all would exalt him. How shall I give thee up, Ephraim? How shall I deliver thee, Israel? how shall I make thee as Admah? how shall I set thee as Zeboim? mine heart is turned within me, my repentings are kindled together. I will not execute the fierceness of mine anger, I will not return to destroy Ephraim: for I am God, and not man; the Holy One in the midst of thee: and I will not enter into the city (Hos. 11:7–9).

Perhaps the reader will remember the sad comment of the Lord when He spoke to the religious leaders: "O Jerusalem, Jerusalem, which killest the prophets, and stonest them that are sent unto thee; how often would I have gathered thy children together, as a hen doth gather her brood under her wings, and ye would not!" (Luke 13:34). God's heart is ever merciful, especially to those that are His, but His holiness demands that His children be obedient before they can enjoy the benefit of His bounty.

The Old Testament book of Malachi is a study in the mercy of God on a people who had all the form of religion, certainly knew the doctrines of God, but were disobedient, not only in their behavior and practices but in their hearts as well. God does not overlook their sin, nor does He execute immediate punishment as they deserved, but will warn and encourage them to obey that they might enjoy His favor and blessing.

> I have loved you, saith the LORD. . . . A son honoureth his father, and a servant his master: if then I be a father, where is mine honour? And if I be a master, where is my fear? saith the LORD of hosts unto you, O priests, that despise my name. And ye say, wherein have we despised they name? Ye offer polluted bread upon mine altar. . . . ye offer the blind for sacrifice. . . .ye offer the lame and sick. . . . And now, I pray you, beseech God that he will be gracious unto us: this hath been by your means: will he regard your persons? saith the LORD of hosts (Mal. 1:2–9).

> If you will not hear, and if ye will not lay it to heart, to give glory unto my name, saith the LORD of hosts, I will even send a curse upon you, and I will curse your blessings. . . . Ye have wearied the LORD with your words. Yet ye say, wherein have we wearied him? When ye say, every one that doeth evil is good in the sight of the LORD, and he delighteth in them; or, Where is the God of judgment? (Mal. 2:2–17).

> For I am the LORD, I change not; therefore ye sons of Jacob are not consumed. Even from the days of your fathers ye are gone away from mine ordinances, and have not kept them. Return unto me, and I will return unto you, saith the LORD of hosts (Mal. 3:6–7).

> Ye are cursed with a curse: for ye have robbed me, even this whole nation. Bring ye all the tithes into the storehouse, that there may be meat in mine house, and prove me now herewith, saith the LORD of hosts, if I will not open you the windows of heaven, and pour you out a blessing, that there shall not be room enough to receive it (Mal. 3:9–10).

As these passages indicate, God's mercy does not force Him to be lenient. His holiness is always foremost in His attributes, and He will never compromise His commandments for the sake or culture or convenience.

But He does delay punishment. He does send corrective instruction through His Word and through the circumstances in our lives.

> My son, despise not the chastening of the LORD; neither be weary of his correction: For whom the LORD loveth he correcteth; even as a father the son in whom he delighteth (Prov. 3:11–12).

> My son, despise not thou the chastening of the Lord, nor faint when thou art rebuked of him: For whom the Lord loveth he chasteneth, and scourgeth every son whom he receiveth. If ye endure chastening, God dealeth with you as with sons; for what son is he whom the father chasteneth not? But if ye be without chastisement, whereof all are partakers, then are ye bastards, and not sons (Heb. 12: 5–8).

The emphasis throughout this section of Psalm 103 is the unlimited reservoir of God's mercy. Two similes are presented to illustrate; the immeasurable distance from the surface of the earth to the reaches of heaven, and the infinity of distance between the east and west. God's mercy is based on His knowledge of "our frame; he remembereth that we are dust." God knows that we are immersed in a matrix of sin and death — "the whole creation groaneth and travaileth in pain together until now" (Rom. 8:22). God knows that our life is short and that the memory of who and what we are is short lived. For these reasons, and for His own love for His chosen, God's "mercy is from everlasting to everlasting."

> Who is a God like unto thee, that pardoneth iniquity and passeth by the transgressions of the remnant of his heritage? He retaineth not his anger for ever, because he delighteth in mercy. He will turn again, he will have compassion upon us; he will subdue our iniquities; and thou wilt cast all their sins into the depths of the sea (Mic. 7:18–19).

Although God's love caused Him to send His Son to die for the sins of the whole world, and His mercy is extended to all humanity through the "seedtime and harvest, and cold and heat, and summer and winter, and day and night" (Gen. 8:22), God's mercy finds its fullest expression in His care and concern for the welfare and spiritual maturity of those who have surrendered their lives to His keeping (John 12:25–26; Matt. 7:11).

Verses 19–22

The LORD hath prepared his throne in the heavens; and his kingdom ruleth over all.

Bless the LORD, ye his angels, that excel in strength, that do his commandments, hearkening unto the voice of his word.

Bless ye the LORD, all ye his hosts; ye ministers of his, that do his pleasure.

Bless the LORD, all his works in all places of his dominion: bless the LORD, O my soul.

This last section of Psalm 103 issues a command to the rest of creation. All are included; none is excepted. The angelic creatures and sundry ministers in His heavenly court are expected to honor their Creator with peals of praise. The very works of creation are to acknowledge God's worthiness. We have little insight into the extent of this reality, other than the occasional words of Scripture.

Praise ye him, all his angels: praise ye him, all his hosts. Praise ye him, sun and moon: praise him, all ye stars of light. Praise him, ye heavens of heavens, and ye waters that be above the heavens. Let them praise the name of the LORD: for he commanded, and they were created. He hath also stablished them for ever and ever: he hath made a decree which shall not pass. Praise the LORD from the earth, ye dragons, and all deeps: Fire and hail; snow, and vapour; stormy wind fulfilling his word: Mountains, and all hills; fruitful trees, and all cedars: Beasts, and all cattle; creeping things, and flying fowl: Kings of the earth, and all people; princes, and all judges of the earth: Both young men, and maidens; old men, and children: Let them praise the name of the LORD: for his name alone is excellent; his glory is above the earth and heaven (Ps. 148:2–13).

And I beheld, and I heard the voice of many angels round about the throne and the beasts and the elders: and the number of them was ten thousand times ten thousand, and thousands of thousands; Saying with a loud voice, Worthy is the Lamb that was slain to receive power, and riches, and wisdom, and strength, and honour, and glory, and blessing. And every creature which is in heaven, and on the earth, and under the earth, and such as are in the sea, and all that are in them, heard I saying, Blessing, and honour, and glory, and power, be unto him that sitteth upon the throne, and unto the Lamb for ever and ever (Rev. 5:11–13).

There will come a day in which all of creation will honor God. It may seem like an impossibility in these days of secular irreverence and mocking defiance. Yet the Scriptures are clear. Even those who die in their irreverence and defiance will bow their knees and proclaim the Lord Jesus Christ as their Creator and rightful King (Phil. 2:9–11).

O Lord God of Heaven and Earth, our finite minds and feeble speech can never produce fitting praise of thee. Although our hearts sometimes fill with gratitude and overflow with the joy of knowing thee, we stumble at our attempts to express our love for thee. Please accept our innermost thoughts. Please hear the groanings of our spirit as we try to hold thee to our breast. Please, Father; receive our childlike thanks and our murmured whispers of love.

We do love thee. But, O Lord, our lives are so impacted by the world and the sin that surrounds us. Forgive us for the constant stumbling and groping in the darkness away from thee. Cleanse us from our sin and bring us into thy light. Direct our steps, God of all wisdom, and keep us from the Evil One. Our soul hungers for thy favor, and we seek to please thee with our days.

Lord God of Sabaoth, our forgiveness stands alone with Thee. We have reached out in sinfulness to respond to thy calling, and have received at thy hand alone the grace of eternal life. We will be unable here in this world to do more than give thee our words of thanksgiving and our lives in thy service. Accept them, O Lord, for it is all that we can do.

And, O Father in heaven, we thank thee for thy mercy. Every day we claim its renewed power. Every day we must have thy mercy extended to our lives. Help us, O God, to heed the promptings of thy Spirit in our hearts and to obey thy Word. We accept the gentle chastening of thy loving hand and yield to thy voice.

O Lord of Hosts, holiness belongs alone unto thee. We would ask as we have been taught to pray that thy will would be done in earth, as it is done in heaven. We gratefully acknowledge that all things come from thee, and we pray that thy bounty would supply our daily bread, and that thy mercy and grace would forgive us our trespasses as we forgive those who trespass against us. And lead us not into temptation, but deliver us from evil, for thine is the kingdom, and the power and the glory for ever. Amen.

Chapter 58

Everlasting Mercy

Psalm 136

This psalm is unique. Every verse ends with the phrase, "for his mercy endureth for ever." The phrase itself is not unique, for it is used some 41 times throughout the Old Testament. Evidently, this was some kind of chorus or chant that was sung during temple worship. Other references in the Chronicles and elsewhere indicate that the phrase was part of songs presented during worship. Psalm 118 uses the phrase 5 times in such a way that it is like an instruction for a "responsive reading" for Israel to follow. Psalm 136 appears to be the same kind of psalm. The Levite would recite or chant an instructional phrase, and the people would respond, "for his mercy endureth for ever."

God's mercy is a monumental theme in Scripture, the English word appearing some 341 times in the Bible. The four Hebrew and three Greek words appear a total of 454 times and are also translated by "kindness," "lovingkindness," "goodness," "favor," "compassion," and "pity." Of the 66 books of the Bible, only 16 do not use one of the words for mercy. Even though "mercy" is an important concept, it is somewhat difficult to prescribe a definition for mercy, especially since "grace" is occasionally closely coupled with it.

In the first reference where "mercy" is used, Lot has just been expelled from Sodom by the angels of judgment. In spite of the command by the angels that Lot and his daughters "escape to the mountain," Lot begs, "Oh, not so, my Lord: behold now, thy servant hath found *grace* in thy sight, and thou hast magnified thy *mercy*, which thou hast showed unto me in saving my life . . . this city is near . . . Oh, let me escape thither" (Gen. 19:17–20). And later, the New Testament saints are told to "come boldly unto the throne of grace, that we may obtain *mercy*, and find *grace* to help in time of need" (Heb. 4:16). In these and other such passages, the two terms appear to address similar subjects.

Although they may appear to be similar, these words are not synonyms. "Grace" is most often associated with the sovereign dispensing of totally undeserved favor, and is specifically connected to salvation. "Mercy" is more often connected to the withholding of judgment: "For he shall have judgment without mercy, that hath showed no mercy; and mercy rejoiceth against judgment" (James 2:13).

Psalm 136 is a teaching liturgy that demonstrates the many ways in which God withholds His judgment from those who deserve punishment.

Verses 1–3

O give thanks unto the LORD; for he is good: for his mercy endureth for ever.

O give thanks unto the God of gods: for his mercy endureth for ever.

O give thanks to the Lord of lords: for his mercy endureth for ever.

God's very nature, when revealed to us through the Scriptures, is an act of mercy. We who are "by nature the children of wrath" (Eph. 2:3), who would "change the truth of God into a lie" (Rom. 1:25), and who love "darkness rather than light" (John 3:19) deserve ignorance of a Holy God, not revelation of His divine nature. We should be "punished with everlasting destruction from the presence of the Lord, and from the glory of his power" (2 Thess. 1:9), not to be "filled with the knowledge of his will in all wisdom and spiritual understanding" (Col. 1:9).

God Is Good!

"It is of the LORD's mercies that we are not consumed, because his compassions fail not. They are new every morning: great is thy faithfulness" (Lam. 3:22–23). "The LORD is gracious, and full of compassion; slow to anger, and of great mercy. The LORD is good to all: and his tender mercies are over all his works" (Ps. 145:8–9). "The LORD will give grace and glory: no good thing will he withhold from them that walk uprightly" (Ps. 84:11). "Trust in the LORD, and do good; so shalt thou dwell in the land, and verily thou shalt be fed. Delight thyself also in the LORD; and he shall give thee the desires of thine heart" (Ps. 37:3–4). "O give thanks unto the LORD; for he is good: for his mercy endureth for ever."

God Is Above All!

He is the *Elohim* of all *elohim*. "The Lord your God is God of gods, and Lord of lords, a great God, a mighty, and a terrible, which regardeth not persons, nor taketh reward" (Deut. 10:17). "Who is a God like unto thee, that pardoneth iniquity, and passeth by the transgression of the remnant of his heritage? He retaineth not his anger for ever, because he delighteth in mercy. He will turn again, he will have compassion upon us; he will subdue our iniquities; and thou wilt cast all their sins into the depths of the sea" (Mic. 7:18–19). "O give thanks unto the God of gods: for his mercy endureth for ever."

God Is Totally Sovereign!

He the "King eternal, immortal, invisible, the only wise God" (1 Tim. 1:17). He is "the blessed and only Potentate, the King of kings, and Lord of lords; Who only hath immortality, dwelling in the light which no man can approach unto; whom no man hath seen, nor can see" (1 Tim. 6:15–16). "The mercy of the Lord is from everlasting to everlasting upon them that fear him, and his righteousness unto children's children. . . . The Lord hath prepared his throne in the heavens; and his kingdom ruleth over all" (Ps. 103:17–19). "O give thanks to the Lord of lords: for his mercy endureth for ever."

God Does Great Wonders!
Verses 4–9

To him who alone doeth great wonders: for his mercy endureth for ever.

To him that by wisdom made the heavens: for his mercy endureth for ever.

To him that stretched out the earth above the waters: for his mercy endureth for ever.

To him that made great lights: for his mercy endureth for ever.

The sun to rule by day: for his mercy endureth for ever.

The moon and stars to rule by night: for his mercy endureth for ever.

The creation of the universe stands out among all of the religions of the world as unique to the God of the Bible. This is that which distinguishes all of the "principalities and powers" of this universe from the one who "created the heavens and the earth." We cannot even understand the triune nature of God apart from what He has revealed of himself in the creation (Rom. 1:20). The very gospel of God has its everlasting foundation in the creation (Rev. 14:6–7). God's "signature" is written throughout the universe, so much so that He used the evidence of His design and authority integrated into the ecosystems of the earth to confirm His deity to Job (Job 39–40).

"He hath made the earth by his power, he hath established the world by his wisdom, and hath stretched out the heaven by his understanding" (Jer. 51:15). The very same power and omniscience that brought the universe into existence now holds it together (Col. 1:17; 2 Pet. 3:7), even though it is falling apart and "the whole creation groaneth and travaileth in pain" (Rom. 8:22). Indeed, the same "Creator" is our "Savior" (John 1:1–3, 14). We do well to honor "Him who alone doeth great wonders: for his mercy endureth for ever."

God Is a Great Deliverer!
Verses 10–15

To him that smote Egypt in their firstborn: for his mercy endureth for ever:

And brought out Israel from among them: for his mercy endureth for ever:

With a strong hand, and with a stretched out arm: for his mercy endureth for ever.

To him which divided the Red sea into parts: for his mercy endureth for ever:

And made Israel to pass through the midst of it: for his mercy endureth for ever:

But overthrew Pharaoh and his host in the Red sea: for his mercy endureth for ever.

The exodus of the nation of Israel from Egypt still stands as one of the most intriguing and awe-inspiring events of history. Nothing in the annals of human events comes close to the intervention of the "I AM THAT I AM" in the affairs of nations. God came "down to deliver" (Exod. 3:8) and to display his "signs and wonders" (Exod. 7:3) "against all the gods of Egypt" (Exod. 12:12). Never before or since has God taken "Him a nation from the midst of another nation, by temptations, by signs, and by wonders, and by war, and by a mighty hand, and by a stretched out arm, and by great terrors" (Deut. 4:34).

In the context of New Testament Christianity, our God has delivered us from "the power of Satan" (Acts 26:18) and "darkness" (Col. 1:13) into "His marvellous light" (1 Pet. 2:9). We have been set free from "the law of sin" (Rom. 8:2) and from "this present evil world" (Gal. 1:4) to the "glorious liberty of the children of God" (Rom. 8:21). The same God who "overthrew Pharaoh " is the Savior who will "deliver the godly out of temptations" (2 Pet. 2:9) and "from every evil work" (2 Tim. 4:18) and has "given unto us exceeding great and precious promises: that by these ye might be partakers of the divine nature, having escaped the corruption that is in the world through lust" (2 Pet. 1:4).

God Is a Great Provider!
Verses 16–26

To him which led his people through the wilderness: for his mercy endureth for ever.

To him which smote great kings: for his mercy endureth for ever:

And slew famous kings: for his mercy endureth for ever:

Sihon king of the Amorites: for his mercy endureth for ever:

And Og the king of Bashan: for his mercy endureth for ever:

And gave their land for an heritage: for his mercy endureth for ever:

Even an heritage unto Israel his servant: for his mercy endureth for ever.

Who remembered us in our low estate: for his mercy endureth for ever:

And hath redeemed us from our enemies: for his mercy endureth for ever.

Who giveth food to all flesh: for his mercy endureth for ever.

O give thanks unto the God of heaven: for his mercy endureth for ever.

There are three specific examples given in this psalm of God's sovereign provision. He protects and shelters during the "wilderness." He makes possible victories over great "enemies." And He gives "food to all flesh." God's detailed provision and the many examples in the Scriptures are inexhaustible. Yet, in these three areas, we may find hope for any situation "in time of need" (Heb. 4:16).

Our "wanderings in the wilderness" are compared to Israel's journey by the apostle Paul (1 Cor. 10) as equal to the many physical and spiritual sins of a people in rebellion against God's control in their lives. Jesus warned that the "cares of this world, and the deceitfulness of riches, and the lusts of other things" would "choke the word" and make us "unfruitful" (Mark 4:19). Yet, even though we may be like the "younger son" in the story of the prodigal (Luke 15:11–32) and would waste our "substance in riotous living," God was still the provider of the "inheritance" that was wasted. God still is waiting for the son to come "to himself" and return home. God still has compassion, forgives, and restores to fellowship all who come home.

And were it not for the promises of deliverance from our enemies so replete throughout the Scriptures, were it not for the hope that we would see deliverance "in the land of the living" (Ps. 27:13), and were it not for the confident knowledge that "evil doers shall be cut off" (Ps. 37:9), we would be in constant fear and torment. God does promise to bring us victory! We are told that He will fight for us! We are not left to our own devices! Jesus said, "All power is given unto me in heaven and in earth. . . . and lo, I am with you alway, even unto the end of the world" (Matt. 28:18–20).

> The steps of a good man are ordered by the LORD: and he delighteth in his way. Though he fall, he shall not be utterly cast down: for the LORD upholdeth him with his hand. I have been young, and now am old; yet have I not seen the righteous forsaken, nor his seed begging bread. . . . Mark the perfect man, and behold the upright: for the end of that man is peace. . . . The salvation of the righteous is of the LORD: he is their strength in the time of trouble. And the LORD shall help them, and deliver them: he shall deliver them from the wicked, and save them, because they trust in him (Ps. 37: 23–40).

Finally, while we are never to take God's provision for granted ("give us this day our daily bread" — Matt. 6:11), we need to be reminded that the mercy of God extends far beyond the care of His own. "He maketh his sun to rise on the evil and on the good, and sendeth rain on the just and on the unjust" (Matt. 5:45). God is "the God of the whole earth" (Isa. 54:5). We often get caught up in trying to make provisions for the "rainy day" in a future that is unknowable and unsecured, but God knows that we "have need of all these things" (Matt. 6:32). Whatever the circumstances may be, God knows, understands, and will make sure that "His mercy endureth for ever."

Chapter 59

God's Loving Kindness and Truth

Psalm 138

God's loving care is a great and expansive theme all throughout the Bible. And, of course, many of the psalms cite incidences of God's faithful help, provision, deliverance, or other evidence that God remains true to His promises and His character. This particular psalm directs our focus on two great pillars of His nature — His loving kindness and His truth.

Verses 1–2

I will praise thee with my whole heart: before the gods will I sing praise unto thee.

I will worship toward thy holy temple, and praise thy name for thy loving-kindness and for thy truth: for thou hast magnified thy word above all thy name.

Praise and worship are not often connected together in the same passage as they are here in Psalm 138:2. Both concepts are widely used in Scripture, but are seldom used to describe the same actions. "Worship" is used to describe an attitude of obeisance and reverence (usually by bowing or prostrating) during a formal act of sacrifice or some other structured observance (as in the idol worship forbidden by the Second Commandment — Exod. 20:5). "Praise," especially this word used in Psalm 138, emphasizes joyous thanksgiving as a result of receiving or recognizing God's specific blessing in a life or God's worthiness in character, power, deed, or authority.

There are only two other events recorded in Scripture where the people of God both "worshiped" and "praised" at the same time. The first was at the dedication of the great temple that Solomon had built. When Solomon finished his prayer of dedication, the fire of God's glory descended on the temple and entered the Holy of Holies. The effect of such an awesome sight was that the people "bowed themselves with their faces to the ground upon the pavement, and worshiped, and praised the LORD" (2 Chron. 7:3).

The other event occurred during the time of Ezra, right after the return of a remnant from Babylon. The people were hearing the Word read to them for the first time in many decades and were trying to celebrate the "festival of booths" properly. During the reading of the Scriptures, the people became so convicted of their disobedience, that they began to cry and confess their sin. Ezra told them that the festival was to be one of joy. The mixed emotions (the festival went on for several days) was such that on one day they stood for about three hours and "confessed (same word as "praise") and worshiped the LORD their God" (Neh. 9:3).

The common factor in both events was the serious and awesome character of the events. Neither of these were ordinary "church services." Something supernaturally special had occurred. God had made himself very evident in the one case through a breathtaking display of His power, in the other through an extraordinary moving of His Spirit. In neither case were the people moved to jump up and down, clap, or otherwise demonstrate exuberance. They were so overwhelmed at the presence of God that they fell down on their faces! Yet the reality of God was so personal that they "praised" (thanked, confessed) — poured out their heart in intimate thanksgiving to the Lord.

This is how we should understand this psalm.

Worship and praise for His loving kindness. Worship and praise for His truth. Worship and praise in His temple — where His name resides. Worship and praise to *the* name — His being, His attributes. Worship and praise *because* God has magnified His word above all His name.

Such an unusual statement! God has, himself, placed such a value on His Word that the Word is to be magnified above His name itself. It is imperative that we gain a perspective from which to view this principle. The name of Jesus is so great that . . .

> God also hath also highly exalted him, and given him a name which is above every name: That at the name of Jesus every knee should bow, of things in heaven, and things in earth, and things under the earth; And that every tongue should confess that Jesus Christ is Lord, to the glory of God the Father (Phil. 2:9–11).

The Word of God is to be magnified beyond the name of Jesus Christ.

382 · Treasures in the Psalms

It is worthy of note that the Third Commandment demands we treat God's name with such honor that we not consider it "vain" (useless, destructive, and profane). God has placed such a high value on His Word that we must approach its use with reverential precision and holy awe.

> Every word of God is pure . . . Add thou not unto his words, lest he reprove thee, and thou be found a liar (Prov. 30:5–6).

> For ever, O Lord, thy word is settled in heaven (Ps. 119:89).

> So shall my word be that goeth forth out of my mouth: it shall not return unto me void, but it shall accomplish that which I please, and it shall prosper in the thing whereto I sent it (Isa. 55:11).

> Heaven and earth shall pass away, but my words shall not pass away (Matt. 24:35).

> The Scripture cannot be broken (John 10:35).

> For all the promises of God in him are yea, and in him Amen, unto the glory of God by us (2 Cor. 1:20).

The point of the worship and praise herein demanded is that we understand that the answers to our prayers, the responses to our needs, even the supernatural deliverance from our disasters are "according to" God's Word (Ps. 119:9, 25, 28, 41, 58, 65, 76, 85, 91, 107, 116, 149, 156, 159, 169–170).

Verse 3

> In the day when I cried thou answeredst me, and strengthenedst me with strength in my soul.

God's responses to our prayers are delivered in two ways: practically, in the circumstances or directions, and spiritually, in the "inner man" (Eph. 3:16). We are often so focused on the physical need or the external circumstance about which we are so insistently praying that when the answer is delivered from the throne, we fail to receive the full blessing — even if we read the practical answer correctly. Our Heavenly Father is committed to providing our needs on earth (Phil. 4:19; Luke 12:30), but such supply must be understood as of minimal significance in the scope of eternity. The "good thoughts" (Jer. 29:11) and the "good gifts" of God (Luke 11:13) are toward the "expected end," our ultimate conformity "to our image of his Son" (Rom. 8:29).

While God will and does respond to our physical circumstances and needs, His heart and his purpose is to fill us "with all the fulness of God" (Eph. 3:19). He blesses us "with all spiritual blessings" (Eph. 1:3) and has chosen us to be "holy and without blame" (Eph. 1:4). God's word is designed to make us participate in the "divine nature" (2 Pet. 1:4). Therefore, God's desire is . . .

> That ye might be filled with the knowledge of His will in all wisdom and spiritual understanding; That ye might walk worthy of the Lord unto all pleasing, being fruitful in every good work, and increasing in the knowledge of God; Strengthened with all might, according to his glorious power, unto all patience and longsuffering with joyfulness; Giving thanks unto the Father, which hath made us meet to be partakers of the inheritance of the saints in light (Col. 1:9–12).

But this private, internal, and spiritual worship and praise must have expression! No one who experiences the blessings of God in his or her life to the extent that the Psalmist is describing can keep it private. There *will* be public testimony.

Verses 4–5

> All the kings of the earth shall praise thee O LORD, when they hear the words of thy mouth.

> Yea, they shall sing in the ways of the LORD: for great is the glory of the LORD.

And please notice, "the kings" will respond in praise. "They" will sing of God's ways. When the wonderful works of God are manifest to us or in us, the resulting testimony brings about a praise response from those hearing of God's action. These testimonies never produce praise for the one giving the testimony! They make those hearing the testimony praise God! Jesus taught us that if we were to learn to love each other as He loved us, then the whole world would know that we are His disciples (John 13:34–35). Solomon let us know that if we would follow the instructions of Scripture, even our enemies would be at peace with us (Prov. 16:7). Everybody in Jerusalem was aware of the powerful witness of the early church (Acts 4:33).

When we are so affected by the working of God in our lives that we "worship" and "praise," others will know about it and will talk about it to God's glory.

Verses 6–8

Though the LORD be high, yet hath he respect unto the lowly: but the proud he knoweth afar off.

Though I walk in the midst of trouble, thou will revive me; thou shalt stretch forth thine hand against the wrath of mine enemies, and thy right hand shall save me.

The LORD will perfect that which concerneth me: thy mercy, O LORD, endureth for ever: forsake not the works of thine own hands.

David's closing application and testimony is finally delivered to his readers. He makes three simple points.

First, God loves His saints, but those with a "pride" problem are not going to gain His attention. This is very basic to Christian doctrine. Pride is one of the seven things that God hates (Prov. 6:16–19). The desire of the humble person is what God responds to (Ps. 10:17). The Lord stays near to those who have a broken heart or a contrite spirit (Ps. 34:18).

Second, God will revive us when we are in trouble. The promise is about the "reviving," and the "saving." That is, we may gain God's sufficient grace to endure (as in the case of Paul's "thorn in the flesh" — 2 Cor. 12:7) rather than a physical cure. We may receive the ability to be victorious in the face of opposition (as during Paul's ministry to Ephesus — 1 Cor. 16:8–9) rather than relief from the circumstances. We may, indeed, be delivered from the pressure of the enemies or have God's miracle performed in our lives, but whatever the circumstantial occasion — God will respond for our good.

Third, God will bring about our "perfection." That term, in both the Old and the New Testaments, relates to "completing" God's work or purpose. Here it is specifically related to "that which concerneth" the saints of God. God will see to it that His "chosen" will make it. There is no question about this. God's mercy is always refreshed. There is no limit to His forgiveness. Nothing about who we are will defeat God's plan for us. Everything has been taken care of. God will not drop the ball.

You have not chosen me, but I have chosen you, and ordained you, that ye should go and bring forth fruit, and that your fruit should remain (John 15:16).

And ye know that all things work together for good to them that love God, to them who are the called according to his purpose (Rom. 8:28).

For we are his workmanship, created in Christ Jesus unto good works, which God hath before ordained that we should walk in them (Eph. 2:10).

Being confident of this very thing, that he which hath begun a good work in you will perform it until the day of Jesus Christ (Phil. 1:6).

Work out your own salvation with fear and trembling, for it is God which worketh in you both to will and to do of his good pleasure (Phil. 2:12–13).

Faithful is he that calleth you, who also will do it (1 Thess. 5:24).

Oh Lord God, we cannot know the end of a thing. We do not have certainty about the plans of our days. Forgive us when we try without consulting thee. Forgive our blundering efforts to make something happen. We do love thee, and we want to please thee, but our lives are so caught up in the things of this world. Help us, Lord. Help us to know how much we need thee. Help us to see the real values of eternal things. Give us a greater awareness of thy Holy Spirit. Give us a holy awe of thy Word. Drive us to our knees more often, Lord. Keep us close.

Oh, our Father. Purge us from the ungodly. Separate us from the sins that hinder and blind. Meet us in the halls of our heart, and sanctify us there.

And then, Lord Jesus, embolden us for the work ahead. Provide our daily bread. Cleanse our sins and enrich our fellowship with the saints. Clothe us in the armor of God and place us where we must stand. Enable us to resist the enemy in the faith, see his strongholds crumble and his minions flee. Grant a fruitful harvest and an effective ministry, in Jesus' name. Amen.

Part IX

The Praise Psalms
of the Redeemed

Chapter 60

The Great Congregation

In chapter 1, the general structural organization of the Book of Psalms was briefly examined, noting that it was composed of five "Books." The last five chapters, however, seem intended as an epilogue to the entire Book of Psalms. They form a fitting climax to this complete, wonderful "Book of Praises of Israel," as the Book of Psalms has been known through the ages. We conclude our studies on the psalms in this volume, therefore, with an exposition of these five remarkable psalms.

These chapters in the epilogue might well be called the "Hallelujah Psalms." Each of them both begins and ends with this exhortation: "Praise ye the Lord." This command, however, is only one word in the Hebrew — "Hallelujah!"

The theme of praise for the Lord permeates the entire Book of Psalms — as it should permeate the entire life of each man and woman — but it reaches its grand climax at the very end. These last five chapters describe nothing less than a great eternal fellowship of heavenly praise beginning at the end of this present age and continuing through the endless ages to come. The words "praise," "praising," and similar forms occur more in the Book of Psalms than in all other books of the Bible put together. But then, in Psalms 146–150 such words occur more than three times as often (44 times) as in any other five chapters, even in the Book of Psalms (13 times in Ps. 115–119).

A number of remarkable patterns are associated with the concept of "praise" in the Book of Psalms. The phrase "Praise ye the Lord" ("Hallelujah") occurs 22 times in the entire book (10 of them in these last five psalms), and this appropriately corresponds to the number of letters in the alphabet of the Hebrew language, the language in which God first revealed His Word to mankind. (See also the discussion on this subject in the expositions of Ps. 22 and Ps. 119). The first occurrence is at the conclusion of the 104th Psalm, the greatest psalm on God's great work of creation and providence.

The key to the interpretation of these five psalms of praise, however, is found in Psalm 22:22, in which the first occurrence of *hallal* ("to praise") in the Book of Psalms is found. There, at the very climax of His sufferings on the cross, these words are prophetically recorded as coming from the heart of Jesus Christ. "I will declare thy name unto my brethren: in the midst of the congregation will I praise thee."

That "congregation" was initially only the pitifully small band of believers grieving at the foot of the cross. This verse is quoted in Hebrews 2:12, however, and there the congregation is said to be the church. During His earthly ministry, Jesus, likewise speaking of the church, had said, "For where two or three are gathered together in my name, there am I in the midst of them" (Matt. 18:20). Each local assembly, where men are "gathered together" in His name, thus has His promise that He is "in the midst of the congregation," leading its praises before the Lord, as it were. All churches are represented by the seven churches of Revelation 2 and 3, symbolized by the seven golden candlesticks, and there John saw "in the midst of the seven golden candlesticks one like unto the Son of man" (Rev. 1:13).

All of these local and temporal assemblies, however, are but types of the grand eternal assembly, when all those who have loved and served Christ through the ages will finally be gathered together before His throne. They all will unitedly praise the Lord forever. "But ye are come unto mount Sion, and unto the city of the living God, the heavenly Jerusalem, and to an innumerable company of angels, To the general assembly and church of the firstborn, which are written in heaven, and to God the Judge of all, and to the spirits of just men made perfect, And to Jesus the mediator of the new covenant, and to the blood of sprinkling, that speaketh better things than that of Abel" (Heb. 12:22–24).

The Book of Revelation also speaks of either the same, or a similar, future assembly. "And I beheld, and I heard the voice of many angels round about the throne and the beasts and the elders: and the number of them was ten thousand times ten thousand, and thousands of thousands; Saying with a loud voice, Worthy is the Lamb that was slain to receive power, and riches, and wisdom, and strength, and honour, and glory, and blessing. And every creature which is in heaven, and on the earth, and under the earth, and such as are in the sea, and all that are in them, heard I saying, Blessing, and honour, and glory, and power, be unto him that sitteth upon the throne, and unto the Lamb for ever and ever" (Rev. 5:11–13).

This heavenly assembly (or similar assemblies) is mentioned several times through the Book of Revelation (7:9–12, 14:2–3, 15:2–4). Finally, at the climax of the judgment on the earth as Christ prepares to return in triumph, we hear a final heavenly exhortation to the assembled multitude to praise the Lord: "And after these things I heard a great voice of much people in heaven, saying, Alleluia; Salvation, and glory, and honour, and power, unto the Lord our God: For true and righteous are his judgments. . . . And a voice came out of the throne, saying, Praise our God, all ye his servants, and ye that fear him, both small and great. And I heard as it were the voice of a great multitude, and as the voice of many waters, and as the voice of mighty thunderings, saying, Alleluia: for the Lord God omnipotent reigneth" (Rev. 19:1–6).

In this glorious passage which begins the 19th chapter of Revelation, the word *Alleluia* occurs four times (verses 1, 3, 4, and 6), and these are the only times it occurs in the New Testament. It is the Hebrew *Hallelujah* ("praise ye the LORD") transliterated directly into the Greek New Testament. This fact confirms our inference that the great "Hallelujah Psalms" of the epilogue to the Book of Psalms should be understood primarily as a prophetic description of that coming day when all believers "shall be caught up together with them in the clouds, to meet the Lord in the air: and so shall we ever be with the Lord" (1 Thess. 4:17). Then we shall no longer be locally gathered together in His name in our respective churches, but will actually experience "the coming of our Lord Jesus Christ, and . . . our gathering together unto him" (2 Thess. 2:1). As the divine judgments of the Tribulation take place on earth, we shall be in His presence in the heavens above the earth, and the great events and testimonies described in Psalms 146–150 will begin to unfold.

Immediately after the mighty victory cry from the cross, where Christ had testified "in the midst of the congregation will I praise thee" (Ps. 22:22), there is noted a change of person in the 22nd psalm, from the first person to the second person. It is as though the Holy Spirit himself interjects the exhortation: "Ye that fear the LORD, praise him!" (verse 23).

To this exhortation, there is the thankful response in the last verses (25–31) of Psalm 22, again in the first person. It is no longer Christ speaking, however, but the believer, for whom He has just died on the cross. David, the author of the psalm, no doubt included himself, by faith, as such a believer. And note how his testimony begins: "My praise shall be of thee in the great congregation: I will pay my vows before them that fear him. The meek shall eat and be satisfied: they shall praise the LORD that seek him; your heart shall live for ever. All the ends of the world shall remember and turn unto the LORD: and all the kindreds of the nations shall worship before thee" (verses 25–27).

We, like David, can look forward to being gathered together in that great congregation, and we, like him, will have abundant opportunity there to express our praise and thanks to the Lord who saved us. We will join, apparently, first of all in a heavenly anthem, never sung before: "And they sung a new song, saying, Thou art worthy to take the book, and to open the seals thereof: for thou wast slain, and hast redeemed us to God by thy blood out of every kindred, and tongue, and people, and nation; And hast made us unto our God kings and priests: and we shall reign on the earth" (Rev. 5:9–10).

From this point on, it seems reasonable to infer that Psalms 146–150 supply a prophetic chronologic framework of the testimonies and events that will be taking place centered there in the heavenly assembly. The Lord Jesus Christ, the Lamb on the throne, will lead these testimonies of praise and will direct the great events both in heaven and on the earth below.

As we proceed to an examination of these remarkable psalms, we may note a tentative and partial outline of their essential respective themes, as follows:

> Psalm 146   Praises of Redeemed Individuals
> Psalm 147   Praises of Redeemed Israel
> Psalm 148   Praises of Redeemed Nature
> Psalm 149   Praises for God's Righteous Judgments
> Psalm 150   Praises Universal and Eternal.

Perhaps we may visualize the scene as a grand heavenly choir, with the Lord Jesus as leader. There is a section for the angels, one for the church, one for Israel, one for the animals, one for the inanimate creation. Every creature of God is there to join in the great fellowship of praise. As the great director signals to one after the other, each responds in song and testimony.

Chapter 61

Songs of the Saved

Psalm 146
Verses 1–10

Praise ye the LORD. Praise the LORD, O my soul.

While I live will I praise the LORD: I will sing praises unto my God while I have any being.

Put not your trust in princes, nor in the son of man, in whom there is no help.

His breath goeth forth, he returneth to his earth; in that very day his thoughts perish.

Happy is he that hath the God of Jacob for his help, whose hope is in the LORD his God:

Which made heaven, and earth, the sea, and all that therein is: which keepeth truth for ever:

Which executeth judgment for the oppressed: which giveth food to the hungry. The LORD looseth the prisoners:

The LORD openeth the eyes of the blind: the LORD raiseth them that are bowed down: the LORD loveth the righteous:

The LORD preserveth the strangers; he relieveth the fatherless and widow: but the way of the wicked he turneth upside down.

The LORD shall reign for ever, even thy God, O Zion, unto all generations. Praise ye the LORD.

First of all, as the heavenly meeting of the great congregation gets underway, the baton points to the Church — that is, to the general assembly and church of the first-born, those individuals whose names are written in heaven and whose spirits have been perfected (Heb. 12:23).

"Praise ye the LORD" (verse 1). And surely, each redeemed soul in that vast body of believers, no doubt numbering many "thousands of thousands," has much for which to praise Him! Each will respond as opportunity affords in the ages to come: "Praise the LORD, O my soul!"

Such testimonies of praise from individuals redeemed by Christ's blood will continue forever. "I will sing praises unto my God while I have any being." Perhaps each will give his individual testimony, recalling in retrospect his experiences on the earth. Though each person has had different experiences in detail, the same great themes will have underlain them all.

The great enemy of true salvation has always been humanism, the belief that man can provide his own salvation. The futility of such a faith is clearly seen in the light of eternity. Put not your trust in helpless man — even in great leaders and princes (verse 3). Great philosophers have sought ways to comprehend and conquer the universe, but they soon die, and their philosophies perish with them. With pitifully few exceptions, the thoughts of even great scientists and philosophers are soon forgotten. How absurd, then, to study — especially to trust — these pitiful products of human wisdom, every one of which will eventually "come to nought" (1 Cor. 2:6).

In contrast, the redeemed soul has rejected all these human inventions and trusted the "God of Jacob," for that God is the only true God, the one "which made heaven, and earth, the sea, and all that therein is" (verse 6). He alone, the God of creation, knows and reveals the truth, and He "keepeth truth for ever." The word of God, which *is* truth, is "for ever . . . settled in heaven" (Ps. 119:89), and does not perish like the philosophies of men.

Furthermore, He "executeth judgment" (verse 7), and it is probably at this very gathering that "we must all appear before the judgment seat of Christ" (2 Cor. 5:10). Each redeemed soul will be able to testify how God has supplied every need, providing food and liberty, guidance and strength, loving those who are "righteous" in Him and who therefore "work righteousness" for Him.

There is still more for which these redeemed men and women can praise the Lord! Their old physical bodies will have been made new in the great resurrection. In the most literal sense, "the LORD openeth the eyes of the blind " and "raiseth them that are bowed down" (verse 8). "Behold, I make all things new," says the Lord Jesus (Rev. 21:5), and the body of each redeemed individual "shall have put on immortality" (1 Cor. 15:54).

At the same time, "the way of the wicked He turneth upside down" (verse 9), and those who have been redeemed can testify of this in a twofold sense. They were once among the wicked themselves, but their lives have been transformed. Second, all opposition from the wicked has finally been swallowed up in victory, and "the LORD shall reign for ever" in the heavenly Zion. "Praise ye the LORD."

Chapter 62

The Redemption of Israel

Psalm 147
Verses 1–20

Praise ye the LORD: for it is good to sing praises unto our God; for it is pleasant; and praise is comely.

The LORD doth build up Jerusalem: he gathereth together the outcasts of Israel.

He healeth the broken in heart, and bindeth up their wounds.

He telleth the number of the stars; he calleth them all by their names.

Great is our Lord, and of great power: his understanding is infinite.

The LORD lifteth up the meek: he casteth the wicked down to the ground.

Sing unto the LORD with thanksgiving; sing praise upon the harp unto our God.

Who covereth the heaven with clouds, who prepareth rain for the earth, who maketh grass to grow upon the mountains.

He giveth to the beast his food, and to the young ravens which cry.

He delighteth not in the strength of the horse: he taketh not pleasure in the legs of a man.

The LORD taketh pleasure in them that fear him, in those that hope in his mercy.

Praise the LORD, O Jerusalem; praise thy God, O Zion.

For he hath strengthened the bars of thy gates; he hath blessed thy children within thee.

He maketh peace in thy borders, and filleth thee with the finest of the wheat.

He sendeth forth his commandment upon earth: his word runneth very swiftly.

He giveth snow like wool: he scattereth the hoarfrost like ashes.

He casteth forth his ice like morsels: who can stand before his cold?

He sendeth out his word, and melteth them: he causeth his wind to blow, and the waters flow.

He sheweth his word unto Jacob, his statutes and his judgments unto Israel.

He hath not dealt so with any nation: and as for his judgments, they have not known them. Praise ye the LORD.

Many saved Jews will, of course, be among this redeemed multitude, as individual believers. But, in addition, God has promised that He will one day restore Israel and Jerusalem as His chosen nation on the earth itself.

This great accomplishment will probably be taking place on the earth as the assemblage at the throne observes it from the heavens. So the great congregation, especially the redeemed Israelites therein, are next called on to praise the Lord. They will sing, "The LORD doth build up Jerusalem: he gathereth together the outcasts of Israel. He healeth the broken in heart, and bindeth up their wounds. . . . Praise the LORD, O Jerusalem; praise thy God, O Zion. For he hath strengthened the bars of thy gates; he hath blessed thy children within thee. He maketh peace in thy borders, and filleth thee with the finest of the wheat. . . . He sheweth his word unto Jacob, his statutes and his judgments unto Israel. He hath not dealt so with any nation: and as for his judgments, they have not known them. Praise ye the LORD" (verses 2–20).

When the promises were first made to Abraham and then to Isaac and Jacob, they must have seemed impossible to fulfill. God had compared their progeny to the grains of sand and the stars of heaven (Gen. 22:17). Such a comparison must have seemed singularly inappropriate and inaccurate, since the number of sand grains was obviously infinitely greater than the 4,000 or so stars that could be seen in the heavens. Now, however, astronomers have calculated that the number of stars in the universe is indeed of the very order of magnitude (roughly 10^{25} in each case) as the number of grains of sand in the world. These cannot actually be counted, of course, only sampled and estimated. God, however, created the stars, so "He telleth the number of the stars; he calleth them all by their names" (verse 4).

Adam was able to name the animals in part of a day, but how long would it take to name all the stars? If there are 10^{25} stars, and if one could name them at the rate of 3 per second, then it would take ten billion billion years (10^{19}) to "call them all by their names"!

It is obvious, therefore, that God named them all at once and, therefore, He must be *omnipresent*. The next testimony (verse 5) recognizes that He is "of great power" — therefore *omnipotent* and that "His understanding is infinite" — therefore *omniscient*. Small wonder, therefore, that He is able both to prophesy and to accomplish the restoration of Israel and the complete fulfillment of His promises to His earthly people.

There is also another testimony in this psalm, affirming His control not only of the physical creation, but also of the biological creation. There had already been one great physical judgment of the earth and its inhabitants, at the time of the great flood, when the Lord "casteth the wicked down to the ground" (verse 6). But then, for that devastated world (in which, according to Gen. 2:5, there had never been any rain until the flood came), He had covered the heaven with clouds, prepared rain for the earth, made grass to grow on the newly uplifted mountains, and given food to the beasts and birds (verses 8–9). After that, following the flood, there had also come a great Ice Age in the northern latitudes. "He giveth snow like wool: he scattereth the hoarfrost like ashes. He casteth forth his ice like morsels: who can stand before his cold?" (verses 16–17).

But the great glaciers, like the waters of the flood, were also under His control. Soon tremendous periglacial winds developed, and the increasing plant life in the lower latitudes sent their air-warming gases (especially carbon dioxide) into the sky, to be translated aloft by the winds, and to gradually restore a partial greenhouse effect to the atmosphere. This would have been similar in kind (but much less efficient) to that which had maintained the warm, calm, beautiful, pre-flood world. "He sendeth out his word, and melteth them; he causeth his wind to blow, and the waters flow" (verse 18).

These testimonies of His control over the physical world are woven in and out among the testimonies of His power to fulfill His promises to Israel. The same Word that could name the stars and command the elements could surely accomplish the redemption of His people. "He sendeth forth his commandment [the same word actually, as 'word' in verse 18] upon earth: his word runneth very swiftly" (verse 15).

And in the heart of this great testimony of God's power, both in creation and among the nations, is the assurance that His greatest joy is not in either one, "The LORD taketh pleasure in them that fear him, in those that hope in his mercy" (verse 11).

Chapter 63

Creation Delivered

Psalm 148
Verses 1–14

Praise ye the LORD: Praise ye the LORD from the heavens: praise him in the heights.

Praise ye him, all his angels: praise ye him, all his hosts.

Praise ye him, sun and moon: praise him, all ye stars of light.

Praise him, ye heavens of heavens, and ye waters that be above the heavens.

Let them praise the name of the LORD: for he commanded, and they were created.

He hath also stablished them for ever and ever: he hath made a decree which shall not pass.

Praise the LORD from the earth, ye dragons, and all deeps:

Fire and hail; snow, and vapours; stormy wind fulfilling his word:

Mountains, and all hills; fruitful trees, and all cedars:

Beasts, and all cattle; creeping things, and flying fowl:

Kings of the earth, and all people; princes, and all judges of the earth:

Both young men, and maidens; old men, and children:

Let them praise the name of the LORD: for his name alone is excellent; his glory is above the earth and heaven.

He also exalteth the horn of his people, the praise of all his saints; even of the children of Israel, a people near unto him. Praise ye the LORD.

Having heard from redeemed mankind, both individually and nationally, the great praise leader turns to His heavenly host: "Praise ye the LORD. . . . from the heavens . . . in the heights. Praise ye him, all his angels: praise ye him all his hosts" (verses 1–2).

Angels are created beings, probably created on the first of the six days of creation (see exposition of Ps. 104), and they "excel in strength" (Ps. 103:20). They "are ministering spirits" for the "heirs of salvation" (Heb. 1:14), and so are interested in the progress of God's plan of salvation, "which things the angels desire to look into" (1 Pet. 1:12). It is highly fitting, therefore, that this "innumerable company of angels" in the heavenly assembly (Heb. 12:22; Rev. 5:11) should desire likewise to give their praises to the Lord.

But then, the exhortation is given even to the inanimate creation, and to the animals also, to praise the Lord. Exactly how this can be done, we do not yet understand, but the same God who made them is the one who gives the commandment, so He will enable them somehow to do so. Certainly in their beauty and order and in the accomplishment of their respective purposes, they speak eloquently even now of God's power and wisdom. "The heavens declare the glory of God" (Ps. 19:1); "the stones . . . immediately cry out" (Luke 19:40); the "lightnings . . . go, and say unto thee, Here we are" (Job 38:35); the "seven thunders uttered their voices" (Rev. 10:3).

However, in the present order of things, "the whole creation groaneth and travaileth in pain together unto now" (Rom. 8:22), and its deliverance from this bondage of corruption is likewise awaiting Christ's work of redemption and His victory over sin and death. It was created "very good" (Gen. 1:31) and the fulfillment of God's purpose in creation requires that it be restored to this original condition. Someday there will be "no more curse" (Rev. 22:3) on the ground, and He will "make all things new" (Rev. 21:5).

When the assembly is gathered in heaven, changes will begin to take place on the earth and in the heavens which will culminate in complete restoration of all to their primeval perfection, which will then last forever. Accordingly, the various stars and all other created things can also join in praise to the Lord both in retrospect and prospect, looking back to the primeval creation and forward to the restored and eternal creation.

First, the sun and moon and stars praise the Lord, with the heavens (atmospheric, stellar, and angelic) in which they function. Also, the "waters above the heavens" have evidently been raised from the earth up into the skies, restoring the ancient "waters which were above the firmament" (Gen. 1:7), which had maintained the ideal environment in the original world. This will probably be accomplished, at least in part, by the great physical upheavals that will have taken place during the Great Tribulation period on earth, when there will be neither rains nor winds (Rev. 11:6, 7:1), but great solar heat (Rev. 16:8), and consequent vaporizing of the lakes and oceans.

Note also the testimony of fiat creation in verse 5. "He commanded, and they were created." True creation is instantaneous. "He spake, and it was done" (Ps. 33:9). Likewise, note the assertion that they would last forever. "He hath also stablished them for ever and ever: he hath made a decree which shall not pass." The idea that this present universe will cease to exist at the judgment day is not the teaching of Scripture. God had a purpose in creating every star, and that purpose would hardly be served by annihilating them. "I know that, whatsoever God doeth, it shall be for ever: nothing can be put to it, nor anything taken from it: and God doeth it, that men should fear before him" (Eccles. 3:14). See also Psalm 78:69, 104:5; Ecclesiastes 1:4; Daniel 12:3; etc.

Then the earth also is exhorted to praise the Lord with all its systems and processes — deeps and mountains and hills, fire and hail, snow and evaporation, as well as the great winds. Most of these systems were not operative in the primeval world, becoming active as agents of judgment when sin came in and especially during and after the flood. They would still be utilized during the period of the Great Tribulation, taking place on earth while the great assembly was convening in heaven, even though ultimately, in the new earth, there would be no further need for them. Nevertheless, in their immediate function as manifestations and implementations of God's judgment, they were, indeed, praising the Lord. Then, attention turns to the plants and animals. The fruit trees and timber trees were to praise the Lord. So were the beasts and cattle, creeping things and birds, even the "dragons" (verse 7). This looks back in retrospect to the original creation of the animals on the fifth and sixth days of creation. The dragons (Hebrew *tannin*) were the same as the "sea monsters" or "great whales" of Genesis 1:21. In all probability, such monsters of the deep still live in modern oceans and deep inland lakes. They will evidently still be living on the earth at the time when the great congregation is gathered in heaven, and so will also be able to add their testimony to God's praise.

The animal kingdom will continue to exist during the earth's great millennial period, but all enmity between man and the animals will have been removed, with harmony prevailing as in the original creation (Isa. 11:6–9, 65:25). In the new earth, however, there will be "no more sea" (Rev. 21:1), so that at least sea animals will evidently cease to exist as well, their purpose having been completed. Whether or not there will be terrestrial animals on the new earth, the Scriptures do not say specifically. But such references as this one, in addition to Isaiah 65:25, as well as the general concept of the originally created fellowship between Adam and the animals he named, make such a thing appear at least possible. If so, of course, they would have to be newly created, not the products of resurrection or reproduction of animals in a previous age.

And finally there is a call to all those people yet on the earth — kings of the earth, judges of the earth (note Ps. 2:10), young men and young women, old men and children. "Let them praise the name of the LORD" (verse 5). There is still time and room, even for these. During both the Tribulation period and the Millennium, there will be people on the earth, in the flesh, needing salvation. The redeemed and resurrected saints in the heavenlies will eagerly hope that those below will respond to the call of the Spirit to come to Christ, whose "name alone is excellent" and whose "glory is above the earth and heaven." Of all these yet on the earth, the people of reviving Israel are His greatest concern, and the psalm concludes with another special testimony of and to them. "He also exalteth the horn of his people . . . the children of Israel, a people near unto him. Praise ye the LORD."

Chapter 64

Praise in God's Judgments

Psalm 149
Verses 1–9

Praise ye the LORD. Sing unto the LORD a new song, and his praise in the congregation of saints.

Let Israel rejoice in him that made him: let the children of Zion be joyful in their King.

Let them praise his name in the dance: let them sing praises unto him with the timbrel and harp.

For the LORD taketh pleasure in his people: he will beautify the meek with salvation.

Let the saints be joyful in glory: let them sing aloud upon their beds.

Let the high praises of God be in their mouth, and a twoedged sword in their hand;

To execute vengeance upon the heathen, and punishments upon the people;

To bind their kings with chains, and their nobles with fetters of iron;

To execute upon them the judgment written: this honour have all his saints. Praise ye the LORD.

Neither God nor His people find any pleasure in the death of the wicked (Ezek. 33:11), and God is long-suffering, not willing that any should perish (2 Pet. 3:9). Nevertheless, He is also a just God, and sin, when it is finished, must bring forth death (James 1:15). God's judgments, as well as His mercy, bring glory to His name: "Fear God, and give glory to him; for the hour of his judgment is come" (Rev. 14:7). After the praises from redeemed believers, redeemed Israel, the angels, and the very creation itself, in the first three of the Hallelujah Psalms, the emphasis in this psalm is on praising God for His righteous judgments on the earth. In God's omnipotence, He is able even to make man's rebellious wickedness an occasion for good. "Surely the wrath of man shall praise thee: the remainder of wrath shalt thou restrain" (Ps. 76:10).

After the initial "Hallelujah," the first exhortation is to "sing a new song." The word "song" occurs more in the Book of Psalms than in all the rest of the Bible put together. Similarly, there are six "new songs" in Psalms (33:3, 40:3, 96:1, 98:1, 144:9, and 149:1), and only three in the rest of the Bible (Isa. 42:10; Rev. 5:9, 14:3). Evidently, all believers in heaven sing this new song; but there is a special exhortation to the children of Israel to rejoice in their great King, Messiah.

The great joy is apparently because of the imminent return of Christ to the earth, when the "children of Zion" shall finally receive the promise of the messianic kingdom. The saints are joyful in the glory in contemplation of His promise that the meek "shall inherit the earth" (Matt. 5:5). "For the Lord taketh pleasure in his people; he will beautify the meek with salvation" (verse 4).

The day is near when heaven will be opened and the armies in heaven will follow Christ to make war against the armies of the kings of the earth (Rev. 19:11–19). This is evidently the meaning of the next verses: "Let the high praises of God be in their mouth, and a twoedged sword in their hands: to execute vengeance upon the heathen, and punishments upon the people; to bind their kings with chains, and their nobles with fetters of iron; to execute upon them the judgment written" (verse 6–9).

It is important always to interpret Scripture in proper context. Unfortunately, the above verses have been badly misused, especially during the wars of the Reformation, with both Protestants and Catholics using them to justify warfare and persecution in the name of Christ. As we have seen, however, the context is really prophetic, looking forward to the great war of Armageddon and the judgment of the nations.

It is indeed true, however, that the redeemed will take part in God's final judgment on the wicked. "Do you not know that the saints will judge the world? . . . Know ye not that we shall judge angels?" (1 Cor. 6:2–3). "And he that overcometh, and keepeth my works unto the end, to him will I give power over the nations; And he shall rule them with a rod of iron; as the vessels of a potter shall they be broken to shivers; even as I received of my Father" (Rev. 2:26–27). "And the kingdom and dominion, and the greatness of the kingdom under the whole heaven, shall be given to the people of the saints of the most High" (Dan. 7:27). "And I saw thrones, and they sat upon them, and judgment was given unto them . . . and they lived and reigned with Christ a thousand years" (Rev. 20:4).

Whether we understand or not, and whether we agree or not, the fact remains that we are now being prepared for just such a ministry in the age to come. The resurrected believer will in that day have been made like Christ (1 John 3:2; Rom. 8:29), in hatred of sin as well as love of righteousness, and thus will be fully capable of participating with Him in judgment.

Chapter 65

Universal Praise

Psalm 150
Verses 1–6

Praise ye the LORD, Praise God in his sanctuary: praise him in the firmament of his power.

Praise him for his mighty acts: praise him according to his excellent greatness.

Praise him with the sound of the trumpet: praise him with the psaltery and harp.

Praise him with the timbrel and dance: praise him with stringed instruments and organs.

Praise him upon the loud cymbals: praise him upon the high sounding cymbals.

Let every thing that hath breath praise the Lord. Praise ye the LORD.

This final psalm looks far ahead to the grand consummation, after all rebellion and wickedness have been purged from God's creation, the Curse has been removed from the earth, and Satan cast forever into the lake of fire.

The heavenly Jerusalem and its inhabitants have already enjoyed the presence of the Lord throughout the seven years of Great Tribulation on earth, the thousand years of peace while Satan was confined in the abyss, the final rebellion of Gog and Magog, and the judgment of the great white throne. Then the holy city had come down out of heaven to the renewed earth, all things in heaven and earth had finally been gathered together as one in Christ, and the dispensation of the fullness of times (Eph. 1:10) had begun. These great events are described in Revelation 19–20.

The time will then finally have arrived for the grandest doxology of all. God's plan of salvation has been completely accomplished and the whole creation is "very good," again and forever.

"Praise ye the LORD." The cry goes forth from the great leader of all praises, the Lord Jesus, and the universe begins to echo His praise. It begins in its center, in the very throne in the New Jerusalem. "Praise God in his sanctuary."

From there it surges forth in all directions. "Praise him in the firmament of his power." The "firmament" (Hebrew *raqia*) means, literally, "stretching out," so that the command is actually to praise the Lord in the stretching-out of His power. His power, of course, stretches out infinitely through all space, so the angelic songs of praise likewise stretch out to the infinite recesses of God's creation.

Verse 1 has outlined the extent of the praises; verse 2 outlines their themes. God is to be praised both for His mighty acts and for His excellent greatness — what He does and what He is. His great work of creation had already been praised by the assembly in Revelation 4:11, and His greater work of redemption in Revelation 5:9. The "abundance of his greatness" must be nothing less than the glory which the Lord had longed for His disciples to see when He spoke to His Father in the upper room (John 17:24). Finally, they have all "seen him as he is" (1 John 3:2–3), and joyous songs of praise sound forth from all the redeemed and purified.

Verses 3, 4, and 5 describe *how* to praise the Lord, as verse 1 tells *where* and verse 2 says *why*. There will evidently be an abundance of musical instruments in the New Jerusalem. The heavenly assembly was already experienced in the playing of harps (Rev. 5:8,14:2, 15:2), and these will be joined by many others. Wind instruments (trumpets and organs), stringed instruments (psaltery, harp, and others), and percussion instruments (timbrel, loud cymbals, and high-sounding cymbals) will all provide a glorious musical background for the universal songs of praise. The music will also serve as an accompaniment for joyful and expressive dancing (verse 3). This will not be sensuous dancing, of course, but dancing which is appropriate as a testimony to the glory and grace of God. "Thou hast turned for me my mourning into dancing: thou hast put off my sackcloth, and girded me with gladness; To the end that my glory may sing praise to thee, and not be silent. O LORD my God, I will give thanks unto thee for ever" (Ps. 30:11–12). "Let them praise his name in the dance: let them sing praises unto him with the timbrel and harp" (Ps. 149:3).

And finally, as the music and singing and dancing resound in ever-expanding waves of joy from the sanctuary and throughout the universe, the climactic exhortation peals forth: "Let every thing that hath breath praise the LORD!" The word "breath" (Hebrew *ruach*) is actually the same word as "Spirit," so this command may well be a reference to the universal presence of God's Holy Spirit in all His creation.

The Book of Psalms ends where eternity begins, with the universal shout: "*Hallelujah!*"

Master Books is proud to publish the following books
by Henry M. Morris:

The Beginning of the World

The Bible Has the Answer
(with Martin E. Clark)

Biblical Creationism

Christian Education for the Real World

Creation and the Second Coming

Defending the Faith

The God Who Is Real

The Long War Against God

Many Infallible Proofs
(with Henry M. Morris III)

Men of Science, Men of God

The Modern Creation Trilogy
(with John D. Morris)

The Remarkable Record of Job

Scientific Creationism

That Their Words May Be Used Against Them

Treasures in the Psalms

What Is Creation Science
(with Gary Parker)

Available at Christian bookstores nationwide